CUBA LIBRE
Breaking the Chains?

CUBA LIBRE
Breaking the Chains?

by

PETER MARSHALL

BOSTON
FABER AND FABER
1987

For Jenny

First published in the United States, 1987, by Faber and Faber, Inc.,
50 Cross Street, Winchester, MA 01890. First published in
Great Britain, 1987, by Victor Gollancz, Ltd.

Library of Congress Cataloging-in-Publication Data
Marshall, Peter H., 1946–
   Cuba libre.
   Includes index.
   1. Cuba—History—1959–   . I. Title.
F1788.M256   1988   972.91′064   87-15678
ISBN 0-571-12985-4

Published by arrangement with Victor Gollancz, Ltd.

CONTENTS

PREFACE AND ACKNOWLEDGEMENTS

To write about Cuba inevitably provokes controversy. The intentions and politics of an author are immediately brought into question. I should like to point out from the start that I undertook this study with considerable sympathy for the original aims of the Cuban Revolution and wanted to find out how far they had been realized.

During my travels in Cuba, I tried to appreciate the Cuban experience with a novelist's eye as much as with a philosopher's mind. I attempted to view the country from within, strongly aware that my own English Protestant background is very different from Cuba's Catholic Spanish and African traditions. I also bore in mind Che Guevara's observation that the first thing a historian must do is 'stick to the truth, like a finger to a glove'. Whether I have been fair and accurate is for the reader to judge.

Since it is usually difficult to travel in Communist states, it might be worth saying something about my two long visits to Cuba in 1984. I travelled with photographer Barry Lewis. In the Cuban Revolutionary tradition of barter, we agreed with the National Institute of Tourism to exchange transport and lodging for photographs. I was able to travel throughout the country and most of my requests for interviews and visits were granted.

I would like to thank Jeremy Gane, Graham Hancock, Kuru Gunawardena, and John Schlapobersky for their interest in this project. Walter Schwartz's comments on part of the manuscript were much appreciated. David Burnett's and Charlotte Greig's editorial advice proved very useful. I would like to thank Sandy, my mother Vera and my brother Michael for their moral support during the composition of the work. My children Emily and Dylan have shown great powers of forbearance. I am indebted in particular to Jenny Zobel for her warm encouragement and critical insight. I am more than grateful to Elizabeth Grzelinska for her skill and speed in typing the manuscript. Finally, the staff of the

University of London Library and of the Institute for Latin American Studies have been very helpful.

Gwynedd
14 November 1986

INTRODUCTION

My keen interest in Cuba dates back to 1968, when I was inspired by the radical enthusiasm of the students of my generation. It was a time of cultural revolution in China, of massive demonstrations in Europe calling for an end to US aggression in Vietnam, of students in Paris storming the Cartesian state, of imagination seemingly about to seize power. In college rooms, the heroic image of Che Guevara peered down from colourful posters, his defiant gaze symbolizing rebellion and hope to the children of the affluent middle class in the West, who despaired of the dull monotony and meaninglessness of the society about them. He seemed an exotic voice calling from the Third World, a kind of secular saint who had given his life to the wretched of the earth and who celebrated the full harmony of being.

I was no particular disciple of Che, but I grew intrigued by reports from Cuba of a kind of pluralist anarchy in the making. I read with great interest Guevara's notes on *Socialism and Man* in Cuba which claimed that 'We are at the head of a people which is at the head of the Americas', and that 'We socialists are freer because we are more complete; we are more complete because we are freer'.[1]

I became fascinated by a revolution that seemed to combine libertarian energy with primitive Communism, to set Marxism-Leninism to a Cuban beat. What was the rhythm of this socialist *rumba* which appeared to make people literate, healthy and confident? What was the nature of this upheaval which proved to be the most radical revolution in the Western hemisphere this century, and the focus of revolutionary hope throughout Central and Latin America? I wanted to find out.

The Cuban Revolution in fact broke most of the traditional revolutionary rules. After only two years' struggle, Havana fell to a small band of guerrillas led by a young lawyer, Fidel Castro, and an asthmatic Argentinian doctor, Ernesto Che Guevara. Amid widespread jubilation, Castro promised an 'olive-green' revolution and a programme of 'humanistic democracy on the basis of liberty with bread for all peoples'.[2] The Agrarian Reform Law which distributed land to the peasants, and the Urban Reform Law which slashed rents, were greeted with great enthusiasm. The large estates and companies were nationalized. With Guevara as head of the National Bank, money was to be abolished and soul-destroying work transformed into meaningful play; as Minister of Industry, Guevara was to break the ancient monopoly of sugar and set up new industries. The whole island was to be transformed into a vast school to forge the New Man and the New Woman, who would be hard working, egalitarian and just. Cuba seemed poised to become a model of self-sufficient, independent socialist development for the Third World. Above all, the greatest promise—and scandal— of the Cuban Revolution was that it brought the youth to power.

Of course the US was unable to let such an original experiment take place in its back yard. After the imposition of an economic blockade, the newly-elected President Kennedy approved the CIA-organized invasion by Cuban exiles and mercenaries at the Bay of Pigs in 1961. The resulting fiasco was hailed by Cubans as 'the first defeat of US imperialism in the Americas'. The Cuban missile crisis in the following year, which nearly provoked a world war, placed Cuba more firmly within the Soviet camp. But the Revolution continued on its own original, erratic path, exasperating orthodox Communists and inspiring Western students and Third World revolutionaries alike.

In its early days, the Cuban Revolution could do no wrong in the eyes of left-wing intellectuals. Those like Ernest Hemingway, who had lived in Cuba for 30 years, gave it their full approval. Jean-Paul Sartre wrote a brilliant series of essays on Cuba in 1961 after a visit there. He counted Castro amongst his few friends, declared Che Guevara to be 'the most complete man of his age', and celebrated the 'profound individualism within the bounds of discipline' that was at work within the Revolution.[3] C. Wright Mills, in *Listen, Yankee* (1960) insisted that the Cuban voice should be heard. The economist René Dumont, the doyen of the French radical Third World commentators, gave his seal of approval. To young radical romantics, Cuba was an inspiration; it seemed to confirm the Maoist view that the peasants could be revolutionary, and the anarchist view that the will of a small, dedicated band of militants could trigger off a revolution.

With the death of Guevara in the Bolivian jungle in 1967, an era of Cuban revolutionary adventurism in Latin America came to an end. Despite the Revolutionary Offensive of 1968 which nationalized the remainder of the private sector and led to the second major exodus of disaffected citizens, the economic policy of the new regime grew more conservative and the political ideology more orthodox. In the same year, Castro gave his support to the Soviet invasion of Czechoslovakia. After the failure of a campaign to harvest ten million tons of sugar in 1970, which severely dislocated the rest of the economy, Castro admitted his mistakes in leadership. Henceforth the government grew more pragmatic and cautious, and the goals of justice and equality grew less important than those of economic growth and defence. Cuba remained a one-crop economy exchanging sugar for Soviet oil.

After the initial flush of enthusiasm, the more staid observers of Cuba started to have second thoughts: gradual socialism, yes; but to abandon sugar and to industrialize at a stroke, to try and abolish money, to run a country through the informal groupings of rebel leaders—that was mere folly and a recipe for economic disaster. When Castro's professed humanism gave way to Marxism-Leninism—on 2 December 1961, he declared 'I am a Marxist-Leninist and shall be until the day I die— when he refused to abandon his military fatigues, when the Committees for the Defence of the Revolution that had been set up in every block began to be the 'eyes and ears' of the leadership, when the Cuban Communist party appeared to identify itself with the army, it seemed that Stalinism was creeping in. All its central features were there: the cult of the personality around Castro, the creation of a centralized bureaucracy, and the silencing of dissidents. Herbert Matthews, the journalist who was the first to track down the guerrillas in the Sierra Maestra and to introduce Castro to the American public, spoke on behalf of most liberals when he wrote in 1964 about 'the tragedy of a revolution that was justified but has been led into the dark realm of Communism'.[4]

Even Cuba-watchers on the left became apprehensive. The American socialists Huberman and Sweezy dedicated their book *Socialism in Cuba* (1969) to the memory of Che, but while recognizing the unprecedented and 'stupendous achievements' of the Revolution, were concerned about the 'paternalistic' nature of the government and the absence of institutions of popular participation and control.[5] After another visit, René Dumont left the country critical of the growing bureaucratic centralism and militarization of the regime. He entitled his next book *Cuba, est-il socialiste?* (1970); and to this question, gave a resounding 'no'. Even the sympathetic K. S. Karol in his *Guerrillas in Power* (1970) accused Castro of abandoning Guevara's ideals and returning to the Soviet-style Communism of the 1930s. Henceforth, customs officers in Cuba were to confiscate these books from visitors who brought them in.

Castro grew increasingly impatient with his critics at home and abroad. In 1968 Heberto Padilla, the Cuban poet and former editor of the Communist party paper *Granma*, wrote:

Instructions for joining a new society
First: be an optimist.
Second: be neat, obliging and obedient.
(be sure to pass all athletic tests.)
And, lastly, march
like every other member:
one step forward and
two or three back,
but always applauding.[6]

Later, an international jury awarded Padilla a prize for his literary work, but he was denounced by the regime as a counter-revolutionary. When he was later arrested in 1971, there was a storm of protest amongst European and Latin-American intellectuals, including Jean-Paul Sartre, Hans-Magnus Enzensbergen, Gabriel García Márquez, Octavio Paz and Carlos Fuentes. Castro replied with a bitter attack on the 'pseudo-leftist bourgeois intellectuals' who dared to criticize his government's cultural policy.[7]

In the 1970s, Cuba moved even closer to the Soviet Union. In 1972 Cuba joined COMECON, the Common Market of the Eastern Bloc countries, and on 26 July 1972 Castro expressed his 'eternal gratitude' for the friendship of the Soviet people. After the First Congress of the Communist party in 1975, a new constitution based on the East European model was drawn up. Since then, the regime has become increasingly institutionalized, following the principles of Marxism-Leninism and 'democratic centralism'.

However, Castro has continued to play an independent foreign policy by his forays in Africa, especially in Angola and Ethiopia, and by his support for Caribbean and Central American revolutions, especially in Grenada, Nicaragua and El Salvador. As an officially non-aligned country, Cuba presents itself as part of the Third World in the struggle between the North and South rather than as a pawn in the East-West confrontation. Cuba will not be silenced or cowed. Few weeks go by without it being mentioned on the front pages of the world's press. Little more than a corrupt colony before the Revolution, Cuba has not only made its voice heard, but now plays a major role in international affairs.

Although it has celebrated 28 years of revolution, Cuba continues to excite controversy and disagreement. The libertarian left has called it a 'totalitarian dictatorship', while from the extreme right it is condemned as a Godless slave state.[8] The historian Hugh Thomas, author of the monumental work *Cuba, or The Pursuit of Freedom* (1971), has recently called it 'the first fascist left regime', by which he means 'a regime with totalitarian left-wing goals established and sustained by methods of fascism'.[9] American universities and institutes, well funded by the US government, pour out endless studies by Cuban exiles and American academics who use a smokescreen of objectivity to attack Castro's regime.

On the other hand, scholars like Carmelo Mesa-Lago and Jorge Domínguez in America have been able to rise above the militant anti-Communism pervading so many studies of Cuba to write fairly about the changing nature of the Cuban Revolution. The British novelist and historian David Caute was able to entitle a book on the subject *Cuba, Yes?* (1974). The West Indian Andrew Salkey opened his sympathetic *Havana Journal* (1974) with the words of the Cuban poet Nancy Morejón, who spoke of 'loving the Revolution's impact on the eyes'. More recently the Christian Bruce Kenrick, in his *A Man from the Interior: Cuba's Quest* (1980) even saw in the Cuban Marxists' attempt to create the New Man an echo of Christ's New Man.

It was with this controversy in mind that I decided to visit Cuba in 1984 and to begin this study. I wanted to get to grips myself with the real nature of the regime which had taken up so much of Guevara's energy, which claimed to be at the head of the Americas, and which appeared to be such a great threat to the US.

In addition, there was the appeal of the country itself which was first excited by the fragrant smell and colourful designs of my grandfather's boxes of cigars. From my Spanish studies I remembered the lines of the Spanish poet García Lorca:

> When the moon is full
> I will go to Santiago de Cuba.
> I will go to Santiago.
> The tops of the palm trees will sing.
> I will go to Santiago.[10]

Cuba further beckoned by its unique culture formed by nearly five centuries of recorded history, a subtle blend of different traditions, religions, languages and customs. It is one of the oldest societies in the New World, more racially mixed and culturally varied than any other country in the West Indies. Unlike other Latin American countries, its culture is not a mixture of Spanish and indigenous cultures but rather a blend of Spanish and African, with only a slight admixture of Indian, French, Chinese and North American. The poet Nicolás Guillén correctly described Cuba as 'this mulatto land of African and Spanish, St

Barbara on one side, on the other, Chango.' Cuba's music, moreover, is the result of the long-standing love affair, as Fernando Ortiz put it, between the African drum and the Spanish guitar. The result of this remarkable process of cultural synthesis is an independent culture which is dynamic, passionate and lyrical. Its uniqueness becomes immediately clear by comparison with the neighbouring English-speaking Jamaica or the French-speaking Haiti.

I at last managed to arrange a visit to Cuba, and as I packed my bags I recalled Guevara's observation:

> Cuba is a socialist country: tropical, unpolished, ingenuous, and gay. It is socialist, without relinquishing even one of its own characteristics, while it adds to its people's maturity. It is worth getting acquainted with.[11]

1

THE LAST JEWEL IN THE SPANISH CROWN

The visitor to Cuba quickly becomes aware that the events of recent years are only the foam on an historical wave. National character and culture are strongly moulded by the past. With nearly five centuries of written history, the country was one of the oldest colonies in the New World. The Cubans, moreover, are profoundly conscious of their tempestuous and varied past and see themselves as actors in a long-running historical drama.

The first European to set foot on the island was Christopher Columbus on 27 October 1492. A Genoese navigator in the pay of the Spanish, he had sailed across the Atlantic with a fleet of three small ships in search of a westerly passage to India.

When he reached Cuba, he landed at Bariay on the north coast of what is now Holguín province. He placed a cross on the beach, took possession of the land 'in the name of Christ, our Lady, and the reigning sovereigns of Spain'. He sent an expedition inland to carry greetings to what he thought would be the Japanese Emperor's court. His emissaries did not discover the famed imperial city, but rather a huddle of 50 huts near the present site of Holguín. The naked Indians there called their settlement Cubanacan, meaning the centre of the island of Colba. Columbus preferred to call it Juana after the daughter of the Spanish monarchs King Ferdinand and Queen Isabella. The country was to remain the 'Jewel in the Spanish Crown' for the next 400 years.

Columbus, disappointed by the inhabitants, nevertheless marvelled at what he saw. The whole island was a stand of precious woods—mahogany, cedar, dagame, quebracho—among which towered giant palms. The Spanish were astonished by the forests, in whose shade one could walk the whole length of the country. Columbus wrote that

The multitudes of palm trees of various forms, the highest and most beautiful I have ever seen, and an infinite number of other great and green trees; the birds in rich plumage and the lushness of the fields make this country of such marvellous beauty that it surpasses all others in charms and graces, as the day does the night. I have been so overwhelmed at the sight of so much beauty that I have not known how to relate it.[1]

Although Columbus returned on a second voyage in 1493, sailed along the south coast, and landed on the Isle of Youth, he died believing that Cuba was part of the continental mainland. The main island was not circumnavigated until 1508.

It soon became apparent that Cuba was the largest island in the Caribbean, situated just below the Tropic of Capricorn. It is placed so strategically at the entrance of the Gulf of Mexico that the Spanish called it the Key to the New World. To the west is the Yucatán Peninsula of Mexico; to the east, 50 miles away, is Haiti. Eighty-five miles to the south is Jamaica, and Florida is 90 miles to the north; both are visible on a clear day.

The main island is, in fact, part of an archipelago which consists of at least 4,195 small islands and keys arranged in four main groups, including the large Isle of Youth. With about 44,200 square miles of land area, the main island is about the same size as Pennsylvania or England. It is long (760 miles) and narrow (ranging between 130 and 22 miles), and shaped like an alligator. The mainland has three mountain ranges: the Sierra de los Órganos in the west; the Escambray mountains in the centre, rising to over 3,000 feet; and the Sierra Maestra in the east, the highest and most rugged range, rising sharply from the coast to 6,500 feet. The land mass is well drained: the rivers are short and small, except for the largest, the Río Cauto which flows parallel to the Sierra Maestra. The country is fortunate in having about 60 per cent of its surface as flat, rolling land. Its soils are deep and fertile; few countries have so much good level land per head of population. Although some coastal areas, particularly in the south, are swampy, there are sweeping bays, beautiful coral reefs and crystal-clear waters swarming with fish.

The Spanish soon found that the climate of the island made it one of the most habitable places on earth. It enjoys temperate sub-tropical weather, with a mean temperature of 25° celsius. Even during the rainy season from May to November, the sun shines most of the day and there are almost constant trade winds from the north east. But the climate can suddenly change. Cold fronts sweep across from Florida in January and February. Droughts, too, can cause havoc to the crops, and from time to time hurricanes swirl across and devastate the land.

The exact number of Indians on the island at the time of the arrival of the Spanish is difficult to establish, and estimates vary from 60,000 to 500,000. The latter figure is probably more accurate. According to archaeological finds at Farallones de Seboraca near Mayarí, Indians had first settled on the island as early as 5,000 BC and had used tools and plates. Little is known of these people, except that their descendants known as Ciboneys and Guanajatabeyes lived in caves as hunters, fishers and gatherers. The Ciboneys were the more advanced, using fire but not ceramics, and living in the western part of the island. The word 'Cuba' is the only trace of the Ciboney language to survive.

At the time of the Spanish conquest, there were also groups of Arawak Indians called Sub-Taínos and Taínos, whose ancestors had come by long canoe from South America in AD 1400 and in AD 1460. Considerably more advanced than the other Indian groups, they built their homes, practised fishing and agriculture, and decorated their bodies. They plotted the sun and moon on elaborate charts; at Punta del Este on the Isle of Youth, some remarkable cave drawings have been found which make up an astonishing map of the solar system. They believed in a supreme being, called on the help of gods, and buried their dead. The Taínos lived in a state of Communism, without classes, although there were chieftains, priests and doctors, among whom were women. According to one Spanish chronicler, they held the outlandish view that 'the earth as well as the sun and water were common property, and that there should not exist amongst them *mine* nor *yours*'.[2] They also had the peculiar habit of smoking leaves from a bush called *cohiba* through their noses during religious ceremonies: tobacco, hitherto unknown in Europe. They lived in groups of ten to 20 in round houses with thatched roofs and palm tree bark walls.

For the most part, they led productive, easygoing and peaceful lives. Although they had recently suffered attacks from Carib cannibals who came from Jamaica and the southerly islands, they were not prepared for fighting. Columbus found them 'very free from wickedness'. They reasoned with their steel-armoured Spanish intruders thus:

Whether you are divinities or mortal men, we know not. You have come into these countries with a force against which, were we inclined to resist, it would be folly. We are all therefore at your mercy; but, if you are men, subject to mortality like ourselves, you cannot be unaware that after this life there is another, where a very different portion is allotted to good and bad men. If, therefore, you expect to die, and believe with us that everyone is to be rewarded in a future state according to his conduct in the present, you will do no hurt to those who do none to you.[3]

But such noble reasoning went unheeded. The Spanish were after riches, for Europe produced no jewels, spices or gold. Columbus reported to his monarch about Cuba: 'It is certain that where there is such marvellous scenery, there must be much from which profit can be made.'[4] When a rumour reached the king of Spain that there was gold in Cuba, the king ordered Diego Columbus, Christopher's son, to conquer the island. Diego Columbus delegated the task to Diego de Velázquez, the richest planter in Hispaniola, the principal colony of the Spanish in the New World (now Haiti and the Dominican Republic). Diego de Velázquez came to Cuba with a force of 300 men in 1512. Like that of the other Spanish *conquistadores* in the New World, it was made up mainly of ex-soldiers, fallen noblemen, adventurers, convicts and criminals. The army landed on the eastern tip of Cuba and set up its first settlement on the present site of Baracoa, calling it La Villa de Nuestra Señora de la Asunción. Within 50 years the Indian population had been virtually wiped out. Most languished in misery, some escaped into the mountains, some committed group suicide, a few fought. One such was Hatuey.

Hatuey was a chief from Hispaniola, where his people had put up a spirited resistance. He had landed in Cuba with 400 men, women and children just before Velázquez, and had tried to rally the local Taíno Indians. According to the Spanish chronicler Bartolomé de las Casas who accompanied Velázquez, Hatuey held up a basket of gold and jewels and declared:

Here is the God which the Spaniards worship . . . They tell us, these tyrants, that they adore a God of peace and equality, and yet they usurp our land and make us their slaves. They speak to us of immortal souls and of their eternal rewards and punishments, and yet they rob our belongings, seduce our women, and violate our daughters. Incapable of matching us in valour, these cowards cover themselves in iron armaments . . . But they are few and we are many. They are fighting in this foreign land, and we on our own soil. They invoke a seditious God of blood and gold, and we have on our side a just and wise God . . .[5]

Hatuey managed to win the support of some of the eastern tribes, and when the Spaniards landed and entered the forest, they attacked. But their spears, arrows and clubs were no match for Spanish steel and guns, and the Indians were quickly forced back into the mountains. Hatuey then resorted to guerrilla tactics and succeeded in besieging the invaders in Baracoa for three months. For the first time since they had arrived in the New World, the Spanish grew afraid. With the help of an Indian traitor, however, Velázquez managed to surround the Indian mountain headquarters and capture Hatuey. He was tied to a stake on 2 February 1512. When asked to embrace the Christian God to win salvation, the captive replied defiantly that he would rather not go to heaven and meet again 'such cruel and wicked people as the Christians who kill and makes slaves of Indians'.[6] The torch was promptly put to the fire. Hatuey has since been remembered as the first Cuban nationalist and revolutionary, and is famous throughout Latin America.

After the defeat of Hatuey, the Indians were an easy and defenceless prey. Velázquez showed no mercy or kindness in his treatment of the Indians. Las Casas records that on one occasion a village of 2,500 Indians welcomed the *conquistadores* and offered them food. When the Spanish guests had finished their meal, they attacked their unsuspecting hosts and slaughtered them until blood ran like a river. They even fed Indians to their bloodhounds for sport. The hapless Indians were forced to work as slaves in the newly-discovered gold mines. They were forbidden to dance, sing, or paint their bodies, and they were exposed to new diseases. They died, victims of overwork, malnutrition and spiritual sickness. Las Casas later commented: 'No tongue is capable of describing to the life all the horrid villainies perpetrated by Velázquez and his men.'[7]

The protests of priests and others eventually led to the liberation of the Indians by royal command, but by then there were no more than a few thousand left. Today only a few Cubans, mainly in the Baracoa region, retain Indian features with black skin, straight hair and slightly oval eyes. The Indian legacy consists mainly of the name of the island and of several of its towns: Baracoa, Bayamo, La Habana, Camagüey. A number of Indian words have entered into international vocabulary such as *hamaca* (hammock) and *canoa* (canoe). The basic design of the *bohío*, the traditional house of the Cuban peasant, made from palm-tree bark and thatch, is based on that of the Indians. Cubans also maintain that baseball is derived from the Indian game *batey* which was played with a rubber ball. The Indians also left their maize, yucca or cassava and boniato or sweet potato.

Unlike other Latin American countries, the Cubans are unable to look back to a great Indian civilization like the Aztecs or Incas in search of their national roots and a national identity. Nevertheless, the memory of the Indians is kept alive, and every child learns of their story in José Martí's romanticized account, *La edad de oro* (1889). The first tourist project undertaken after the Revolution was to build a replica, with statues, of an Indian village on the shores of Lake Tresoro in the Zapata swamp. Built on the original site, the village is called Guamá after an Indian chief who resisted several Spanish attempts to subdue him, and who was eventually killed in his sleep by his brother.

For their part, the Spanish *conquistadores* quickly imposed their own civilization. They had come with iron, gunpowder, the horse, the wheel, the sail, the printing press and money. They gave the island its language, its dominant religion, its pattern of family life, and its political and legal institutions. Initially, the most important powers were the army which guaranteed the privileges and rule of the Spanish, and the church which tried to preach the submission of the Indians.

At first, the economic development of Cuba was slow. Velázquez was authorized by the Spanish Crown to distribute land for use, not ownership, amongst the Spanish settlers. The Crown granted the right for each landholder to have 40 to 200 Indians as free labourers, which made the Indians slaves in all but legal status. From 1536, *cabildos* or municipal councils were able to give grants of land, some of which were *hacienda comunera* or communal properties.

After failing to grow the crops of their native Andalusia in Cuba, the settlers began to cultivate and cure the native tobacco. The great hardwood forests were cleared for cattle ranches and for their superb timber. Cattle from India, known as Zebu or Brahman, were introduced throughout the island. Leather became the major export. When the Indians had been exterminated, their labour was replaced by black African slaves who first arrived in 1524 to work the Jagua gold mines. They staged their first revolt in 1533 in gold mines near Bayamo, when four slaves fought to the death against a large force of soldiers.

At the beginning of the sixteenth century, seven important towns were founded on Cuba—Baracoa, Bayamo, Santiago de Cuba, Trinidad, Sancti Spíritus, Puerto Príncipe and San Cristóbal de la Habana. In 1514, Velázquez moved the capital of the new colony to Santiago, (so named after the patron saint of Spain) because of its natural harbour and proximity to the fledgling colonies in Hispaniola and Jamaica. The 16th century is known as the 'Century of Huts' because of the predominant type of building. But fine stone houses were built around the central square which was first marked out in the new towns. Velázquez's house in Santiago, constructed between 1516 and 1520, is still standing, with its florid stone façade, stark Moorish-style balconies, and magnificent stained-glass windows. Significantly, the first floor was used as a house of commerce and as a gold foundry. But the Spaniards were in the New World in search of souls as well as gold. In 1528 the first cathedral was erected nearby and has been there in some form ever since.

The Spanish mainly used Cuba as a base for their operations in the New World. The gold soon ran out, and despite the threat of the death penalty for leaving Cuba without permission, *conquistadores*, merchants and adventurers moved on to richer pastures. Cuba, with its strategic position at the entrance to the Gulf of Mexico and its fine harbours and roads, proved an ideal stepping stone for the *conquistadores* and for the treasure fleets returning to Spain.

Havana was founded by Pánfilo de Narváez in 1514 on the south coast, but moved to its present position in 1519. It grew rapidly as a transit port to Central and South America, and in 1589 Villa de San Cristóbal de la Habana, to give its full name, was proclaimed by royal edict as the capital of Cuba. It adopted a coat of arms showing three castles above a gold key and became known as the 'Key of the Old World to the New World'.[8]

The growing trade with the transient *conquistadores* suited the merchants but not the other settlers. As one of the governors wrote to the King of Spain in June 1581, 'This place [Havana] is the most expensive in all the Indies; this is because of the great number of ships that pass through here and the people travelling on them who cannot refrain from spending, even if they wanted to.'[9] In order to protect the Spanish fleets in the harbour, vast fortresses were built at its entrance. But the Spanish settlers and the *criollos*, their Cuban-born descendants, who remained on the island were isolated and had to be self-reliant. They were constant prey to the buccaneers and privateers from competing European powers, who were a law unto themselves on the Spanish Main. The inhabitants of Cuba never felt secure in the sixteenth and seventeenth centuries, although they were part of the richest and most powerful empire on earth.

In the eighteenth century the Spanish empire began to crumble as British power grew. As a result, Spain's attitude to Cuba turned from one of neglect to monopoly—especially in commerce and the export crop of tobacco. Now that Spain was virtually bankrupt, and gold had run out in the New World, the Spanish turned to agricultural wealth. In this, Cuba was worth more than all the gold mines of Mexico and Peru. Cuban growers and traders were thus, under the threat of death, obliged only to trade with certain cities in Spain. By a strange quirk of fate, the best tobacco in the world grows where Europeans first discovered it. Columbus found the Indians cultivating a bush called *cohiba* whose leaves, known as *tabacs*, they rolled in bunches and smoked through the mouth or stuffed into hollow forked reed pipes inserted directly into the nostrils. Smoking was an integral part of their religious practices and used medicinally.

By the early 1700s, tobacco had become Cuba's most important export. But it was not without difficulty. Tobacco is one of the most difficult crops to grow and requires constant and careful attention. The delicate work could not be carried out by forced labour, so most tobacco workers were white *criollos*. They remained fiercely jealous of their independence. When the Spanish government's edict of 1717 imposed a monopoly on the island's commerce, 500 outraged tobacco growers rebelled in the first armed insurrection in Cuba. They rose up again in 1718 and 1723, but they were ruthlessly crushed. In 1723 the governor general hung the bodies of executed rebels from trees along the road to Havana as a warning.

Spanish merchants prospered, but the economy languished and most of the population suffered. The trading monopoly encouraged smuggling, especially with the neighbouring islands of Haiti and Jamaica, which came to be known as the *comercio de rescate* (barter trade). When Havana was taken after a 44-day siege in 1762 by the British Fleet under the Earl of Albemarle during the Seven Years' War, it was therefore something of a blessing in disguise. Under Spanish rule, about 15 ships a year pulled into Havana; during the 11-month British occupation, about a thousand ships unloaded their cargoes. They established a plantation economy and in one year introduced as many African slaves (5 to 10,000) as normally would have entered in 12 to 15 years. At the end of the war, in 1763, the British exchanged Cuba for Spanish Florida at the Treaty of Versailles. The Spanish flag was once again raised in Havana, but the British had ended the oppressive commercial restrictions there and given a tremendous boost to the economy.

It proved a turning point in Cuban affairs. Hitherto the country had been a moribund and neglected colony, but from 1763 it began to develop a dynamic agrarian economy. The English had freed the *criollos* from the yoke of the Spanish merchants. The departure of the English may be considered as marking the beginning of Cuban history in a modern sense. Havana was rebuilt with splendid plazas and palaces, and in 1777 the governor was made formally independent of the Spanish Crown. Soon after the Spanish government permitted the independent ownership of land by the *criollos*. When the great geographer and naturalist Baron Alexander von Humboldt visited Havana in 1800, he described the harbour with the great fortresses at its entrance and forest of masts within as 'one of the gayest, most picturesque and enchanting vistas' that could be seen in the New World north of the equator. Eighteen years later, Cuban ports were open to free trade with all nations.

The type of society which had emerged by the second half of the eighteenth century was complex, both ethnically and economically. At the bottom were black and mulatto Cubans, both slaves and free men and women. The free black Cubans (who had either bought their freedom or run away) were forced into day labour, although a few rose to be small landowners and merchants. Above them were the *criollos*, born in Cuba, and often descendants of Spanish settlers who had had children with Indian and African women. They controlled and directed the economic production of Cuba, as cattle ranchers, tobacco and sugar planters in the country, and as the professionals in the cities. They might be rich landowners or poor peasants living side by side with the free blacks. At the top of the social hierarchy were still the Spanish-born *peninsulares*, the monopoly merchants and government officials. They believed in the natural superiority of the pure-bred Spaniards, despised the *criollos*, and ignored the blacks.

At this time, a new agricultural commodity was developed which was to determine the course of Cuban history: sugar. Sugar and tobacco are the economic basis of Cuba, and yet the two could not be more different. Tobacco is indigenous to Cuba and, in a sense, represents national sovereignty. Sugar is foreign to Cuba and for many years made it dependent. Tobacco was cultivated by free white men, sugar by black slave labour. Tobacco requires great care to grow, sugar takes care of itself. Tobacco is processed by people, sugar by machinery. Cuba has produced the finest quality of tobacco in the world, but the greatest quantity of sugar. The contrast between the two is so great that it inspired the Cuban historian Fernando Ortiz to call his study of tobacco and sugar *Cuban Counterpoint* (1947).

Columbus had brought sugar from the Canary Islands to the New World on his second voyage. It was initially cultivated in Hispaniola and the first box of refined sugar was sent back to Spain in 1517. It was introduced five years later into Cuba which was ideally suited to the crop, and from the beginning it was exempt from royal taxes and given every legal and financial encouragement. Even so, the Cubans were unable to compete with the English growers in Jamaica and the French in Haiti.

Towards the end of the eighteenth century, increased demand in Europe and the newly independent colonies in North America meant that sugar quickly overtook hides, tobacco and coffee as the principal export. With the destruction of the sugar industry in Haiti following the slave rebellion in 1793, Cuba soon became the world's sugar bowl and a great devourer of slaves. It immediately enjoyed a world sugar boom;

in five years, from 1790 to 1795 the price of sugar increased sevenfold. King Sugar, despite periodic attempts to dethrone him, has maintained his tyrannical and absolute rule in Cuba ever since.

Sugar production rapidly transformed the face of Cuba. Cattle ranches were turned over to the white gold, and Cuba's vast forests of precious woods were cut down to release more land and fuel the sugar mills. The plunder culture which had always prevailed in Cuba suddenly took on devastating proportions. The method of cutting and burning forests to achieve high yields and then moving on resulted in widespread soil erosion, an irreversible change in the climate and the long-term destruction of Cuba's legendary fertility. Almost nothing remains today of Cuba's hardwood forests and its fabled mahogany.

The boom in sugar not only caused the death of the forests but also resulted in a sudden influx of African slaves to work the plantations. Whereas tobacco spelled liberty, sugar meant slavery. African slaves had of course been brought in steadily from the beginning of the sixteenth century to replace the exterminated Indian workforce. By the middle of the eighteenth century, however, Cuba still had the fewest slaves in the West Indies. But with the expansion of the labour-hungry sugar industry at the end of the eighteenth century, it was not long before the black and mulatto population began to outstrip the white population, leaping from about 30,000 (out of a total population of 171,620) in the year 1774 to 313,203 (out of 533,033) in 1817. Whites, mainly due to renewed immigration, only caught up in the 1850s.

The slaves came from the whole range of West African slave centres: from Senegal in the north to the Congo and Angola in the south, and as far away as Mozambique on the east coast of Africa. The sources were particularly varied in the nineteenth century, when the majority of slaves were shipped to Cuba. The most lasting influences have however come from the Congolese, from the Yoruba of southern Nigeria (called *Lucumis* by the Cubans) and the Efik and the Efo of the Niger delta (called the *Carabalís*, that is the people from Calabar). The Arara also came via Haiti and left their mark particularly in the east of the country.

Under Spanish law, slaves were at least legal persons: they could own and exchange property (although it would revert to their masters on their death). The murder of a slave was a crime. Slaves could marry. They could buy their own freedom and the freedom of their children and parents by instalments through the *coartación* (obligation) system. White masters, who took black mistresses on a lavish scale, usually freed their offspring.

Nevertheless, this did not prevent the slaves from being brutally ill-treated. Their families were systematically broken up; one typical advertisement went: *'Una nodriza de dos meses de parida, con su cria o sin ella'* (Nursing mother, two months from child's birth, with or without child). Slaves could be beaten while it was forbidden to beat oxen: animals were considered more important. In Havana there was a special building just outside the old gates of the city which received town slaves from their masters to be whipped. There were regular slave revolts and breakouts. A few escaped slaves, or *cimarrones*, managed to live in the mountains, alone or in groups; often they preferred to kill themselves by hanging or by eating earth than to be caught by the professional hunters and their bloodhounds.

The sugar barons who benefited from the boom at the end of the eighteenth century were quick to innovate. Unlike in the British West Indies, the expansion of the sugar industry did not originate in, but took place in spite of, the metropolis. The *criollos* in Cuba more readily welcomed the new technology than their Spanish counterparts. The steam engine was introduced to the mills as early as 1820 and the railway first came to Cuba in 1837, even before Spain. Within 20 years, all Cuban sugar areas were linked by railroad. Paradoxically, however, these technological innovations and capitalist techniques of organization were based on the institution of slavery which provided inefficient labour. This economic contradiction prevailed until the end of the nineteenth century. Indeed, rather than freeing the slaves, the partial mechanization in the industry meant that more labour was required to feed the mills, and conditions became worse in the nineteenth century. Sugar merchants were not only obliged to finance slaving expeditions themselves, but were forced to import indentured Indians from Yucatán and Chinese from Mongolia (about 140,000 in the middle of the century) to maintain the momentum. Even stud farms with black women and white immigrants were planned to increase the working population.

The drive for profit soon tore away the religious and feudal veils which had helped to hide the brutality of slavery, as sugar growers and mill owners exploited slave labour to the full. The failure to mechanize the mills fully meant that the only way to make a profit was to squeeze the last ounce of labour from the slaves. The semi-patriarchal regime of the eighteenth century gave way to naked barbarism in the first half of the nineteenth century. This is reflected in the changing names of the mills. In the eighteenth century they were founded under patronage of protecting saints, but in the following century the new mills portrayed the godless audacity of their owners with names like *Nueva Esperanza* (New Hope) or *Casualidad* (Chance). One was even called *Amistad* (Friendship) although other names such as *Angustia* (Anguish) or *Desengaño* (Warning) better reflected the attitudes of those who worked in them.

The sugar mills resembled small towns. There were large houses for the different stages of processing the cane—for grinding (*casa de trapiche*), for boiling (*casa de caldera*), and for draining (*casa de purga*). The owner usually had a magnificent mansion, sometimes like a palace or a Greek temple. There were handsome houses for the *mayoral* who supervised the mill; the *administrador* who was responsible for the practical running of the mill; the *mayordomo* who was responsible for the paperwork; the sugarmaster who maintained the quality of the sugar, and the machinist who looked after the technical side. The waged artisans had more basic accommodation, but were at least free men. The slaves lived at first in primitive *bohíos* or thatched huts clustered in *bateyes*, but increasingly they were moved into *barracones*, huge parallelograms with locked rooms like cells whose barred windows looked in on the inner courtyard. The cemetery was often an abandoned spot in the centre of a field where the remains of slaves were buried without a name, marker or cross.

The regime on the sugar plantation was simple and hierarchical. The *mayoral* ruled with an iron hand with the help of whips, dogs and black overseers. The slaves were overworked and cruelly punished. Because they worked badly and constantly threatened to rebel, physical force became the sole motivating power. Both rulers and ruled were caught up in an atmosphere of terror, brutality and ignorance. Longing for flight and freedom, the slaves were forced into a state of impotent rage, adopting a crippling attitude of submission and pretence. They were uprooted and crushed, like the cane in the field, with the last drop of their labour extracted. The early nineteenth-century saying 'sugar is made from blood' is not an exaggeration. The conditions of the slaves were appalling. As the demands of the mills grew, the slaves were worked up to 20 hours a day, seven days a week, with no respite on Sundays or saints' days to work their traditional plots known as *conucos*. They lived in a permanent state of semi-somnambulance. The plantation bell ruled their lives—waking them up, sending them to work, calling the overseer, and from time to time announcing the departure of another slave to the cemetery. A contemporary writer described the incessant work rhythm of the slaves as:

> Cutting cane if it is harvest time, in the full heat of the sun, feeding it into the grinding mill, minding molds and kettles, stoking the furnace, heaping up cane; loading it on the *burro*, carrying bagasse;

at night doing these tasks in the cold and dew and pre-dawn and dawn hours, dying of sleeplessness since there are but five rest hours for each nineteen of toil; and after the harvest, planting cane and clearing the canefields—one of the mill's toughest jobs, for the body must be bent over, not permitting the machete, the implement regularly used, to be wielded freely; and all this time enduring the tremendous downpours of the rainy season, the mud underfoot; that, although seen from a great distance, is a picture of the kind of work which is done on these farms . . .[10]

Not surprisingly, the slaves died in shoals. The death toll was about ten per cent a year, and an official report in 1823 admitted that there was hardly a mill without a quarter of the workforce useless, injured and sick. It was seriously discussed whether it was better to sacrifice the slave to the work or the work to the slave. Indeed, the slaves were treated worse than the animals: in the detailed production reports of the mill there were entries for the sex and name of the mules which died or were bought or sold, but the slaves were merely divided into *Negros* and *Negras* with columns for the numbers of 'received', 'new born', 'sick', 'dead', 'escaped', 'captured' and 'jailed'.[11] Life in the sugar mills was so bad that there were not only numerous uprisings and breakouts, but cases of collective suicide, where slaves killed themselves in the hope of being resurrected in Africa.

The lot of the male slaves was all the more grim since they could find no solace amongst the women or children. As slave prices rose, some women were brought into the mills, but they had to work as hard as the men and were defenceless prey to the overseers. A contemporary Spanish visitor wrote:

They rest neither on Sundays nor saints' days; they seem to be made of iron. What with only five hours' sleep in the grinding season; rising before dawn has even begun to display its splendours; toiling in the canefields without let-up save for the short noon break to come in and eat; cutting cane in the melting tropical sun interspersed with torrents of rain; in winter suffering cold which penetrates to the bones of an African; and then, on Sundays and saints' days, nursing the baby, washing and mending clothes, cooking the food—well, I just don't know how they stand up to it! Yet with it all, my friend, would you believe it? They always look happy—smiling faces, never that heavy expression that the males have—and it is quite rare for them to get desperate and hang themselves . . .[12]

They could only meet clandestinely with their men; the *tumbaderos*, the felling place where wood was collected for the furnace, was a favourite spot to meet, so that even now the word *tumbadero* is used in Cuba for a brothel and *pulo* (log) for sexual intercourse. These conditions meant that the slaves did not reproduce themselves in great numbers. If female slaves became pregnant, they would often prefer to abort rather than bring a child into such a world of suffering and misery. If the child was born, it had little chance of survival, with the mother being sent back to work after a couple of days. If the child reached five or six, he or she would join the production crew. Cuban mills during the first half of the last century were undoubtedly the most barbaric in the world.

The local church was weak and inactive; indeed a traveller in 1859 declared that Roman Catholic worship was at a lower ebb in Cuba than almost anywhere else.[13] Nevertheless, the priests justified the institution of slavery: it could not but be a noble task to bring black savages from Africa, to redeem them by work, and to teach them the road to Christian salvation. The priests pictured Jesus as an ever-watchful, all-powerful overseer who would condemn them if they failed to perform their work. Their message to the slaves was simple, even if their logic was faulty: 'God made me a slave; He wants me to serve my master; so I will work because God wants it . . . ' Since idleness exposed them to sin, it was better for them to work. Some priests even argued that if the slaves obeyed their masters, their souls would become pure, like white sugar. 'Your body may be enslaved,' they proclaimed, 'but your soul remains free to fly one day to the happy mansion of the elect'.[14]

If some owners did show some Christian humility, it tended to rebound on them. When Count de Casa Bayona washed 12 of his slaves' feet, it ended with his mill being burnt down. The heads of the rebels were later stuck on pikes as a warning to others. In general, priests and owners left slaves without any organized religion. As a result, the slaves formed themselves into nations or *cabildos*, practising their traditional rituals and customs in semisecret societies. The Yoruba religion in particular was grafted onto Roman Catholicism to form Santería, a cult in which white saints were matched to black gods while African drums beat time to Catholic prayers.

The relative isolation and neglect of Cuba in its long history meant that towards the end of the eighteenth century a distinctive Cuban identity began to emerge, based on a racially mixed society, a blending of Spanish and African cultures, folk Catholicism and an agricultural economy. Those in Cuba who were benefiting from the sugar boom were tired of Spanish interference and prided themselves on their technological superiority over the mother country. They were developing their own way of life, architecture and culture which was not Spanish but Cuban. The *criollos* were increasingly realizing that their interests were different from those of the Spanish officials and *peninsulares*. The American War of Independence further inspired national Cuban sentiment.

The outbreak of the French Revolution was to have a great effect, as Alejo Carpentier has brilliantly described in his novel *El siglo de luces* (1963). But while it was an inspiration to some *criollos*, it was also a warning to other large landowners. In 1791, the slaves revolted in neighbouring Haiti and, led by a black general in Napoleon's army, Toussaint L'Ouverture, they drove the French out. Many *émigrés* settled with their coffee, sugar and slaves in Oriente province in eastern Cuba.

The worst fears of the Spanish authorities were confirmed when the Spanish Governor of the Bayamo region in Oriente was told by an informer in June 1795 that one Nicolás Morales, a free black, 'tall in body, very robust, of dark colour, marked with smallpox, straight hair, very cunning, and about 56 years old', was urging black slaves and white farm workers to unite, arm themselves, and demand that the Spanish king should declare the equality of races, the abolition of excise taxes, and the distribution of the land to the poor.[15] The uprising which followed was quickly crushed, but it united whites, blacks and mulattos in a new way.

It was a time of sudden change in the Western hemisphere as well as in Europe. Two leaders emerged in the Venezuelan Simón Bolívar and the Argentinian José San Martín who were to topple the Spanish Crown in Latin America. Their armies swept the Spanish authorities out of Colombia in 1819, out of Central America and Venezuela in 1821, and out of Mexico in 1822. After the battle of Ayacucho in Peru in 1824, the Spanish armies never set foot on the Latin American continent again. Only the islands of Cuba and Puerto Rico remained in their hands.

With the example of neighbouring Haiti, where a Negro Republic was established in 1803, the wealthy *criollos* were reluctant to follow the other Spanish colonies in Latin America with their demand for independence. 'Remember Haiti!' was the cry; they feared a black revolution more than Spanish domination. This fear was made real by an uprising in 1812. It was followed by a series of slave revolts which culminated in 1844 in the movement known as the Conspiración de la Escalera in the province of Matanzas, (so named because suspects were tied to *escalera* or ladders and whipped to obtain confessions), during which several thousand slaves died and many more were imprisoned.

The majority of the *criollo* bourgeoisie therefore called only for reform, demanding land property rights and control over the development of private capital while rejecting the freedom of contract between capitalist and worker. They wanted to manage their own affairs in their own interest, but with the Spanish sword there to maintain their privileges. Some of the wealthy Cuban landowners, however, called for an annexation with the slave-owning US as the best bulwark against abolition—an idea first mooted by Jefferson in 1808. A secret representative of the Cuban annexationists met President James Monroe and his cabinet in September 1822. In the following year, the Secretary of State John Quincy Adams made the policy of the US absolutely clear by declaring that Cuba and Puerto Rico are 'natural appendages of the North American Union'. He added:

> There are laws of political as well as physical gravitation, and if an apple, severed by the tempest from its native tree, cannot choose but to fall to the ground, Cuba, forcibly disjoined from its unnatural connection with Spain, and incapable of self support, can gravitate only toward the North American Union, which by the same law of nature cannot cast her off from her bosom . . .[16]

In December 1823, President Monroe further enunciated the doctrine which bears his name: 'We should consider any attempt on their part [the European powers] to extend their system to any portion of this hemisphere as dangerous to our peace and safety.'[17] The immediate effect of this was to warn off all European rivals and the Latin American countries, notably Mexico and Colombia. It preserved Cuba as an apple on the Spanish tree until it was ripe enough to fall into the hands of the United States.

In the period of American expansion in the middle of the century, when California and Texas were acquired, the US government was no longer prepared to wait patiently. President Polk offered Spain a hundred million dollars for Cuba in 1848. When that failed, the military option was tried. The southern states supported the expeditions of the Venezuelan Narciso López, who landed in 1850 in Cárdenas in Matanzas province with a force of 600 Americans and five Cuban exiles. No local support was forthcoming and the invaders were quickly defeated, but Cárdenas is remembered as Cuba's 'Flag City', for it was here that the Cuban flag was raised for the first time, even if it was in the annexationist cause. With the victory of the abolitionists in the Civil War, the issue of annexing another slave state was dropped.

In the meantime a growing number of intellectuals, professionals and landowners called for the abolition of slavery and complete independence from Spain. The particularly ruthless rule of the Spanish governor Francisco Lersundi triggered off a rebellion in 1868 which was to become the Ten Years' War of Independence, and which cost the lives of more than 200,000 Spanish and 50,000 Cubans.

The legacy of the war is an integral part of modern Cuba, and the Castro regime has rewritten national history to present itself as the natural heir to the aspirations of the patriots who took part. 'There has been one revolution,' Castro declared on its hundredth anniversary, 'that which was begun by Carlos Manuel de Céspedes on 10 October 1868, the revolution which our people are still carrying forward.' Nowadays, its leaders are numbered amongst the deities in the revolutionary pantheon and are honoured by magnificent monuments in the capital. The principal events and battles in the war are retold endlessly in museums, school textbooks and in the press.

Carlos Manuel de Céspedes was the 50-year-old leader of the rebellion. After studying in Havana he had gone to Spain and became a lawyer. He travelled throughout Europe and returned in 1844, imbued with ideas of independence inspired by the French Revolution. In an attempt to put these into practice, he symbolically freed all his slaves on his small plantation La Demajagua near Bayamo in Oriente province in October 1868. He then attacked the village of Yara with less than 40 men, of whom only 12 survived. Afterwards, in the famous *Grito de Yara* or Cry of Yara he declared that all men are equal and that the people are sovereign. He called for complete independence from Spain and the establishment of a republic based on universal suffrage. At the same time he respected the private ownership of property and religious observance and desired the gradual emancipation of slavery with compensation. He is remembered as the *padre de la patria*, and has a splendid monument over his grave in Santiago de Cuba and a fine statue in Havana.

Céspedes' message and example immediately spread and within a month 12,000 men had joined the rebel army. The movement inspired by Céspedes was directed mainly by landowners in the east of the island, and the bulk of the fighting was done by *criollo* peasants, slaves that had been freed and Chinese labourers recently brought into the country. Among its leaders was Ignacio Agramonte, a young *criollo* lawyer from a wealthy family in Camagüey. The most effective popular generals of the Ejército Libertador (the Army of Liberation) to emerge were Máximo Gómez and Antonio Maceo. Gómez was an exile from Santo Domingo (now the Dominican Republic); he is remembered as the first internationalist fighter and has a vast equestrian statue raised in his honour in

Havana. Antonio Maceo was the son of a free black Venezuelan merchant in Santiago de Cuba. Poorly educated and at work for his father
by the age of 16, he joined a Masonic lodge which was a centre of
nationalist sentiment. He soon made history halting a column of Spanish
troops on their way to relieve Bayamo which had been occupied for
three months soon after the uprising. Bayamo fell, but Maceo went on
to become the most audacious general of the rebel forces. He was called
the 'Titan of Bronze' because of the 28 bullet holes he had received in
his body. As a mulatto, he did much to unite black and white in the
nationalist cause; in 1870 he had declared *No hay negritos ni blan-
quitos, sino Cubanos*' ('there are no blacks or whites, but Cubans').

The rebel forces were called *mambises* after an African word meaning
'children of vultures and apes', but for them the name was a title of
honour. At first they were no match for a well-trained professional
army, but what they lacked in arms they made up for in courage. Most
of them were equipped only with machetes. Some even went into battle
and fought with their bare hands. They soon changed their tactics to
guerrilla warfare and became virtually unbeatable: at Las Guásimas in
1874, 250 men under Maceo decimated a Spanish column of 5,000
troops. They successfully confined the Spanish to the cities and towns
and hid in the forests and mountains. But they were unable to get a
supply of arms or aid from abroad (President Grant of the US overruled
a Congress favourable to the rebels) and the struggle died down.

The Spanish, determined to hold on, at whatever cost, to the last and
most precious jewel in their Crown, turned the island into a heavily
fortified garrison, adding 250,000 troops to the population of one million. They did their best to exploit regional differences and the potential
disagreement amongst the leaders. The resulting stalemate caused the
rebels to lose heart. Agramonte died fighting in 1873, and Céspedes
was killed a year later. The *criollo* landowners, who distrusted blacks
and poor whites, agreed in the Zanjón Pact of 1878 to lay down their
arms in return for certain reforms. In the same year, municipal government was introduced, in 1881 parity with Spanish provinces was
granted, and in 1886 slavery was abolished.

Maceo, however, in his famous Baraguá Protest in Oriente, declared
his intention of fighting on to the Spanish commander. Every Cuban
knows Maceo's words: 'Liberty is won with the blow of the machete,
it is not asked for; to beg for rights is the way of cowards who are
incapable of exercising them.'[18] But with his support withering, he was
soon forced into exile in Costa Rica. Máximo Gómez returned to Santo
Domingo. Nevertheless, his protest symbolized the radical development
among Cubans during the Ten Years' War: Céspedes, the wealthy land-

owner, was the originator; Maceo, the mulatto of humble origin, was the last to give up. He made sure that the cries *Independencia o Muerte* and *Patria y Libertad* reverberated down through the next century; Castro's favourite slogan *Patria o Muerte* is a composite of the two.

The war which cost a quarter of a million lives had a profound effect on the Cuban people. It gave birth to the national flag, with its red triangle, which is said to symbolize the blood spilled in the struggle for liberty, and its single star which signifies that Cuba will always be a free and sovereign country. It also produced *La Bayamesa*, the warlike national anthem which calls its citizens to arms with the words: *'morir por la patria es vivir'* (to die for your country is to live). Above all, the war not only united black and white, but saw the first call for the full emancipation of women. At the Guáimaro Assembly in 1869, Ana Betancourt declared:

> Everything was slavery here—the cradle, colour, sex. You want to destroy the slavery of the cradle by fighting to death. You have destroyed the slavery of colour by emancipating the slave. The moment of women's liberation has arrived![19]

During the Ten Years' War, Cuba had undergone considerable changes. It was of course still a slave society, and although a Cuban middle class was emerging, many visitors were struck by the polarization of the social groups. The Comtesse de Merlin, a Cuban who went to live in Paris, wrote after a return visit in 1840 that:

> There is no populace in Havana; there are only proprietors and slaves. The first are divided into two classes: the land-owning gentry and the mercantile middle class. The latter is composed for the greater part of the Catalans who, arriving without patrimony on the island, end by making great fortunes. They begin to prosper by their industry and thrift and at last get possession of the finest hereditary estates, as a result of the high interest at which they lend their money.[20]

By 1861, largely due to the immigration of poor Spanish workers and peasants, the whites formed the majority again. Blacks and mulattos made up 43 per cent of the population, of which 26 per cent were still slaves, and 17 per cent were free, either because they had bought their freedom, or because they had been freed by their masters.

By the middle of the nineteenth century, coffee had replaced tobacco as the second most important crop, but it was still sugar which dominated the economy. Coffee and tobacco were mostly grown by sharecroppers or small tenants. The large livestock ranches which remained required little labour. The sugar plantations, which had been amalgamated by trusts of owners, were by far the greatest devourers of labour. Although seasonal wage workers were taken on, the slaves still provided the backbone of the sugar industry. The workforce was inefficient, un-educated and rebellious. One contemporary observed:

> There came into being a sort of practical code of absurd principles, in which the farm worker's stupidity became the guarantee of the farm's security, physical force the sole motive power, routine the only agricultural law.[21]

The inefficiency did not prevent vast profits from being made, which were invested in magnificent buildings. Havana, in particular, grew rapidly during the nineteenth century, its baroque style of architecture giving way to an explosion of the neo-classical.

The introduction of steam-powered mills started a process which led in the end to the abolition of slavery. Initially, the new machinery speeded up the work process, but as the mills became more and more productive the burden of the slaves only grew worse. 'Why are there more slave risings in steam-powered mills than in those which grind their cane with oxen?' the priest asked observantly in Cirilo Villaverde's great novel about plantation life, *Cecilia Valdés* (1882).[22] When Cuba eventually abolished slavery in 1886—it was the last country to do so in the Caribbean—life for the new wage-earning labourers was not much improved. Most of them would only be employed for a few months each year during the harvest and they were left in their *bohíos* (small huts) without decent clothing, food, education or health care. Life for the most part remained poor and uncertain.

The machinery in the mills came from the US. By 1850, Cuba's trade with the US was greater than with the mother country, Spain. Given its geographical position, the US became Cuba's economic centre as well as the principal consumer of its products. Although politically governed by Spain, Cuba increasingly became an economic colony of the 'colossus to the north'. With the abolition of slavery without com-pensation in 1886, the industry had to be modernized to remain com-petitive. Cuban landowners did not have enough capital, so US interests naturally stepped in and expanded the railways, introduced new sugar mills, and took over many of the *centrales* (large centralized mills) which had replaced the smaller sugar mills. With the growth of large estates or *latifundia*, many peasants lost their land to absentee and foreign owners.

The US not only imported 94 per cent of the sugar, but also invested heavily in mining. Its investments reached $50 million and its exports $100 million in the 1890s. Towards the end of the century, it completely dominated trade with Cuba: in 1887 Cuba's exports and imports to the US were greater than those of Mexico, twice as great as all five Central American republics taken together, and were only exceeded in South America, by Brazil and Argentina.

In the meantime, a labour movement began to emerge as Cuba moved from a slave, agrarian society governed by Spain to a capitalist one dominated by the United States. Anarchist ideas prevailed, brought over by Spanish immigrants influenced by Michael Bakunin and Elisée Reclus. The most militant of the skilled workers who adopted their views were the *tabaqueros* (tobacco workers). This was partly because of the more social nature of their work and partly because of their high level of education. The latter was made possible by the widespread practice of daily reading to the workers at their work tables in cigar factories, which began in Bejucal in 1864. The reading table became a pulpit of liberty, and through it the workers became familiar not only with national and international news, but with novels as varied as those of Cervantes, Cirilo Villaverde and Dickens. From 1865, the *tabaqueros* published the anarcho-syndicalist weekly *La Aurora* and a year later formed in Havana the first trade union in Cuba: the Asociación de Tabaqueros de la Habana.

The tobacco workers became the most politically conscious group in Cuba and, during the nineteenth century, formed the spearhead of the working-class movement. During the Ten Years' War of Independence, many fled to the neighbouring island of Key West or to Tampa in Florida, but the *tabaqueros* remained a *criollo* stronghold, contributing ten per cent of their earnings through the union to the independence struggle. Symbolically, the order to launch the second War of Independence in 1895 was rolled in a cigar in Key West and sent to Havana.

It was not only the tobacco workers who were organizing themselves. In 1885 the Círculo de Trabajadores de la Habana, the first Workers' Congress of Havana, was founded, an informal federation of workers' clubs. In the following year, the anarcho-syndicalist newspaper *El Prouctor* appeared. At the regional Workers' Congress in 1892, which was closed down by the Spanish authorities, resolutions calling for independence drafted by the Cuban anarchists Enrique Cresci, Enrique Suárez and Eduardo González recognized that: 'The working class will not be emancipated until it embraces revolutionary socialism, which cannot be an obstacle for the triumph of the independence of our country.'[23]

At the end of the Ten Years' War of Independence, a Spanish

lieutenant-general had observed: 'The country is totally in insurrection; and from the roots of this war will emerge another'. His words were to be only too prophetic. An uneasy peace ensued, broken by periodic uprisings. In 1879 another rebellion took place, led by the veteran Calixto García and the black general from Santiago, Quintón Banderas, but it was brutally crushed after only ten months. War erupted again in 1895. It was to prove the undoing of the Spanish authorities.

The political leadership this time fell to José Martí, one of the most original and influential writers of Latin America. Martí was born on 28 January 1853 to a poor family of Spanish stock in Havana. Inspired by the 1868 War of Independence, at the age of 16 he published a magazine called *La Patria Libre*. Imprisoned, with a sentence of hard labour for his anti-Spanish activities, he was deported from Cuba three years later and remained an exile for most of his life. At first, he finished his studies in law in Madrid and Saragossa. He then travelled extensively in Spain, France and Mexico, earning his living as a teacher and journalist, and writing. He returned to Cuba in 1878 under a general amnesty, but oppressed by the air of despondency he left and eventually settled in New York in 1881. Eleven years later in Key West he founded the Partido Revolucionario Cubano (Cuban Revolutionary Party) with the tobacco workers. In his *Manifiesto de Montecristi* on 25 March 1895 he called for the realization of the goals of Céspedes and for the absolute economic and political independence of Cuba.

Though Martí's writings are endlessly quoted to support the goals of the Castro regime, he was not strictly speaking a socialist, let alone a Marxist. If anything, he was a liberal, believing that all classes should collaborate and that government should serve the interests of all. At the same time he was interested in anarchist ideas; he reprinted the articles of the French anarchist Elisée Reclus in his magazine *La Patria*, and he worked closely with and admired the anarchist tobacco workers in exile in Florida. While not opposed to free enterprise, he criticized the 'rich capitalist' for forcing the workers to labour for low wages and declared that it was 'the duty of the state to put an end to unnecessary misery'.[24] He was a staunch advocate of racial equality: 'Whoever foments and propagates antagonism between races', he wrote, 'sins against humanity'.[25] He stressed the dangers of trading with one nation: 'Whoever says economic union says political union,' he declared in 1891, with prophetic truth.[26] But above all, he was a great internationalist and, like Simón Bolívar, saw himself as a citizen of the Americas. He rightly feared the 'colossus to the north'. A few days before he died, he observed in his diary:

I have provoked the war, my duty has just begun rather than ended. The liberation of the Antilles will assure the long-term independence of our America. At last, I can give my life to my country to obtain freedom that will stop the expansion of American imperialism.[27]

Martí contacted the veteran generals Máximo Gómez and Antonio Maceo in exile and planned an uprising early in 1895. On 24 February, when they were still out of the country, an insurrection broke out in Baise about 50 miles from Santiago. Five days later Maceo landed with a handful of men by the River Duaba near Baracoa, having declared on the high seas: 'I am on my way to my homeland, ready to serve it free of the contagion of personal ambitions and to prevent with energy and resolution its useless transactions with Spain.'[28] His arrival was electrifying. The news spread like wildfire. *'!Maceo esta aquí. Viva Cuba libre!'* Thousands of poor peasants and farm workers joined the Liberation Army.

Ten days later on 11 April, Martí and Gómez landed with four companions at Playitas on the south-eastern coast of Oriente. At last Martí was putting his ideas into action. But on 9 May he was ambushed while riding down Dos Ríos to his first battle, betrayed ignominiously by a Cuban guide. Disobeying Gómez's order to retreat, he was killed by Spanish soldiers. The Spanish buried the 42-year-old writer who had never fired a shot with full military honours. Martí has been variously celebrated as the 'Apostle of Revolution', 'Martyr of Freedom', 'National Hero' and the 'Intellectual Author of Moncada'. His bust is to be seen in every school and square, in every village and town of Cuba. His works have been rifled for slogans to fit each change in the course of the Cuban Revolution. His body lies in a grand mausoleum in Santiago's cemetery, so designed that sunlight always falls on it, thereby fulfilling his wish:

> Don't lay me in the dark
> To die like a traitor.
> I am good and like a good man
> I shall die with my face to the sun.[29]

Like Bolívar, he is a symbol of the struggle for independence throughout Latin America. The Cuban Constitution of 1976 declares in its preamble the intention of realizing his wish: 'I want the first law of our republic to be the Cubans' worship of complete human dignity'.[30]

Despite Martí's premature death, Maceo continued the struggle. He rapidly put the Spanish on the defensive. As they retreated to the towns and cities, the forests and mountains became thick with rebels. Although greatly outnumbered, Maceo's forces beat their professional enemies in a dozen pitched battles. In September 1895, Maceo led a force of 1,500 men out of Oriente to the westernmost point of the island, Pinar del Río, thereby encircling the capital. Despite the numerically superior Spanish troops under General Valeriano Weyler who had about 250,000 men compared to 10,000 rebels, and the introduction of concentration camps into which the Spanish herded whole villages, they were unable to regain the offensive. But Maceo was killed in battle in December 1896, to be remembered later as 'the personification of protest and heroism, a man made of duty, the Herculean arm of the invasion, a tempest on horseback'.[31] A year later Spain granted Cuba autonomy, but the rebels this time refused to lay down their arms; the war had already cost 40,000 dead.

It was at this stage that the United States decided to intervene. It already dominated the Cuban economy; President William McKinley now saw the advantages of dominating the Gulf of Mexico. He was fearful of a 'Negro Republic' in Cuba, as 75 per cent of the rebels were black. He was also influenced by those who insisted that it was the manifest destiny of the United States to civilize the 'lesser breeds'. The blowing up of the American battleship *Maine* on 15 February 1898 in Havana harbour which killed 260—by whom, it is still not clear—provided the excuse for US intervention. To a reporter who cabled that all was quiet, the American press tycoon Hearst replied: 'PLEASE STAY THERE STOP SUPPLY PICTURES I WILL SUPPLY WAR STOP'. A jingoistic press, especially Hearst's *New York Journal* and Pulitzer's *New York World* whipped up war fever. The slogan 'Remember the *Maine*, to hell with Spain' was often heard. War was declared on 25 April 1898 and soon after US Marines landed on the island, engaging Spanish troops at El Carey village and San Juan Hill. The US Navy defeated the antiquated Spanish fleet under Admiral Cerrera off Santiago de Cuba. Although they had intervened when the Spanish were on the verge of defeat, the US forces refused to let the Spanish surrender to the Cubans, and kept General Calixto García and the *mambises* out of Santiago.

The conflict was naturally glorified by the US press; the charge up San Juan Hill by Teddy Roosevelt's 'Rough Riders' was given maximum coverage. In fact, no more than 500 men were killed in battle in the whole Spanish-American war, which lasted only 114 days; on the other hand, thousands on both sides died of yellow fever and malaria.

In the Treaty of Paris signed on 11 April 1899, the US gained possession of Cuba, Puerto Rico, Guam and the Philippines, with the loss of 266 dead. It was, as US Secretary of State John Hay put it, a 'splendid little war'.[32] Lenin, on the other hand, saw it as giving birth to the imperialist stage of capitalism. It also marked the entrance of the US on the international stage as a world power.

It was not the intention of the US to grant immediate independence; Spanish rule was replaced by military occupation under General Leonard Wood. Four years later, nominal independence was granted when Washington imposed a US-style constitution based on universal suffrage and an all-powerful President. The infamous Platt Amendment of 12 June 1901 was also included, which was to hang like a millstone round the neck of the new republic. It not only retained the use of certain naval stations to be leased 'in perpetuity' but declared that the United States could exercise 'the right to intervene for the preservation of Cuban independence, the maintenance of a government adequate for the protection of life, property and individual liberty'. The United States had completely ignored the Revolutionary Government-in-Arms and none of the leaders of the independence movement, which had cost the lives of ten per cent of the Cuban population, were consulted. The Amendment reduced the independence and sovereignty of Cuba to a sad myth.

2

THE PSEUDO REPUBLIC

The Pseudo Republic, as the newly independent Cuba of 1902 came to be known, could not have got off to a worse start. Two out of three people could not read, while only a sixth of the school-age children were receiving an education. Half the cultivated land had been ravaged. There were virtually no health facilities outside the towns: poverty and disease were rampant.

The American military governor General Wood himself recognized that the Platt Amendment added to the new constitution left Cuba with little or no independence. The Cuban government could not enter certain treaties without US consent, nor secure loans above certain limits. It was even obliged to maintain the sanitary conditions which had been introduced by law. General Wood noted frankly:

> With the control that we have over Cuba, a control which without doubt will soon turn her into our possession, soon we will practically control the sugar market of the world. I believe that it is a very desirable acquisition for the United States. The island will be gradually 'Americanized', and in due course we will have one of the most rich and desirable possessions existing in the world . . . [1]

Rough-riding Roosevelt, now President, concurred, and wrote, albeit more circumspectly, in a message to Congress on 10 November 1903:

> It was provided that when the island became a free and independent republic, she should stand in such close relations with us in certain respects to come within our system of international policy; and it followed that she must also to a certain degree become included within the lines of our economic policy.[2]

The country indeed was an American colony in all but name. In 1898, US holdings were 50 million pesos; in 1906, 160 million pesos; in 1927, they had reached 1.45 billion pesos. Americans influenced the price of Cuban exports and flooded the Cuban market with their manufactured goods. Under the Reciprocity Treaty of 1903, Cuba received a 20 per cent preferential reduction in US tariffs, while many products received a 20 to 40 per cent cut in Cuban tariffs. Within 15 years, 74 per cent of all Cuba's imports came from the US.

The sugar industry had undergone major changes and came under US control. Until 1870 it was mainly run by small mills, but with the introduction of new technology and railways, it became more profitable to have big centralized mills (*centrales*) fed by large estates. The *latifundia*, as the massive sugar plantations were called, grew up early this century, squeezing out the small farmers. The new owners then leased out their land to large tenant farmers known as *colonos* who produced the cane for the *centrales*. In 1899, there were 15,000 *colonos* feeding just over 200 *centrales*; in 1936, the figure had almost doubled. The overriding monopoly of sugar meant that the Cuban economy became fundamentally distorted. With the US the main customer for sugar, US investment in the industry also became dominant. The Cubans were then obliged to give further tariff concessions for American exports in exchange for sugar quotas (at two US cents a pound above world market price). As Nicolás Guillén wrote in *Caña* (Sugar-Cane):

> The black
> next to the cane
>
> The Yankee
> over the canefield
>
> The earth
> beneath the canefield
>
> The blood
> we are losing.

Sugar became a symbol of Cuban dependence on the 'colossus to the north'. The Spanish administration had never been particularly clean and honest, and the circumstances of the birth of the new Republic hardly made for a fresh start. Cuban political life became corrupt and lackadaisical; public office was seen as a source of personal profit; the trade of *botellas* (jobs for the boys) became the order of the day. Differences tended to be settled by violence. Several attempts at revolution were checked by US intervention.

When the first Cuban President Tomás Estrada Palma held fraudulent elections in 1906, the coup led by liberal politicians which deposed him, known as the *Guerrita de Agosto*, provided an excuse for the second intervention of US troops. They remained until 1909 under the governorship of Charles Edward Magoon. Marines landed again in 1912 when fear of a 'negro rising' swept the island and 3,000 rebels were killed. The US returned when another liberal insurrection occurred in 1917, and were on the island until 1922.

On the surface, Cuba liked to pose as an independent and sovereign nation. But the hold of the US over the economy and politics of the country was dramatically symbolized in 1929 by the completion of the Capitol to house the slumbering legislature. This was a replica of the Congress building in Washington, fittingly placed at the top of the Spanish Paseo del Prado. Martí's question: 'Once the United States is in Cuba, who will get it out?' was proving only too problematical.

With the fall in sugar beet production in Europe during the First World War, Cuba enjoyed a sugar boom which was called the 'dance of millions'. The 'golden twenties' in Cuba created a mad orgy of extravagance and saw the growth of the western suburbs of Havana— Miramar, Marionao, Cubanacan and Siboney. New buildings, hotels, clubs and casinos went up. Havana's most famous hotel, the Nacional, a palace of opulence and luxury, was opened in 1930. La Tropicana, billed as the largest nightclub in the world, began to swing. And then, of course, there were the brothels. In the 1880s a visitor called the display of prostitution in Havana 'more nude and shameless than even in the bazaars of Malta and the Eastern ports'.[3] In the 1920s, prostitution was no less widespread but a little more sophisticated and discreet.

The grand buildings which were erected might have seemed a sign of wealth, but they were in fact symbols of poverty, dependence and uneven development. As property in Cuba traditionally meant wealth and stability, the emerging middle class preferred to invest in real estate rather than in the risky world of industrial enterprise. The result was that the Cubans sold the Americans their sugar and let the Americans provide their services and their manufactured goods for them. Cuba had the first automatic telephone system in the world, but it was built by a US company which repatriated all the profits. Each new car unloaded at the Cuban docks benefited Detroit, not Havana. The palatial residences, like the skyscrapers after them, stand as graphic symbols of the failure of the Cuban middle classes to develop their own country.

The 1920s also saw the rise of large banking institutions, the growth of a central railway network, and development of electricity. It marked the triumph of the *centrales* in the sugar industry. By 1926 the *centrales* owned about a fifth of the total area of Cuba. And yet the conditions for the sugar workers were abysmal amidst all the new wealth. The wages of the cane cutters were even reduced. The *tiempo muerto* (fallow period) between the harvests was stretched to almost nine months, and some families were even obliged to eat roots and bark to stay alive, and to live in caves or woods.

The election of Gerardo Machado in a landslide victory in 1924 brought about a new low in political *gangsterismo*. Half a million dollars of his campaign expenses had been supplied by a US-owned electrical company. Ironically, he had campaigned as a liberal in his election for 'honesty in government', and promised to develop 'water, roads, and schools'. He extended his rule unconstitutionally after 1929, and in the following year governed by martial law. He became the first real Cuban dictator.

The labour movement which had emerged towards the end of the nineteenth century did not remain quiescent during the first two decades of the new Republic. From the 1890s and during the first quarter of this century, it was the anarcho-syndicalists who led the class struggle. The Cuban labour movement was predominantly anarchist.[4] Many anarchists, mainly peasants, were in the forefront of the struggle for independence, including Rafael García, Armando André (a commander in the rebel army) and Enrique Cresci. At the turn of the century, the group publishing *El Mundo Ideal* invited the Italian anarchist Enrico Malatesta to the country. In his farewell address before being deported, he traced a very different path for the independence movement from that of Castro's:

I assume that the libertarians fighting against the existing government will not put another government in its place; but each one will understand that as in the war for independence this spirit of hostility to all governments incarnated in every libertarian will now make it impossible to impose upon the Cuban people the same Spanish laws which martyrs like Martí, Cresci, Maceo and thousands of other Cubans died to abolish . . .[5]

In the first two decades of this century, the anarchists with their influential journal *Tierra* spread the ideas of Bakunin, Reclus and Kropotkin. They led the 1902 strike of the apprentices, the first major one of the new Republic. In 1907, they spearheaded the agrarian co-operatives and built up peasant organizations. They were especially strong amongst tobacco and construction workers. The first general secretary of the Confederación Nacional Obrera Cubana, (CNOC) (National Confederation of Cuban Labour) was the anarchist typographer

Alfredo López. However, when President Machado cracked down on the anarchists in the 1920s they began to lose ground to the Communists. With their prestige enhanced by the success of the Russian Revolution, the Communists grew in strength and managed to seize control of the CNOC. In 1925 the Cuban Communist party was also founded. Thereafter the Communists dominated the labour movement.

The students at the University of Havana, the only centre of higher education, were at the forefront of the opposition to Machado's tyranny. Julio Antonio Mella helped organize the first Congress of Cuban Students, the Federación Estudiantil Universitaria (FEU) (University Students' Federation) in 1923. Two years later he was a founding member with veteran socialist Carlos Baliño, of the Communist party, but in 1929 he was assassinated by a Machado gunman when exiled in Mexico. Other clandestine groups, like the Directorio Estudiantil Universitario (University Students' Directorate) and the ABC maintained the pressure on Machado by linking up with the liberal nationalists and the labour movement and by organizing demonstrations. These culminated in a general strike on 4 August 1933, which forced Machado to leave Cuba.

Carlos Manuel de Céspedes, the only son of the leader of the Ten Years' War, was proposed as President by the new American ambassador Sumner Welles. The top-hatted and fur-collared Céspedes, who was more at home in Paris than Havana, immediately assumed supreme power and moved into the florid presidential palace. The period of Cuban political history that followed was complicated and fast-moving. A provisional government was set up, but with revolutionary aspirations on the crest of a wave, it was taken over a month later on 4 September 1933 in a coup organized by groups of students, workers and soldiers. A group of army sergeants, including a young Sergeant-stenographer called Fulgencio Batista y Zaldívar, seized the main Columbia garrison in Havana. Ramón Grau San Martín, a member of the ABC, became President and governed with a 27-year-old expelled student, Antonio Guiteras, as Secretary of the Interior. Under the impetus of Guiteras, the government granted Havana University autonomy, ended the Platt Amendment (except for the right of the US to use the naval base at Guantánamo), created a Ministry of Labour, gave women the vote, introduced the eight-hour day, and a minimum wage, and granted peasants the right to the land they were farming. In more than 30 mills the well-organized sugar workers set up councils of self-management, modelled on the soviets of the Russian Revolution.

But this was to be known as the 'frustrated revolution'. Although a government full of nationalistic fervour and keen to benefit the people, it had no real political base. Ambassador Welles, who had Roosevelt's ear, was moreover not impressed by its irresponsibility and refused US recognition of the new regime. The last act of Guiteras was to nationalize an American-owned electric company. The next day, on 15 January 1934, Batista (now a colonel) overthrew the regime with army and US support. It had lasted only 100 days.

Batista maintained his political influence for the next 17 years through four puppet Presidents. He broke the traditional officer class in the army and maintained his sway over the new leaders which emerged. Although he crushed the general strike of March 1935 and assassinated Guiteras, he found it useful to co-operate with the Communists in the so-called Anti-Fascist front, legalizing the Communist party and freeing political prisoners in 1938. In the following year a new labour organization, the Confederación de Trabajadores de Cuba (CTC) (Confederation of Cuban Workers) was founded. It was heavily dominated by Communist leaders. Its black secretary-general from 1939 to 1947, Lázaro Peña, was a Communist, as was the black president of the powerful sugar workers' union, Jesús Menéndez. When Batista became President himself in 1940, he actually introduced a new constitution which protected individual and social rights, supported full employment and a minimum wage, extended social security, called for equal pay for equal work, and limited the huge *latifundia* plantations. The national assembly which drafted the new constitution had Blas Roca, the leader of the Communist party, as one of its members, while the Communists, Carlos Rafael Rodríguez and Juan Marinello, served as ministers in Batista's government. All three were to come to prominence under Castro. As Batista was a mulatto, many of the non-white Cubans identified with him at this stage. The main opposition to Batista fell to the Partido Revolucionario Cubano (Auténtico) led by the veteran politician Grau, who based his reputation on his participation in the 1933 revolution. In the elections of 1944, Grau was voted into power once again, but this time with the support of conservatives and big business.

Grau simply failed to stem the graft, nepotism, violence and gangsterism which characterized political life in Cuba. When, for instance, the son of a government minister was assassinated by one of the proliferating groups of hired thugs known as *bonches*, Grau complained cynically: 'In the Ministry of Education, there is a payroll devoted especially to support these gangsters. But I cannot permit one of my collaborators to be attacked in this manner.'[6] He also tried to curb the power of the rejuvenated CTC after its elections of 1946. Two years later the sugar union leader Jesús Menéndez was shot by an army captain under his orders.

The situation did not improve during the presidency of Carlos Prío

Socarrás, formerly Grau's Minister of Labour, when he was elected in 1948. He closed down the Communist party paper *Hoy* and tried to divide the labour movement. A group of purists within the Auténtico party led by Eduardo R. Chibás therefore decided to break away to form the rival Partido del Pueblo Cubano (Ortodoxo). They claimed to be the repository of the ideals of the 'frustrated revolution' of 1933, calling for economic independence, political liberty and honest government, under the banner *Vergüenza contra Dinero* (Dignity versus Money). In a dramatic gesture, Chibás ended one of his Sunday evening speeches on the radio in August 1951 by accusing the government of Socarrás of being the most corrupt ever in the history of the republic; he cried: 'Comrades of the Ortodoxo party move forward for economic liberty, political liberty, and social justice! Sweep away the thieves in the government! People of Cuba, arise and walk. People of Cuba, awake. *This is my last knock at your door!*'[7] And with that, the microphone still on, he whipped out a revolver from his pocket and shot himself dead. A young lawyer who had just graduated from Havana law school, called Fidel Castro Ruz, listened in amazement.

If anything, this increased the popularity of the Ortodoxo party. But when the party seemed poised to take power in the 1952 presidential elections, Fulgencio Batista—who was running a poor third—decided once again to resort to his old violent methods. He met up with a group of dissatisfied officers and on 10 March 1952 they staged a coup by taking control of most of the military garrisons. The students rushed to the university to defend the government, but Socarrás had already left the country in the fine tradition of Cuba's political game of musical chairs. The following seven years of Batista's dictatorship plumbed new depths of corruption and oppression.

In the 1940s and 1950s, there was rapid economic growth on the island. Sugar production expanded so that Cuba became the largest producer in the world. New investment was made in the mining of nickel and cobalt, and in the development of tourism. After the Depression, there had been a world glut of sugar in the 1930s. Under the Sugar Defence Act of 1927, the Cuban government interfered in the free market economy to encourage a reduction in sugar-cane production and an increase in coffee production. Because of the drop in profits there was a relative US withdrawal from ownership, and Cuban ownership in the sugar industry increased from 22 per cent in 1939 to 55 per cent in 1952. But sugar continued to dominate the economy: from 1949 to 1958 sugar accounted for about 30 per cent of GNP and 85 per cent of exports. Land was also held in the hands of a few, with the vast estates of the *latifundia* becoming larger and representing in 1940 average investments of $3.5 million dollars. By the early I950s the sugar market was largely controlled by two big speculators, Francisco Blanco (who administered Batista's 'Washington' mill) and Julio Lobo. The latter possessed 14 mills, controlling 100,000 acres worth $50 million a year, and had interests in hotels (financing the hotels Capri and Riviera in Havana), banking, radio and shipping. He sold annually 35 to 50 per cent of Cuban sugar.

Cuba continued to be greatly dependent on the 'colossus to the north' for trade. US sugar quotas were bought as before with Cuban tariff concessions for importing manufactured goods which seriously impaired the growth of domestic industry. In the 1950s about 75 per cent of imports came from the US, which took 65 per cent of Cuba's exports. In addition virtually all of the telephone and electric services, one half of the public service railways, one fourth of all bank deposits, about 40 per cent of sugar production, and much of mining, cattle ranching and oil production were in US hands. And with economic control came American cultural influence, which began to change many customs, distort the folklore and affect the language. Throughout the country, and especially in the towns, *tienda* became stores; *escuela*, schools; *liceos*, clubs; and even *funerias*, funeral homes.

The result of Cuba's dependence on the US was an extremely unequal society. By Latin American standards, the people were reasonably well provided with food; daily average consumption was only exceeded by Argentina and Uruguay, and the country had good telephones and roads. But the wealth was poorly distributed. While the Cuban sugar barons and the American-sponsored middle men lived a grand lifestyle, the majority of the population eked out a subservient and miserable existence. Unemployment was high; work in the sugar industry was seasonal. The differences between town and country were vast: Havana, now known as the 'Monte Carlo of the Caribbean', was one of the most sophisticated cities in the West; the rest of the nation lived in profound poverty with little provision for education and health. New housing was almost entirely limited to suburban residences and apartment blocks in Havana, while rural immigrants poured into the shanty towns around. As the song of Carlos Puebla put it, for most people 'The roads of Old Cuba lead nowhere'.

Batista could count on the support of the middle class, and some peasants and workers, especially amongst the Communist leaders, some of whom had served in his former cabinet. Nevertheless, his political base remained narrow. The anarcho-syndicalist Asociación Libertaria de Cuba (ALC), founded in 1950 at the third National Liberation Congress, attacked in their widely circulated paper *El Libertario* the collaboration between Batista and the Communist leadership of the CTC. In addition, his seizure of power also coincided with celebrations in 1952 of the 50th anniversary of the establishment of the Republic, and in 1953 of the centenary of Martí's birth. The hopes of the founding fathers of the Republic—Céspedes, Maceo, Gómez and Martí—were reawakened and contrasted cruelly with the increasing repression and censorship of Batista's rule.

The lawyer Fidel Castro had attempted to get charges against Batista's coup taken seriously by the courts. When he failed, he and others decided that the only answer was armed struggle. With a group of Ortodoxo dissidents, he helped organize simultaneous attacks on army barracks in Bayamo and Santiago de Cuba in Oriente to coincide with the summer carnival, hoping that this would be the spark that would ignite a new revolutionary fire over the country.

On 26 July 1953, Fidel, his brother Raúl, a young black bricklayer Juan Almeida, a recently graduated law student Melba Hernández, a business studies student Abel Santamaría and his sister Haydée, and 125 others took part in the assault on the Moncada Barracks in Santiago de Cuba, the second most powerful stronghold of the dictatorship.

It was never the intention of the young revolutionaries to engage the soldiers in combat; they wanted to seize control of the garrison and the weapons by surprise, and then call the soldiers to embrace the 'banner of liberty'. Raúl was to take over the Palace of Justice with five men; Abel Santamaría, the neighbouring Military Hospital. In the event, the attack on the Moncada Barracks proved a disaster—only one car penetrated the barracks and the soldiers quickly responded. The Bayamo assault did not even get that far. Fidel Castro and Juan Almeida managed to escape with some others to the Sierra Maestra but were rounded up a few days later. Three of the group were killed in the Moncada attack. Out of a total of 165 prisoners, 61 were murdered within hours of their surrender or capture.

Many were cruelly tortured. Haydée Santamaría was only one victim of the brutality surrounding their trial: having refused to divulge the secrets of the group, she was given the gouged-out eyes of her brother; when she refused again, she was presented with the testicles of her lover. Orders were given not to take Fidel alive, but he was; the officer who captured him proved to be an acquaintance from his university days. Even the Archbishop of Santiago appealed for mercy. Despite continued rumours, said to originate with the CIA, that Castro was castrated, it seems he was not tortured. At his trial he was sentenced to 15 years' imprisonment.

Although a military disaster, the dramatic gesture had a galvanizing effect. Batista could shrug it off as the futile effort of some young hotheads, but it marked the beginning of the Cuban Revolution. Today, 26 July is the most important celebration in the revolutionary calendar and the Moncada Barracks has been turned into a school. The wing attacked by the revolutionaries has had the bullet holes on its façade restored, and houses a Museum of the Revolution. The farmhouse outside Santiago where Castro and his comrades met the night before the attack is also a museum, and a monument stands for each martyr alongside the new road to the city.

In an eloquent five-hour address at his trial to the secret tribunal of officers and soldiers, the young and unknown lawyer Fidel Castro Ruz gave a devastating survey of Cuba's ills and outlined a political programme of renewal. It was afterwards published clandestinely as a pamphlet prophetically entitled: 'History Will Absolve Me'. Despite the prospect of capital punishment, Castro declared Batista to be the worst dictator in Cuban history. With an impressive array of largely accurate statistics, he described the sorry plight of the Cuban people: 700,000 people without work, 500,000 peasants employed seasonally for only five months in a year, 200,000 families without an acre of land, 30 per cent of peasants illiterate, unable even to sign their name. Placing himself firmly within the tradition of Martí and Chibás, he called for a return to the 1940 Constitution, national sovereignty, honest government, universal education, and agrarian reform. He looked to state legislation, not workers' struggle, to increase popular participation, to bring about a limited degree of nationalization, and to speed up the process of industrialization. While expressing solidarity with the peoples of Latin America, he declared that 'the island of Cuba will sink in the sea before we shall consent to be slaves of anyone'.[8] Castro finally perorated with great courage:

> I know that imprisonment will be as hard for me as it has ever been for anyone—filled with cowardly threats and wicked torture. But I do not fear prison, just as I do not fear the fury of the miserable tyrant who snuffed life out of 70 brothers of mine. Sentence me, I don't mind. History will absolve me.[9]

The pamphlet became a major document of the Cuban Revolution, and was translated into many languages. Cuban officials have seen a 'magisterial Marxist interpretation of the composition of class' in every word of it and called the author a 'fighter armed with all the Leninist artillery', but there is little evidence of this in Castro's analytical perspective.[10] Castro appears rather as a liberal constitutionalist threatening violence only if good laws are not enacted. Significantly, it is Tom Paine who is referred to, not Marx.

At the time of his trial, Fidel was only 26 years old, a recent graduate in law from the University of Havana. Born on 13 August 1927, he was the son of Angel Castro, a soldier from Galicia in Spain who had been sent to quell the independence movement in the 1890s and had decided to settle. He soon acquired considerable cattle and sugar lands in the district of Mayarí along the north coast of Oriente. He married a schoolteacher and had two children; he then had five illegitimate children by his cook, Lina Ruz. Fidel was the second of these. He grew up barefoot but sturdy on his father's farm, and went to the village school. He was sent to a Catholic secondary school in Santiago, and then to the Jesuit Belen High School in Havana. Here he encountered Falangist ideas and read the works of the Spanish writer Primo de Rivera who had founded in 1933 the *Falange Española*, the Spanish fascist group. As well as a scholar, he had grown up to be a powerfully built young man and was proclaimed the best high school athlete in Cuba for the year 1943–4. When he graduated, his high school year book said:

> Fidel distinguished himself always in all the subjects related to letters. His record was one of excellence, he was a true athlete, always defending with bravery and pride the flag of the school. He has known how to win the admiration and affection of all . . . the actor in him will not be lacking.[11]

Castro went on to study law at the University of Havana in 1945. Whilst a student, he was active in the struggle against the regimes of Prío Socarrás and Batista, although he never became a prominent student leader. He also married Mirta Díaz Balart, the sister of a male friend in the university law faculty. They had a son a year later, but the couple divorced soon afterwards. Although he has shown keen interest in women's emancipation, Castro has been described as a man without women.

The young Castro's internationalism and radicalism revealed themselves when he enrolled himself in 1947 in the abortive expedition against the dictator Rafael Leonidas Trujillo of the Dominican Republic; the expedition of Dominican exiles and Cubans never got beyond a key off the coast of Cuba. Elected in 1948 President of the Law Students' Association, Castro went in the same year as a delegate to the first meeting to establish an anti-imperialist Latin American Congress of University Students in Bogotá, Colombia. When the Liberal party leader

Jorge Eliecer Gaitán was assassinated in front of him in a newspaper office, he grabbed a gun in the riots that followed, though he did not fire a shot, and eventually took refuge in the Cuban Embassy.

After graduating from law school in 1951, he started practising as a lawyer and began to participate in parliamentary politics. He joined the Ortodoxo party led by Chibás, and still had sufficient confidence in the parliamentary system to allow himself to be selected as a candidate for the abortive 1952 elections; a photograph taken of him talking to the police during a demonstration at the time shows the young lawyer looking spruce and ultra-respectable in a smart suit and dark tie, with carefully polished shoes. But Batista's coup soon confirmed Castro's suspicion that the only way to achieve justice and equality in Cuba was through armed struggle, and in 1953, he and others of the Ortodoxo party stormed the Moncada barracks. After his arrest and trial, Castro went to serve his 15-year sentence with other young comrades in the Presidio Modelo (Model Prison) built by the dictator Machado on the Isle of Pines. Designed after Juliet Prison in Illinois, it was Cuba's most notorious and corrupt prison. The new political prisoners were separated from the rest of the inmates for fear of the subversive influence they might have on them, and were kept in a dormitory in the hospital block. The political prisoners were allowed to spend each day in the small adjoining courtyard, but at night they had to sleep with the lights on in the iron-barred dormitory.

They made good use of their time, dividing each day into periods of academic study, cultural activity and sport. They formed an academy amongst themselves named after Abel Santamaría, who had died after the Moncada attack. Like the young Martí before him, Castro became a teacher, mainly in philosophy but also in mathematics, Spanish, geography, economics and politics.

Despite their circumstances, the prisoners were buoyed up by an absolute conviction in their ultimate victory. Whoever might fall in the struggle, Castro wrote on 12 December 1953, there were thousands to take their place: 'the masses are ready, it is only necessary to show them the right path'. Already, Castro had developed his view of the committed vanguard group which would lead to the triumph of the Revolution. At the same time, he also wrote rather ominously on 23 March 1954, after studying the French Revolution, that Robespierre was an idealist and an honourable man until his death: 'he had to sin on the side of excess, never on the side of moderation, because he might be the cause of total loss. A few months of terror were necessary to end a terror that had lasted centuries. Cuba needs many Robespierres.'[12] While Castro may have seen himself in the role of a tropical Robespierre, he rejected at this stage the traditional Latin American dictator or *caudillo*:

> The great obstacles to the integration of such a movement [the revolutionary movement] are: cult of personality, group ambition, and *caudillos* . . . The conditions indispensable for the integration of a true civic movement are: ideology, discipline and leadership.[13]

The kind of revolution he was preparing was clearly not one with a great faith in the spontaneous creativity and political intelligence of the people. But while he was already stressing the need for powerful leaders he does not seem to have been a convinced Marxist-Leninist at this stage.

After four months of studious collective living, a totally unexpected event happened which galvanized the young revolutionaries. By chance, one of them saw through the bars of the windows none other than President Batista who had come to inaugurate a nearby electric plant. They immediately broke into their revolutionary 'Hymn of 26 July'. At first, the dictator thought that it was some sort of homage and smiled complacently. When he realized the meaning of the words, his smile became a ferocious scowl; he said nothing, but left immediately.

The result of this spontaneous demonstration was that the composer of the hymn, Agustin Díaz Cortaya, was beaten unconscious and Castro was placed in solitary confinement. His cell was situated so that from one side he could hear the cries from the wing of the hospital which housed mental patients where prisoners were tortured, and on the other he could see the bodies of the dead laid in the mortuary. It was, however, a square, roomy cell with its own toilet. At first he had no light, but he was eventually given one, and even allowed books to read. These included Victor Hugo, Michelet, Thackeray, Turgenev, and Jorge Amado. He was even allowed to read, by default, Marx's *Capital*; a guard who checked the book over is said to have left it with Castro, declaring that it was a good idea to learn about capitalism, since capitalism would make Cuba rich! Castro certainly was impressed by Marx, as much for his style as his theory:

> After breaking my head on Kant for a good while, Marx seems easier than saying an Our Father to me. He, like Lenin, had a terrific appetite for polemic, and I really enjoy myself and laugh as I read them. They were implacable and terrifying to their enemies. Two real revolutionaries . . .[14]

Although Castro has been accused of being a philistine, his reading in prison certainly reflects a wide-ranging interest. Indeed, he readily acknowledged that 'literary, philosophic or artistic genius has a considerably wider area in time and history than the world of action and reality, which is the only stage that political geniuses possess.'[15]

Castro's pamphlet 'History Will Absolve Me' was completed in prison, but it did not have a great influence at first. The official Communist party, renamed the Partido Socialista Popular (PSP) in 1944, dismissed the attempt to spark off a revolt by the attack on the Moncada Barracks as a form of 'putschist' adventurism, 'peculiar to bourgeois factions', which was opposed to the 'interests of the people'.[16] Since the Communist party had already collaborated in previous Batista administrations and espoused a gradual and parliamentary road to socialism, it is easy to see why they disliked the Ortodoxos' move, and why Castro and his colleagues should have been so impatient with the Communist party at this stage. But events moved quickly. A sugar strike in 1955 was followed towards the end of the year by a series of student riots which were brutally suppressed. The University of Havana was then closed for three years.

Castro was fortunate in 1955 to be released in a general amnesty engineered by Batista as a publicity stunt after serving only 20 months of his sentence. The young revolutionaries returned to Havana in triumph, greeted by the Ortodoxo party and the University Students' Federation. But when he was prohibited from making speeches and some released prisoners were re-arrested, Castro decided to go into exile. On 7 July 1955 he wrote an open letter to the political leaders, informing them that he was leaving Cuba because all doors of peaceful struggle had been closed to him. As 'a follower of Martí', he added, 'I believe the hour has come to take rights and not to beg for them, to fight instead of pleading for them.'[17]

In Mexico, Castro launched the 'July 26 Movement' (M-26-7), named after the date of the attack on the Moncada Barracks. 'It is not a political party but a revolutionary movement,' Castro wrote. 'Its ranks are open to all Cubans who sincerely desire to see political democracy re-established and social justice introduced into Cuba. Its leadership is collective and secret, formed by new men of strong will who are not accomplices of the past . . . ' Although Castro stressed above all that the revolution must be 'a revolution of the people, with the blood of the people and the sweat of the people', it is clear that he saw his role already as a powerful leader leading a group in the Leninist vanguard mould.[18]

He travelled up and down the east coast of the US in November

1955, trying to win support for the movement amongst groups of Cubans living in exile. In Mexico, Alberto Bayo, a Cuban instructor at the School of Military Aviation, agreed to help train a guerrilla force which would land in Cuba just as Maceo and Martí had done a century before. A small nucleus gradually began to form, who were later to form the leadership in the Revolution.

The most important of these men was a 26-year-old doctor from Argentina called Ernesto Guevara. Born in 1928 into a privileged family of Spanish and Irish descent, he was a brilliant student and, despite suffering terrible asthma attacks, he quickly graduated in medicine, studying for half the normal time. As a student he travelled through Latin America leading a hobo's life. He felt at home anywhere: 'I felt Guatemalan in Guatemala, Mexican in Mexico, Peruvian in Peru.'[19] It was not a reaction to his family but to the conditions of the continent which made him a radical; he wrote:

> I came into close contact with poverty, hunger and disease. I discovered that I was unable to cure sick children through lack of means, and I saw the degradation of under-nourishment and constant repression. In this way, I began to realize that there was another thing which was as important as being a famous researcher or making a great contribution to medical science: and that was to help those people.[20]

In Guatemala, Guevara was impressed by the progressive government of Jacobo Arbenz, which was distributing land to the peasants and which recognized that man hungered for dignity as well as bread. When a CIA-backed *coup* by a right-wing general overthrew the Arbenz government in 1954, Guevara tried to organize resistance. Although this failed, the experience proved a turning point in Guevara's life and he left for Mexico a convinced revolutionary.

Guevara had hitherto been impatient of bureaucracy and rejected all political parties. The overthrow of the Guatemalan government now led him to a study of Marx and Lenin and to a whole pantheon of Marxist thinkers in his search for an explanation of the workings of imperialism in Latin America. It also convinced him of the need for armed struggle to take the initiative against imperialism. When Guevara came across Castro in the summer of 1955 in Mexico City, they talked all night; it was immediately agreed that Guevara would be the doctor in Castro's planned expedition to Cuba.

Che (Argentinian for 'buddy') as he came to be called by the Cubans, was the second to join the group after Fidel's younger brother Raúl who had participated in the attack on the Moncada Barracks. Another recruit was 23-year-old Camilo Cienfuegos, who had emigrated illegally to the US but had been deported back to Cuba as Fidel was leaving for Mexico. He had then been shot in the leg in a student demonstration in honour of Antonio Maceo. On recovery, Cienfuegos decided to join Castro in Mexico. José Antonio Echeverría, the 24-year-old president of the University Students' Federation in Havana, and the leader of the militant student group, the Directorio Revolucionario (Revolutionary Directorate) also visited Castro in Mexico to find out his plans.

It was decided that the M-26-7 would stage an uprising in Santiago de Cuba to coincide with the landing of the invasion force in Oriente. Frank Pais, a 21-year-old teacher from Cuba was recruited to co-ordinate the plan and came to Mexico City in 1956. The group chose 30 November 1956 as the date for the event which would trigger off, they hoped, an insurrection across the country. País then returned to Santiago to help organize the growing underground movement.

In the event the plan for Revolution in Cuba could not have got off to a worse start. Castro and Guevara set out with 81 other comrades in a leaky cabin cruiser called *Granma*, built only to hold eight. They were still at sea when the uprising in Santiago took place on 30 November 1956, and although Frank Pais and his comrades (wearing M-26-7 armbands) attacked the police station, naval headquarters and the Moncada garrison with some success, they were forced to retreat and go underground. *Granma* landed two days later, some 30 miles south of the agreed spot in almost impenetrable mangrove swamps near the village of Las Coloradas.

The tired, disorientated band of revolutionaries who had lost most of their equipment, tried to make it to the refuge of the Sierra Maestra mountains, but they were discovered by Batista's forces at Alegría de Pio on 5 December 1956. It proved a baptism of fire: the group were mown down in a hail of bullets. For Guevara, who was badly wounded, it was again a turning point: 'I was faced with the dilemma of choosing between my dedication to medicine and my duty as a revolutionary soldier. At my feet were a pack full of medicines and a cartridge box; together, they were too heavy to carry. I chose the cartridge box . . .'[21]

The scattered survivors moved, as planned, eastwards to the Pico Turquino, Cuba's highest mountain, stumbling through the lush vegetation of the dense forests. The five comrades with Che, including Ramiro Valdés and Juan Almeida, made a formal pledge to fight to the death. Only 12 of the original band managed eventually to meet up; ten others had survived and were in jail.

Although conditions in Cuba were ripe for revolution, with unrest amongst the city workers and anger amongst the peasants, the odds against the small band were apparently insurmountable. For six months they were constantly on the move, intent on keeping alive, on trying to win the support of the local peasants, and on linking up with Frank País and the M-26-7 movement in Santiago. They opened the war of the Revolution on 14 January 1957, with a successful attack on a small army garrison on La Plata river. After so many setbacks, the effect on morale was electrifying. They managed to survive a few more skirmishes, and on 28 May they won their first major battle when they attacked and overcame a garrison in broad daylight at El Uvero, on the narrow coastal strip to the south of the Sierra Maestra. The guerrillas, who now numbered 80, were in business.

Although Castro and Guevara believed that a guerrilla group in the country should be the flag-bearer of Revolution, the support of an urban underground was essential to supply arms, money and recruits. Cuban official historians, wise after the event, have blown up the military importance of the guerrilla band out of all proportion: the heroic 'battles' which are recounted in such exhaustive detail were in fact little more than skirmishes involving 20 or so guerrillas. The opposition in the cities was probably much more significant in keeping relentless pressure on Batista's regime. Without the struggle in the cities, there would have been no guerrilla army. At the same time, it is equally true that without the myth of the invincible guerrillas in the Sierra, the urban movement would not have been so effective or inspired.

Frank País came to meet the guerrillas with other leaders of the urban wing of the M-26-7 who included Armando Hart Dávalos, Vilma Espin, Haydée Santamaría (who had survived her ordeal after the Moncada attack) and Celia Sánchez. The American journalist Herbert L. Matthews also managed to contact the guerrillas, bringing back photographs and an interview with Castro which, through wild exaggerations of their actual threat, gave the guerrillas great publicity.

Apart from the M-26-7, the more radical members of the Auténtico party were active in the cities. There was also a Civic Resistance Movement (made up mainly of professionals) and the students' clandestine Revolutionary Directorate. On 13 March 1957, 40 members of the Revolutionary Directorate stormed the presidential palace in the centre of Havana, almost managing to kill Batista. At the same time, a group headed by the student leader José Echeverria (who had visited Castro in Mexico) took over a radio station and announced the death of Batista, before being gunned down by police. While Castro criticized the action at the time as 'a useless expenditure of blood', the students who died have subsequently became venerated martyrs of the Revolution.[22] Survivors of the attack joined other members of the Revolutionary Directorate and of the M-26-7 to open up an independent guerrilla front in the Escambray mountains above Trinidad. It became increasingly clear to the guerrillas that the correct strategy was to sap gradually the morale of Batista's army from their stronghold in the mountains.

While the victory at El Uvero in May 1957 increased morale enormously in the Sierra Maestra, the war between the guerrilla forces and Batista's army in the mountains entered a period of stalemate which lasted nearly a year. The urban struggle also had its setbacks. On 30 July 1957, Frank País was identified to the police by an informer and was shot dead in the street in Santiago. A photograph in the Moncada Museum shows the blood from his corpse running in the gutter. At his funeral a spontaneous general strike took place, and a riot erupted at the cemetery which was eventually quelled by the police.

A couple of months later on 5 September, an uprising occurred in the important port of Cienfuegos. A group of young naval officers had organized a nationwide plan to take over several towns and cities early in September, but at the last minute the plan had been postponed. The rebels in Cienfuegos were not notified of the decision. In the event they managed to seize the naval base and take over the city for a few hours before being brutally crushed by reinforcements brought up in an armoured troop train.

After the battle of El Uvero, Batista's troops withdrew from the outposts in the Sierra Maestra. The guerrillas were no longer intent on surviving at all costs and keeping up morale; the nomadic phase was over. They were able to set up a permanent camp at La Plata near the mountain Pico Turquino. At last they had hammocks to sleep in, and regular meals. New recruits joined them, bringing arms and equipment, but life was hard. Camilo Cienfuegos used to test them by offering them cooked cats to eat. A government in miniature was established, and justice was administered by popular courts. They supported themselves by small cottage industries which turned out shoes, knapsacks, ammunition and even cigars. A hospital and school were set up.

The guerrillas were extremely careful in their treatment of the enemy. Castro and Guevara insisted that they should behave as humanely as possible towards wounded enemy soldiers, prisoners and civilians. But discipline was strict. All food was paid for and no drinking was allowed. When one over-zealous guerrilla accidentally killed a comrade when he held a revolver at his head as a threat, he narrowly escaped being executed by a vote of all the guerrillas, Castro and Guevara taking his defence. But the revolutionaries executed informers and some bandits, and even used simulated execution as a punishment. Castro also announced that the crimes of insubordination, desertion and defeatism were to be punishable by death. Guevara later defended the 'iron fist' of that time by asserting: 'We were obliged to inflict exemplary punishment in order to curb violations of discipline and to liquidate the nuclei of anarchy which sprang up in areas lacking a stable government!'[23] But while the punishments meted out were severe the guerrillas earned a reputation for fair treatment.

The guerrillas quickly realized that, if they were to survive, the support of the peasants around them in the mountains was crucial. Contact with the peasants and a knowledge of their problems also had a profound influence on the guerrillas' political consciousness. Guevara later wrote:

> The people in the Sierra grow like wild flowers, untended and without care, and they wear themselves out rapidly, working without reward. During those consultations we began to grow more conscious of the necessity for a definitive change in the life of the people. The idea of agrarian reform became clear, and oneness with the people ceased to be theory and was converted into a fundamental part of our being.[24]

In order for the peasants to become rebels, the rebels became peasants: the middle-class city boys donned palm-leaf straw hats. Guevara was deeply impressed by the changes wrought by the experience of the Revolution amongst the peasants. For him, the greatest miracle of the Revolution was the discovery by Cuban peasants of happiness within the liberated zones:

> Whoever has witnessed the timorous murmurs with which our forces were received in each peasant household, notes with pride the carefree clamour, the happy, hearty laughter of the new Sierra inhabitant. That is the reflection of his self-assurance which the awareness of his own strength gave to the inhabitant of our liberated area. That is our future task: that the concept of their own strength should return to the Cuban people . . .[25]

The experience of guerrilla warfare in the Sierra Maestra only confirmed for Guevara his faith in the peasantry. He rejected Marxist theory which stressed the need for an uprising in the cities led by the urban proletariat. Indeed, in defiance of Marxist-Leninists, he argued that it was for the country to liberate the city and not the other way round. In his book *Guerrilla Warfare* (1961), he concluded that:

1. Popular forces can win a war against the army.
2. It is not necessary to wait until all conditions for making a revolution exist; the insurrection can create them.
3. In underdeveloped [Latin] America the countryside is the basic area for armed fighting.[26]

The failure of the urban insurrection and the pragmatic compromises of the Cuban Communist party also led Guevara to reject the idea of Communist party leadership. He went beyond Mao in *Guerrilla Warfare* in advocating the autonomy of a guerrilla group outside the central control of the urban-based Communist party. The position echoes that held by the anarchists in their dispute with the Communists during the Spanish Civil War. But unlike the anarchists, Guevara declared that the success of the guerrilla group depended on the unquestioned leadership of a *jefe máximo*—which betrays the old Latin American respect for a *caudillo* or boss. This contradiction runs through all of Guevara's writings on guerrilla warfare; one minute he stresses that the rebel group must remain autonomous and that every guerrilla must be 'his own general', the next, he demands rigid discipline and uncritical obedience to an all-powerful leader.

The guerrillas fully realized that the Revolutionary war was not only fought with arms but also with ideas. Once established in La Plata, they began to print a newspaper, *El Cubano Libre*, named after the paper of the nineteenth century *mambí* independence fighters. They put up handmade signs around the mountain range of the Sierra Maestra denoting the *Territorio Libre de Cuba*. And then, on the night of 24 February 1958, the 63rd anniversary of the beginning of the Second War of Independence, a voice broke into the radio waves of Cuba: '*¡Aquí Radio Rebelde! ¡Transmitiendo desde la Sierra Maestra, en territorio libre de Cuba!*' ('Here is Radio Rebelde! Broadcasting from the Sierra Maestra, the free zone of Cuba!'). Following Guevara's advice that truth is the best policy in Revolutionary propaganda, it was soon to become the most popular radio station in the country.

As their strength grew, the guerrillas in the Sierra Maestra split up into five columns with Fidel Castro holding the centre, Guevara on the northern slopes, Juan Almeida on the heights above Santiago de Cuba, and Camilo Cienfuegos on the plains near Bayamo. Meanwhile Raúl Castro opened up a new front in the mountains north of Santiago, the Sierra Cristal. A general strike, hastily organized by the leaders of the M-26-7 movement and the Civic Resistance Movement in the cities, failed on 9 April 1958. It became clear that it was only the guerrillas who would be able to break the military basis of Batista's tyranny.

Batista decided to launch an all-out attack on the guerrilla stronghold in the Sierra Maestra. During May 1958, 10,000 soldiers supported by aircraft massed in the foothills, north and south of the rebel headquarters near Pico Turquino. Castro called in the columns except for Raúl's and was able to count on only 300 men for his defence. For two and a half months, the two armies tried to outmanoeuvre each other, Castro's forces making up in morale what they lacked in numbers and equipment. The turning point came at the battle of Jigüe which lasted ten days. The rebels surrounded a battalion camped at a river fork close to their headquarters, and despite aerial bombardments managed to hold back reinforcements. Eventually the soldiers surrendered and their leader, Major Quevedo, joined the Revolutionary forces.

The spirit of the Batista army was broken; the soldiers fled from the Sierra Maestra mountains in disarray. The rebels, by contrast, had suffered only 27 dead. The rebels could only count on 800 men by August 1958, but it was now just a matter of time before the dictatorship collapsed. Following Antonio Maceo's strategy, two invasion columns led by Che Guevara and Camilo Cienfuegos were despatched to carry the revolution westwards to the capital. Castro, leading the José Martí column, then moved towards Santiago. He managed to defeat Batista's forces in late November in a frontal battle around the central highway. In late December, Guevara routed an armoured train bringing reinforcements and arms in the town of Santa Clara. Batista's demoralized army refused to fight, thus dealing a death blow to the regime.

Realizing that all was lost, Batista slipped away by plane in the early hours of 1 January 1959 to the Dominican Republic taking with him, allegedly, the tidy sum of $300 million. In the end, his regime had collapsed without a real struggle: there had been no peasant revolts, no general strikes, only the constant pressure of the urban underground and a tiny guerrilla force.

Fearful that Batista's generals would try to establish a military government, Castro called for a general strike and announced on Radio Rebelde: 'The story of 1895 will not be repeated! This time, the *mambises* will enter Santiago de Cuba!'[27] On the following morning the rebel army entered the jubilant city. Carlos Franquí recalled: 'People rush out to meet us. They are wild; they touch us, they kiss our filthy beards.'[28] Castro walked slowly through the doors of the Moncada Barracks which he had tried unsuccessfully to storm five years, five months, and five days earlier, and accepted the surrender of Batista's army in Oriente from General Cantillo. In Havana, the road to the airport was jammed with abandoned Cadillacs and Chryslers. At noon the gates of Príncipe prison were opened. The political prisoners rushed down the stone steps crying 'Freedom! Freedom!'

Then, at the head of the columns of his rebel army, Castro entered Havana on 8 January 1959. The ill-kempt, bearded guerrillas, with colourful beads about their necks and shining stars on their foreheads, swept through the broad and elegant boulevards. There was wild rejoicing; they were welcomed everywhere as heroes and liberators. Pure and beautiful youth had taken over, and all would be well.

3

THE FIRST FREE TERRITORY IN THE AMERICAS

Castro's march on Havana, which appeared so spontaneous and joyful, was a well-orchestrated event. His army, which numbered only 1,500 at the end of the fighting, did not enter Havana immediately after the departure of Batista. His first move was to make Santiago the new capital. He then ordered Camilo Cienfuegos, with a force of 300, to occupy the Columbia military base in Havana after 12,000 of Batista's troops surrendered. Guevara took over La Cabaña fortress, and Raúl became provisional commander of the Marina de Guerra naval station in the capital. Castro's most reliable close *comandantes* occupied the key military posts; power was in his hands. It was only then that he staged the massive propaganda stunt of marching 350 kilometres along the central highway to enter Havana.

The guerrillas not only had the enthusiastic support of the overwhelming majority of Cubans but also of the revolutionary left everywhere. Even *Time, Life,* and the *New York Times* gave Castro their blessing. The Church genuflected. The toast of 'Cuba Libre' with rum and coke at last had real meaning. Beards sprouted all over Cuba in solidarity with the guerrillas, and razor-blade sales plummeted. The prevailing atmosphere of gloom and cynicism was suddenly transformed into euphoria. Roberto Fernández Retamar evokes something of the mood in his poem *No word does you justice*:

> Tremor stronger than coupling
> Company intenser than solitude,
> Conversation richer than silence,
> Reality stranger than dream,
> Truth pervading day and night,
> Song without stop-note,
> Sky flushed with banners,
> Reason for being here:

> You see that no word does you justice,
> Revolution.[1]

Castro was hailed as a new Messiah, having led the 12 apostles who survived the *Granma* expedition down from the mountains. He seemed to offer something for everybody: in his manifesto issued from the Sierra Maestra in 1957, he had promised free elections within a year, the recognition of all individual rights guaranteed by the 1940 constitution, and the guarantee of a free press. On his entry into Havana, he described his programme as 'humanistic democracy on the basis of liberty with bread for all peoples'.[2] When he went to Columbia barracks held by Camilo Cienfuegos, he gave his famous speech, 'Who Needs Guns?'. As all Cubans remember from history, in the middle of his speech, he asked the uneducated Camilo, 'Camilo, am I on the right track?' 'Fidel, you are on the right track,' came the answer and nearly everyone agreed.[3] Castro was launched at the head of a Revolution which was to reverberate throughout the Western hemisphere.

During his visit to New York in April 1959 at the invitation of leading newspaper publishers, he described the ideology of the Cuban Revolution as humanist, democratic and libertarian:

> Our revolution practises this democratic principle [of the majority] and is in favour of humanist democracy. Humanism means that in order to satisfy the material needs of many, it is not necessary to sacrifice man's dearest desires, which are his freedoms, and that the most essential freedoms of man mean nothing if his material needs are not satisfied as well. Humanism means social justice with liberty and human rights; humanism means what is usually meant by democracy, but not theoretical democracy—real democracy, human rights with the satisfaction of the needs of man . . . No bread without liberty, no liberty without bread; no dictatorship by one man, no dictatorship by classes, groups, castes. Government by the people without dictatorship or oligarchies; freedom with bread, bread without terror: that's what humanism is all about.[4]

The slogans went up all over Havana: 'Freedom with bread, bread without terror'; 'Neither dictatorship from the right nor dictatorship from the left'; 'Neither capitalism nor socialism—Revolutionary humanism'.[5] The Cuban Revolution was a local one made in the particular circumstances of the tropical isle: 'Our Revolution is olive green, just like the mountains in Oriente province,' Castro had declared in New York.

It seems that at this stage Castro was genuinely no Marxist. Indeed, much of his experience and strategy ran counter to the Marxist-Leninist tradition with its stress on the urban proletariat as the agency of revolution and the vanguard party as their leaders. Guevara emphasized the primary importance of the peasantry, while Castro maintained that the revolution had been 'won with the help of men of all ideas, of all religions, of all social classes'.[6] They both saw the need for armed struggle and regarded the rural guerrilla group as the autonomous motor force of the revolution outside the control of political parties. Finally, they felt it was not necessary to wait until the conditions for revolution were ripe: a determined guerrilla group could precipitate the necessary conditions for revolution.

If anything, their tactics were more typical of the anarchist tradition than the Marxist, and not surprisingly they were accused of left-wing opportunism by the Partido Socialista Popular (PSP), the official Communist party of Cuba. Unlike the anarchists, however, Guevara stressed the need for the unquestioned leadership of a supreme chief as more important than a whole party organization. Castro, with his great gifts of oratory and undoubted charisma, perfectly fitted the role.

Both Castro and Guevara were also determined not to share power with the other groups who had been in the forefront of revolutionary struggle against Batista. 'The authority of the Sierra', as Guevara called it, had to prevail. The students' Revolutionary Directorate had turned the university into an armed camp on the fall of Havana, but they were obliged to give up their arms. The second guerrilla front opened by a splinter group in the Escambray mountains was similarly dissolved, as was the Civic Resistance movement. The Cuban Communist party, the PSP, which had compromised with Batista and which disapproved of the guerrilla strategy, was kept waiting in the cold. As Guevara acknowledged:

> The Student Directorate took the path of insurrectional struggle, but their movement was independent of ours and they had their own line. The PSP joined with us in certain concrete activities, but mutual distrust hampered joint action and, fundamentally, the party of the workers did not understand with sufficient clarity the role of the guerrilla force, nor Fidel's personal role in our Revolutionary struggle.[7]

With the M-26-7 movement virtually undisputed, Castro assumed command of the armed forces. He appointed the former judge Dr Manuel Urrutia as President, and José Miró Cardona, president of the Havana Lawyers' Association, as Prime Minister to organize the new govern-

ment of largely moderate and liberal middle-aged men. A militia was
then formed in May to counterbalance the professional army. Its uniform
of blue shirts and trousers—once that of common labourers—came to
represent the spontaneous and voluntary organization which marked the
early libertarian phase of the Revolution. The armed people were seen
as both a symbol and instrument of Revolutionary democracy.

In the same month, the new regime rewarded its rural supporters by
passing the first Agrarian Reform Law and Castro returned to the rebel
headquarters in La Plata to sign the bill which established the Instituto
Nacional de Reforma Agraria (INRA) (National Institute for Agrarian
Reform) and which limited private land ownership to a maximum of
1,000 acres. The plantations, large farms, and major properties were
nationalized (just eight per cent of landlords had previously held 70 per
cent of the land). Co-operative and state farms were set up as examples,
and small farmers were given credit and taught improved methods of
cultivation. Agricultural diversification became the fi rst priority in order
to lessen the dependence on sugar. A central planning board was set
up to direct the rapid industrialization of the country.

These measures were widely popular. On the announcement of the
Agrarian Reform Law, the black Cuban poet Nicolás Guillén issued a
warning to the landlords on behalf of his peasant ancestors:

> Yesterday, I sent you a letter,
> written in my blood,
> to tell you that I want back
> the mountains and the plains
> and the rivers you stole from me,
> the ones that run between the trees,
> swaying in the wind,
> full of birds
> and my life
> which is nobody's but mine.
>
> Lord, you'll have to reckon with me.
> From the sugar cane to the rose bush,
> and from the rose bush to the sugar cane,
> you've staked your claim, and
> you'll have to reckon with me;
> Lord, how you're going to reckon with me.[8]

At the time, US interests possessed 75 per cent of Cuba's fertile soil,
90 per cent of public services, mining and oil production, and 40 per

cent of the sugar industry. The US took 75 per cent of all Cuban exports and supplied more than 80 per cent of imports. US investments were worth about $800 million. In order to break the American stranglehold on the economy, the government on 13 October 1960 nationalized foreign enterprises, the banks, and most large and medium-scale industrial and commercial enterprises. Urban rents were halved, and a low-income housing programme started. Brothels and casinos closed down, and prostitutes were rehabilitated in special schools. The mass communication media were taken over. Education was made public and expanded, many of Batista's garrison camps being converted into schools. A massive literacy campaign was launched to help the estimated one third of the population who could not read or write. The beaches, hotels and clubs were opened up to all Cubans, and racism was publicly decried as an odious ideology of the past.

To radical observers abroad, it seemed that in the Cuban Revolution a pluralist anarchy was at work, in which a genuinely original path to socialism was being mapped out and a model of development forged which could pave the way for other undeveloped countries. Cuba was the first country in the Americas which had genuinely broken away from the US; it appeared to be in no hurry to align itself with another power. When Sartre visited Cuba in 1960 he was overwhelmed with enthusiasm. He declared Guevara to be the 'most complete man of his age'.[9] He saw in Castro's rule 'a direct and concrete democracy . . . the revolutionary rulers converse directly with the people, thus establishing a direct and permanent bond between the will of the great majority of the people and the government minority . . . '[10] Sartre was fascinated by a living, spontaneous revolution without a bureaucratic structure or hierarchical party machine. He was reassured by Castro's claim 'I will never sacrifice this generation for the next. That would be abstract'. He pictured the young Revolutionaries romantically as on 'a long march, against the wind, under the clouds, in the night, toward a still unknown fate: victory or extermination'.[11] It seemed that Cuba at last was beginning to break the chains of underdevelopment, imperialism, and poverty. Could the island become, as the new regime insisted, the 'first free territory in the Americas'?

Initially, there were two visible centres of power in Havana: Castro and his commanders in the Hilton Hotel (renamed Habana Libre), and the President in his palace. It soon became clear who had the real authority. Unhappy about the slow implementation of the reforms, Castro became Prime Minister in February 1959 and forced President Urrutia to resign in July in favour of Dr Osvaldo Dorticós. Dorticós was a former member of the Civic Resistance movement and M-26-7, and also a lawyer. Although older than most of the guerrillas, at 40 he was Cuba's youngest ever President. Other moderates began to be eased out and replaced by comrades from the Sierra Maestra. Che Guevara became Director of the National Bank, and then Minister of Industry. As the Revolution began to bite, Castro's ideology and tactics began to take a new direction.

Hubert Matos, an intellectual who had fought in the Sierra Maestra and who became a governor of Camagüey province, sent a letter of resignation to Castro on 20 October 1959 complaining of Communist infiltration in the government: 'Everyone who has spoken frankly to you about the Communist problem has had to leave or be dismissed.' He called on Castro 'to rectify his errors—if there is still time'. Camagüey city was immediately surrounded by Castro's troops. After being accused of treason for having conspired to stop agrarian reform, Matos and 34 other officers were sentenced by a Revolutionary tribunal to 20 years' hard labour.

Matos' fears were not however entirely without foundation. On 1 May 1960, Castro reneged on his promise of free elections within a year, saying that they were a corrupt and fraudulent betrayal of the people. The press was censored. On 2 December 1961, he publicly declared his allegiance to Marxism: 'I am a Marxist-Leninist and shall be until the day I die.'[12] What had begun as a nationalist revolution was clearly becoming a Communist and militaristic one.

The political leadership which emerged in the crucible of the Revolution in its early days was made up of Castro and the commanders of the Sierra. Scarcely a year passed before the anarchist press, especially El Libertario of the Asociación Libertaria de Cuba (ALC) was suppressed. According to Simone de Beauvoir, who visited the island with Sartre, Castro purged his own M-26-7 movement 'because it was petty bourgeois and could not keep pace with the Revolution . . . the party had to go, to be replaced by reliable elements'.[13]

As a widespread urban movement, M-26-7 clearly threatened Castro's power base, so in July 1961 it was merged with the students' Directorio Revolucionario and the small Communist Partido Socialista Popular to form the Organizaciones Revolucionarias Integradas. This was eventually replaced in 1965 by a new Cuban Communist party, which reigned alone and supreme with Castro as its undisputed leader. Régis Debray, a French Marxist philosopher who took up a chair in Havana University, later justified this process in his *Revolution in the Revolution?* (1967), proofs of which were corrected by Castro. Debray argued that the guerrilla force is the nucleus of the people's army, and hence the arm of a revolutionary party in embryo:

Cuba Libre

Any guerrilla movement in Latin America that wishes to pursue the people's war to the end, transforming itself if necessary into a regular army and beginning a war of movement and positions, must become the unchallenged political vanguard, with the essential elements of its leadership being incorporated in the military command.[14]

In other words, Communists and socialists are expected to take their orders from the guerrilla force without discussion once the armed struggle has been victorious.

Although the liberals accused Castro of betrayal, his move towards Communism seems to have been a result of 'living the revolution'. Officials like Antonio Núñez Jiménez now like to argue that Castro was a *comunista autodidacta* and that he had adopted a liberal and democratic programme to begin with merely for tactical reasons, so as not to isolate himself from the masses who were prejudiced against Communism.[15] Certainly, Castro had read the *Communist Manifesto* as a student, and Marx's *Capital* in prison, but he admitted in a speech on 2 January 1962 that he only reached page 370 of the latter! Indeed, he told Herbert Matthews in October 1963 that he became a Communist after the Revolution was under way.[16] This development was no doubt encouraged by his brother Raúl, who had long been an orthodox and disciplined Communist, and Guevara, who was a highly unorthodox and imaginative Marxist. Guevara had written from the Sierra in 1957 to a friend:

I belong, because of my ideological background, to that group which believes that the solution to the world's problems lies behind the Iron Curtain, and I understand this movement as one of the many provoked by the desire of the bourgeoisie to free itself from the economic chains of imperialism. I shall always consider Fidel as an authentic left-wing bourgeois leader . . . [17]

It seems likely that Communism for Castro was not a deeply felt and carefully thought-out philosophy. It offered him however a useful analytical tool and a convenient radical programme. He told Chilean students in 1971, 'I was a man who was lucky enough to have discovered a political theory, a man who was caught up in the whirlpool of Cuba's political crisis long before becoming a fully-fledged Communist . . . discovering Marxism . . . was like finding a map in the forest . . . '[18]

If Castro's early attitude to Communism is subject to debate, his attitude towards the US is much more clear-cut. During the guerrilla war, he wrote to Celia Sánchez on 5 June 1958 that after a friend's house had been hit by rockets, he swore: 'The Americans would pay dearly for what they are doing here. When the war is over, I shall begin a longer and greater war: the war I'll wage against them. I realize that this is my true destiny.'[19]

At first Castro insisted that Cuba was with the West in the Cold War. The United States, however, was soon alienated from Cuba by the appropriation of US interests, by the trial and execution of hundreds of Batista's supporters, by the threat of a Communist state in its back yard, and by Castro's boast that he would turn 'the Cordillera of the Andes into the Sierra Maestra'. The US simply could not tolerate the prospect of a radical revolution right under its nose.

The CIA was quick to support the counter-revolution: Havana was bombed by a low-flying aircraft piloted by Diaz Lanz, once head of the Revolutionary Air Force. He had taken off from Florida. On 4 March 1960, the ship *Le Coubre* loaded with Belgian arms and ammunition, exploded in the harbour killing 70 people. The next day Castro declared ominously, 'we shall answer counter-revolutionary terror with Revolutionary terror'.[20] The slogan 'Bread without terror' had already been forgotten as tensions increased within and outside the country. For the first time Castro used the slogan *Patria o muerte* (Our country or death!).

Oil supplies were cut by the US. Cuba was obliged to turn to the Soviet Union for oil, but the refineries owned by Standard Oil and Shell refused to process it. The US government reduced sugar quotas and suspended exports to Cuba, except for food and medicines. Then on 17 April 1961, in an uninhabited area surrounded by swamps on the south coast of Cuba, a CIA-organized invasion force landed in the Bay of Pigs.

A year previously, President Eisenhower had ordered the CIA to begin training Cuban exiles, mainly in Guatemala. The CIA also began infiltrating counter-revolutionary guerrillas in the Escambray mountains in the central southern part of the island, where bandit gangs had given the Revolution a bad name amongst the local farmers.

When the Revolution began to bite and the Cuban government nationalized US interests, the newly-elected John F. Kennedy sanctioned, early in 1961, a CIA plan for a direct invasion of Cuba from Nicaragua. Five small exile organizations were patched together under the direction of a hastily formed Consejo Revolucionario (Revolutionary Council) to lead an invasion force consisting of five merchant ships, 1,500 men with landing craft, anti-tank guns, and thousands of automatic rifles. As the Nicaraguan dictator Luis Somoza came to see them off, he allegedly joked: 'Bring me a couple of hairs from Castro's beard!'[21]

In the meantime the regime in Havana was prepared for counter-revolutionary activity. When bombs went off during a rally after Castro's return from addressing the United Nations in September 1960, he called for a 'system of revolutionary collective vigilance'.[22] The result was the setting up of the Committees for the Defence of the Revolution (CDRs) in every neighbourhood to keep a watch out for imperialists and counter-revolutionaries.

The army and the new militias were on the alert. The first indication that something was afoot came on 15 April 1961 when eight aeroplanes with Cuban air force markings attacked three bases around Havana. The following day, Castro declared for the first time that the Revolution was a socialist one. He was speaking to a crowd of armed militia outside Havana cemetery. 'The imperialists', he exclaimed, 'can't forgive our being right here under their very noses, seeing how we have made a revolution, a *socialist revolution*, right here under the very nose of the United States!'[23] The enthusiastic crowd raised their rifles, shouting '¡*Venceremos, Venceremos!*' That same night Castro was awakened in the early hours to be told that fighting had broken out on the beaches of Playa Girón and Playa Larga in the Bay of Pigs.

The CIA chose the Bay of Pigs for the landing because it was ideal for a defensive bridgehead; the soil is rocky on the coast and hard up to six miles inland, where it becomes impassable. There were only two roads through the swamps which could easily be covered. Once landed, the invasion force planned to declare a provisional government and then wait for a US economic blockade to bring the revolutionary regime to its knees.

The first Cubans to encounter the invaders were small groups of the local militia and a battalion of the Revolutionary armed forces stationed at the Australia sugar mill on the edge of the Zapata swamp. The Cuban forces immediately proceeded down the road to Playa Larga, but were cut off by paratroopers landing behind them. Castro made the sugar mill his headquarters, ordering a battalion of militia leaders, who were attending a school in Matanzas, to move up; they managed to secure a foothold in the swamps despite being strafed by B-26 bombers with Cuban air force insignia.

In the meantime six Cuban planes launched a counter-attack, sinking landing craft and a ship which was carrying all the supplies for the first 10 days of the campaign.

The next day saw the militia and the newly arrived tanks forcing the invaders to retreat south to the Playa Girón. US Sabre jets were unable to check their momentum. On the third day, they arrived at the beach only to find the invaders had abandoned their equipment. Some of the routed troops tried to make it to the two US naval destroyers which had come to pick them up; most made for the swamps. The battle of the Bay of Pigs was over: it had lasted just 72 hours.

Along the 20-mile stretch of road from Playa Larga to Playa Girón there is today a monument for each of the 80 Cubans who died, the martyrs and heroes of the Revolution. There is also a great hoarding which lists, next to a skull and crossbones, the professions of the 1,197 prisoners taken: 100 plantation owners, 67 landlords of apartment houses, 24 large property owners, 112 big businessmen, 194 ex-soldiers of Batista's regime, 179 'idle rich' and 35 industrial magnates. In a typical gesture, Castro exchanged the prisoners for baby food and medicines from the US government.

On 25 April 1961, President Kennedy imposed a total trade embargo on Cuba. *'¡Viva Cuba Libre!'* responded the headlines of the newspaper *Revolución* in Havana. The US government also tried to isolate Cuba diplomatically: Cuba was expelled from the Organization of American States (OAS) and eventually all its members except Mexico severed relations.

The abortive invasion at the Bay of Pigs was a turning-point for the regime. As the poet Fayad Jamís wrote, it revealed the combatants' love for their country:

> Many of us shoulder our weapons
> at whispering outposts
> or in the dark corner of a workshop,
> behind a sturdy tree,
> beside the throbbing waves,
> under tree limbs and the stars,
> and everywhere love flourishes,
> as wide and as blue as the night,
> the love a man feels for his woman,
> the love of being here,
> our love of Cuba.[24]

Moreover, the Bay of Pigs invasion united the people behind Castro as never before, showing him to be a great soldier and man of action as well as a revolutionary leader. In a public discussion on television, the majority of the prisoners taken at the Bay of Pigs even ended up applauding Castro! The event not only led Castro to stress the socialist nature of the Revolution, but made the Cuban people aware of what the Revolution meant to them. Above all, it gave them the lasting confidence to stand up to the 'colossus to the north'. The Bay of Pigs is remembered as the first defeat of US imperialism in the Americas.

The threat of counter-revolution did not, of course, disappear with the defeat of the invasion force. The Escambray mountains were full of counter-revolutionary rebels—at least a thousand. They were supported by peasants who had been alienated by those guerrillas who had acted more like bandits than freedom fighters. But the counter-revolutionaries were contained and eventually swept out of their stronghold. However, Camilo Cienfuegos, the most popular of the guerrilla commanders, known as the 'lord of the vanguard', disappeared in mysterious circumstances on 28 October 1959 during a plane flight. There were several attempts on Castro's life. Outrageous anti-Communist rumours were circulating in the country, that all children were going to be taken to the Soviet Union, that the anti-polio vaccine was really a chemical to turn people into Communists and that white girls would be forced to marry black men.

Castro's attitude was simplicity itself when it came to opposition to his rule. 'A revolution is not a bed of roses,' he told a vast crowd on the second anniversary of the triumph of the Revolution in the Plaza de la Revolución in Havana. 'A revolution is a struggle to the death between the future and the past. The old order always resists to the death, and the new society fights with all its energy to survive. Either the counter-revolution destroys the Revolution, or the Revolution destroys the counter-revolution.'[25]

The threat of the counter-revolution, so dramatically symbolized by the Bay of Pigs invasion, led to a witch hunt of anyone who might oppose the Revolutionary regime—which included former members of the Ortodoxo party, the Revolutionary Directorate, the independent trade unionists and anarchists. Immediately after the Bay of Pigs, there were mass jailings of suspects, often denounced by the Committees for the Defence of the Revolution (CDRs), organized by Raúl Castro and Ramiro Valdés through the new organ of state security, the Ministry of the Interior. Most were released within a week or two, but Castro admitted in 1965 that there were at least 20,000 political prisoners in Cuban jails. A new Revolutionary puritanism also became discernible. Operation P, denoting pederasts, prostitutes and pimps, was organized to clean up the bohemian quarters of Havana in 1961. Homosexuals were rounded up, insulted, and denied influence in culture and education.

The Revolution was clearly moving into a more authoritarian stage. The right to strike was abolished by Guevara, and the freely elected independent leadership of the Confederation of Cuban Workers (CTC) was replaced by Communist appointees. Even some of the old guard of the Sierra Maestra, like Carlos Franquí who had run Radio Rebelde and the popular newspaper *Revolución*, began to fear that the Revolution might 'devour its own children'.[26] It became increasingly clear that instead of a new society created from the grass roots by the workers and peasants themselves, Cuba might become a society in which they were expected to be an obedient and docile workforce loyal to their all-powerful military leaders.

In the year following the Bay of Pigs invasion, Cuba became the focus of world attention in a potentially much more serious crisis. The Soviet Union agreed to step up its aid to Cuba now that the island was economically and politically isolated by the US. After a visit from Guevara, the Soviet Union began to introduce nuclear weapons onto the island, ostensibly to deter a direct US invasion. The Kennedy administration, however, saw this as offensive and felt Cuba was threatening the hemisphere with Communist subversion. As the second Declaration of Havana of 4 February 1962 put it, there was a fear of 'Latin American Revolution . . . [a] fear that a plundered people will seize the arms from the oppressors and, like Cuba, declare themselves free people of America'.[27] In these circumstances, it was not surprising that Kennedy saw the presence of nuclear weapons on Cuba at this time as dangerously changing the political balance of power in the region. His response was to impose a naval and economic blockade. This sparked off the so-called Cuban missile crisis in October 1962.

Kennedy refused to negotiate; Soviet ships were steaming towards Cuba; the world seemed on the brink of World War III—a war, this time, to end all wars. On 26 October, Khrushchev wired, 'only lunatics or suicides, who themselves want to perish and to destroy the whole world before they die' would start a nuclear war. He proposed withdrawing the missiles inside Cuba on the understanding that the US would not invade the island. It was agreed.

At the time Castro was furious. He had been uncompromising and belligerent in face of the US threat: 'If they attack us, we will resist. If they totally blockade us, we know how to resist. Anyone who wants to inspect Cuba had better come prepared to fight their way in.'[28] The Cuban people were entirely behind Castro. They brought out the drums and sang to the *rumba*:

> Nikita, Nikita, [West] Indian giver,
> You don't take back what you once deliver.
> Fidel, go ahead;
> Bop the Yankees on the head![29]

The agreement between Kennedy and Khrushchev had been made without Cuba being consulted, and Castro felt cheated. He was ready to involve the world in a nuclear conflagration rather than to compromise his Revolutionary principles. It was only years later that Castro admitted the wisdom of the Russians' decision and that the Cuban position had not been correct.

With the immediate threat of US invasion removed, Cuba could turn its energies to carrying through the socialist revolution. This second stage of the Revolution was undoubtedly the most original and adventurous, a time when socialism and Communism were to be built simultaneously. Guevara and Castro saw the Revolution as one that would transform human relations; it was not only an opportunity to increase production but also to create the 'New Man'. Work, Guevara asserted, should not be something to be avoided like the plague, but a 'true human pleasure and the ultimate act of creation'.[30] Again, just as human labour should not be seen as a commodity to be bought and sold, so people should not work only for material incentives: 'Volunteer work is nothing less than the fountainhead of the socialist education of the masses'.[31] As a result, the Cuban people not only adjusted to austerity but also participated voluntarily in mass mobilization campaigns, especially during the sugar harvests.

But despite the energy of the people, the bold attempt to industrialize ground to a halt. The exodus of capital and skilled personnel, and the lack of spare parts due to the blockade, severely upset the economy. The failure to understand precise technology and economics rendered the new industries inefficient and wasteful: for instance, toothpaste went hard in the tubes. Shortages became commonplace and rationing was introduced. The expropriation of thousands of small businesses early in 1968 made distribution worse. It was eventually decided that sugar would have to remain the backbone of the economy for the foreseeable future. Every effort was then directed to the target of a massive ten million ton sugar harvest in 1970. In the event, the production of only eight million tons was achieved, while the rest of the economy had been seriously neglected.

The failure of the harvest led to an important and thorough reappraisal of the objectives and means of the Revolution. Castro squarely laid the blame on himself and the bureaucracy. 'We have a certain underdevelopment in leadership,' he declared. Thereafter the regime became more pragmatic and cautious. It set more realistic production targets and reintroduced material as well as moral incentives. The days of revolutionary idealism, when will and fervour seemed enough to overcome the greatest of challenges, were over.

As a result, Cuba moved closer to the Soviet Union and adopted its style of economic planning. In 1972 the country became a member of the Council for Mutual Economic Assistance (COMECON). It also made long-term economic agreements with the Soviet Union, exchanging sugar and nickel for oil on terms favourable to Cuba. The 1970s in Cuba became a period of economic advance and political consolidation, with greater government control in terms of ideology, culture and education.

There was a similar process of reefing in the sails in foreign policy. Following the US blockade and the missile crisis, Cuba inevitably had close relations with the Soviet Union, but still maintained an independent line. Cuba continued to trade with China, at least until 1966 when a reduction in rice shipments from China led to a breakdown in relations. Castro's wish to export revolution throughout Latin America also provoked Soviet disapproval, particularly as he quarrelled with the pro-Moscow Communist parties committed to parliamentary action in the region by calling for armed struggle as the only path to socialism. At the Tricontinental Solidarity Organization Conference in Havana in January 1966, he insisted on an independent line, calling for guerrilla struggles throughout Latin America.

Guevara died trying to foment rebellion in Bolivia the following year, and when the 'many Vietnams' he had called for failed to erupt in the region, Castro tacitly recognized that there were different paths to power. His qualified support of the Soviet invasion of Czechoslovakia in August 1968 marked a renewed friendship with the Soviet Union.

But despite the economic difficulties and the growing Soviet influence, the Cuban leadership continued to see itself in a historical role as the Revolutionary vanguard. 'We are at the head of a people,' Guevara wrote in 1965, 'which is at the head of the Americas.'[32] Castro reiterated this view in 1968 on the commemoration of the centenary of the beginning of Cuba's Wars of Independence:

We are no longer the last to abolish slavery—the ownership of man by man—today, we are the first people of this continent to abolish the exploitation of man by man! . . . We were the last to break the chains of the colony, but we have been the first to throw off the chains of imperialism.[33]

Castro's regime constantly insists that Cuba is 'the first free territory in the Americas'. But despite its great and genuine advances, has it really broken the chains of the past? Or has it forged new shackles to replace the old?

4

STEERING THE REVOLUTION

To begin with, the Cuban Revolution appeared like a sudden cataclysm rather than a deliberate act of creation. It was preceded by no prolonged political struggle, no peasant uprising, no workers' general strike. Batista's corrupt regime collapsed from its own internal contradictions, and Havana fell like a ripe peach into the hands of the small band of Revolutionaries. They were moreover predominantly young, middle-class, urban intellectuals who had no mass following.

The principal participants in the cities were the July 26 Movement, (M-26-7) which was made up of a motley combination of radicals, ranging from anarchists to liberals; by the Civic Resistance Movement, a mainly professional democratic group; and the students' Revolutionary Directorate. In the country, there was the guerrilla band led by Castro and Guevara in the Sierra Maestra, and a second front mainly consisting of a splinter group from the Revolutionary Directorate in the Escambray mountains. There was no clear ideological party line in the early days, except that of Revolutionary humanism which offered bread, liberty and a fresh start to the Cuban people.

From the beginning, however, Castro and his *comandantes* took power and quickly eased out the moderates and anyone who opposed the 'authority of the Sierra'. This was partly achieved by the charisma of Castro himself, who used the media extremely effectively, and partly by his control of the rebel army. Once having discovered Marxism as the 'map of the forest' in the Revolutionary upheaval, he and his group quickly began to orientate the course of the Revolution towards Communism.

By July 1961, the Revolutionary Directorate, the July 26 Movement and the small Communist PSP were merged to form the unified whole known as the Organizaciónes Revolucionarias Integradas (ORI) (Integrated Revolutionary Organizations). In December of the same year, Castro publicly declared his firm allegiance to Marxism-Leninism. Henceforth, the Communists in the regime gained increasing power, even those like Blas Roca, the leader of the PSP who had been dismissed as too pragmatic and compromised during the Batista era. The ORI gave way in 1963 to the Partido Unido de la Revolución Socialista (United Party of the Socialist Revolution). In 1965, the purged coalition of Revolutionary groups controlled by Castro was eventually replaced by a new Cuban Communist Party (PCC) which reigned alone and supreme. Its tiny membership was appointed without election and followed Castro as its *jefe máximo* or leader. The political leadership was part of the military command; the party was intimately connected to the army. The army gave the regime its ultimate authority and guarantee of power. This situation was justified in Régis Debray's *Revolution in the Revolution?* (1967), a work inspired (and corrected) by Castro. The book argued that the guerrilla force, once in power, should become the 'unchallenged political vanguard' of the Revolution, with control of the regular army:

> Under certain conditions, the political and the military are not separate but form one organic whole, consisting of the people's army, where the nucleus is the guerrilla army. The vanguard party can exist in the form of the guerrilla *foco* itself. The guerrilla force is the party in embryo.[1]

Che Guevara also saw the guerrillas as the 'motor force' of the Revolutionary movement, which had to mobilize the 'sleeping mass of the people'.[2] In his essay *Socialism and Man* (1965) he correctly observed that the 'mass follows its leaders, basically Fidel Castro, without hesitation', and that 'the initiative generally comes from Fidel or from the Revolutionary High Command, and is explained to the people who adopt it as theirs'.[3] While Guevara hoped that the people would not act like a 'tame flock of sheep' and called for 'close communion between the vanguard and the masses', he recognized that the party would only become a mass party 'when the masses have reached the level of the vanguard, that is, when they are educated for Communism'.[4]

But Guevara's position was not entirely authoritarian. He was a subtle thinker; indeed, there is something paradoxical about his thought and action. By temperament he was an individualist, and as a guerrilla fighter he saw the need for spontaneous action and personal choice. The chief departure from Marxist orthodoxy in his manual *Guerrilla Warfare* (1961), based on his experiences in the Sierra Maestra campaign, was its stress on the autonomy of the guerrilla group outside the central control of the monolithic Communist party in the cities. At the same time, Guevara put forward the view that the guerrilla groups were the flag bearers of the Revolution and talked incessantly of the need for strong leaders of the vanguard. Following the tradition of Latin American *caudillismo* or dictatorship as much as that of Marxism-Leninism, he argued in his essay on *Socialism and Man* that unquestioned leadership by a chief or *jefe máximo* was more important than a whole party organization of anonymous cadres.

The same tension between individual self-reliance and obedience to a leader is apparent in Guevara's thinking on economics. On the one hand, he insisted on the need for state control and centralized planning; yet he was the first to criticize the bureaucracy which inevitably arose from this and which checked local initiative, by imposing its will from above. He was also very impatient with traditional governmental procedures. Despite his emphasis on central control he was undoubtedly sympathetic to certain aspects of anarchism. But while part of him seemed to revel in spontaneity and sudden change, another part deeply feared the possible anarchic developments of the Revolution in its early stages. It was as if he were instinctively an anarchist, but unconsciously felt, perhaps because of his middle-class background and scientific training as a doctor, the need for authoritarian and centralized control of 'unruly' elements within himself and within society.

In the final analysis, Guevara's stress on the need for the individual to subordinate him or herself to all-powerful leaders separates him from the anarchist tradition. He also departs from anarchists in his belief that the individual should submerge him or herself in communal solidarity. For Guevara, the notion of Western individualism is merely a product of capitalism which has developed 'a route for wolves', in which success is only achieved at the expense of others.[5] The individual in such a society is not free or fulfilled; he or she is inevitably alone and alienated; relationships are governed by the market which transforms people into objects to be bought and sold.

Guevara argues that, rather than standing apart as an isolated atom with unsatisfied yearnings, the individual should become one with the masses and follow the leaders in building the new society. He declared in a speech in 1960 that individualism, 'in the form of the individual action of a person alone in a social milieu, must disappear in Cuba. In the future, individualism ought to be the efficient utilization of the whole individual for the absolute benefit of a collectivity.'[6] The goal of the Revolution was to set people free from that alienation from their society and fellow human beings, which they mistakenly call 'individualism'.

Like Plato, Rousseau and Marx, Guevara believed that men and women are social beings who can only realize themselves as full members of society. The opportunity provided by the Revolution to enable the individual to become integrated into society therefore not only offered a chance of personal freedom from alienation, but of self-realization. It is in this sense that, in spite of the apparent standardization of people under socialism, the individual is more complete: 'We socialists are freer because we are more complete; we are more complete because we are freer.'[7]

In a genuine socialist society, Guevara argued, the divisive barriers which at present separate individuals, such as competition and working for money, would disappear. Work would become a social duty and people would work for each other. Again in a socialist society, he believed that while some 'moral coercion' would be needed in the transitional period to get people to work, this would no longer be necessary when the social conscience of people became fully developed.

As President of the National Bank, Director of the National Planning Board, and Minister of Industry, Guevara set the country on the audacious and heretical course to realize socialism and Communism simultaneously. He tried to turn the degrading and alienating work which most people are compelled to do into 'meaningful play'.[8] He rejected the narrow considerations of profit and efficiency, wanted to abolish money, and tried to make the chief criterion of an economy its contribution to society as a whole. He saw in socialism not only a way of increasing material well-being, but of transforming social relations and creating the New Man and Woman, who would be self-sacrificing, egalitarian and cooperative. During the height of his influence in the 1960s, these aims were official policy, and their partial realization proved the most original and creative phase of the Revolution.

But above all, Guevara was an internationalist who felt that imperialism is a world system and must be fought wherever it spreads its tentacles. Despite his ministerial responsibilities, from 1960 he often served as a roving ambassador for Castro on important missions, to Moscow, to North Vietnam and to other Communist or non-aligned countries. He increasingly felt, however, that the real contradiction in the world was not between capitalism and Communism, but between the developed and underdeveloped countries. At a speech to the General Assembly of the United Nations in December 1964, he argued that the doctrine of 'peaceful co-existence among nations does not encompass co-existence between the exploiters and the exploited, the oppressor and the oppressed'.[9] He soon after decided to leave Cuba to become a permanent revolutionary fighter on behalf of those oppressed and impoverished people in the Third World whom Franz Fanon has called the 'wretched of the earth'. At the Afro-Asian Solidarity Conference at Algiers in February 1965, he rejected even more forcibly the tacit complicity between East and West and declared that in the attempt to build socialism,

> there are no boundaries in this struggle to the death. We cannot be indifferent to what happens anywhere in the world, for a victory by any country over imperialism is our victory; just as any country's defeat is a defeat for all of us. The practice of proletarian internationalism is not only a duty for the peoples struggling for a better future, it is also an inescapable necessity.[10]

Determined as ever to combine theory with action, Guevara went to the Congo to train and fight alongside the guerrillas opposed to President Tshombe. But he found that the experience of the Cuban Revolution was of little use to them and his thoughts turned increasingly to a plan of starting the liberation of Latin America from the central country of Bolivia. Returning to Cuba secretly in the autumn of 1966, he decided at the end of October to join a group of Cuban guerrillas in the jungle of Bolivia.

Jungle life proved very different from his days in the Sierra Maestra. Guevara's *Bolivian Diaries*—the most human and unrhetorical of his writings—record how for 11 months the small band of about two dozen guerrillas struggled to survive in the mountainous jungle against an enemy trained and co-ordinated by the CIA. The local Indians remained distrustful of the white foreigners, it was difficult to recruit reliable Bolivians, and even the Bolivian and Cuban comrades fell out with each other. Moreover, Guevara, true to his principle that the guerrilla nucleus outside the control of parties should lead the Revolution, refused to compromise with Mario Monje, the head of the Bolivian Communist party, which meant that there was little urban support. The harassed guerrillas were eventually forced to split up into two groups, and then the final disaster took place in the Yuro Ravine. Guevara and his band were surrounded by a large contingent of the Bolivian army. They fought bravely, but Guevara finally ran out of ammunition and was wounded and captured. The next day, on 9 October 1967, he was shot in the village of Higueras by a sergeant. However, the care that the army authorities took to burn his body and scatter his ashes showed their fear of his legend and of his vision of a united and liberated Latin America.

Their fear was not groundless. Guevara's sordid death made him a martyr. In a message sent to the Tricontinental Solidarity Organization in Havana in April 1967, he had already made his Revolutionary testament. In the global struggle against imperialism, he called on Latin America, Africa and Asia to liberate themselves at any cost. All must fight together in genuine proletarian internationalism so that many Revolutionary wars like the one in Vietnam at the time might flower on the face of the globe. He ended on the prophetically chilling note:

> Wherever death may surprise us, let it be welcome if our battle cry has reached even one receptive ear, and another hand reaches out to take up our arms, and other men come forward to join in our funeral dirge with the chattering of machine guns and new calls for battle and for victory.[11]

After his death in 1967, Guevara was transformed into the foremost god of the revolutionary pantheon, as powerful a symbol as Bolívar and Martí. Castro remembered Guevara in his funeral oration as 'an extraordinarily capable leader, as a master, as a virtuoso in the art of revolutionary war', as well as a man of 'visionary intelligence'. In addition to his rare qualities as a man of action and of thought, Castro saw Guevara's great legacy as providing 'the ideal model of our people'.[12]

It was the poet Nicolás Guillén, however, who expressed most eloquently the feeling of the majority of Cubans on hearing of Guevara's death:

> In spite of your fall,
> your light is undiminished,
> A horse of fire
> celebrates your glory as a guerrilla,
> between the wind and the clouds, in the Sierra,
> Even though they've silenced you, you speak,
> and even though they burned you
> and let you rot in the earth,
> and lost you in the cemetery
> in the forest,
> in the swamp,
> they can't stop us from finding you,
> *Che Comandante,*
> *Amigo.*[13]

In Cuba today, Guevara's Christ-like image looks down from posters along motorways; it decorates postcards and stamps; it dominates Revolution Square in Havana and is a constant reminder of the ultimate sacrifice that Revolution demands. On the anniversary of his death, Guevara's speech 'Colonialism is Doomed', which was delivered to the United Nations on 11 December 1964, is broadcast every year. Children in Cuba are urged to behave like Che and to enact his writings; his death has immortalized him as the outstanding example of the New Man he wished to create. Every child learns by heart the last letter that Guevara wrote to his parents before he set off to fight in the Bolivian jungle, in which he declared that his Marxism had taken root and become purified: 'I believe in the armed struggle as the only solution for those people who fight to free themselves, and I am consistent with my beliefs. Many will call me an adventurer—and that I am, only, one of a different sort—one of those who risks his skin to prove his platitudes.'[14] Equally well-known is Che's last letter to Fidel, when he bids farewell to the Cuban people and admits that: 'My only serious failing was not having trusted more in you from the first moments in the Sierra Maestra, and not having understood quickly enough your qualities as a leader and a revolutionary.'[15]

If Guevara was the most important theoretician of the Revolution in its early days and its greatest inspiration, Castro has proved its most powerful leader. He has been so closely identified with the Revolution in the popular imagination that many foreign commentators have talked of 'Castro's Cuba' and described Cuban socialism as 'Castroism'.[16] Most people who have met Castro have been struck by his personal charisma. The American journalist Herbert Matthews, who joined him in the Sierra Maestra, described him as a great talker and a 'powerful six-footer, olive-skinned, full-faced, with a straggly beard'. He found him an 'educated, dedicated fanatic' as well as a man of ideals and courage.[17] Indeed, Castro has completely given himself to the revolutionary cause. He has abandoned family life and all private interests in order to shape the course of the Revolution.

'What is man if he has no goal beyond himself? A *desoladora nada* (a pitiful nobody)', Castro once said.[18] But this almost religious search for a purpose in life beyond oneself is combined with an elitist spirit. It is not for the people to reach the goal for themselves through revolutionary praxis, or even in exchange of ideas between the leaders and the rank and file; the truth is to be handed down from the vanguard. All his arguments, as K. S. Karol has observed, betray a faith in the role of the Revolutionary elite. In this, he remains in his smart army uniform very much the Jesuit he was brought up to be. Indeed, his erstwhile comrade Carlos Franquí went so far as to suggest that he has imposed on Cuba 'all the punishment he suffered as a boy in his Jesuit school: censure, separation of the sexes, thought control, a Spartan mentality.'[19] His fanaticism also betrayed itself in the way he fought in the Sierra Maestra. According to Franquí, while Che never forgot the first man he shot, Fidel allegedly killed 'in a cold way, without emotion' and set up symbolic executions.[20]

Castro's hold over his guerrilla comrades and then the Cuban people attests to his remarkable powers of persuasion and eloquence. From the beginning he has calmly explained, in his legendary speeches, the developments of the Revolution to the people, who have largely responded with rapt admiration and enthusiasm. He was the first revolutionary leader to make full use of the media—especially the television and radio—and in the early days of the Revolution had the world's longest-running chat show. He was equally skilful at rallies. Cabrera Infante has called Castro with some truth 'the greatest actor in Cuba, playing Macbeth to the biggest captive audience in the Americas'.[21]

By rushing about the country, ready to talk to peasants and workers, by always being present in the most dangerous situations, by cutting cane with the best of the boys, he gave the impression of being part of the people, sharing their trials and tribulations, and articulating their problems. It was this daily sympathetic contact with the people that impressed Jean-Paul Sartre so much and led Sartre to talk of the direct democracy present in the early days of the Revolution. Sympathetic visitors saw Castro as 'a sort of permanent opposition', representing the people against any injustice from state structures.[22] He was an agitator, criticizing other leaders and the bureaucracy; he was also an 'ombudsman', the people's court of appeal, the gallant righter of wrongs. Significantly, no Cuban calls him Dr Castro; he is always known as Fidel. As with all so-called 'great men' in history, he undoubtedly expresses and interprets the aspirations of a whole social movement.

Another endearing aspect of Castro's character is his readiness to acknowledge his mistakes. A study of his speeches and decisions amply shows how he practises self-criticism, thinks against himself, and develops his theory according to his experience. Whenever the Revolution changes course, he is the first to explain and apologize to the Cuban people. After the abortive attempt to achieve the ten million ton sugar crop in 1970, he laid the blame squarely on himself, declaring that 'we have a certain underdevelopment in leadership', and that the people could change their leaders 'right now, at any moment they wish'.[23] It sounded good, even if there was no mechanism to change the leadership, short of insurrection. Again in 1982, Castro acknowledged that 'there were some idealistic moments when we did want to make short cuts. We had the chance to see the consequences and were honest enough to recognize our mistakes and rectify them.'[24] In the following month, he declared 'the first, most sacred duty of every revolutionary is to admit his mistakes.'[25] Castro may be erratic and quixotic but his obvious sincerity and honesty are quite disarming.

Nevertheless, the very qualities which have made Castro a popular leader have prevented the development of a genuinely democratic political culture in Cuba. He is not, as Matthews suggested, 'by temperament an anarchist', but rather a military *caudillo* or boss in the Latin American mould.[26] A vertical power structure emerged quickly in Cuba, with Castro as much its victim as its master. Despite his energy, his many interventions in the field of agriculture have proved ill-advised. His attack on the bureaucracy towards the end of the 1960s only put greater pressure on middle officials and further concentrated power in the elite, creating a system of authoritarian centralization.

Above all, Castro has kept strict ideological control. His dictum 'Everything within the Revolution, nothing against the Revolution' has been narrowly interpreted, with the 'Revolution' coming to mean whatever he decides it to be.[27] In 1959, he tried his former comrade Hubert Matos and 34 other officers for creating an anti-Communist scare; in 1968, he jailed the veteran Communist Aníbal Escalante and others for forming a 'microfaction' within the Communist party. Castro can challenge or change his own policies, but it is difficult for others to do so.

For all his towering presence, Castro's role in the Cuban Revolution has been absurdly over-estimated: he is not at once 'the creator, motor force, guide and spokesman for the Revolution'.[28] Though key political decisions have always come from the top, there were from the beginning mass organizations that implemented policy and had some influence. The most important of these were the Comités de Defensa de la Revolución (CDRs) (Committees for the Defence of the Revolution) which were set up in every neighbourhood in 1961 just before the Bay of Pigs invasion, to maintain revolutionary vigilance. As the 'eyes and ears' of the Revolution, they are an important means of social control, checking on anything from children playing truant to adult shirkers. They have emerged to play a vital role as a link between the government and the community, especially in implementing health and education programmes. They also act as local self-help groups in organizing voluntary work, providing services, resolving disputes, discussing policies, and looking after the environment. Their membership now includes about 80 per cent of the adult population.

Another mass organization to have exerted an important influence is the Federación de Mujeres Cubanas (FMC) (Federation of Cuban Women) formed in 1960 to help women participate in the economic, social and political life of the country. The organization was at the head of the struggle to abolish prostitution and to prepare women for non-domestic work. It played a key role in the literacy campaign in 1961. Since then it has successfully fought for equal rights and jobs for women, and brought about in 1975 a radical law known as the Family Code which assigns both sexes equal obligations. The FMC is now the main vehicle for expressing the aspirations of women within the Revolution, and has a membership of more than 80 per cent of Cuban women, recruited from the age of 14.

The trade unions might have been expected to play an influential role in shaping government policy in a socialist society, but they were quickly suppressed for fear that they might become an alternative power base to Castro and his inner circle. Communist leaders were imposed on them in 1961 and they shortly lost the last vestiges of their independence. The unions had virtually ceased to function by the end of the 1960s. At the Congress of the Central de Trabajadores de Cuba (CTC) (Central Organization of Cuban Trade Unions) held in 1973, it was decided to develop their role in order to improve the flow of communication between workers and management. Their principal role, however, remains as an agency to stimulate productivity and to encourage political and educational development. The Asociación Nacional de Agricultores Pequeños (ANAP) (National Association of Small Farmers) has played an important role in expressing the wishes of the private farmers and cooperatives, but it, too, remains entirely state-controlled and is merely an advisory body.

While the Committees for the Defence of the Revolution and the Federation of Cuban Women started as mass organizations they were and are now mainly used as means of mobilizing and directing the people rather than as vehicles to express their will. For the first 15 years, Castro ruled virtually alone except for the Communist party, a small tightly-knit vanguard organization which was controlled by the old guard of the Sierra Maestra. The members were chosen from the hardest-working, best-behaved and most reliable individuals. The structure remained hierarchical. Power in the party was concentrated in the Central Committee, which in turn was dominated by the *jefe máximo*, Castro.

Castro was at first in no hurry to create state institutions; indeed, Guevara had specifically argued against the immediate institutionalization of the Revolution. For most of the 1960s and early 1970s, the Cuban government remained more or less improvisational, characterized by its guerrilla mentality. It was an entirely secret affair, with Castro announcing its decisions to the people. When the economy reached a new footing, however, it became clear that there was a need to fill the political vacuum within the country. The Communist party therefore held its first Congress in 1975 and adopted a set of statutes for the first time.

The party in its statutes sees itself as heir to the struggles for Cuban independence from the nineteenth century, but defines itself unequivocally as a Marxist-Leninist party, 'the organized vanguard of the working class of our country'.[29] Its fundamental principles include 'absolute fidelity to the interests of the working class', 'fidelity to Marxism-Leninism as its vanguard theory and guide for action', defending itself against 'all rightist and leftist deviations', fidelity to 'proletarian internationalism', and close ties with the 'masses whom it guides and directs'.[30]

In addition, the party places great stress on the need to educate the masses in the values of Communist morality, and to create the New Man who governs his conduct by 'collectivism, self-sacrifice, love of work, hatred of exploitation and parasitism, and the fraternal spirit of co-operation and solidarity.'[31]

Although the statutes call for members of the party to develop criticism and self-criticism, it is above all concerned with maintaining 'unity and purity in party ranks by weeding out those who do not deserve to belong', and insists that members should never establish relations with individuals who are 'detractors of the Revolution'.[32] There seems to be a prevailing fear of contamination by deviationists and critics—a threat which can only be dealt with by excommunication and the erection of an ideological *cordon sanitaire*.

To become a member of the party is a protracted and difficult affair. A person must first be nominated by his fellow workers after much discussion at the workplace, but it is the party organization in the end which makes the final selection. As an 'aspirant' (as the person who wants to join the party is called) told me, a worker will only be chosen by his fellows if he is 'a vanguard worker, undertakes voluntary work, participates in meetings, saves money for the state, is of good behaviour and a living example of responsibility'. An aspirant must have been a member of the Union of Young Communists for at least three years, or be supervised by a party nucleus for at least a year, during which time he must attend meetings but have no vote. If after exhaustive investigations, he can prove his revolutionary worth as a Marxist-Leninist, he is eventually accepted into the honoured ranks of the party.

The party's structure is organized on the principle of 'democratic centralism' and the leaders of the party are chosen from the members. Each member belongs to a nucleus in his or her place of work, which in turn is affiliated to branches at the municipal and provincial level. The highest-ranking body of the party is the Congress which elects the

Central Committee, and the Central Committee elects the Politburo. All branches, however, are bound by party discipline, and the decisions of the higher levels are binding on those subordinate to them. The party has an extremely thin base with a membership of only about five per cent of the population, although it is supported by the Union of Young Communists which embraces about a third of the young between 14 and 26 years of age. The power structure is therefore vertical and hierarchical; crucial decisions are handed down from the Politburo and Central Committee. The party is also monolithic, allowing no other political grouping or faction to exist outside its Marxist-Leninist vision. 'The party is a synthesis of everything,' Castro declared at the first Congress in December 1975. 'Within it, the dreams of all the Revolutionaries in our history are synthesized . . . The party today is the soul of the Cuban Revolution.'[33]

The party, in theory, is separate from the state; it does not have direct control of the army, police force, and courts. Its authority is political and ideological, and it is meant to lead by persuasion and example. Nevertheless, what the party decides at its Congresses defines the course of the Revolution, and the party is taken by the people to be the source of the crucial decisions and the ultimate authority in the land. Nothing can be done without the party's consent, and party members are both respected and feared for their obvious power by their fellow workers.

The years following the first Congress of the Communist party in 1975 saw a further institutionalization of the Cuban Revolution. A new Constitution was adopted in 1976. It had a twofold purpose: to support the socialist legal system which had been reformed since 1973, and to clarify for the first time the nature and role of the Cuban state and its bodies. It was also decided to redraw provincial boundaries and to decentralize the political and administrative functions of the state. To this end, 14 new provinces were created out of the six old provincial divisions inherited from the Spanish.

Original drafts of the Constitution were circulated amongst the mass organizations, party branches, and work centres for discussion. Several suggestions were incorporated. The Constitution was ratified in a referendum in February 1976 by voluntary secret ballot open to all over the age of 16: 98 per cent of eligible voters went to the polls; 97.7 per cent of those who voted approved.

The Constitution is shaped on the East European model, although it re-established a presidential system more consistent with Latin American practice. It declares that the 'Republic of Cuba is a socialist state of workers and peasants and all other manual and intellectual workers' (Article 1). While following the desire of José Martí to base the first law of the republic on the 'worship of complete human dignity', it is unequivocably guided by 'the victorious doctrine of Marxism-Leninism' and supported by 'proletarian internationalism'. It states in no uncertain terms that:

> The Communist party of Cuba, the organized Marxist-Leninist vanguard of the working class, is the superior guiding force of society and the state, organizing and steering communal efforts towards the high ends of the construction of socialism and the advance towards Communist society (Article 5).

The positive rights it includes are a right to a job, health care, free education, to be cared for in old age, and to be free from discrimination because of race, colour or sex. The Constitution also guarantees the right to one's earnings and savings and to one's home and personal property. At the same time, the Constitution does not guarantee the right to adequate housing, simply because the country doesn't have the necessary resources to fulfil this goal. In addition, the rights are tempered by duties. While the right to work is guaranteed, it is also a duty; every able-bodied male Cuban must work by law. The Constitution decrees that the supreme duty of every Cuban is to defend the socialist homeland: military service is compulsory, and it is illegal to refuse to fight with arms on religious grounds.

There are clear limits to certain freedoms guaranteed by the Constitution. The right to artistic creation and belief is proclaimed but only as long as it is not 'contrary to the Revolution' (Article 44). The freedom of speech and press is recognized—'conforming', that is, 'to the ends of the socialist society' (Article 52). The right to religious belief and practice is upheld, but it is 'illegal and punishable' to oppose such faith to the Revolution (Article 54). Indeed, it is clearly asserted that the state bases its educational and cultural policies on the 'scientific conception of the world, established and developed by Marxism-Leninism' (Article 38). It comes as no surprise to read that none of the freedoms recognized can be exercised against the Constitution, the existence and ends of the socialist state, or against the decision to build socialism and Communism (Article 61). There can be no doubt that with its Soviet-style Communist party and Marxist-Leninist credentials, Havana can offer Moscow a reliable hand of friendship.

While giving a clear definition of the nature of the Cuban state and the role of the Communist party, the Constitution also set out the structure of new popular assemblies. During the first 15 years, the Revolutionary government was self-appointed. Whatever their rhetoric about governing in the interests of the people, they certainly were not a government by the people in the sense that Cuban citizens were able to elect directly their rulers, or to demand their accountability. Indeed, Castro told K. S. Karol in 1967 that the very word 'election' had become discredited on the island, and that the Cuban people would never stand for such a 'comedy'.[34] Be that as it may, it was decided to reintroduce the principle seven years later, and provide some sort of institutional vehicle for the so-called 'dialogue' between the 'vanguard leaders' and the 'masses'.

The new assemblies were intended to decentralize political power to a degree and to increase popular participation. For the first time, the people were not merely to be listened to, but to be given a say in running their affairs. It was an attempt to overcome the difficulties arising from the over-centralized government of the 1960s. In the absence of any criticism, there was no organized way of testing public opinion, gaining current information, or benefiting from new ideas. Within the Marxist-Leninist framework, the new assemblies are also seen as deliberative and consultative institutions embodying the 'dictatorship of the proletariat' in the transitional socialist stage towards Communism.

The assemblies, called Asambleas del Poder Popular (People's Power Assemblies), have been established at municipal, provincial and national level. There are no political parties or professional politicians, but there are different candidates who distribute their photographs and biographies stressing their work and achievements. The people elect one person from a list of candidates who will represent their constituency or *circunscripción*, each of which consists of about 500 to 1,000 citizens. The delegates make no promises and express no personal ideas. Their task is to represent fully the wishes and opinions of those who elect them. They are elected every five years by secret ballot of all citizens over 16 years old. They are always accountable to their constituents, and subject to immediate recall. Every delegate must meet with the people in his or her *circunscripción* to account for their work done, and are expected to meet individuals more regularly to take up their problems or suggestions.

Although the municipal assemblies in Cuba have more bite than the soviets in the USSR, they are more a forum for expressing public opinion than a source of strategic decisions. The municipal assembly decides how the municipal property and services are run, and is mainly concerned with implementing policies in health, education, housing, transport, sport, tourism, and so on. The assemblies appoint trained personnel to administer them.

Delegates are elected from the municipal assemblies to the two higher levels of government—the provincial assemblies and the national assembly (one delegate to the provincial assembly for each 10,000 citizens; one to the national assembly for every 20,000). The council of state and the head of state are chosen by the national assembly, which is the supreme organ of power in the state. But the head of state proposes to the national assembly the members of the council of state.

As with the Communist party, the key decisions are also passed down from the top. While the provincial and municipal assemblies can decide how to solve local problems, the administrative methods are regulated at the national level, to ensure uniformity throughout the country. At all levels, the principle of democratic centralism is also upheld; that is to say, decisions are made by a simple majority after discussion. Since the decision is binding on the minority who must carry it out, there is a real danger of creating the tyranny of the majority and of corrupting judgement by forcing people to do things they do not believe in. The official Cuban answer is that, since there are no longer classes in Cuba, the people have common interests, and so feel no need to oppose each other.

The new assemblies have undoubtedly been welcomed by the Cuban people. As with the Constitution, their structure was fully discussed before being adopted; a trial election was first held in Matanzas province in 1974. But it has taken some time for people to get used to elections; the process was undermined for 15 years. During recent elections, posters appeared everywhere with ten white and three brown hands (presumably representing the racial mix of the population) stressing that *'El Poder del Pueblo ese Sí es Poder'* (People's Power, that's Power Indeed). Other posters call on the people *'A Nominar a los Mejores'* (To Nominate the Best).

There is a feeling that the new People's Power Assemblies could offer a real opportunity for political participation, and could be strengthened at the municipal level in the future. Politics have long been fundamental to the way Cubans look at the world, but now the views of the people can be heard by the leaders—it is no longer necessary to have private access to Castro's ear in order to exert an influence.

But despite the establishment of the assemblies, real power lies with the armed forces, who ultimately guarantee Castro's rule and the position of the Communist party within the state. From the beginning, the line between the civilian and the military in Cuba has been smudged, if not erased. It was both Guevara's and Castro's view that the guerrilla band should be the Revolutionary party in embryo, and that on seizing power they should become the unchallenged political vanguard with control of the regular army. Significantly, the guerrillas in government did not abandon their olive-green fatigues; Castro controls both the Communist party and, with his brother Raúl as Minister of Defence, the armed forces. Even the Ministerio del Interior (MININT) (Ministry of the Interior) responsible for state security is a direct part of the Fuerzas Armadas Revolucionarias (FAR) (Revolutionary Armed Forces). While some commentators have argued about the relative rate of militarization of Cuban society in the 1960s and 1970s, it should be pointed out that from the beginning the Cuban Revolution was steered by civic soldiers. Significantly, the journal of the armed forces, *Verde Olivo*, not only carried many of Guevara's most important political and economic articles, but regularly comments on social matters. Today, Cuban society is as highly militarized as it has ever been, but the guerrilla mentality of the 1960s, with its improvising and unorthodox approach, has given way to the authoritarian, hidebound mentality of the professional soldier.

Carlos Franquí has recalled that amongst the guerrillas in the Sierra Maestra there was a strong feeling of egalitarianism between the *comandantes* and the soldiers: 'Rank had no privileges. We were family, and we worked together out of respect instead of mere obedience.'[35] The highest rank in the rebel army was *comandante* or major. Although a high command was set up and discipline became stricter on the arrival of new recruits, there was always a feeling of camaraderie and everyone was free to express his or her view. Those who became leaders did so simply because of their better skills or greater courage.

On Castro's triumphant arrival in Havana, in his first speech at Columbia Barracks, he pledged an end to militarism in Cuba: 'Arms? What for? . . . the military barracks will be converted into schools.'[36] With the foundation of the Milicia Popular (People's Militia) who wore the traditional blue of workers' overalls, it was hoped that the regular army would eventually be abolished. This, of course, did not happen. Some of Batista's garrisons were turned into schools but with the threat of counter-revolution—highlighted by the struggle in the Escambray mountains and the Bay of Pigs invasion—the army and the militia went from strength to strength. Compulsory military service began again in 1963. The *comandantes* of the guerrilla band took over key positions in the Revolutionary government, while many of the top commanders in the army had served under Raúl in the Sierra Cristal. Even economic activity became militarized; the army spent a great deal of time in agricultural tasks, on army rather than civilian pay. Between 1969 and 1970 the armed forces were 'mobilized for the sugar harvest as they would have been in case of war'.[37]

The 1970s saw a relative demilitarization of Cuba; the militias were abolished in 1973 and regular troops were no longer used as a pool of labour. The power of the civilian bureaucracy increased, especially after the new Constitution of 1976. The 1980s, however, have seen an upswing in the role of the military. The armed forces have increased in strength, and with Raúl still as Minister of Defence and Fidel as Commander-in-Chief, its members make up a large proportion of the party's Central Committee. High command is still in the hands of the 'old guard' of the Sierra Maestra and Escambray campaigns. The army, moreover, has developed since 1973 a classical hierarchical structure, inspired by the language, methods and discipline of the Soviet Red Army. Long gone are the old guerrilla days when all were part of a caring and egalitarian family, living like peasants.

The army is now a highly disciplined, highly stratified, extremely efficient military machine. The modest olive-green fatigues of the guerrillas have given way to resplendent uniforms. Soldiers form an elite in Cuban society, both in status and privileges. They are paid very well; officers earn more than teachers (a major received in 1985 400 pesos a month to a teacher's average of 250) and about the same as doctors. Their accommodation is free and they can buy consumer goods at half price.

The Cuban government has always been committed to the need for armed struggle, partly no doubt because that was the way it came to power itself. From the beginning, it has supported guerrilla movements in Latin America, although with the failure of 'many Vietnams' to erupt in the area and the death of Guevara in Bolivia in 1967, it grew more cautious about direct assistance. Nevertheless, in the 1970s, Cuban armed forces have become increasingly involved in Africa. Cubans have helped with military programmes in Syria, South Yemen, Algeria, Congo, Somalia (until 1976) and in Guinea-Bissau. Their greatest commitments have been in Ethiopia, where they helped to check the Somalis in the Ogaden war and in Angola, where they have supported the MPLA government against the South African backed UNITA rebels. More recently, Cuba has given military aid to El Salvador and sent military advisers to Nicaragua. Its forces also engaged US Marines during the invasion of Grenada in 1983.

The Cuban armed forces are not all made up of volunteers. All able-bodied men (except students) must undergo three years' military service, after which they stay in the reserve army and must spend 45 days training every two years. In addition there is an Army of Working Youth in which conscripts work in construction or agriculture for three years under military discipline and conditions. Since 1980 the reintroduced Territorial Militias have also grown considerably, largely financed by people's donations. Each member must spend a couple of weeks every two years, and one day a month, training.

To make sure that the need for war preparations is understood, a Society for Patriotic-Military Education was created in 1980. A propaganda organ for the armed forces, it promotes everything from sports for civilians to free target ranges in towns and villages. It has ensured that Castro's dictum, 'each Cuban must know how to shoot, and to shoot well', is plastered on hoardings throughout the country.

With what is seen as an increased military threat from the United States, the country has been turned into a veritable porcupine. 'Defence' and 'Production' are now the two watchwords of the Revolution. With arms provided free from the Soviet Union, Cuba now possesses the best-equipped military force in Latin America, capable of mobilizing more troops than Brazil, Mexico or Canada. It has increased its militia to 1.2 million, 48 per cent of whom are women. Whereas Batista's army was only 30,000 men, Cuba can now count on 250,000 professional combatants and 190,000 reservists; nearly 15 per cent of its people are prepared for military action. Civil defence involves the entire population throughout the country.

Cuba has not only expanded its armed forces, but the whole society is militarized from top to bottom. From an early age, children are brought up in a world in which the threat of war is ever present, and in which they will be expected to fight. As soon as they reach primary school, they are trained in the use of arms. Once in the Pioneers organization, which every child joins at eight, children undergo patriotic military training and are taught to sing,

> We are pioneer explorers
> Our watchword is to be like Che,
> Long live socialist Cuba!
> Fatherland or death! Long live Fidel!

Their magazine *Pionero* carries endless stories of the battles of the Cuban Wars of Independence; on a double-page spread of one issue, there is an enormous figure of a faceless, charging soldier below which two smart Pioneers (a white girl and a black boy) are saluting. The whole is intended to illustrate the message taken from the national anthem, 'to die for your country is to live'.

Students at secondary and university level undergo compulsory military training every week; their motto is *Estudio, Trabajo, Fusil* (Study, Work, Gun). The guerrilla fighter has become the model of revolutionary virtue. Significantly, the logo for the Federation of Cuban Women is a young mother carrying a baby, with a rifle slung over her shoulder. The bookshops are full of manuals on guerrilla warfare, as well as military histories. A whole generation has been brought up to see the US as a ruthless Goliath about to attack the gallant Cuban David.

In these circumstances it comes as no surprise to learn not only that pacifism is a concept totally alien to present Cuban society, but that the Constitution specifically states it to be illegal; it is punishable not to carry arms in defence of the homeland. Far from preaching the Christian attitude of turning the other cheek, the regime goes beyond the 'eye for an eye' principle of revenge in the Old Testament to uphold José Martí's assertion: 'Every righteous man should feel on his cheek the blow given to the cheek of any man.'[38] After seeing the film *Gandhi*, a Cuban friend told me simply that he must have been a masochist. Even the non-violent approach of Martin Luther King is quite incomprehensible to most Cubans.

There is a sense of constant military activity going on in the background of everyday life in Cuba. This comes across in the regular civil defence exercises reported on television; in the hoardings which declare 'as long as there is a Revolutionary and there is a rifle, no cause is lost'; in the museums of the Revolution in every town; and in the photographs in village squares of the dead in Angola and Ethiopia. The sign *No pase* (Do not pass) is common throughout the country, often attached to mysterious stretches of barbed wire. During a visit to the Isle of Youth, I was often not allowed to take photographs of apparently innocuous landscapes, which suggested eerily that there were missiles behind every bush, and radar aerials on every hilltop. I was refused permission to go anywhere near the huge Guantánamo Naval Base in the south-east of the mainland, which has been occupied by the US since the Platt Amendment of 1902. Since it provides an ideal bridgehead for a US invasion of Cuba it is called by Cubans the 'First Trench of the Revolution'.

With the coming to power of Reagan in the US, and the deepening hostility between the two countries, Cuba has felt obliged to double its planned defence spending in the first half of the 1980s. It claims to have tripled its defence capacity as a result. It takes the threat of US invasion very seriously: in 1983, the Cubans thought that the invasion force sailing towards Grenada was heading for Cuba itself. There were plans to keep all tourists in their hotels and if necessary to issue them with arms, it being presumed that anyone holidaying in Cuba would be sufficiently inspired by a spirit of internationalism to help defend their socialist comrades. Since the invasion of Grenada, the country has been on a war footing, with its regions organized into defence zones as in Vietnam. Civil defence exercises have been organized involving the whole population. At a time of acute housing shortage, it was even announced in 1984 that 15 per cent of the concrete production would be used for defence fortifications. 'Defence', Castro announced at the fourth Congress of the Federation of Cuban Women in March 1985, 'has been turned into a task of all people, with everyone organized and prepared.'[39]

The permanent state of military preparedness also affects personal relations. People are often reluctant to talk frankly about their views and feelings, especially to foreigners. They are not only watched by their Committees for the Defence of the Revolution, but agents from the Ministry of the Interior (modelled on the KGB with personnel trained in Moscow) keep an eye and ear open for careless talk which might benefit the enemy. In local Communist party headquarters, I also saw the signs: 'He who is indiscreet is an unconscious collaborator with the enemy' or 'He who divulges what he shouldn't is the most faithful agent of the enemy'. The result is secrecy amongst bureaucrats and officials, and a deep suspicion of those who are curious and question.

The threat of external war and internal subversion is also used as an excuse for the limits on freedom of the press, of expression and of movement. This state of affairs has of course been one of the principal criticisms of Castro's regime in the West. But Cubans resent this. 'Why do you Europeans always complain about our censorship?' I was asked by an exasperated official. 'We are in a state of war. When you are at war, certain freedoms have to be curtailed. In England during the Second World War, Churchill imposed censorship and no one complained, so why complain about us now?' The Cuban leadership knows only too well the advantages of promoting the threat of the enemy within and without in order to unite the people and to excuse the continuing restrictions. Castro could thus boast early in 1986: 'Military training has contributed to the development of discipline in Cuban culture.'[40]

The steering of the Cuban Revolution has thus become increasingly rigid in the last decade. The Communist party has had its role defined and its base widened. The new People's Power Assemblies have given the people a say in running their affairs for the first time. The Constitution has clarified the nature of the Cuban state. But while this makes for more stable rule through known procedures, it checks the future development of the Revolution, prevents the former spontaneity and innovation which were its hallmarks, and sends the railroad of state along a straight and narrow Marxist-Leninist track. At the same time, the increasing strength and influence of the armed forces and the continued rule by civic soldiers means that the military will have the final word. Cubans, who were once allergic to uniforms, violating rules of dress at every opportunity, have had to adjust to a society where the clothes provided by the state to a large extent define one's worth and status. Some of Batista's garrisons may have been turned into schools, but Cuba as a whole has become highly militarized.

Moreover, political power still remains centralized in the hands of the elite. The Communist party remains the highest authority in the land. It holds supreme political command and gives direction to the state and the whole society. At the head of all remains Fidel Castro, the *jefe máximo*, the undisputed leader, with his brother Raúl as his Minister of Defence and designated successor. In the meantime Fidel Castro is Commander-in-Chief of the armed forces, First Secretary of the Communist party, President of the council of ministers, and head of state. He controls the Communist party which in practice dominates the mass organizations and People's Power Assemblies.

After more than a quarter of a century he is more firmly ensconced than ever, and the majority of the people remain his enthusiastic followers. 'Commander-in-Chief,' the crowds shout during his speeches, 'we await your orders.'

5

MANAGING THE ECONOMY

The management of the economy in Cuba has undergone several distinct phases, reflecting the shifts in political ideology and practice as well as the underlying economic conditions. The economy, especially in the early years of the Revolution, was in such flux that its direction only becomes clear with hindsight.

In the first phase from 1959 to 1963, when the popular, democratic and nationalist Revolution rapidly took an anti-imperialist and socialist turn, the economy was increasingly collectivized and brought under state control. The most important act during this initial period was the First Agrarian Reform Law of May 1959, which established the Instituto Nacional de Reforma Agraria (INRA) (National Institute of Agrarian Reform), expropriated the large and medium estates, limited land owner-ship to less than a thousand acres, and distributed some land to tenants, share-croppers and landless peasants. The Urban Reform Act which followed halved rents and forbade speculation on them. Those who lived in houses in the country were given them. Foreign-owned busi-nesses were appropriated, the credit system and 90 per cent of industries nationalized, and the transport network taken over.

The economic aims of the Revolution gradually became clearer: to reduce dependence on sugar, to diversify agricultural production, to develop the industrial sector, to achieve a high rate of economic growth, to attain full employment, to improve living conditions, and to break the country's dependence on the United States.

Under the influence of Che Guevara who became the Head of the National Bank and then Minister of Industry, the economy became strongly centralized. A central planning board, the Junta Central de Planificación (JUCEPLAN), was set up in 1960 to transform the private enterprise system into a socialist one. Guevara argued that centralized planning should be the way of life in a socialist economy; he there-fore insisted on rigid central control of the economy as well as ex-tensive planning, and on the complete collectivization of the means of production. 'If the people must benefit,' he declared, 'and we are the people's representatives, we, the government, should carry the weight and the direction of industrialization, so that there will not be anarchy.'[1]

He feared any economic activity which was not directed by the state as a threat to the new socialist society he was trying to build. He therefore tried to regulate specifically all production units in order to bring to an end 'the mystification, murkiness and anarchy' which the Revolutionary regime had inherited.[2]

Unlike orthodox Communists, Guevara rejected the notion that a socialist country cannot develop its institutions faster than its economy. It was absurd to attempt to build Communism with 'the rusty arms inherited from capitalism'.[3] More importantly, he did not believe that it was first necessary to build a socialist economy before trying to change human relations and attitudes to work. Within the Marxist conceptual framework, he argued that growth in the consciousness of people was as important as the development of the economic base of society. Indeed, 'without this consciousness, which encompasses his [man's] awareness as a social being, there can be no Communism'.[4]

In a famous controversy with the Marxist academic Charles Bettelheim on socialist planning, Guevara later clarified his position. Bettelheim adopted the traditional Marxist argument that the relations of production (social relations) cannot outstrip the development of productive forces (the economic base) of society, and that it is therefore necessary to use some categories inherent in capitalism (the market, the medium of money, and the notion of profit and loss) during the socialist period of transition towards Communism. Guevara, on the other hand, felt that with the skilful leadership of the vanguard, it was possible to skip certain historical stages and move directly to Communism, since 'consciousness results from the development of all productive forces in the world, not just within a country'.[5] In other words, Guevara felt that it was possible to develop rapidly towards Communism despite the underdevelopment of the Cuban economy. Guevara believed however that this could be achieved only by rigid and centralized state control of the economy. He would have no truck with workers' control or self-management in the place of production. He also rejected the use of the market to regulate supply and demand, and did not allow individual enterprises to function as autonomous self-financing units. Instead, he set up a budgetary system of financing, which financed enterprises directly through the National Bank in order to plan and co-ordinate their activities within the national plan. An enterprise therefore had no funds of its own nor did it receive bank credits; it was intended to be nothing more than a specialist in its administrative area. The worth of its product, moreover, was not its market value as defined by the mechanisms of supply and demand, but was to be its moral and social usefulness. Profitability was not the overriding goal of an enterprise; its contribution to the national plan was more important. In Guevara's scheme of values, a book was more important than beer, (whatever the workers might think). The National Bank therefore budgeted according to social value of goods, not according to capitalist notions of economic efficiency and growth. Indeed, Guevara despised material wealth and always put people before things. He understood perfectly that 'the life of a single human being is worth a million times more than all the property of the richest man on earth'.[6]

But in order for this scheme to prevail, it required a fundamental change in people's attitudes to work and money. Like Marx, Guevara saw the individual as fundamentally creative, a productive being. Human beings, he felt, define their relationship to each other and to nature through work. He therefore felt it essential to change the attitudes to work developed under slavery and capitalism: that work was something one did only for money, or that one avoided it like the plague. This attitude, Guevara argued, was a hangover from the old, evil times. Slavery did not lie in the need to work, but in the failure of workers to own the means of production. After the Revolution, the worker could see himself as important in the social mechanism and become 'happy to feel himself a cog in the wheel'. Somewhat optimistically (though to be fair, he was trying to inspire the troops) Guevara declared that Cubans had left the old attitude to work behind them in their desire to 'return to nature, to change daily chores into meaningful play'; in Cuba, he said,

> man, after passing through all the stages of capitalist alienation, and after being considered a beast of burden harnessed to the yoke of the exploiter, has rediscovered his way to play. Today, in our Cuba, everyday work takes on a new meaning. It is done with new happiness.[7]

Guevara therefore proposed an economic system in Cuba in which production would be based on voluntary labour and distribution take place without the medium of money. Such a system would be both practical and educational. Rather than leaving the decision to work extra hours or without pay a private, individual matter, Guevara promoted it through campaigns of mass mobilization and 'socialist competition'. Professors and clerks were expected to go to sugar fields to help with the harvest; workers were encouraged to outdo each other in their productive tasks. Unlike capitalist competition, which is based on every individual maximizing profit for his private interest, 'socialist competition' (or 'emulation' as it came to be called) requires each person to do his best for the good of the whole. As such, it too is a weapon to increase production, and an 'instrument to deepen the consciousness of the masses'.[8]

Under Guevara's influence, the Cuban people began to work extra hours and without pay. The line between what was done 'voluntarily' or through moral coercion was thin, and in some cases nonexistent. Money was also phased out to a degree, with *libretas* or ration cards ensuring equal distribution of goods and food, and with free services such as telephones, transport and medicine.

There was clearly a great deal about all this which disturbed Moscow-style Communists. Indeed, Guevara was accused of Marxist revisionism, of Maoism, even of Trotskyism. He did not try to deny the similarities:

> In lots of other things I have expressed opinions that may be closer to the Chinese side: guerrilla warfare, the people's war, the development of all those things, voluntary labour, being opposed to material reward as a stimulus, all that series of things that the Chinese take up, and since they identify me with the budgetary system, all that stuff about Trotskyism gets mixed in. They say the Chinese, too, are nationalistic and Trotskyites, and I've been tarred with the same brush.[9]

But while Guevara was undoubtedly influenced by Trotsky, Mao and, on his own account, by 'a whole pantheon of Marxist thinkers', he made theoretical progress of his own. He was above all concerned about placing the Cuban Revolution on a sound foundation for independent development—a model of development which, he stressed was 'based on our own experiences'.[10] In so doing, he made a lasting contribution to socialist theory and practice, even though his ideal was only partly realized, as it turned out.

The initial response to the collectivization measures was generally enthusiastic. As part of the industrialization programme, Guevara toured Soviet bloc countries early in 1960 and obtained large-scale credit and commitments to build some 70 factories in Cuba from the USSR, Czechoslovakia, Romania, Bulgaria, Poland and East Germany. The fishing fleet was expanded, and mining developed—especially nickel. The emphasis in factories was on import substitution and heavy industry. The first new factory to be opened by Guevara in 1964 was, symbolically, a barbed wire factory in Santa Clara. All seemed propitious; the people awaited the expected industrial take-off. Unemployment receded, and unskilled urban workers received an increase in real income though some skilled workers suffered losses.

With the economic blockade from the US, however, spare parts for US machines became a major problem, especially in the sugar industry. Many of the commitments from the socialist countries failed to materialize. With the exodus of many skilled and professional people, there was a growing shortage of planning and technical expertise. There was inflation, waste, and production bottlenecks. The over-hasty programme ground to a halt. Guevara acknowledged later that they had mistakenly tried to become self-sufficient in a whole series of consumer products which could easily have been obtained in friendly countries.

After the initial euphoria, similar problems emerged in agriculture. Again, the aims were admirable: to increase agricultural production, to redistribute wealth, to introduce technological progress, to reduce food imports and, above all, to break the monopoly of sugar by diversification of crops. The land reform was also extremely impressive. The First Agrarian Reform Law of 17 May 1959, which had been drafted by the guerrillas in the Sierra Maestra, limited land holdings to 933 acres (402 hectares) and expropriated the *latifundia*; some land was distributed to the most impoverished tenants, share-croppers and landless peasants. The National Institute of Agrarian Reform (INRA) was set up to oversee the process and to administer provisions: within a year it had acquired about half the farmland in Cuba. The cattle ranches were taken over.

To begin with, several co-operatives were set up to operate the sugar-cane plantations with managers appointed by INRA. The members worked for a daily wage, and had a share in the annual profits according to the amount of work done. But neither Castro nor Guevara were happy about co-operatives, since they were based chiefly on material incentives and divided the peasantry; they preferred to turn peasants into wage-earning workers on state farms. Ostensibly because the co-operatives lacked 'political consciousness' and because they were run by inexperienced and incompetent administrators, they were dissolved and turned into state farms in August 1962. Whereas the co-operatives might have given the farmers more control over their work, they now became employers of the state rather than of the old absentee landlords. Most of the land passed into the hands of the state as 'people's property'. Only a few deeds were handed out to tenants and share croppers after the initial dividing of land.

Late in 1963, under the Second Agrarian Reform Law, all farms over 165 acres (67 hectares) were nationalized, and small farmers were organized into the Asociación Nacional de Agricultores Pequeños (ANAP).

Agrarian reform proved the boldest and most radical measure of the Revolution in its early stages. It is understandable that since sugar symbolized slavery, colonialism, dependence and unequal development, the revolutionaries should want to end its rule once and for all. There were two good sugar harvests in 1959 and 1960 which produced a surplus. Towards the end of 1961, Castro urged the farmers to destroy the cane fields and plant vegetables and fruit. The farmers took him at his word: half the cane fields were ploughed up and half the sugar crop was lost. Sugar production fell from 6.8 million tons in 1961 to 3 million tons in 1962. Again in the following year, only 3.8 million tons were harvested. It took years to repair the damage to the sugar fields. From 1959 to 1963 there was also a serious depletion in cattle herds including breeding stock, due to excessive slaughter (meat consumption rocketed as a just Revolutionary reward) and the export of cattle to Venezuela.

Typical of the many unplanned schemes, which contrasted with the careful central planning advocated by Guevara, was Castro's vision of a green belt around Havana of coffee, fruit and beans. It was suddenly decided to mobilize half a million citizens from Havana and the same number from neighbouring Las Villas province to plant seedlings, but nearly all the seedlings planted died because the conditions were simply not appropriate. A similar situation prevailed in rice production. If it had been intensely cultivated like southern China, Cuba could have produced enough food for 50 million people, but it failed to feed a population one fifth that size. Unfortunately Cuba's leaders had a guerrilla mentality, acting on sudden inspiration and ill-conceived ideas, focussing energy first in one direction and then in another. The mismanagement of agriculture—mainly due to Fidel Castro and the inexperienced officials at the National Institute of Agrarian Reform—was further compounded by a drought in 1961 and a hurricane in 1964.

The production difficulties in agriculture and industry soon had their effect in the shops. The goods inherited from before the Revolution eventually ran out and the spree abruptly stopped. Rationing had to be introduced in 1961 for the first time in Cuban history, although it had its positive side in showing the regime's determination to share equally the country's resources. The *libreta* or ration book has remained ever since; it is an everyday part of Cuban life and is necessary for buying food, clothing, shoes and other essential items. At first, rationing was all part of the heady experience of the Revolution. When there was a shortage of oranges, President Dorticós contributed to the Revolutionary debate by saying that an orange is a bourgeois fruit! (Ironically, Cuba has since agreed to provide all the COMECON countries with citrus fruits.) When people asked where the most common foods were to be found, the answer was 'In the future!' in the future!' Castro declared simply, 'If there's nothing else to eat, we'll eat *malanga*.' He may have shown more realism than Marie Antoinette, but even *malanga*, the tough root crop which had kept the guerrillas alive in the Sierra Maestra, was in short supply.

The population boom in Cuba which followed the Revolution—now called the 'Fidel generation'—was put down to a shortage of condoms. Cuban *machos* joked that the condoms sent by the Chinese were too small for them; while lines of pregnant *mulatas*, dancing to the *conga*, would chant:

> Fidel, Fidel, watch me swell.
> Here you see the Revolution;
> Now please give a smart solution![11]

But despite the economic disruption and the shortages, the Revolution was still at least in its carnival stage.

Clearly something had to be done about the economy. The plans for heavy industrialization were abandoned. Guevara also admitted that in agriculture he had made the fundamental error of undervaluing sugar, Cuba's national product, in trying to push through diversification. After making a deal with the Soviet Union to supply sugar for oil, agriculture was given high priority once again, and the country returned to its traditional monoculture. The brave experiment to diversify had failed; henceforth King Sugar was back on his throne. When Castro returned from Moscow in 1964 with an agreement from the Russians to purchase 24 million tons of sugar during the period 1965–70, the subsequent rule of sugar was assured.

The years from 1963 to 1965 saw a period of discussion and experimentation in planning. In some areas a certain degree of decentralization and market socialism was partially tested. Guevara, with characteristic frankness, analysed the mistakes of his policy which had resulted in a loss of production and mismanagement. He still believed in democratic centralism but recognized the need for middle-level cadres 'to interpret the general directives issued by the central power, to assimilate them and to transmit them as ideas to the masses'. Such cadres should be the 'driving force of the ideological engine'. At the same time, he was ready to admit errors in the administration of the executive body, and mounted an attack on the 'peaceful and cosy bureaucracy' in the political apparatus.[12]

In 1963, Guevara criticized the pluralist anarchy that had so beguiled Sartre and others in the early stage of the Revolution. He saw it as a negative form of *guerrillerismo*, the guerrilla style of working developed in the Sierra Maestra, in which the way to solve specific problems was left to each of the leaders, using experimental methods. The resulting disruption in the economy had led to the counter-measure of setting up a strongly centralized bureaucracy in the Ministry of Industry and INRA. Such a policy of centralization was understandable, Guevara argued, owing to the lack of middle structures and to the 'former anarchic spirit'. However, it had resulted in an over-zealous compliance with directives, put the brakes on any spontaneous action, and led to a lack of individual motivation. Guevara therefore called in 1963 for a 'war against bureaucratism, streamlining of the state apparatus, production without any restraints, and responsibility for production'.[13] Impressed with the gains of the Chinese Revolution, he now advocated their slogan for self-reliance and initiative: 'Use your own two feet.'[14] Just as in his political thought there is a contradiction between direct democracy and strong leadership, so in his economic thought Guevara failed to reconcile his theoretical belief in central planning in a socialist society with his practical recognition of the benefits of self-management and workers' control.

After the limited experiments with decentralization and market socialism in 1964 and 1965, the rest of the 1960s saw the development of Guevara's economic model. This had been partly inspired by the young Marx's humanism and by the Chinese Cultural Revolution under Mao, but was adapted to the peculiar nature of the Cuban economy. The system that emerged was a radical and idealistic one, which combined Guevara's stress on centralized planning with Castro's addition of special plans, and which sought to raise political consciousness through mass mobilization and voluntary work. Moral, not material incentives, were to become the order of the day. Castro coined Guevara's slogan: 'We must create wealth through a new consciousness, and not a new consciousness through wealth.'[15]

In a hurry, inspired by the enormous advances made by a few dedicated revolutionaries in the Sierra Maestra, Castro and his comrades were confident that Communism could be created with the same speed and ease that Batista was defeated. Capitalism was doomed, they thought, and the Communist utopia was round the corner. As President Dorticós told K. S. Karol in 1967:

We are about to build Communism. The aim of the Revolution is not to build a socialist state, but to move with minimum delay toward full Communism. It is pure illusion to think that Communism will come automatically, just as soon as all the conditions are right. We have to prepare for it here and now, by partial transformations of our society. . . . We have our little heresy.[16]

The period also marked the high point of the regime's attempt to create the New Man and Woman, fully integrated into the community, and hence capable of expressing their true nature as social beings.

Despite the death of Guevara in Bolivia in 1967, Castro and his associates continued Cuba's radical economic policy. The Great Revolutionary Offensive of March 1968 saw the takeover of 57,000 enterprises and the nationalization of individually-owned businesses such as bars, shops, restaurants and garages, the last vestiges of petty capitalism. 'Gentlemen,' Castro declared to applauding crowds, 'we did not make a Revolution here to establish the right to trade! . . . When will they finally understand that this is a Revolution of socialists, that it is a Revolution of Communists?'[17] This, according to the Communist party daily *Granma*, was a final attempt to root out the 'nests of parasites, hotbeds of corruption, illegal trading, and counter-revolutionary activity'.[18]

The result of this Guevara-style campaign was to create a radical brand of egalitarianism. Class distinctions were being eroded by the partial neglect of the wage scales, work quotas and labour norms which had been established in 1964. Socialist emulation, not capitalist competition, became the order of the day. Bonuses for overfulfilment of quotas were replaced by comradely pats on the straining back. Social goals were constantly promoted over individual ones, and the moral values of altruism and sacrifice extolled. Castro also took up Guevara's criticism of the bureaucracy which put a brake on Revolutionary action. Indeed, the battle against bureaucracy came to be seen as decisive as the battle against underdevelopment.

The eventual outcome, however, was not altogether positive. The de-bureaucratization campaign led to a further erosion of the power of the middle cadres whom Guevara had promoted, and put great pressure on top state officials, thereby making political power even more hierarchical and vertical. The French economist I. Joshua described the resulting system as one of 'authoritarian centralization coupled to anarchic decentralization' with, I would add, the disadvantages of authoritarian centralization cancelling out the benefits of anarchic decentralization.[19] The leadership kept issuing orders and appeals, yet lacked the means of discovering whether they were understood or heeded. At the same time, the workers were denied any real self-management or control.

The zigzag course of economic development in Cuba, which had borrowed often incompatible practices from different traditions, also led to certain contradictions. In order to boost production the regime followed the Russian precedent by adopting a national competition of vanguard workers based on the Stakhanovite model geared to material incentives. But this clearly conflicted with Guevara's project to abolish money and promote moral incentives in the form of socialist emulation. It was, as K. S. Karol observed after a visit in 1968, a policy which consisted of 'coining slogans of the Chinese type while staking everything on developments of the Russian type'.[20]

In such a thicket of problems and contradictions, Castro decided in 1968 to revive the economy and the energies of the people by mass mobilization on militaristic lines. He opened the year with a speech at the Cultural Congress in Havana in which he attacked the 'calcified pseudo-Marxist church' and outraged old Communists by declaring that 'no one has a monopoly of revolutionary truth'.[21] In March the Great Revolutionary Offensive was begun. This was followed by a speech in September when the whole capital was invited to celebrate the anniversary of the foundation of the CDRs. 'Today I can see an immense army,' Castro exclaimed, 'the army of a highly organized, disciplined, and enthusiastic nation, ready to fulfil whatever tasks it is set, ready to give battle to all who stand in the way.' Criticizing the behaviour of young people, he declared that military law would apply to all youngsters over 15 who were not engaged in studies: 'In future they will be put in uniform.' As for anyone who tried to threaten his rule, he issued the stark and sinister warning: 'The heads of all who try to destroy the Revolution will fall.'[22] Castro even apologized for having given the mistaken impression of being a liberal. All the talk about the freedom of thought amongst Marxists earlier in the year was quickly forgotten. Castro remained silent about the student rebellion in Paris and the massacre of Mexican students at Tlatolco, but supported in August the Russian invasion of Czechoslovakia. Three months later he signed a common declaration with a delegation from the East German Communist party calling on the 'necessity of fighting against all forms of revisionism and opportunism'.[23]

Castro then made one last great effort of Revolutionary will: he threw all the energies of the Cuban Revolution behind the attempt to make a sugar harvest of 10 million tons. The year 1969 was called the Año del

Esfuerzo Decisivo (Year of the Decisive Effort). In so doing he not only abandoned most of Guevara's ideas, but began to extoll the virtues of discipline and work. The whole campaign was run on military lines, and the apparent solution to Cuba's problems was found: conscription.

In the event, the campaign to achieve the 10-million-ton harvest proved a disaster. By backing the honour of the Revolution on such a Herculean task, Castro made a physical impossibility into a serious moral and political defeat. In an outstanding speech on 26 July 1970, Castro informed the people that total sugar production for that year had only reached 8.5 million tons. He further admitted that insufficient production in the face of increasing expenditure had resulted in growing difficulties in the economy, and that there were large imbalances in their foreign trade, especially with the Soviet Union. But rather than placing the responsibility on the lack of political consciousness amongst the people, or on the bureaucracy, this time Castro placed the blame firmly on himself and the leadership.

The major crisis precipitated by the sugar harvest failure caused Castro and his leaders to reassess their policies. On a visit to the Soviet Union in the same year, Castro acknowledged again that Cuba had not previously fulfilled many pledges, and that there was 'accordingly—very naturally and justifiably—a certain scepticism about our economic plans'.[24] The response was to accept more economic and military aid from the Soviet Union and to adopt more closely its system of planning and management. Russian-trained technical advisers and technocrats replaced the Cuban political cadres. In 1971, a Cuban-Soviet Commission of Economic, Scientific and Technical Collaboration was created. Cuba's new economic orthodoxy was symbolized in the following year by its membership of COMECON. Three years later, the Organization of American States (OAS) lifted its trade embargo against Cuba and welcomed it back into the economic fold.

All this was a clear and irreversible retreat from Guevara's ideal of creating a moneyless, co-operative society based on the voluntary labour of workers and peasants. On May Day in 1971, Castro argued 'the way to Communism is not a question of consciousness alone. It also has to do with the development of the forces of production . . .'[25] In the new spirit of pragmatism he felt compelled to argue in July 1973: 'Along with the moral stimulus, we also have to use material stimulus without abusing one another. The first would lead to idealism, the second would lead us to develop individual selfishness.'[26]

The Cuban economy thus entered the 1970s plagued by low productivity, poor planning and mismanagement. There were shortages of almost every item, especially bread, milk, vegetables and clothing.

Long-term trade agreements with the Soviet Union had perpetuated Cuba's role as a sugar producer after the failure of the early ambitious programmes of industrialization and agricultural diversification. The workers and peasants, without any genuine trade union organization, could only express their discontent by absenteeism and slackness. The attempt to stimulate production by mass mobilization on a military scale and model had further alienated many workers. The romanticism of the 1960s, with its bold and heretical experiments inspired by Guevara to build socialism and Communism, had ended. The Marxist innovators had lost the struggle.

The 1970s thus saw a return to the post-reform, Soviet-style of planning, with technocrats organizing production, and the country geared to monolithic five year plans. The new economic plan for Cuba was based on high investment and low consumption. The call for sacrifice, frugality and hard work was reiterated, coupled with incentives in the form of wages and consumer goods. The moribund trade unions were revitalized but more to enable the managers to direct the workers than to give the workers greater power. And just as the economy followed the Soviet model, so new institutions were set up to transform the nation into a fully-fledged Marxist-Leninist state based on the East European model. The new watchwords of the Revolution became production and defence.

The entire economic system of Cuba was reorganized in the middle of the 1970s. The enthusiastic economic experiments of the 1960s were replaced by the Sistema de Dirección Económica (SDE), an organization with a careful system of book-keeping and management based on methods developed in the Soviet Union. Instead of Guevara's budgetary system of financing which tried to do away with money (and therefore with book-keeping) the 'rusty tools' of capitalism which had been abandoned as useless were reintroduced: rigorous accounting and the use of categories such as profit, interest, prices, wages, and even taxes. If a factory used a commodity from another factory, it was not just taken, but paid for at a 'price'. It borrowed 'money' from the National Bank at an 'interest' and was expected to make a 'profit'. Workers' hours were recorded and they were paid 'wages' accordingly. In keeping with the new economic orthodoxy, the schools of public accounting in the university (which had been closed in the mid-1960s) were reopened for students to study crisp, heavy textbooks on economic theory, translated from Russian.

The only difference between Cuba's economic system now and capitalism is that so-called 'profits' theoretically go to benefit the people as a whole rather than individual owners or shareholders, and that every aspect of the economy is developed according to an inflexible five year plan. The Communist party draws up an outline after weighing the various political and economic options, while the central planning board JUCEPLAN fills in the details. The final plan has the force of law which the workers are obliged to carry out.

There has been a slight but significant easing of the state control of the economy in the last decade, within the rigid overall framework of the five year plans. In 1976, the co-operative movement was revitalized and has been developing successfully, with members sharing their profits. The principle of payment according to work done and a policy of making more consumer goods available have been adopted as material incentives for workers to produce more. In 1980, free markets for excess agricultural produce were allowed to stimulate production, and fill production gaps. A parallel market based on the mechanism of supply and demand also operated alongside the subsidized and rationed one in an attempt to undermine the black market. Self-employment was even allowed in services, and tradespeople such as gardeners, mechanics and masseurs advertised for work after hours. In early 1985 Castro announced a plan to sell state properties to their tenants on a mortgage scheme so that all Cubans would be able to own their own houses.

While threatening the egalitarian gains of the Revolution—Castro admitted at the tenth session of the National Assembly in July 1986 that 'we have created a class of newly rich'—the liberal measures undoubtedly improved services and increased output. However, no doubt to disarm hard-line critics in the party, Castro has firmly rejected the capitalist system as 'rotten and disgusting' and pledged that the 'hell of capitalism' would never return to the country.[27] In June 1986, the Politburo in a major policy shift further squashed the recent liberal measures by clamping down on the private sector, putting an end to house sales, and dissolving the free agricultural markets. It would seem to mark a return to the idealism of the sixties when moral incentives were stressed more than material ones.

Despite the upheavals and changes of course in policy and planning, the Cuban economy has done rather well in conventional capitalist terms, especially in comparison with neighbouring countries in Central and South America. Some Western experts claim that the figures published in Cuba are unreliable (the Cold War exists in economics as well as politics), but even making allowances for certain exaggerations, economic performance in the last 15 years has notably improved. The 1980 World Bank Report suggested, on US Intelligence sources, that Cuba's GNP growth rate per capita for the years 1960–79 was − 1.2 per cent. The 1981 COMECON report put the growth rate at 4.4 per cent. Cuba's own national accounts employ what they call the Global Social Product (GSP) to measure growth; these figures show that in the first half of the 1970s there was a real boom which has since levelled out. At the same time there was a great increase, almost an explosion, in expenditure devoted to satisfying the basic needs of the people. With these different figures, a more reliable way of calculating growth might be to take both the indices for GSP and basic needs, in which case from 1958 to 1980, the annual growth rate per capita would work out at 2.9 per cent, rising from $743 to $1421.[28]

In the second half of the 1970s, the economy performed less well, with the GSP contracting from 10 per cent on average for the first five years of the decade to four per cent. Many of the targets for the first five year plan (1976–80) were not fulfilled, largely owing to errors in planning, bad management, mistaken incentive policies, low productivity and labour difficulties.

Outside factors also adversely affected the economy. Since Cuba still sold a significant portion of its sugar on the open market, the collapse in the value of sugar to almost half the cost of its production had serious repercussions. Then, from 1976, Cuba was deeply involved in costly African wars in Angola and Ethiopia. Towards the end of the decade, agriculture also suffered from a series of natural disasters: blue mould devastated the tobacco crop in the year 1978 to 1979, destroying almost a third of it; a fungus disease attacked the sugar cane in 1979; there was a serious outbreak of swine fever on the island; and in 1984, Hurricane Kate badly hit the sugar crop. But despite the failure to fulfil its projected targets, Cuba made some significant advances during the first five-year plan, with sugar production up, and investment in industry increased by half. There were also important areas of growth in housing, public health, education, culture and defence. Cuba was fortunate in being virtually the only non-oil-producing, underdeveloped country that could be certain, with Soviet aid, to meet its fuel needs.

Despite general economic decline in Latin America, the Cuban economy has continued to expand moderately in the 1980s. At the second Congress of the Communist party in Cuba, the annual growth rate for the second five year plan (1981–5) was projected at 4 per cent. In the event, the rate fluctuated dramatically: in 1981 the GSP jumped unexpectedly to 15 per cent, the best performance since the Revolution, but in 1982 it dropped to 2.5 per cent after agricultural production had been lowered due to disease. It then rose steadily to 5.2 per cent in 1983, 7.4 per cent in 1984, and 4.8 per cent in 1985. Overall, a seven per cent growth rate was achieved between 1981–5, more than expected. Considerable economies were made in the use of energy and raw materials during this period which resulted in a seven per cent increase in productivity. Since 1978 the balance of trade has shown large surpluses, mainly due to a cutback in imports. The 1986–90 five year plan projects an annual average growth rate of 5 per cent.

Cuba's total estimated debt is about $7.5 billion owed to the Soviet Union and about $3.2 billion owed to Western governments and commercial banks. It is not a huge debt by Latin American standards, and Cuba is considered a good customer who meets its commitments. It has adjusted its economy to low sugar prices and the world recession, and managed its debt prudently: by 1986 it had refinanced most of its debts successfully. But while it would like to increase its trade with Western countries, this has dropped from 22 per cent in 1981 to less than 10 per cent in 1986. Japan, Canada, Spain and France remain Cuba's chief trading partners in the West.

Cuba's economy is, of course, protected from the ups and downs of capitalist countries by its special relationship with the Eastern bloc countries. Most of its trade (88 per cent) is with socialist countries and continues to grow. It is, with Vietnam, the only member of COMECON outside the Eastern bloc, and as such is given special treatment as a valued and prestigious addition; indeed, Cuba has been called the 'spoiled brat' of COMECON. In 1985, the COMECON summit took place for the first time outside Eastern Europe, in Havana, even though Castro was the only leader of member countries not to have attended the previous meeting in Moscow. Cuba benefits from special aid and soft loans with less developed countries like Vietnam and Romania. Since 1972 COMECON has made credit worth more than $1.2 billion available for the development of Cuba's sugar mills, citrus production, nickel and cobalt plants. Cuba can also earn substantial amounts of hard currency by reprocessing and reselling cheap Soviet crude oil on the world market.

Industrialization is still the principal aim of the government. Since the initial burst in the early 1960s, the stress has been on the gradual development of Cuba's natural resources and on import substitution. The industrial sector now employs over 20 per cent of the national workforce. The country has developed its computer knowledge and intends to keep up with the new technology. It has diversified its exports during the past decade, especially to capitalist countries: in 1976 it exported a range of 60 products and now sends abroad some 150 products and a number of semi-manufactured goods. Further major investment is being made in export diversification. The country is exploiting its rich reserves of nickel (said to be the largest high-quality deposits in the world) and its considerable reserves of copper, iron ore, and marble. Cuba is hampered by a lack of oil, producing only

10 per cent of its needs, but is now building in Cienfuegos, with Soviet aid, the first nuclear power station in Central America. Cuban officials are impatient to reap the so-called benefits of industrialization; they wax lyrical, for instance, about the 'majestic constructions of steel and concrete rising among the smoking chimneys' in the new industrial zone in Cienfuegos. Never having experienced large-scale industrial pollution, smoke from factory chimneys is seen as a sign of progress and prosperity.

However, Cuba will remain a predominantly agricultural country for the foreseeable future. Despite the efforts to diversify, the processing of agricultural products remains the most important industry, and accounts for about 80 per cent of the total volume of exports. Cuba is no longer the world's sugar bowl, but it is still the fourth largest producer, representing about 8 per cent of total world production. On average, eight million tons are harvested, but the magic ten million ton crop is on the cards by the end of the decade.

Tobacco remains the second most important foreign exchange earner, although the production of citrus fruits for COMECON has doubled since 1981 and may eventually displace tobacco in importance. Tourism is increasing, both from East and West, and is now in third place as a foreign exchange earner. The country's rich fish stocks are being exploited for the first time. But although great efforts have been made to increase food production, Cuba still has to import half of its total needs.

Cuba thus finds itself in the 1980s with a moderately expanding economy which is beginning to make full use of its resources and in a position to make sustained industrial growth in the next century. But it is closely integrated with the COMECON economies and follows their style of economic management and planning. It is set on an orthodox Soviet course, not deviating too much to the left, to Mao or Guevara, or to the right, to Tito. The dominant theme is still one of frugality and austerity. Castro calls his people ceaselessly in neat slogans plastered all over the island: to save more (*hacer mas con menos*); to produce more (*mas que nunca: la producción*); to take more care (*para tener, hay que cuidar*); and to carry the spirit of sacrifice and dedication to even greater levels. The predominant mood is one of pragmatism and caution. The workforce is expected to be loyal, hard-working and obedient, carrying out the centrally planned policies issued by the new technocrats.

And yet there is an enormous residue from the experience of the 1960s, reinforced by party ideology. Many Cubans will undertake voluntary labour and place national interests above their personal ones. The use of material incentives has recently become more pronounced, but it has not entirely replaced the power of moral motivation: consciousness still helps to create wealth. A new generation of Cubans has grown up with a strong socialist conscience. Daily chores may not have been turned into 'meaningful play' as Guevara hoped, but a more positive attitude to work has undoubtedly emerged. After nearly three decades of Revolution, the political consciousness and economic values of the Cuban people have been fundamentally changed.

6

THE WORKER AND PEASANT ALLIANCE

On the outskirts of Camagüey in central Cuba, alongside the Havana to Santiago highway, I came across a noisy crowd of people on a piece of waste ground next to a factory. It was a local rodeo. *Vaqueros* (cowboys) were standing on their saddles drinking beer out of bottles, more at home on their horses than on the warm earth, trying to get a better view of the corral over the heads of the milling, jostling crowds. Women and children sat by the wooden fences, shading themselves against the fierce sun with bits of cardboard. Boys dashed between the legs of the horses, impervious to dung and dust in their hectic play.

Inside the corral, young men pitted their skill against each other in riding unbroken horses, lassoing cattle and dodging bulls. All was noise and mayhem; the smell of manure, beer and sweat filled my nostrils. Then a tiny, black, greased pig was released into the ring, which ran about squealing, looking absurdly vulnerable in the empty space within the throng of humans. Suddenly a great roar went up from one end of the corral, and a cavalcade of bare-chested and bare-footed toughs came charging down on the terrified pig. They fell in an enormous tangle of arms and legs. The squeals of the tiny pig buried under this mass of sweating, cursing humanity were like a child's. 'They'll kill it! They'll kill it!' screamed some of the excited women onlookers. But no. Suddenly a grease-covered man emerged from the scrum carrying the squealing and struggling pig aloft by its trotter. It was his by right of force. A great roar of applause went up.

The rodeo was over; it had been a good afternoon. The *vaqueros* slipped into their saddles and with a flick of their reins slid away like shadows to the central plains, their cattle and their thatched huts. Most of the other spectators walked home to their prefabricated apartment blocks to watch the news on their television sets.

The afternoon was not just an age-old bucolic sport, a picturesque custom, but a politically motivated event. The *vaqueros* put on the rodeo for the workers of the beer-bottling factory nearby. It was a show of town and country solidarity, a way of forging the new 'alliance of workers and peasants' in Revolutionary Cuba.

Visitors to Cuba who only stay in Havana often get a completely distorted picture of the country. Although a large number of Cubans (about 70 per cent) live in towns, Cuba is fundamentally an agricultural country. Havana has been correctly described by Castro as the over-developed capital of an underdeveloped country. Sugar barons who used to entertain in the grand neo-classical palaces in the Havana suburbs were living off the surplus of the Cuban peasants who subsisted in *bohíos*—wooden thatched cottages with dirt floors and no plumbing which had not changed since pre-Columbian times. The city dweller moved amongst the greatest luxuries the West could create; the peasant lived in a state which was often worse than that of the most remote African village. But the real Cuba is to be found on the veranda of the Indian-style *bohío*, not in the air-conditioned skyscraper built by American capitalism. The visitor to Cuba who sees only Havana, leaves without knowing Cuba.

Before the Revolution, there were great differences between the town and country. Nearly all government expenditure was directed to Havana while provincial towns and rural districts were seriously neglected. There were few, if any, sewers or paved roads in the villages. A very large part of Cuba's population was ill-fed, ill-housed, ill-clothed, and provided with few amenities of modern civilization. Many rural people lived virtually incommunicado, separated from the rest of the Republic, with no roads and no mail. Visits from the town were few: the priest might come once a year to baptize children for a fee or politicians would appear at election time. Living conditions were atrocious. According to the 1953 census, most people had dirt floors and no piped water or sanitary facilities. The water which had to be collected from springs and rivers was invariably exposed to pollution. The illiteracy rate in the country was four times that of the towns, running at 42 per cent compared to 11 per cent. Outside the towns, housing, education and health were poor and life uncertain. Not surprisingly, there was a steady migration to the cities, especially to Havana in the 1950s, where sprawling shanty towns mushroomed.

The laws of land tenure, crucial for the well-being of peasants, were heavily weighted against them. By the first part of this century, most of the traditional small farms had been merged into large-scale cattle ranches and sugar plantations known as *latifundia*, which were owned by *hacendados*, absentee Cuban landlords or American interests. By 1959, the *hacendados* controlled 40 per cent of sugar-sown land and 10 per cent of cultivable land on the whole island. Large tracts of land were also rented by *colonos*, tenant farmers who grew sugar for the mills. Those peasants who were lucky enough to rent a plot of land lived in constant insecurity: they could not even plant a cedar or an orange tree, for they never knew when the Rural Guards would come and evict them. And then there was a vast army of dispossessed itinerant agricultural workers, more than half a million, who formed a kind of rural proletariat. Most of them worked in the sugar plantations and had no choice but to be seasonally employed. Cuba was thus a rich country with a poor people. The *campesinos* (peasants) were not only forgotten but despised—dismissed with the derogatory term *guajiro*.

Unlike Mexico where Zapata led a peasant uprising in 1910, there was no general peasant revolt in the Cuban Revolution. Only about a thousand of the half million peasants at the time joined or helped the rebel force. Indeed, the Revolution was made principally by urban middle-class youth. Nevertheless, the experience of the Revolutionaries living amongst peasants in the Sierra Maestra led the Revolutionaries to make agrarian reform their foremost pledge and to put the peasants in place of the urban proletariat as the chief revolutionary class.

The First Agrarian Reform Law of 1959 expropriated the large *latifundia* without compensation, placed a maximum limit of 933 acres on land holding, and distributed some land to tenants, share croppers and landless peasants. A short-lived attempt to set up some rural co-operatives failed largely because of lack of political direction, incompetent administration, and Castro's prejudice against them. The Second Agrarian Reform Law of 1963 further limited private land holdings to 165 acres, but guaranteed the security of the peasant land holdings in perpetuity. These measures marked one of the most thoroughgoing agrarian reforms ever, and was welcomed enthusiastically by the peasantry. Camilo Cienfuegos rode into Havana after the declaration of the First Agrarian Reform Law in an astonishing cavalcade of ten thousand peasants on horseback, in a demonstration of worker-peasant solidarity. The literacy campaign of 1961 also brought a hundred thousand young city dwellers into the country to teach the peasants, enabling them to break down their mutual prejudices and fears.

For the first time in Cuba's history, the regime concentrated its resources in the country rather than in the towns. Since the Revolution $11.6 billion have been invested in rural development: the number of tractors has increased eightfold, the use of fertilizers tenfold, the use of pesticides fivefold, and the water supply capacity has multiplied by 125. Annual sugar harvests have sent city dwellers into the country. Secondary schools in the country also have pupils who spend half their time working the land. By continuing to provide full amenities in the countryside, Cuba has been able to avoid the steady drift to the towns which has bedevilled so many other developing countries.

Most of the *latifundias* worked by seasonal labour, and the cattle ranches patrolled by a few *vaqueros*, have been made into state farms with wage-labourers guaranteed work all the year round. There has been no attempt to collectivize the land forcibly as in the Soviet Union in the 1930s. Indeed, about 30 per cent of cultivable land is still in the hands of private farmers who produce more than a quarter of livestock, less than a fifth of sugar, half the fruit, vegetables and coffee, and almost three-quarters of the tobacco. The Asociación Nacional de Agricultores Pequeños (National Association of Small Farmers) (ANAP) was set up in May 1961 to express the interests of small farmers and co-ordinate their production.

Although Castro personally preferred to see all agriculture state-controlled, at the beginning of the Revolution he went out of his way to respect the farmer's traditional individualism. When ANAP was founded, he declared:

> What is the policy of the Revolution? The most absolute respect for the will and the desires of the *campesino*. If he wants to spend his life alone, working and cultivating as he wishes, as he sees fit, the Revolution respects whatever the *campesino* thinks is best for himself, what he likes best.[1]

This respect has meant that in some cases an access road to a state dairy farm will go round a small private plot complete with *bohío*, rather than across it. The government recognizes the need to woo the peasants and convince them of the need for change. Where peasants must be moved, as for the construction of a dam, they will be offered an equivalent holding. Unlike the Soviet Union, China, or even Tanzania, voluntary persuasion, not coercion, has been the approach adopted by the government with regard to the private farms. It was recognized in 1977, at the fifth Congress of ANAP, that any change in agricultural practices requires prior knowledge and consent. As Castro made clear to the República de Chile co-operative in the same year: 'It is up to the peasants . . . their decision will be respected. Only on the basis of persuasion and respect of each peasant's free will can such change be effected.'[2]

While the cultivation of crops remains under the direct control of the farmers, production is co-ordinated and information distributed through ANAP, which has about 201,000 members. The government provides inputs and sets crop quotas. From 1980–6, free markets for agricultural produce were permitted. All crops in excess of the quota set by the government in the national plan targets were sold at any price that the market allowed. The markets proved a financial breakthrough for the peasants, and more than 60 per cent of food was distributed through these markets. Because of the excessive profits made by the middlemen, however, it was announced in July 1986 that the free markets would be closed and the State would take-over distribution as before.

After the Revolution, all the big sugar estates were nationalized. Although there was a bold attempt to diversify agriculture, it soon became apparent that Cuba could not escape the conditions imposed by its geography and history so easily. Sugar would have to remain the principal source of foreign exchange for the foreseeable future. Every effort was therefore made to increase production; the mass mobilization of 'voluntary' workers became a regular feature of the annual *zafra* (harvest). But office workers were clearly more at home with pens than machetes. After the failure to reach the magical figure of ten million tons in 1970 more realistic targets were set.

In the last decade, a considerable amount of investment and modernization has taken place in agriculture. Nearly all the planting is now mechanized, while Cuban-built sugar-cane combine harvesters have reduced the workforce from 350,000 in 1970 to about 70,000. Only 20 per cent of the crop is produced by private farmers. In 1984, 8.2 million tons were harvested, the third best total so far, and it seems likely that ten million tons will be reached before the end of the decade. There are now 150 sugar mills, with at least ten new ones under construction; 60 per cent of their components are manufactured in Cuba.

Few other nations are so dependent on a single crop: sugar accounts for 80 per cent of Cuba's exports, 80 per cent of its foreign exchange earnings, and takes up half the cultivable land. The old saying *sin azúcar, no hay país* (without sugar there would be no country) is still as valid today as it was 50 years ago. The Soviet Union has replaced the United States as the principal customer, exchanging oil for sugar at fixed prices. Cuba has to launch only a quarter of its crop on the uncertain world market.

The *zafra* takes place from November to May. Traditionally, the cane is cut from the ground by one stroke of the machete, trimmed of leaves, and then cut into pieces to await collection. The cutters swing their machetes with apparently effortless grace, but in fact the work is back-breaking; the sun and scorpions also take their toll. But the new great bulldozer-like *combinada* cane harvesters mean that where a master cutter produced about 200 *arrobas* (5,000 lbs) a day, a truckload of 600 *arrobas* can now be produced in eight minutes. Once the cane is cut, its juice begins to ferment immediately, so there is a breathless haste to get it to the mill by truck or railroad. Modern mills work 24 hours a day during the *zafra* and the whole processing of the sugar takes place under one roof.

Although the slavery has been taken out of the sugar industry, and its trials and benefits are spread more evenly, little has changed in its production and processing. This became apparent during a visit to a sugar mill at Palmira near Cienfuegos, one of the oldest in the country, founded in 1830. Slaves worked there until 1886, when slavery was abolished. Today, the steam engines bringing the cane from the fields are vintage—all made in the United States at the turn of the century when American interests started to control the large *centrales*. Although now being replaced, some of the generators for the enormous grinding machines date from before the Second World War (their maintenance shows how well the Cubans managed to circumvent the US economic blockade by manufacturing their own spare parts for their American-built machines). The rhythm of work in the mill continues as before. The machines turn 150 days a year during the *zafra*, from November to May, day and night, non-stop. Only during the slack period are they overhauled and holidays taken. The working day is organized into three shifts of eight hours. There are four brigades of 150 workers per brigade, making 600 workers attached to the mill. Three brigades work while one rests. The mill can produce 30,000 tons of crude sugar a day.

I had the impression that the workers got on well with the managers who were friendly, relaxed and good-humoured. They all seemed to be proud of their work and respected the plant. While little had changed physically in the mill since the days of slavery and American ownership, the Revolution had clearly changed the attitude of those who toiled there. On a newly-painted boiling vat, a poster of Castro carried the words *Frente a las Amenazas Imperialistas no se Puede Retroceder* (Faced with Imperialist Threats, no one can Retreat). The old manager's house, beautifully set in gardens, is now a workers' centre with a permanent exhibition of photographs and posters depicting the heroic strides made in the economic development of Cuba in recent years. There is also a large recreation area for workers' children, complete with swimming pool and coloured parasols, run by the local branch of the Central Organization of Cuban Workers.

After sugar, tobacco is Cuba's second most important export crop. The country's unique combination of climate and soil produces the best tobacco in the world. The word 'Havana' evokes for the connoisseur of cigars an indescribable blend of sensual associations. Most Europeans, including myself, usually first see the word on a fragrant,

colourful cigar box. The trade names of the cigars are as exotic as the
cedar and pine boxes in which they are packed: Romeo y Julieta, Punch,
Fonseca and Montecristo, to name but a few. The Havana cigar has
always been a symbol of wealth and power. It has traditionally been
associated with the fast-talking gangster, the fur-coated millionaire or
the elderly statesman but only recently with the revolutionary. Ironically, Cuba's Marxist regime has been compelled by history and
geography to produce the best cigars in the world for the bourgeoisie.
Advertisers in the West are forced to joke at the paradox, offering
'Havana cigars at revolutionary prices'. The Cuban government warns
its own people that smoking damages health, and Castro has given up
the habit but it has to rely on tobacco as its second most important
foreign-exchange earner. In a good year, 45 to 50 thousand tons of
tobacco can be harvested, producing up to 200,000 million cigarettes
and 300 million cigars of 140 varieties. All in all, tobacco represents
about ten per cent of Cuba's exports.

Tobacco is one of the most difficult crops to grow and requires
constant and careful attention. Although most of Cuba's agriculture has
been collectivized, about 80 per cent of the tobacco crop is still grown
by private farmers who take a personal interest in the cultivation of
each plant on their small family plots of land or *vegas*. The most
important growing areas are the lowlands in the west known as Vuelta
Abajo, Semi-Vuelta near Havana, and Vuelta Arriba in the centre of
the island.

The size of tobacco factories varies. They can be small workshops
employing a score of people or vast factories like the H. Upmann factory
in Havana which produces 23.5 million cigars a year in 39 different
varieties. Machines have been introduced so that now, for instance,
four workers can roll 9.5 Montecristos per minute, while the average
hand-rolled is 110 in eight hours. Only hand-rolling, however, can
produce the best quality. As a result, about 70 per cent of Cuban cigars
are still hand-rolled. The tobacco industry is therefore labour intensive,
employing some 50,000 workers, more than half of them women.

The tobacco factory I visited was a small one in Pinar del Río where
Serbio cigars were being made for national consumption in a former
prison of the Batista era. The factory was named after Francisco Dona-
tien, a boxer and cigar-roller who became a martyr of the Revolution.
The manager who greeted me had a small badge of Lenin pinned to his
hat. Ribbons, medals and awards won by the workers of the factory
were displayed in a special room, a kind of shrine to socialist emulation.

Although cigar rollers used to work individually, they are increasingly
grouped into brigades. Here they were divided into brigades of eight

or ten members each. The principle of payment according to work done operated: they were paid a basic salary, and after completing a daily quota (150 medium-sized cigars in an eight hour day) the workers received a bonus calculated on a piecework basis.

The workforce was made up of about half men and half women; the women tended to be younger than the men. The manager admitted that it was now difficult to recruit tobacco rollers because of the dangers to health and the monotony of the work. Certainly some of the older men smoking cigars (they could smoke as many as they liked at work) looked ill, producing immaculate cigars with rapid deft movements with their shaking hands. The *tabaqueros* used to be the elite of the working class, the most educated and politically conscious, but their skills are no longer being passed down from generation to generation in one family; the children of the Revolution have wider horizons.

But not all has changed. The old tradition of reading, established in the nineteenth century, which made the *tabaqueros* such an educated class, continues. From a desk with a microphone in front of the lines of work tables, every day a fellow worker reads the newspapers in the morning, for a period of 45 minutes (20 minutes national news, 15 minutes international news, five minutes for culture and the same for sport). In the afternoon the workers listen to a reading from a book of their choice for half an hour, usually a novel. The *tabaqueros*, despite their changing work conditions, retain a special place in Cuban folklore and they are widely respected for being well-informed, independent thinkers.

The third great traditional product of Cuban agriculture is cattle. Before the late eighteenth century, hides were the island's most important export, and vast tracts of forest were cut down to make room for the rolling pastures in the central plains. With the growth of sugar, some of the ranches were ploughed up, but at the turn of the century there were still great *haciendas* often owned by American interests or absentee landlords. The *vaqueros* have now become salaried workers on the state-owned ranches, but their way of life in the saddle has changed little. A *vaquero* may still be seen cantering down the middle verge of the central highway, his straw hat pulled hard over his forehead, with his machete slapping on the side of the large saddle on his small *criollo* horse.

At the beginning of the Revolution, the cattle were badly managed: too many were slaughtered for the Revolutionary feast in the first couple of years while some were unwisely exported to earn foreign exchange. Indeed, the ratio of cattle head per inhabitant in 1967 was less than the ratio in 1958. Today, the Cuban beef herd is still primarily made up of

Cuban Charolais bred early this century and reared largely on unim-
proved ranch land. The increase in numbers has not been able to satisfy
the Cuban appetite for meat, and beef is rationed to once every two
weeks or so. Cattle breeding at one time became Castro's chief hobby,
but his intervention was not always felicitous; he rejected, for instance,
the finding of some visiting British geneticists in 1969 that corn was
cheaper than grass or sugar cane as cattle fodder. His elder brother
Ramón, however, has been more circumspect, and now runs a successful
genetic breeding centre in the Valle Picadura near Havana.

Climate, particularly the dry season, continues to hinder the development of cattle rearing. Because of the massive deforestation of Cuba
and other Caribbean islands in the past, the boundary between the
continuous rainfall tropical climate and the seasonal subtropical climate
has moved from the middle of Florida to south of Jamaica. The result
is that Cuba now has a winter dry season lasting from November to
April, and its natural grasses have evolved to be more drought-resistant
than nutritious.

Nevertheless, there has been marked improvement in milk production. The old Cuban dairy cows—the Brahman or *zebu* cow of Indian
ancestry and the *criollo* of Spanish origin—produced about four pints
a day, barely enough for a peasant's family. The Brahman has been
successfully crossed with the Canadian Holstein, to produce an animal
that is well adapted to the tropics and capable of giving 20 to 40 pints
a day. Cuba has now developed a modern dairy industry and is self-
sufficient in dairy products, with cheap milk and cheese freely available.

But while sugar, tobacco and cattle have always been Cuba's traditional agricultural products, a new crop has begun to exert its influence:
citrus fruit. In order to lessen its dependence on sugar, Cuba has agreed
to meet the needs of COMECON for this product, and may well soon
become the second largest producer in the world after Spain. Many
parts of the Cuban mainland and the Isle of Youth have been turned
into neat plantations. Like Cuba's other crops, citrus fruit also has its
special workforce: mainly secondary school children in boarding schools
in the country, who combine studies at their desks with work in the
fields.

The most interesting recent development in Cuban agriculture has
undoubtedly been the co-operative movement. Although they proved
unsuccessful at the beginning of the Revolution, the new co-operatives,
known as Colectivos de Producción Agropecuaria (CPA) have since
1977 been going from strength to strength. The state now owns 70 per
cent of the land, and the rest is still in the hands of private farmers and
co-operatives. But the number of private farmers has been halved since

1977; there are now more than 1,450 co-operative societies with an average of about 1,700 acres of land each. Members own shares in the co-operative according to the material contributions they have made in the form of land, equipment or livestock. Profits, on the other hand, are distributed according to the amount of work done. Unless the soil requires special crops, the co-operatives try to become self-sufficient first, and then sell their surpluses to the state.

The state does not directly coerce the peasants but makes the formation of co-operatives attractive by offering direct investment based on need, by helping to build the infrastructure, and by providing loans for equipment, fertilizers and seed. In addition, members of a co-operative get better access to education and health care, as well as enjoying social security benefits, including old age and disability pensions. Then, of course, there are the advantages of a more communal way of life which at first are not so obvious to the strongly individualistic Cuban peasant. Indeed, the cooperatives are particularly attractive to the young generation, which has tended to leave the private family farms over the past two decades. The small farmers' union, ANAP, is a mouthpiece for their interests and their president is a member of the Politburo of the Cuban Communist party, ensuring that their views are heard at the highest level.

About 25 miles from Camagüey, I travelled along a new road through sugar fields to visit one of the new agricultural co-operatives. The members were all part of ANAP and called their co-operative the Alianza de Obrero-Campesino (Worker–Peasant Alliance), promoting the official policy of uniting town and country. New prefabricated bungalows of the co-operative bordered the road, each with a neat garden in front and a television aerial on the roof. There was a pleasant air of prosperity and simplicity about the place. In the distance amongst the trees could be seen the older thatched *bohíos*. Waiting to meet the leaders of the co-operative, I could see one middle-aged man giving another a haircut amongst some tractors in the shade of the communal workshops.

The president of the co-operative arrived on horseback at the agreed time, a stocky man with heavy glasses, who jumped nimbly down from his horse, tied it to a tractor, and sauntered over with his spurs clicking. He took off his straw hat to wipe his brow; his deeply-lined face burnt nut brown by the sun contrasted starkly with the white of his skin where his hat had been. We went into the communal dining room which served as the meeting place for co-operative business and as a social club. A board, with posters from ANAP giving information and slogans, stood on a small dais. A picture of Raúl Castro visiting the co-operative was given pride of place. One slogan read *El Respeto es Parte de la*

Educación (Respect is Part of Education). Some drums were also visible in a corner, brought out no doubt to celebrate the key dates on the Revolutionary calendar. We were joined by some other members of the co-operative, who all addressed each other by the familiar *tu* form. The president, who was introduced as 'comrade', *Compañero* Jiménez, quickly reeled off the basic facts and figures of his co-operative:

> The co-operative now has 142 members, 32 of which are women. There are 87 families and a total population of 1,553 people. In 1979, we had only 18 members with 8 *caballerías* [285 acres] of land; now we have 136 *caballerías* [4,500 acres]. About half the land is for sugar cane, but we have also 513 head of cattle, 250 goats, pigs and a chicken farm as well as 50 horses. We produce 260 litres of milk by hand. We are self-sufficient in food, and grow rice, *yucca* [cassava], sweet potatoes and fruit. What we do not need, we sell to the state.

He was very proud of what the co-operative had achieved in five years. Although I was clearly visiting a model farm, it was not untypical of the new developments in the Cuban co-operative movement. As we visited the nearby workshops, the president overflowed with enthusiasm as he sang the praises of the new machines: 'In the old days, the farmer's tools were simply his hands, his hoe and his machete. He spent every day in back-breaking toil. When we first began the co-operative, there was only one old tractor. But now we have 20 Russian tractors, seven Japanese trucks, two cane-cutters made in Cuba, and (here he smiled, kissed his hand and slapped a steel box) an English welding machine'. I could see dark oil being soaked up by the red dusty earth. 'This workshop shows the real alliance which exists today in Cuba between the peasant and the worker,' he said, beaming. Jiménez had a strong proprietary sense, but it was a deep satisfaction in collective rather than private ownership, as he talked about the assets of the co-operative.

I asked him how the co-operative was organized.

> It is all very democratic. There is an elected managing council which consists of 13 members and includes a president, a vice-president, a production secretary and a secretary for education and ideology. The council meets twice a month to discuss the problems and to analyse the situation. A general assembly of all comrades is also held once a month, to decide what is to be done. The proposals of the council are then put to the vote; we usually get about 80 or 90 per cent

agreement, as all issues have been thoroughly discussed beforehand by our fellow members. Whether you are on the council or not, we're all partners; we're all equal.

Jiménez was quick to point out the advantages of the co-operative. Social services were more accessible: there is a clinic nearby, and a doctor visits regularly. Before, the farmers were all illiterate; now they have reached the equivalent of the sixth grade in Cuba's schools and are working for the ninth grade by studying in evening classes. They have built a primary school for their children. Each family will eventually have a new concrete house with three rooms, a toilet, large kitchen and running water in the back yard. Houses are built by the microbrigade system, that is, members of the co-operative are supported by their neighbours while they construct their houses. In addition, they have built communal sport facilities like volleyball courts and a baseball pitch.

It is work which principally unites members of the co-operative. But the increased mechanization—only 30 per cent of the sugar cane is now cut by hand—means that there is more time to grow other crops and pursue other interests. Diet has improved and is more varied, and the members can sell their surplus food to the state. Standards of living have increased so much in the past few years that some city dwellers are beginning to complain that the farmers are becoming the new aristocrats. Sharing tasks has also meant that the work is not so monotonous. 'Everyone is paid according to the amount of work they do.' Jiménez explained. 'A *norma* is set for each task, and any work done over the *norma* is paid extra. We usually have an eight-hour day. During the school holidays the children can help their mother do her *norma*.'

I asked about how private farmers became members of the co-operative and what happened to their property when they joined. He explained that after the Agrarian Reform Laws, there emerged three different types of farmer: there is the old-fashioned private farmer who owns all his land and tools, but sells his surplus produce to the state; next there are the 'co-operatives of credits and services', where the tools are owned privately but the land is worked collectively, these being still most common. And then there are the new co-operatives like this one. 'In our co-operative the land and tools are both collectively owned. When a new member applies to join, we value his land, stock and equipment, and pay him 35 per cent of its worth. He then gets paid according to the amount of work he does, and after three or four years he becomes a full member. In our region about three-quarters of the farmers are in co-operatives. The problem is that some private farmers here are doing so well that they don't feel the need to join a co-operative.'

Although once an illiterate peasant, Jiménez has now a remarkable grasp of modern agricultural methods and economic principles. He has also a clear idea about the future direction of Cuba towards a Communist society. But whereas my visit to the co-operative only confirmed my view of the advantages of small self-managing communities in a de-centralized society, Jiménez, for all his enthusiasm, follows the Communist party line:

> The eventual goal of co-operatives is to become integrated with the state. Co-operatives and private property will go and we'll all eventually work for the state. We will give our land to the state and become salaried workers; then we will no longer be selfish. Everyone will then be an owner of the means of production. One day though the state and the army will also disappear, and with them money relations.

Then he said, looking wistfully at the crowns of the royal palms which were turning gold in the setting sun, 'It won't be in my lifetime, that's for sure!'

Cuban leaders, including Castro, would like to see all agriculture controlled by the state. The co-operatives are encouraged as a stepping-stone from private land ownership to state ownership, and as a way of eradicating the individualism of the Cuban peasants. The ultimate aim is to overcome the differences between town and country, between farmers and workers, so that all Cubans become salaried proletarians under the umbrella of the Cuban state. The private farmer in Cuba is undoubtedly a dying breed. In the meantime, the Cuban agricultural policy, by only nationalizing the *latifundia*, by giving tenure to private farmers, and by encouraging the co-operative movement through per-suasion rather than coercion, has given the Revolution a strong base in the countryside. It remains to be seen whether Jiménez's vision of all farmers working for the state will improve either their material or psy-chological well-being; the experience of the wage-earners on the large nationalized estates does not suggest that a radical transformation of their consciousness will take place, or that their work will suddenly become more meaningful.

While the independence of the peasants was recognized from the beginning of the Revolution, and in general they have been persuaded rather than coerced into becoming part of the Revolutionary process, the same cannot be said about the workers. Just as there was no mass peasant uprising to inaugurate the Revolution, so the urban proletariat played a small role. Indeed, the general strike called in April 1958 by the July 26 Movement in the cities failed. Fearful of alienating what support he had, Castro promised independent trade unions on coming to power. In the free elections held at the tenth Congress of the Central de Trabajadores de Cuba, (CTC) in November 1959, many new leaders were chosen and nearly all the Communist candidates were rejected. However, purges began soon after that. In a speech on 'Sacrifice and Dedication' to a Havana assembly of workers on 18 June 1960, the new Minister of Industry, Che Guevara, made it clear that the unions would no longer be allowed to struggle against the state to protect the interests of the workers. Guevara argued that many workers, especially in the new industries, were privileged individuals compared to the rest of the population. It was therefore necessary for the regime to engage in 'arduous struggles' against the representatives of the 'old CTC gang' which had halted the advance of the workers' movement. He proudly boasted that already by June 1960 the old representatives were 'in the process of being destroyed'. He lamented the fact that:

> in the process of industrialization, which gives such great importance to the state, the workers consider the state as just one more boss, and they treat it as a boss. And since this is a state completely opposed to the state as boss, we must establish long, fatiguing dialogues between the state and the workers, who although they certainly will be convinced in the end, during this period, during this dialogue, have braked progress . . . The best labour leader is not the one who fights for his work comrades' daily bread, but for everybody's daily bread. In these circumstances, it is inadmissible, and it would be the start of our failure, for the workers to have to go on strike . . .[3]

The Cuban workers would therefore have to get used to living in a collectivist regime, without the right to strike.

At the eleventh Congress of the CTC, now temporarily renamed the CTC-R (with the extra 'R' denoting *Revolucionario*) held in November 1961, the right to strike was officially abolished. Only one list of candidates was allowed—all carefully chosen for their Communist orthodoxy and loyalty—and the veteran Communist Lázaro Peña was appointed general secretary. It became crystal clear that the new regime would not allow an independent trade union movement which might offer a separate power base. The Marxist-Leninist corporate state became real; as Raúl Castro explained: 'The best union is the state—the workers don't need unions when they have a friendly government, their government, to protect them.'[4]

Henceforth, the chief task of the CTC was as an instrument of the state to increase production and tighten labour discipline. In a series of laws passed between 1960 and 1962, the state took complete control of employment, determining where workers went, what they should do, and what wages they should receive. The new legal system for the trade unions introduced in 1961 reorganized the unions no longer according to occupation but by economic or industrial sector. In one factory, for instance, all the 'intellectual' and 'manual' workers would become members of the same union. Grievance Commissions were established at the same time, consisting of five reliable workers to mediate in any local disputes or complaints at work.

A decree in August 1962 prohibited workers from changing their occupation or employer, and made absenteeism a major crime. By Law 647, the Ministry of Labour was further authorized to take full custody of any union or federation and to appoint or dismiss officials. By the twelfth National Congress of the CTC held in mid-1966, the unions had become part of the state apparatus. The Congress approved a declaration of principles and union statutes which include the principle that: 'The labour movement, directed and guided by the party, must effectively contribute to the mobilization of the masses in the fulfilment of the tasks assigned by the Revolution and to strengthening Marxist-Leninist ideology.'[5] The trade union movement rapidly lost its traditional role of defending the interests of its members, and was now there in order to promote the collective national interest, as conceived by the Revolutionary government and party. Unions were incorporated into the overall system of central planning and used as a vehicle to increase production and labour discipline. Guevara called for a close relationship between the workers and administrators in the state-owned factories, for the administrator to get to the work bench, and the worker to rise to the administrator's desk. But in practice, there was virtually no worker participation in management decisions, in planning, or in distribution.

The desired performance of the workers was achieved through a system of punishments or rewards, by a mixture of legal sanctions and moral and material incentives. A code of labour discipline was drawn up, with violations penalized by law, in order to ensure that the workforce was hard-working, obedient and docile. The rules forbid tardiness, absenteeism, disobedience, negligence and lack of respect to superiors as well as physical offences like damage to equipment, fraud and robbery. From 1965 the offences were dealt with by Consejos de Trabajo (Labour Councils) which replaced the old Grievance Commissions.

From 1975, under the new judicial system, special labour courts have been operating at municipal and provincial level. Sanctions for indiscipline can vary from admonitions, wage deductions and transfers to another job to being discharged. For serious crimes like harming public property, the death penalty exists.

As part of the campaign inspired by Guevara to promote equality, by the end of 1965 a new system of work quotas and labour norms had been established, together with a new series of wage scales. Henceforth, a worker was expected to fulfil a set quota in terms of output, quality and time in order to receive a basic wage rate according to his or her particular scale. Every worker was given a quota; if it were not fulfilled, wages would be proportionally reduced; if exceeded, they would be increased. The system still exists more or less in the same form.

In the latter half of the 1960s, however, *estímulos morales* or moral incentives were promoted more than material ones in order to develop political consciousness. The most important of these was the socialist emulation programme, first introduced in 1963, in which workers are encouraged to 'emulate' each other, that is, to outdo each other in productivity, correct behaviour, voluntary work, and so on.

Developing the Stakhanovite system introduced in the Soviet Union, from 1965 a vanguard workers' movement was also developed, in which exceptional workers are given honorary titles, diplomas and banners. More than 26 orders and medals now exist, which includes medals for 'labour feat', or 'for friendship', as well as the highest order of 'hero of the Republic'. They are taken very seriously and are much coveted. But while individual feats of outstanding work are rewarded, the government today still prefers to promote 'socialist emulation' between groups—work brigades, factories, even provinces. During every sugar harvest, *Granma* carries the daily results of each province in the collective battle to maximize production. The province with the highest overall annual productivity is chosen to host Castro's speech on July 26 which always begins with fulsome praise of the achievement of the vanguard workforce. Although the province is theoretically chosen strictly according to merit, privately it is admitted that different ones are chosen each year to stimulate emulation.

In addition, Guevara saw the principle of voluntary work as a crucial weapon to elevate the 'consciousness of the masses', and a way of preparing the road to 'a new stage of society where classes will not exist, and therefore where there will be no difference between a manual worker and an intellectual worker, between worker and peasant'.[6] Voluntary work thus became a symbol of Cuban Revolutionary consciousness; the *millonarios* (workers who cut more than a million *arrobas* of cane) were made into national heroes. There were mass mobilizations of workers during the sugar harvest, which sent professors and students alike into the cane fields.

But while the mass mobilization of voluntary workers was undoubtedly a great outburst of collective energy, it was increasingly organized along military lines, particularly after the death of Guevara. Already from 1964 to 1967 labour camps had been established which were called Military Units to Aid Production (UMAP). The Revolutionary Offensive of 1968, which took over the remaining small businesses and trades, was organized throughout the country on the model of the army: command posts were set up and the directives issued. In September 1968, when the whole capital was invited to Revolution Square to celebrate the anniversary of the foundation of the CDRs, Castro told the vast crowd that he was delighted with the progress so far in unequivocal military terms: 'Today I see an immense army, the army of a highly organized, disciplined, and enthusiastic nation, ready to fulfil whatever task it is set, ready to give battle to all who stand in the way.'[7] This was followed by the further rapid militarization of labour. Students were expected to work under strict military discipline. Labour brigades were organized into battalions. The culmination of the militarization process was the Youth Army of Work (EJT), founded in 1973 as part of a branch of the regular army. Guevara's voluntary labour had given way to Castro's military conscription.

After the failure in 1970 of the ten-million-ton sugar crop, there was a reassessment of strategy in the labour movement, as well as in economic planning; penal laws were added to the moral principle of socialist emulation to get the workers moving. With absenteeism a major problem, a law against loafing or *vagrancia* was introduced in 1971, making it a social duty for all able-bodied men between 17 and 60 to work. Now, penalties for being absent for 15 or more days from work without justifiable excuse can vary from admonition, to house arrest, to up to two years' forced labour.

In order to keep track of workers, it was also announced in August 1969 that every worker had to register a *carta laboral*. The *carta laboral*, which is both an identity card and work file, has remained the principal means of controlling the workforce. It contains a full record of a worker's behaviour, and lists 'demerits' such as poor discipline, neglect at work, or disrespect to superiors, as well as 'merits' such as overfulfilment of work quotas, voluntary labour, defence of state property, and perhaps most important of all, 'political consciousness'. They are carefully guarded and deeply respected documents, essential to get a job. However their very nature means that the past of any worker will inevitably cast a shadow over his future, that no one can escape his former 'crimes'.

By the end of the 1960s, the trade unions had become moribund; they were non-representative organizations aimed at directing and regulating the workforce. From 1970 to 1973, the party and the government decided to reanimate the movement after the failure of the mass mobilization for the ten million ton sugar crop. Meetings were held at work centres, 21 new national unions were formed, and new elections were held. It was clear that something had to be done to prevent the increasing alienation of the workers. Discussions on wage policies, moral and material incentives and economic planning culminated in the thirteenth National Congress of Cuban Workers in November 1973. The Congress approved nine theses and 22 resolutions which have defined the role of the trade unions ever since. The ninth thesis maintains that in a socialist society the state, the management, the party, and the trade unions are all organizations of the 'working class', representing their interests and therefore there cannot be any conflict between them. They must be partners, not antagonists, in a corporate state.

The principal role of the trade unions is thus still to increase production, to improve state services, to promote workers' discipline and attendance, to raise political consciousness, and to implement party policy and directives. While there has been an attempt to improve the flow of communication between workers and management, there is no talk of workers' control or self-management. No Solidarity-style trade union movement has emerged in Cuba as in Poland.

The most important decision at the Workers' Congress in 1973 was to reintroduce the extensive use of material incentives. Under Guevara's system of moral incentives, voluntary labour and mass mobilizations, wages had little relation to work done. At the First Congress of the Communist Party held in 1975, the socialist slogan was hung in huge red letters above the tribunal: 'From each according to his ability, to each according to his work'.

Workers now receive wages according to the amount of work they do, not, as Marx foresaw in a Communist society, according to their needs. The principle has not only reactivated material incentives, but provides a way of measuring productivity. Reliable and productive 'vanguard workers' are thus rewarded by increased wage packets, as well as privileges such as special holidays, better access to housing, or subsidized consumer goods. The latter are the most coveted, and are distributed by the labour councils at the work centres according to the criteria of a worker's behaviour and productivity. One out of every three cars is distributed in this way.

In order to see the conditions of the workers for myself, I arranged a visit to a cement factory in a new industrial zone in Nuevitas in the north-east of the country. The factory, capable of producing 470,000 tons a year, was built in 1968 with East German aid, and is named July 26. In the local Communist party office, which every visitor must pass through, there were the usual portraits of Marx, Engels and Lenin on the notice-board, and the stirring message to the local workers: '*¡Elevemos a planos superiores los conocimientos teoréticos sobre la doctrina del proletariado!*' (Let's take the theoretical knowledge of the doctrine of the proletariat to higher levels!).

Although using local materials, the factory, like most of Cuba's, was imported. It had been partly shut down in the past because of lack of spare parts, but it was now making its own parts. The factory was in full swing during my visit, with men working with protective helmets and eye shields in the unbelievable heat. But the whole place was covered in a thick layer of cement dust; even the struggling saplings outside were completely coated. 'This is Cuban snow,' joked the works manager. There were 720 workers in all at the factory, 110 of whom were women. The men tended to do the manual work while the women worked as administrators and technicians. Other women were repairing electrical equipment in a laboratory. As usual, there was one labour council for the whole factory, with a representative from each workshop.

In the director's office, I raised the question of the dust pollution. 'Yes,' he readily admitted, 'we must reduce our dust problem. Two tons are wasted every day. We must put in new filters, and build a hangar so that the loading of the cement is done inside.' But did it affect the health of the workers? Apparently not. 'We have no cases of lung disease,' he insisted, 'and some of the workers have been here for 25 years.' It seemed to me however that the constant drive to improve productivity and maintain production could very well involve a health risk to the workers.

While the techniques of production were the same as in capitalist countries, the management was very different. In the director's office, the trappings of a Communist society were all there: a bust of Lenin stood on a Russian television; on the walls were hung honorary certificates commending the superior quality of the factory's product. In a prominent position, there was a letter personally signed by Castro dated 15 February 1984, urging the workers of the factory to do their best to save energy as part of the national plan.

A very different factory I visited, but also built by East Germany, was one on the Isle of Youth in the main town of Nueva Gerona. It was an extension of the first ceramics factory in Cuba opened by Che

Guevara in 1964. Built in 1980, it was called 'Il Congreso' in honour of the second Congress of the Communist party held in that year. It has been supplied on a ten year credit, and still has East German technicians working in it. Unlike the cement factory in Nuevitas, 80 per cent of the workforce are women.

The working norm is set at seven and a half hours with two 15-minute breaks, for a basic wage. Any extra work done is paid accordingly, although there is a maximum of 64 hours a week. If the norm is over-fulfilled by more than half, there is a special bonus. The ceramic artists get a special rate and are paid by the hour, and some can work on their own designs. There are therefore strong material incentives to work hard.

Despite the efforts of the regime through money, persuasion, propaganda and plain bullying to establish a socialist work ethic, the Cubans have refused to be turned into super-efficient work machines. The country, for instance, imported over 50,000 tractors between 1959 and 1970, but these were employed as transport for all sorts of non-productive uses, despite the high cost and scarcity of petrol. Castro admitted in 1970 that formerly a privately owned tractor could last for 20 years, whereas when owned by the state their average lifespan was two to four years. President Dorticós also acknowledged early in 1972 that Cuba had the highest per capita consumption of spare parts in the world, due to the poor maintenance of equipment.[8]

In November 1979, Raúl Castro admitted that the principal cause for the 'notorious lack of efficiency' in important areas of the Cuban economy was the 'presence of indiscipline, lack of control, irresponsibility, complacency, negligence and buddyism which . . . generate justified irritation on the part of broad sectors of the population'.[9] In his speech to the third Congress of the Communist party in February 1986, Fidel Castro was even more outspoken in his criticisms of the waste, poor planning, insensitive service and excessive bureaucracy in sector after sector of the economy.

In a sense, the inefficiency, the go-slows, the absenteeism so lamented by the leaders, are all positive signs of the human dimension to the Revolution, a reflection of the revolt of individuals who do not want to become unquestioning and docile cogs in the industrial machine or the super-state. Cuban workers can really work hard if they are committed, as the *millonario* brigades of sugar cutters and the national labour heroes demonstrate. But just as the Stakhanovite system did not really succeed in the Soviet Union, so socialist emulation run on militaristic lines seems to have rebounded to a degree in Cuba. In addition, the new emphasis on self-interest by relating wages to work in order to

improve production and discipline has resulted in a great step backwards
from Guevara's vision, partially realized in the sixties, of motivating
people by the love of society. Cuban workers in the third decade of
the Revolution are again becoming money-conscious and consumer-
orientated in the incessant drive of the state to achieve economic growth
and military strength.

It cannot be denied that Castro's regime has created a more egalitarian
society. This is especially true of the relationship between the worker
and the peasant. The countryside has benefited from a considerable
amount of investment in agriculture and from a startling expansion of
social services. Schools and clinics reach areas entirely neglected before the Revolution. Seasonal unemployment has been eliminated. The
countryside has been less affected by rationing, and some of the once-
despised *guajiros* are becoming envied for their wealth, thanks to the
rewards offered by the state for their surplus produce.

Owing to the literacy campaign, the mass mobilizations, the nationwide militia and the schools in the country, the political consciousness
of the farmers has been developed and their traditional suspicion of the
city dweller eroded. The farmers have gone to the cities, and the urban
workers to the fields. The expanding co-operative movement shows
how they are being brought into the social and economic mainstream
of the country, although the significant number of private farmers remaining demonstrates that the traditional individualism of the Cuban
peasant has not been entirely overcome. But while there is more equality, the farmers still do not have direct control over production and
distribution, or participate in the making of national economic policy.

The cities, historically privileged in Cuban society, have not fared
so well. Many cities, especially Havana, were left to decay whilst
resources were being poured into the countryside. Many high status and
well-paid urban workers left, and those who remained have lost their
privileged positions and no longer have trade unions to represent and
defend their interests. While the 'aristocracy of labour' has been over-
thrown, the urban workers still remain at the bottom of the economic
and political scale. They have problems with overcrowding and shortages of accommodation, and they are expected to work long hours for
low wages. At the same time, many of their real sacrifices have been
compensated for by free social services, security of employment, and
greater equality.

Many peasants and workers now feel that working for the community
is more important than working for themselves, and they have discovered a meaning in their work which was lacking before, as Guevara
hoped. The prospect they have is of improving services, better housing,

and a widening range of consumer goods; the future appears full of promise for their children, if not for themselves. They do not have to worry about their old age, with community services and pensions provided. It is no longer necessary to look inwards to family for protection and security—the community at large is there ready to help. For all its shortcomings, the alliance of workers and peasants is undoubtedly more than a mere slogan in Cuba today.

7

HEALTH CARE FOR ALL

The way a society looks after its weaker members—the sick, the elderly, the mentally ill and the handicapped—vividly reflects its fundamental values. Cuba has developed a remarkable system of health care which looks after citizens from the cradle to the grave. It is not only one of the greatest achievements of the Revolution, but one of the principal reasons for the regime's continued popularity. The Cuban health care system is, moreover, recognized by international organizations as the best in Latin America, and one of the best in the world.

Medical care was a profitable business in Batista's era. There were 6,300 doctors practising at the time of the Revolution, 64 per cent of them in Havana. The rich had their private physicians and psychiatrists, the poor had to make do with a few poorly-run hospitals and costly medicines. In the remote countryside, medical care was virtually nonexistent. When the Revolution triumphed, half the doctors left the country.

The new regime had to start from scratch. From the beginning it was committed to a state-run system of health care available to all citizens. The Ministerio de Salud Pública (MINSAP) (Ministry of Public Health), set up in 1960, took as its fundamental principles the need for full social participation, respect for human dignity, and the opportunity for self-realization according to each person's capacities. It continues to recognize the article of the Constitution that 'Everyone has a right to the care and protection of their health' (Article 49).

The result is that today the Cuban people enjoy a network of medical services which is comprehensive and preventive, free of charge and open to all. A new attitude to healing has developed amongst the doctors. No longer primarily a means of making money, the practice of medicine has become a genuine service to humanity. As a group of Cuban doctors declared in 1968: 'Our medical services must be made more humane and scientific; each sick person should be cared for as if he or she were our own father, mother, spouse or child. In this way, we will enrich ourselves, being more human to others.'[1]

Before the Revolution, the average life expectancy of a Cuban was around 55 years, compared with around 73 today. Inoculation campaigns, improved diet, better sanitation and living conditions have eliminated the diseases like tuberculosis, gastro-enteritis, polio, diphtheria, malaria and tetanus, which still devastate Third World countries. The main causes of death in Cuba are now those of the developed West: accidents, heart disease, cancer, strokes, asthma and bronchitis. AIDS has not reached epidemic proportions, although after three deaths in 1987, victims are being kept in quarantine.

Cuba, in fact, not only offers the best medical service in Latin America but is fast becoming a world medical centre. The ratio of doctors per head of population is now one to 400, with one to every 125 families in Havana. Of dentists, the ratio is one to 1,746 people. While only 3,000 doctors remained after the Revolution, Cuba now has more than 17,000. The number of dentists has quadrupled to more than 4,000. The country even sends its medical personnel on missions all over the world.

The new Hermanos Ameijeiras Hospital in central Havana, standing 24 storeys high with 1,000 beds, symbolizes the regime's concern in providing the best and most modern medical treatment. Furnished like a hotel, it includes a million-dollar scanner as well as a computerized administrative and records service. Apart from this showpiece, each province has several hospitals backed up by a series of 'poly-clinics' scattered throughout the country. They offer general medicine, paediatrics, gynaecology, obstetrics, dental care, control of contagious diseases, hygiene and health education, and support the work of doctors and dentists who live in the local communities.

In order to find out more about this remarkable medical system, I visited the new hospital in Cienfuegos. Founded in 1979, it is the first of its type to be designed by a Cuban architect, and will be the model for future hospitals in the country. It has all the latest equipment, and I was shown around the radiological department and physiotherapy unit by the director, Miguel Avel Díaz. The wards all have balconies and can accommodate up to 669 patients. There are 27 beds to each ward, which are divided into cubicles for three to six patients. The atmosphere was one of quiet, relaxed friendliness. Walking down one corridor, I came across a remarkable innovation: an operation could be seen in progress through a wide window. It let in natural light and enabled the staff to communicate with the outside world and to train students. In another ward, dying patients could be seen through windows as in an

aquarium. Even in hospital, however, you cannot escape Cuba's political culture, and posters on walls urge staff and patients alike to work
harder for *La Producción y la Defensa*.

I also visited a surgery in the country with a doctor and dentist.
The surgery consisted of two plain rooms in worker flats, on an estate
built next to a sugar mill near Vertientes in Camagüey province. It
was a typical medical post in the countryside, with one doctor to 480
people and one dentist for 2,000. The most important illnesses in the
region were acute respiratory diseases, especially bronchitis and asthma,
cardio-vascular complaints, and high blood pressure.

The young doctor lived in a simple flat on the same estate as his
patients, and was expected to work a 10-hour day for about the same
salary as a manager in the local mill. Like all doctors, he was expected
to spend at least three years in the country. His training would already
have taken five years: two in medical school with visits to the hospital,
and then three in a teaching hospital. He explained that obstetrics and
paediatrics are considered the most important branches of medicine in
Cuba. Ironically, some measures criticized by feminists in the West are
considered major achievements in Cuba. In a country where most women
in the country used to give birth in unhygienic shacks with dirt floors,
with only the help of a local woman acting as a midwife, the regime
proudly boasts that all women now have their babies in public health
institutions. Breast-feeding is actively encouraged. Natural birth is also
encouraged, and women are taught breathing exercises. As a result of
these measures, the infant mortality rate has been reduced from 70 to
17 per 1,000.

A paediatrician will visit the home of a mother with her newborn
child once a month during the first year of its life. The mother is expected
to call once a month at the local clinic where she receives training in
diet, hygiene and so on. With the country doctor, I went to visit one
such mother who lived in a neat flat at the top of a seven-storey block.
Her husband was working in the sugar mill and her eldest son had just
returned from Angola. Her mother was also living with her in their
four-roomed flat, but they seemed to manage. The doctor chatted with
the mother in a relaxed way, joking, and clearly enjoyed playing with
the young baby.

Mothers also enjoy generous maternity benefits: they are on full-paid
leave for two months before and three months after the birth, and their
jobs will be kept open for them to return to for a year at least. There
are also child care centres for working mothers which take infants from
45 days old. Regular smear tests for cervical cancer are carried out.

Contraception and abortion are freely and easily available while sterilization, especially for women, is becoming increasingly popular. As a result, the net growth in population has fallen to less than one per cent in recent years.

While all facilities are provided for the cure of patients, the main priority in health care is given to preventive medicine. Popular participation is encouraged at all levels: 'To give blood is one of the most beautiful forms of human solidarity', I read on the wall of the doctor's surgery. With the help of the mass organizations, countrywide inoculation campaigns have been undertaken. There are regular public health programmes recommending exercise, careful diet and hygiene. 'War on the sedentary life' is a popular slogan, and people are reminded to use the stairs whenever they can. In a country producing tobacco, people are warned by posters that smoking can damage your health, although a symposium of Cuban scientists recently claimed that sugar does not rot your teeth! While Cuba has begun manufacturing its own drugs most of them are still imported from socialist countries. To deter over-use, patients have to pay for their medicines, and posters warn them not to turn their organisms into 'pharmacies'.

While the young get special attention, and the medical needs of all adults are met, old people are also looked after. Old people do not share the poverty and the insecurity of the majority of their counterparts in Western industrialized societies. They tend to live with their families, helping with domestic chores and the upbringing of children, but they also have a considerable social life outside. They spend much of their time seeing friends in the city squares, chatting on porches, or undertaking voluntary work. Above all, they participate in running local affairs through the mass organizations, especially the Committees for the Defence of the Revolution (CDRs) and the Federation of Cuban Women (FMC). They therefore have a meaningful role to play in society after retirement. Unlike in the West, it is virtually impossible in a Cuban neighbourhood for old people to remain locked alone in their rooms, poor, frightened and anxious. With improved living conditions there are, of course, many more old people in Cuba now, and mortality rates have altered: more than ten per cent of the population are over 65 and life expectancy is now about 73 years.

Voluntary retirement for women is at 55, for men at 60, but part time work is often available for old people. Retired people receive a guaranteed pension which is 50 per cent of their previous income, although many pensioners claim this is not enough to pay for their transport, medicines and entertainment as well as their board and lodging. Even so, their basic needs are undoubtedly met, especially the need for physical and psychological security. And they do not have to worry about the cost of their funerals.

If old people are in poor health, living alone, or unable to look after themselves, they can now enter state-run homes or Hogares de Ancianos, where everything, including food, medicine, toilet articles, clothes, hairdressing and recreation, is provided free. The guests keep their own pension cheques and can do what they want with them.

I visited such a home on the outskirts of Santiago de Cuba. It was called Antonio Maceo after the famous local nineteenth-century rebel leader. It seemed more like a hotel than a home, set in spacious gardens. It had a very friendly and positive atmosphere, with staff and inmates cheerful and informal. The ages of the guests varied from 60 to 103 years, although the average age was 70. There were 620 full-time inmates and 150 who came each day. People are able to work in small workshops, making handicrafts, repairing equipment and so on, as well as in the grounds, producing food and flowers. The permanent medical staff include nurses, doctors, physiotherapists and psychiatrists. There is even a beauty salon and a barber's shop. The old people live in different wings according to sex, though they can meet during the day. There is also accommodation for couples; I met one recently married couple who had met each other in the home, and they proudly showed me around their comfortable two-roomed apartment. Privacy is respected and staff must always knock on doors before entering. The inmates are incorporated in the running of the home as much as possible. They elect representatives who sit on a council and express their needs and grievances to the management. They also help to arrange entertainment and recreation. The old people are taken out on visits to the beaches or mountains, or to visit the local cinema, music or cultural centre. In the home itself there are dances and concerts, and the inmates often entertain each other—I saw one old man singing and playing a guitar to friends as I passed through.

Although the homes meet the needs of the old people and provide a sheltered community for them, they are not cut off from the outside world. 'We try and maintain family relationships as much as possible,' I was told by the resident psychiatrist, a young woman. Members of the family can visit the old people at any time and are encouraged to take them out on trips. There are even special social workers to deal with the families.

I could not help being impressed. While old people in the West are often abandoned by their families in lonely flats or uncaring institutions, where the permanent noise of the unwatched television bears witness to the lack of real communication, Cubans can look forward to a secure, sociable and sheltered old age. Old people are integrated, respected and useful members of society. When they can no longer contribute directly to the community, the community looks after them.

The same caring attitude and generosity with resources is applied to the mentally ill in Cuba. The Cuban way of life certainly has its fair share of stress and tension, and although no official figures are published, the cases of mental disorder are undoubtedly high. Most officials appear harried, suspicious and edgy. People have several roles to fulfil—as parents, workers and Revolutionaries. Outside work and the home, most people are members of the mass organizations, especially the CDRs, Militia and FMC. They are even expected to do extra voluntary labour. In the rushed daily round, few have time to stop and stare.

Then there are other causes for anxiety. Firstly, there is a constant threat of war, and most families have had a member involved in one of Cuba's foreign wars. Families have been disbanded, with ten per cent of the Cuban people living in exile abroad. Secondly, the social pressures to conform in the new collective society are strong. Parents have high expectations of their children, and are in turn expected to be models of socialist morality. Thirdly, widespread social and psychological disharmony is inevitable in a rapidly changing society. Indeed, the experience of the revolutionary upheaval has for some, particularly the elderly, been traumatic. Finally, the higher the hopes in a new society, the greater the frustration can be when they are not realized.

In the circumstances, it is therefore not surprising that the diseases linked with stress—heart disease and strokes—are, with cancer, the main causes of death. The divorce rate is high (four out of ten marriages are dissolved). Above all, suicide is the seventh most important cause of death. The Cuban saying *¡No cojas lucha, que la vida es corta!*, 'Take it easy, for life is short', has never been so apt.

In Communist states, the issue of mental disorder has also become entangled with the question of dissidence, particularly as claims are made in the West that Soviet psychiatry, for instance, is used as a means of social and political control. By a twisted logic, if the party is said to be the sole possessor of truth, the state the only possible reality, and Communist society the only path to happiness, then it follows that people who disagree with the party, see an alternative to the existing state, and who feel unhappy in a Communist society, must have something seriously wrong with them: in short, they must be mad. Moreover, in Communist as well as capitalist societies, it is those in power who tend to define what is sane, rational and acceptable conduct.

In order to explore some of these misgivings and to see how Cuban psychiatry works, I visited the Psychiatric Hospital of Havana, the largest institution of its kind in the country. It consists of a large community adjacent to the highway from the airport to the centre of the capital. Every visitor is shown the large billboard made by the patients which arches over the highway and which depicts the attack on the Moncada Barracks. As we swept in through the gates, we could see men in similar clothes working in the spacious and neatly kept grounds. One patient at the centre of a circle was leading a group for physical exercise.

I was met and introduced to Dr Ricardo González Menéndez, who was responsible for the senior teaching programme of physicians and specialists in the hospital. He was casually dressed, quietly spoken, and with a warm and friendly manner. We were ushered into the board meeting room, which was suitably panelled in dark wood. Dr Menéndez took the seat at the head of the long table; he quickly defined his position of power as a young woman brought in coffee and a tray of exquisite pastries made, I was told, by the patients.

He explained that the hospital had been opened in 1857 and used mainly as a jail for old slaves and vagrants who were no longer productive. In this century, it had become a notorious asylum for the mad who had no family to look after them or pay for the expensive private mental hospitals. To enter the Mazorra Asylum, as it was called, meant that life had come to an end. It was run like a jail, with patients locked in their cells, young and old together, without proper food, care or hygiene. Promiscuity was widespread. Pictures in an exhibition showing the history of the place show naked women wandering about their cells or lying on the floor. Six thousand patients were crammed in cells with only 2,500 beds. Disease was rampant and there was no treatment. Life expectancy for inmates was 39. The asylum was little different from a concentration camp and when Castro entered it following the triumph of the Revolution, he said that it could only be compared to Dante's Hell.

Today, all that has changed. The bars and the cells have gone. The Psychiatric Hospital is now a therapeutic and rehabilitation community with glass windows. The patients live in airy spacious wards, which combine social life with privacy. They work voluntarily and mix freely during the day. Everything is immaculately clean, freshly painted and cared for. The gardens are spacious and full of flowers. The hospital now has 3,800 patients and 4,100 beds and also acts as a teaching and research centre.

There are hospitals with 1,000 beds each in Camagüey and Santiago de Cuba and ten others with 200 beds scattered throughout the country. It is intended to decentralize further the hospitals, with the patients helping to build new hospitals themselves. The care of the mentally ill is now entirely state-run, except for one private health institution in Havana with 1,500 beds, called San Juan de Diós, which is run by Catholic priests.

As the director of the Psychiatric Hospital, Dr Eduardo B. Ordaz Ducungé has made clear, mental treatment, like the rest of the health service, is in line with directives from the Revolutionary government, 'based on the theoretical and methodological principles of Marxism-Leninism'.[2] These principles, according to the official literature, assume that the massive rehabilitation of the chronic mentally ill in Cuba is only possible under the conditions of a socialist system; that work is the fundamental condition of all human life; that the essence of humanity is its social nature, which presupposes a regular exchange between individuals; and that all mentally ill patients, however severe, are in some degree rehabilitable.[3]

Dr Menéndez gave a similar account of the principles on which the hospital had been run since the Revolution, although he made no mention of Marxism:

> The hospital is involved in teaching as well as caring, so it has helped develop the policy towards the mentally ill in modern Cuba. Our fundamental principle is the 'dignity of man', and the end of treatment is to enable the patients to recover their sense of worth and to be able to shape and be responsible for their own lives. Although patients may be broadly divided between the acute and chronic, it is a working rule that every patient can be rehabilitated to some degree, however ill. Since the ultimate aim is to rehabilitate the patient into the community, the milieu of the hospital is made to resemble as closely as possible the external social environment. Work is therefore central to the treatment—not just as a form of recreation but in a constructive sense of having a social meaning and earning a salary.

Although mental treatment is officially based on a Marxist concept of man, Dr Menéndez stressed that the specialist took a syncretic approach to the origin of mental disease:

> We consider man as a bio-psychosocial unit. Our approach is multidisciplinary; we look at the biological, social and psychological factors in the rehabilitation of mental patients. This is the main area of our research—to see the relative importance of these factors. Just as

there are different kinds of mental disorders, so there are different causes. At the psychotic level, we have found biological factors—inheritance and constitution—to be the most important, although we recognize that social and psychological factors also exert an influence. But whatever their state, we deal with patients on the psychological as well as the social level.

Methods of treatment are as varied as in the West. Drugs are used extensively. The use of electro-convulsive therapy is limited to cases of deep psychiatric depression with a high risk of suicide, or for schizophrenics who do not respond to drugs. While individual treatment is given, group therapy is preferred. The great originality of Cuban psychiatry, however, is the stress placed on occupational therapy—work—as the cornerstone of treatment. It is also a means of rehabilitating the patient as a participating and productive member of society.

Occupational therapy as practised in the hospital is based on the principles that it is carried out in a collective form in order to promote social interaction; that it is selected according to the patients' own interest; that it is real and socially useful work so that the patients can feel satisfaction in recognizing the product of their own activity; and that it is managed in a progressive way, allowing the patients to see their own development. The environment in which the work takes place in the hospital resembles as closely as possible that of similar work done outside.[4]

The patients are motivated in the same way as other Cuban workers. They receive money for their work according to the amount done, but there are also moral incentives such as being elected as outstanding workers, or being invited to attend community activities. The system of emulation, in which groups and individuals are encouraged to compete with each other, prevails. Rewards are always preferred to punishments, but the latter are applied in the form of admonitions before the group, limitation of passes, temporary wage deduction and so on, in order to stimulate self-criticism. At the same time the staff go out of their way to offer affection, guidance and respect.

Work is offered in a progressive form at different levels; as the patient progresses, it becomes increasingly like real work in the outside society. Work is also supplemented by sports, recreation and art. Music is considered particularly important, since it has been found to reduce stress, fatigue, hostility and to enhance group integration. A new and interesting innovation has been psycho-ballet—a form of group therapy developed by Alicia Alonso which has proved particularly effective for children. It is said to release tension, develop self-knowledge, and help patients to adapt to their milieu.[5]

During my visit to the hospital, I was shown rows of women making plastic flowers or painting pots in well-lit halls, while in the grounds outside, men in overalls were gardening or doing exercises. Some of the patients helped in running the place—the women's hairdressing salon, for instance. While many patients responded warmly to Dr Menéndez's friendly greetings, several appeared apathetic and listless at their work benches, no doubt as a result of drugs. There were special workshops for the chronic patients.

I was told that the hospital grows its own food and runs a chicken farm. There are opportunities to gain an education up to the sixth grade of the country's schools. The hospital has a good baseball team and band. Patients are also taken on trips around Cuba for holidays in the best hotels, and can attend outside cultural and political activities.

Since one of the primary aims of the hospital is to encourage the self-esteem of the patients, they are incorporated in the management of the hospital. Representatives are elected from among the patients who have weekly meetings with members of the staff to organize activities and to solve any problems. Dr Menéndez insisted, 'We try to ensure that each patient does not see him or herself as an object but as an active participant in the work and administration. The hospital as a whole is considered to be a therapeutic community, and each ward is a community in itself.'

When ready, the patients go to sheltered rehabilitation centres with lodgings, where they live as a democratic community of 60 to 70 members. They are free to call on their relatives who can also stay. If they prefer, they can join centres for both sexes. To encourage responsibility and participation, the entire group meets in the early morning to plan the day's activities. There is a weekly administrative meeting, and a monthly 'emulative' meeting in which the collective assessment of the most outstanding workers is carried out. In their work, the patients have a choice of becoming park keepers, gardeners in the city's green spaces or in vegetable plots, or can be employed in beach cleaning, construction or light industry. They often help with the sugar harvest. While they work alongside people who appreciate their problems, they are otherwise treated as responsible and full members of society.

The system seemed admirable in theory and much of what I saw in practice only confirmed my positive impression. But as in all countries, a close connection exists between psychiatry and politics in Cuba. The aim is not only to help the patient to readjust to existing social reality, but to rehabilitate him as a productive and participating member of a specifically collectivist and socialist society. Thus, while the official literature accepts the principle proposed by the World Health Organization Committee on Mental Health in 1952, that therapy must 'preserve the patient's individuality', it is based, as Cuban society itself, on 'the organizational principle of democratic socialism'. Therapy therefore pursues what is called 'the suppression of stress-causing ambiguities' and seeks to develop 'the collective mind of the participants'. While 'dialectically reinforcing individuality as regards self-respect and the delimitation of rights and duties', it seeks to promote 'collective decisions, according to the majority criterion', to encourage the 'emulative mind' through material and moral remuneration, and to facilitate 'a feeling of group belonging to avoid alienation'.[6] The basic principles of therapy are therefore those of the wider society.

With this and the vivid mural of the attack on the Moncada Barracks outside the hospital in mind, I raised with Dr Menéndez the thorny question of political influence in therapy. 'There is no direct political influence,' he explained, 'but there is naturally a general diffusion of socialist culture. Patients live in groups as workers, and are unavoidably in touch with what is happening in our society through television, the press, family visits, and work in the community. There is, however, no overt political education done here.' Since some states have been accused of pacifying dissidents by having them defined as mentally ill, I then asked how patients were hospitalized. Dr Menéndez replied:

We only hospitalize patients when all other treatment fails and their adaptation to family, work and society deteriorates seriously. In the case of neurotics, if the patient is not too severe, he or she will be admitted on his or her own request. At the psychotic level, the family's permission must be obtained. Conversely, if a family requests for a patient to be discharged, he or she will be, even if there is a high suicide risk. The state does intervene, however, in the case of delinquents, and a judge can ask for a doctor's report and recommend admission.

He admitted, on the other hand, that there was an important link between revolution and mental disorder. Many people, particularly the wealthy and powerful, who would have been at risk because of the sudden transformation in their lives, left the country. But for the rest, in the first five years of the Revolution there was a high incidence of reactive psychosis produced by stress in those who were suddenly given great administrative responsibility without proper training. Since then the rate of schizophrenia has levelled out to about the same as in the rest of the developed world. Drug dependence and alcoholism, it is claimed, have also been drastically reduced. I saw no evidence of drug taking, despite US accusations that Cuba is involved in the trade from Colombia. The practice of drug taking not only carries a heavy penalty (possession of marijuana means at least seven years in jail) but there are constant campaigns in the media against the danger of drugs. The elimination of the once serious drug problem is considered one of the major successes of the Revolution. The incidence of alcoholism is also said to have been reduced from five per cent of the population to 0.7 per cent. Nevertheless, Cubans are still heavy social drinkers and can often be seen drunk in public.

The overall success rate is in fact impressive by any standard. In the last 10 years, the hospital has discharged 700 patients each year. There is about a 20 per cent success rate among chronic patients. In the wards for the acute, the average stay is 45 days, amongst the medium severe, about six months. The average stay for the chronic is about two and a half years. The hospital has had particularly good results in the last five years with the five per cent who are usually considered to be hospitalized for life. About a third of all patients are in rehabilitation centres outside hospital.

This treatment of the mentally ill, by trying to rehabilitate them into society as fully as possible, has helped change the attitude of Cubans in general to mental illness. Traditionally, Cubans often treated the mentally ill as figures of fun. As a result, during the initial rehabilitation programmes outside the hospital, people took a hostile and defensive attitude which led to the admission of many patients into the hospital. But over the years the way in which mental patients do socially useful work and live in sheltered lodgings within the community has helped change the attitude of the population to mental illness. Patients are treated with much greater tolerance and understanding. Both the mentally ill and healthy have therefore benefited.

It would appear that Cuban psychiatry, like the rest of the medical services, has made astonishing progress. Not only has the first Cuban *Glossary of Psychiatric Illness* and the first Cuban *Thesaurus of Psychology* been compiled, but original research and teaching are taking place. The Cuban experience of rehabilitating patients through work, with its high success rate and innovative methods, is proving a major contribution to an understanding of the value of occupational therapy. While Cuban psychiatric principles are based on a Marxist concept of humanity, and the aim of therapy is to rehabilitate the patient as a productive and participating member of socialist society, there seems little evidence of the political abuse of psychiatry in dealing with dissidents. Above all, the resources made available by Cuban society to deal with the mentally ill are very impressive and stand as an indictment of materially richer but socially poorer societies in the West.

8

EDUCATING THE NEW MAN AND WOMAN

'To be educated is the only way to be free,' wrote José Martí. The principle has become one of the most popular of the Revolutionary slogans. Following in Martí's footsteps, Castro has been a teacher as much as a leader, and has from the beginning realized the necessity of changing the consciousness of the people as well as their material conditions. Whilst in prison on the Isle of Youth after the attack on the Moncada Barracks in 1953, he and his fellow revolutionaries formed themselves into a study group to learn from each other, and as soon as the guerrillas set up a permanent base in the Sierra Maestra they established a school. Many of the Revolutionary leaders had been students themselves and education, not surprisingly, became one of their primary targets for reform after their triumphant entry into Havana.

The state of Cuban education at the time was abysmal. The rich sent their children to private schools, many of which were Catholic; the middle class did their best to follow suit, while the poor had to make do with badly organized and sparsely established general schools. The three main universities turned out lawyers, but few scientists or engineers. In the 1953 census, nearly 24 per cent of the total population were illiterate, and while illiteracy ran at nine per cent in the capital, in Oriente it was 35 per cent. The gap between town and country was even worse: 11 per cent to 42 per cent.

One of the first acts of the Revolution was to expand and improve the public schools while planning one nationwide system which would be state-run, universal and free. By 1961, all the private schools had been nationalized. Havana University lost its autonomy and two-thirds of the professors left to go abroad. The universities were then reorganized to produce more technical and vocational graduates who, it was felt, would be more appropriate for Cuba's development. As for the students, the revolutionary youth groups were first organized into the Asociación de Jóvenes Rebeldes, then renamed in 1962 the Unión de Jóvenes Comunistas (UJC) (Union of Young Communists). Within four

years, the entire face of Cuba's educational system had changed in order
to prepare new generations of Cubans to live in a socialist society.

The most impressive and lasting educational initiative in the early
days of the Revolution was the literacy campaign. The campaign was
launched throughout the country in 1961: 100,000 young people, over
30 per cent of them women, formed brigades and poured into the
countryside in order to live with the peasants and teach them. The
slogan of the day was, 'If you don't know, learn; If you know, teach'.
The opportunity for political propaganda was not missed: the letter 'F'
was introduced with '*El Fusil de Fidel Fue a la Sierra*' (Fidel's rifle
was in the Sierra); the letter 'R' with '*Raúl el Faro*' (Raúl the Beacon);
and 'Ch' with '*Los Muchachos y Muchachas quieren mucho al Che*'
(The boys and girls like Che a lot).

The campaign proved to be an unparalleled success: the pencil and
notebook became as much a symbol of the Cuban Revolution at this
stage as the rifle and the beard. The campaign not only taught people
to read and write, but began a process of adult education which has
never ceased: 'Education will not blossom if it is not continuous and
constant', declare the posters. About 98 per cent of the population
are now literate, the highest rate in the Americas. Having achieved the
sixth grade, the whole populace is engaged in the battle for the ninth
grade. The literacy campaign not only brought the peasantry into the
mainstream of the Cuban Revolution, but by taking the young city
dwellers into the country it helped them become aware of the problems
of underdevelopment. So successful were the Cuban experiences that
they were recommended by a UNESCO mission for a world literacy
campaign.

During the campaign, it became increasingly clear that the leaders
were not intent merely on extending education and making people literate, but that they wanted to use the education system to shape political
consciousness and to create new men and women for a new society.
The old ideas of religious or liberal education were replaced by an
overriding drive for political education. Both Guevara and Castro based
their educational views on the belief of the eighteenth-century Enlightenment in the 'perfectibility of man'. They therefore were convinced
that human beings are products of their circumstances, and if you change
their circumstances, you can change their nature. Like Marx, they also
recognized that while the economic base of society influences consciousness, consciousness also influences the economic base: the revolutionary must therefore work on shaping consciousness through education
as well as changing economic relations.

From the beginning of the Revolution, Guevara had an ideal vision of the type of person who would be capable of transforming the consciousness of his fellows and of building socialism. 'To build communism', he insisted in his essay *Socialism and Man*, 'you must build new men as well as the new economic base.'[1] Capitalist man of the nineteenth century had been a selfish, alienated individual who followed the 'route of wolves'; as such he was an unfinished product.[2] The man of the twenty-first century, on the other hand, will have undergone a complete change in his attitude towards his work so that it would become a 'true human pleasure and the ultimate act of creation'.[3] He would also no longer think in individual or personal terms, but be able to bend his efforts towards the good of the whole—even extending his commitment to others beyond the narrow ties of family or nation to embrace 'proletarian internationalism'. Such a man would be capable of realizing his true nature as a creative and social being. He would be freer because he would be more complete, and more complete because freer. And since man is a product of his environment and culture, Guevara laid the greatest stress on education: 'Society as a whole must be converted into a gigantic school'. It follows that youth are of supreme importance since they provide 'the malleable clay from which the New Man can be shaped without any of the old faults'.[4]

These principles became both a programme for and the ideological foundation of the Cuban Revolution. By taking up Guevara's challenge to create the New Man (and Woman), Castro and other leaders attempted one of the greatest experiments this century to change human nature through education.

The power of education to change society was not a new idea in Cuba. Martí had written: 'Anyone who wants to forge peoples must forge human beings.'[5] The concept of the New Man had appeared at least as early as 1920 when a radical labour journal was published with the title *Hombre Nuevo*. It was not until 1965, however, that Castro and his leaders seriously tried to create Guevara's vision of the New Man which was inspired by the humanist philosophy of the early Marx. In the same year that Guevara was killed in the jungle of Bolivia, Castro declared in his speech of 26 July that:

The most difficult task is the one we are engaged in today: the task of building a new country on the basis of an underdeveloped economy; the task of creating a new consciousness, a New Man, on the basis of the ideas that prevailed in our society for centuries . . .[6]

Whereas Guevara followed Marx in believing that Communism would enable man to realize his species-being as a productive and social creature, Castro talked less of fulfilling man's true nature, but more of overcoming his 'instincts'. It is as if the Catholic upbringing of his youth made him see man to be in a state of sin. Thus in a speech on 13 March 1968 he insisted that 'we cannot encourage or permit selfish attitudes among men if we don't want them to be guided by the instinct of selfishness, of individuality . . . by the wolf, by the beast instinct. . . . The concept of socialism and communism, the concept of a higher society, implies a man devoid of those feelings; a man who has overcome such instincts at any cost'.[7] Not long afterwards he confided to the visiting Nicaraguan writer Ernesto Cardenal that he thought capitalism very dangerous precisely because it attracts people by encouraging all their instincts, including 'egoism, greed, sensuality, laziness, prostitution of all sorts, usury'. Socialism, on the other hand, is '*anti-instinto*' and involves sacrifice. The aim therefore must not be to create a consumer society which is really one of waste, but a socialist one which necessarily involves 'distribution, and therefore sacrifice'.[8]

The first Congress on Education and Culture was not held until April 1971, but it reaffirmed the commitment made in Guevara's and Castro's speeches to create 'a new kind of human being, a new people, who, as they shook off the burden of the past, would be able to consciously create superior conditions of individual and social existence'.[9] The Congress also asserted that in a Communist society there would be no barriers standing in the way of the 'integral formation of human beings', which calls for the development of all capacities that society can promote in each person.

These vague principles were clarified at the first Congress of the Communist party, held in December 1975, when the exact goals and objectives of Cuban education were set out for the first time. Although the document calls for an educational policy based on the 'multilateral and harmonious development of each individual', its goals are Marxist-Leninist. To use its own jargon, Cuban education is officially based on the 'historic mission and the interests of the working class', and is designed to inculcate new generations and the entire Cuban people to a belief in 'the scientific conception of the world, that is, that of dialectical and historical materialism'. It seeks to transform the 'ideological, political and moral principles of Communism into personal convictions and daily habits of conduct'. Young people must not only be taught to combat 'all manifestations of bourgeois ideology and morality' but they must be brought up to have 'a Communist attitude towards work, social property, study and society; as well as a love of the working class, the socialist homeland and the practice of proletarian internationalism'.

Finally, the party document on educational policy insists that children and young people must be taught 'love and respect' for the combatants of the Revolutionary Armed Forces, and the Ministry of the Interior (the internal security forces) who are depicted as the 'permanent defenders of our Revolution and of the future of our working people'.[10] No document perhaps reveals better the type of society the Communist party is trying to create in Cuba today—a society in which leaders are loved, the workers are productive and loyal, and history, nature and society are seen only through Marxist spectacles.

These principles were further enshrined in the Cuban Constitution drawn up in 1976. Article 38 of the Constitution asserts that education is a function of the state, and that its educational and cultural policy is not only based on the 'scientific conception of the world, established and developed by Marxism-Leninism', but is intended to promote the 'Communist formation of new generations'. Indeed, Article 39 adds that 'the education of children and young people in the spirit of Communism is the duty of the whole of society'.

The creation of the New Man has not been left as a vague goal for educationalists to pursue as they see fit. The Communist party has gone out of its way to describe how the New Man should behave. Indeed, this concept of socialist morality is at the heart of the Cuban Revolution and is what distinguishes Cuba from other Communist states. The leaders, especially Castro, place as much stress on the moral reform of the individual as on changing economic conditions. This is not only evident in Communist party documents but in the regular public campaigns to inculcate the new morality. The result is that the Castro regime has adopted a strong moral tone which is often highly puritanical.

The statutes of the Communist party for instance insist that one of the primary tasks of the party is to educate the people in the values of socialist morality and to help create the New Man

who, stripped of bourgeois and petit-bourgeois morality and ideology (based on individualism and egotism), governs his conduct by the most noble principles of collectivism, self-sacrifice, love of work, hatred of exploitation and parasitism, and the fraternal spirit of co-operation and solidarity among all the members of society and among the socialist countries and workers and peoples throughout the world.[11]

Castro insisted from the beginning on honesty in the government bureaucracy; the misuse of funds became a capital offence. Prostitution was forbidden immediately after the triumph of the Revolution, and prostitutes were rehabilitated in special schools. Not only gambling but traditional and immensely popular Cuban institutions like lottery and cockfighting were banned.

In the drive to establish 'socialist morality', the regime even interferes in personal sexual relations. Party members who are known to be unfaithful to their spouses will be admonished by the party. If it happens again, then the guilty adulterer can get three to six months suspension from the party and the mass organizations. Sexual misdemeanours are also marked down on the worker's file which is kept in the work centres, and may influence future promotion prospects. Again, any sexuality which is not heterosexual is considered suspect: homosexuals and lesbians have been derided as 'unnatural'. In 1965 there were even public campaigns against homosexuals, some of whom were drafted into Military Units to Aid Production.

The New Man must also be sound in body as well as mind. Castro firmly believes in the principle *mens sana in corpore sano*. 'Young people need sports', he argues, 'to burn off the excess energy they have . . . Sports are an antidote to vice'.[12] The result is that a huge amount of scarce resources has been invested in sports. There are not only special schools for budding sportsmen and women, but Havana boasts a vast Sports City with the latest equipment, and every major town has a stadium for up to 30,000 spectators.

Cuba now holds the world amateur title in baseball and women's volleyball. It has held first place in the Central American and Caribbean games since 1966, and second in the Pan-American games since 1971. It came fourth in the 1980 Olympics, and its runners and boxers did exceptionally well in the 1984 Alternative games for socialist countries in Moscow.

The attempt to forge the New Man and Woman with a 'socialist morality' has become one of the most ambitious efforts of the Cuban Revolution. The whole of Cuban society, as Guevara recommended, has become one 'gigantic school'. This process is undertaken through an impressive education system which is universal, compulsory and free until the sixth grade. Youth organizations are also backed up by well-produced propaganda and carefully arranged activities.

To deal with the latter first, every child between six and 13 is expected to be a member of the José Martí Pioneers Organization, a kind of socialist Boy Scouts and Girl Guides. Children under eleven wear uniforms of blue and white, and those above eleven, known as Moncadistas, wear red and white. The Pioneers Organization is intended to initiate Cuban children 'in social tasks and activities and organize a portion of their free time, promoting their participation in sports, cultural and recreational activities'.[13] There are 'Pioneer Palaces' throughout the country where the young can gain work experience. In Lenin Park, on the outskirts of Havana, there is a mini-city for Pioneers, with scaled-down working models of sugar mills, railways, offices and laboratories. Here the young spend one afternoon a week, combining study and work, and enabling their teachers to find out about their aptitudes and interests. To the east of Havana there is a vast Pioneers Camp with an artificial lake for boating and an aerial cable car. The Pioneers are also taken on camping trips in the country or to the beach in the holidays; the children certainly seem to enjoy these camps.

But the Pioneers are not just an organization to get young children to have fun together in the fresh air. Children are taught the principal values of the Revolution: hard work, patriotism and internationalism. Their weekly comic *Pionero*, first set up in 1961, is aimed at encouraging 'love of country, love for work and study' as well as 'solidarity and close friendship with the children of the entire world'.[14] The decadent and corrupting models of Superman and Batman of American cartoons have been replaced by a Cuban character called Elpidio Valdés who is a brave, wisecracking rebel modelled on the *mambí* combatants who fought in the nineteenth-century.

Young Cubans are brought up to see themselves continuing a revolutionary tradition which dates back to the Wars of Independence. Overriding all is the model of the guerrilla who is self-sacrificing, courageous and patriotic. It is Che, Camilo and Fidel whom they must strive to be like; they are the new apostles of the Revolution. Every year Che's death is commemorated by reading out his last letter to Fidel; every year Camilo's death is commemorated by children throwing flower petals into the sea. Fidel stands as the towering father figure who punishes and rewards his children depending on how they behave.

The best behaved and most ideologically committed of the Pioneers can enter the Union of Young Communists (UJC), founded in 1962. About a third of the population between 14 and 26 are chosen to join this privileged group. It is often seen as a stepping-stone to membership of the Communist party, although only about five per cent of the population eventually managing to scale these dizzy heights. The UJC is thus seen as the vanguard of youth and its members are expected to influence, by example and persuasion, all young people into adopting the principles of socialist morality and into building the future Communist society. Their slogan, first announced by Guevara, is 'Work, Study and the Gun'. They must see themselves as carrying the torch for others to follow: 'Grandchildren of *mambises*, sons of rebels, brothers of workers, we will be exemplary,' they declare, and it applies equally to the girls who make up half the number of Young Communists. The principal organ of the UJC is *Juventud Rebelde*, a daily evening paper which has the same national distribution as the Communist party's *Granma*.

The youth organizations of course only complement the state education system, which is entirely geared to creating the New Socialist Man and Woman. As we have seen, it is based on a psychological theory that the characters of human beings originate in their circumstances, and that it is possible through education to bring up children who are generous, hard-working and patriotic. While some children may prove more intelligent than others, Cuban educationalists see no scientific grounds for believing that one race or sex is inherently more intelligent than another, or that heredity plays a significant role compared to environment in influencing a child's potential.

Cuban educational theory is also based on a developmental model that assumes children pass through certain phases as they grow up, and different activities and experiences are appropriate to different phases. Underlying all, however, is a traditional Cuban concern for children. 'We work for children', Martí wrote on behalf of many of his compatriots, 'because children are the ones who know how to love, because children are the hope of the world'.[15] As the hoardings of today declare, 'there is nothing more important than a child'.

The most original aspect and one of the basic principles of Cuban education is the combination of study and work which is seen as a development of the thinking of Marx and Martí. It is intended to shape mental and physical skills in the harmonious development of the whole person. 'Human beings grow with the labour that emerges from their hands,' Martí wrote. 'In school,' he went on, 'people must learn to handle those forces with which they will have to struggle in life'.[16] At elementary level, this is done mainly through a school garden; at the intermediate level, by taking city schoolchildren to the countryside for six weeks each year, or by situating boarding schools in the countryside.

Combining work with study in Cuba is both an ideological and an economic objective. In the first place, the work helps pay for education and contributes to the material base of society. Secondly, it is seen as invaluable experience by breaking down the traditional opposition between theory and practice, and ending the elitist concept of intellectual work totally divorced from material production. In the society of the future, it is hoped that all will be intellectual workers, and worker intellectuals.

One of the less endearing aspects of Cuban education, however, is the control and surveillance the state maintains over young people.

Throughout their academic careers, pupils are carefully monitored. From 1973 every pupil has been issued with a cumulative file prepared by teaching and professional personnel, which includes details of his or her medical history, academic ability, personality traits and political opinions. The files are reviewed yearly: teachers evaluate the holder's academic progress, vocational training and behaviour, while ideological and political assessments are made by the youth organizations mass organizations, and the School Council. The file follows the student throughout his or her academic career, and then becomes part of the work dossier which every citizen must have during adulthood. The files are consulted in order to decide who goes on to further education and who does what kind of work: correct conduct is almost as important as academic ability in making the choice.

The Cuban state has invested a vast amount of its limited resources to develop a remarkable system of education from pre-school to university. Infants can be accepted from the age of 45 days in day-care centres. Primary school is then available for children from the age of five to 12. Secondary school is divided into three cycles: basic secondary education, senior high school and pre-university education. At the secondary level, there are schools in the country as well as vocational and technical schools. Special secondary schools exist to develop particular talents in such subjects as dance, sport, music, science and art. There are even schools for the handicapped.

In order to see how the principles of Cuban education were being practised, I managed to arrange visits to several representative institutions. The most impressive was a day care centre in the Santa Barbara district of Santiago de Cuba, which takes infants from 45 days old to five years. It was called *La Edad de Oro* (The Golden Age), after a famous work by Martí. Not surprisingly, a portrait of Martí dominated the stairway, while Che looked on in the infants' playground. Both Che and Camilo were to be found in the director's office.

The school building was pre-fabricated, airy and light. Outside were gardens, a grass area, sand pits, and a concrete yard. Places are allotted to infants of working mothers who do not have a grandmother to look after them. With 75 per cent of mothers working, demand still outstrips supply, and priority is given to soldiers or technicians working abroad or away from home, and single parent families. The school consisted of 55 workers: 30 teachers, 23 service staff, a director and a nurse. The children are arranged in classrooms according to their year. The last year is seen as a pre-school year in which they begin to wear school uniforms and are introduced to mathematics, reading and writing.

There seemed a friendly atmosphere about the place, with a lot of

toys, bricks and clay. The teachers had made papier-mâché models of
a hospital, dental surgery, laundry, shop, pharmacy, dining-room and
hairdresser's, so the children could gain 'work' experience. It was all
very well organized: the children's combs were neatly hung up in a
row, and each had its owner's photograph attached to it. At lunch, the
children sat quietly at their tables, with nurses dressed in white helping
the babies and toddlers. As the children seemed so subdued and orderly,
I asked the director about discipline. 'There are no rules of discipline
and we never beat anyone. We just persuade them to be sociable. If a
boy likes to fight others, we try and find out why and help him over
it.' I then asked her about the type of gender model that was being held
up to the children and whether there were any men working in the day
care centre:

> Well, no, not exactly; the gardeners are men. At present there aren't
> any men who would like to work in a day care centre. You must
> understand that it will take a long time to change *machismo* in Cuba.
> Although we are all equal, and there is no discrimination, people are
> still prejudiced and follow their old customs. The tradition is for the
> mother to be in the home and the father in the street. The new
> generation are being brought up to do both things. Boys and girls
> can decide what they want to do, to become a pilot, a hairdresser,
> an engineer or a cook.

She agreed, however, that in order to eradicate *machismo* from the
minds of the young, it was essential to show men and women in similar
roles, which included looking after young children: 'One of the greatest
obstacles to equality today is the care of the children. There is a great
conflict in the country about it. Both parents, mother *and* father should
look after them! In the meantime we do our best not to encourage one
kind of work for the boys and another for the girls in their games.'

The question of men working in day care centres was raised at the
fourth Congress of the Federation of Cuban Women in 1985; but the
day a man wipes the bottom of another man's baby will signal a major
step in the fight against *machismo*.

The next step up the educational ladder is the primary school, which
all children enter at the age of five. The curriculum and methods are
standardized throughout the country. The one I went to was in the centre
of Havana at the back of the offices of *Granma*. The school was called
El Ejército Rebelde (The Rebel Army). It consisted of a pre-fabricated
building surrounded by a low-rise housing estate. In the corner of the
concrete schoolyard stood the inevitable bust of Martí, which graces

every primary school in Cuba. Below were engraved the words '*Estimo a quien un revés echa por tierra a un tirano; lo estimo si es cubano; lo estimo si aragonés*' (I respect anyone who strikes to the ground a tyrant; I respect him if he be Cuban; I respect him if he be from Aragon). From an early age the children imbibe a readiness to fight tyranny, and a spirit of internationalism.

The director was a dynamic and efficient lady in her 30s. On the wall in her simple office were portraits of Fidel and Raúl Castro. The school could take up to 700 pupils from the age of five to twelve. The staff consisted of 20 teachers and 20 assistants, only five of whom were male. The teacher/pupil ratio was high, with 35 to 40 pupils per teacher. The pupils attend six classes each day which last for 45 minutes. The subjects covered in the first cycle are Spanish, reading, mathematics, physics and plastic arts. They also learn about work in a class devoted to *educación laboral* and by tending the school garden. In the second cycle from the third and fourth grades, pupils learn about Cuban history and natural sciences; and in the third cycle, from the fifth and sixth, literature and botany. A *matutino* session is held every morning for the whole school, when moral and political issues are raised, and there is a Friday meeting analysing the school's progress.

As in secondary schools, the children are stimulated to study and behave correctly through a system of 'emulation' which involves them being praised or criticized in front of the other children. Corporal punishment is not allowed. The discipline of the school, however, is backed by a number of organizations. There is a school council which represents the mass organizations, especially the Movement of Exemplary Parents of the CDRs, and the Movement of Mothers for Education of the Federation of Cuban Women. In this way, families are encouraged to participate in the education of their children, while the organizations make sure the pupils attend school punctually and take care of 'social property'. After all, the school is seen not only as a tool of the state but also as part of the community.

Looking around the school, I found it again neat, orderly and quiet. The teaching was traditional and authoritarian. The little children in their uniforms sat silent behind their desks looking at their books. In one classroom a child stood up and read some passage out of a book in what was clearly a well-rehearsed event. In a class of five-year-olds, I saw a box full of wooden machine-guns. I was taken aback when I entered a class of eight-year-olds by a powerful chant of young Revolutionaries in red shorts and white shirts: 'We will follow the heroic example of the Cuban international construction workers in Grenada! We will be like them in work, study and war! Commander-in-Chief, give us our orders!' The little ramrod figures saluted with perfect precision as if their Commander-in-Chief Fidel Castro were present.

This was one of the most chilling experiences of my whole visit to Cuba—the spectacle of young and tender minds trained to obey uncritically the orders of their head of state, even unto death. But this was no temporary aberration of an over-zealous teacher. War and peace are topics learned from an early age by all Cubans. At first, the children are taught songs in which they learn the word 'peace' and an elementary notion of what it means. Then, as the official document *Children in Cuba* points out, they become aware of the world in which they live and learn to understand 'the full meaning of the concept of peace, who fights for it, and who are its enemies'.[17] The effectiveness of this type of indoctrination was vividly brought home to me by an exhibition of war paintings by primary school children put on in Lenin Park. They were clearly chosen more for their ideological than their artistic content. One seven-year-old had painted a Cuban plane shooting down an American one, and strafing the four crew who tried to escape by parachute. The most imaginative and macabre painting, however, was done by a five-year-old. It showed an American surrounded by rockets wielding a club with blood dripping from a nail in its end, and a bloody hatchet stuck in the island of Grenada which is placed between Florida and Cuba. Opposite, a cool Cuban militia man held up to the American a mirror which reflected a skull in it. The slogan of this five-year-old Cuban super-patriot was '*El que comienza como Adolfo, termina como Hitler*' (He who begins like Adolf, ends up like Hitler). Clearly children in Cuba are brought up to see the world in eternal conflict between the forces of evil represented by the United States and those of good represented by Cuba and her allies, with the inevitable outcome of the conflict being war.

After the sixth grade, children move at the age of eleven from primary school to secondary school. One of the most controversial and interesting developments has been the setting up of basic secondary boarding schools in the country where pupils combine work and study. The first one was established in 1970 and called 'Los Martires de Kent' (named in commemoration of the students shot by the US National Guard at Kent State University in that year). Since then, they have developed rapidly—all made to the same design—and now nearly half of Cuba's secondary school students attend them. From the southern approach to Havana's José Martí airport, the H-shaped pre-fabricated buildings with their swimming pools can be seen scattered amongst green citrus plantations.

I went to visit one of them near Havana, called the Che Guevara School. The school buildings were set in beautifully kept gardens and were clean and tidy with wide, open-air walkways. One side of the 'H' was used for the classrooms, the other side for the dormitories, while the kitchen and dining-room were in between. In addition to well-furnished classrooms, there were laboratories, workshops, a cinema, hairdresser's and even a 'beauty parlour' for the girls. The school had 614 students, 360 of whom were girls. There were 36 teachers and 72 extra workers, but the classes were big—about 45 students to each teacher. The teachers were young and the director was only in his twenties. Children of the Revolution themselves, they were Cuba's answer to the dilemma posed by Marx about who will educate the educators in a socialist society.

The school is governed by a council made up of representatives from the administration, the Union of Young Communists, the students, the Communist party, and the workers of the school. Another council involves parents and community organizations in the area.

The students come from the towns and villages in the surrounding area and can go home at the weekend. But with only six weeks' holiday in July and August, they spend most of their lives in blue and white uniforms at school. Their days are vigorous and full. They wake at 6 a.m. and after breakfast line up in columns for *matutino*, a 15-minute session of uplifting political and cultural news. Then half the school will spend the morning working three hours in the fields, while the others are in class, and vice versa in the afternoon. After a shower, everyone studies for a couple of hours until dinner. Then they can do more or less what they want—singing, watching TV, chatting—until they go to bed.

The schools are co-educational, but the boys and girls sleep in separate dormitories and work in different brigades. The boys are generally given harder physical work to do than the girls; they dig while the others weed. Senior students co-ordinate the work. Most of the schools have their own gardens and are self-sufficient in food, but the main production is usually done in citrus plantations—work which is both monotonous and gruelling. The brigades I met in the fields seemed happy enough; they were certainly extremely fit-looking. When they returned to the canteen for lunch, served by their fellow students on a rota basis, they wolfed down the large quantities of fish, white rice, white bread, and bananas.

The reason for all their sweat and toil was spelt out on the notice-board by Martí: 'Schools should be called workshops, the pen used in the morning in the classroom, and in the afternoon the hoe'. The experience is intended to show Cuban youth the necessity of labour and to make city dwellers aware of the toil of the country folk which has supported them for centuries. The primary aim of the work experience, I was told by the director, is not so much to increase production but to help in the 'harmonious development of the personality'.

Over the entrance to the school there was a vast portrait of Che as a constant reminder to the students of their revolutionary ideal. On the notice-board was his famous exhortation to the coming generations: 'You are young creators of the perfect society, human beings destined to live in a new world'. Every day, the students are reminded of their responsibility and privilege of being the vanguard of a society which is at the head of the Americas. Castro's advice is also there, although less utopian and more puritanical, echoing even the ideal of the traditional English public school: 'We want to form pure and clean men, loyal and honest men, men of principles' (and presumably women).

'La emulación, motor impulsor de la revolución socialista.' This slogan, found on hoardings throughout Cuba, is also on the notice-board in the Che Guevara school. Socialist emulation is Cuba's answer to capitalist competition, and is applied in schools as much as in factories to motivate people. The students are formed into groups of 25 to 40 individuals, and then compete with each other in the work in the fields, in the maintenance of the grounds, in the cleanliness of their dormitories, and in sports. The winners, chosen at weekly meetings, are rewarded with extra privileges such as cultural outings, visits to Lenin Park or the beach, or going home early at the weekend. At the same time individual emulation is encouraged, with results of work and behaviour recorded on every student's cumulative file.

A student must get high marks if he or she wishes to go on to higher education, and only the very best students can study popular subjects like medicine at university. The choice of career also depends on school performance: a student chooses ten careers in order of preference, and is then allotted one by the state depending on the needs of society and the abilities of the student.

Although socialist emulation is intended to encourage individuals or teams to do their best by outdoing others, success is inevitably achieved for some at the cost of failure for others. The strong beat the weak and the intelligent leave the less bright behind. The winners are rewarded, those who fail punished. In the long run, it does not seem very different from classic competition: it is based on similar psychological drives, involves contests, and ends in a hierarchical ordering of individuals according to their abilities and conduct.

The actual method of training in the school is largely traditional; students are expected to regurgitate what they have been taught. The limited political, historical and philosophical perspective leaves little room for independent and critical thinking. The curriculum, too, is conventional for the most part: Spanish, history, geography, literature, mathematics, chemistry, physics and biology. Sex education is left to the initiative of the teachers. Russian however is now as important as English as a foreign language. The Marxist orientation of school further comes through in the study of politics, economics and the basis of contemporary production. In addition, every student must undertake a course in Marxist studies when they reach the ninth grade, during which they learn about the nature of capitalism, imperialism and socialism, and the history of labour movements. Religion is only considered as a historical phenomenon in the context of Marxist studies and its roots are traced to the economic problems of the past.

The ideological nature of the teaching is plain even in texts for teaching English. On the cover of a second-level textbook entitled *My English Book*, there is a brown schoolboy with a blonde girl, both wearing red scarves. Each lesson is centred around an amusing sketch intended to carry a moral. They include a black worker looking for a job in a garage in Chicago who is rejected because of his colour and an imaginary news report by a New York journalist who finds out that the captured mercenaries at the Bay of Pigs were not soldiers but cooks. A more direct and revolutionary note is struck in a letter from the Soviet Union sent by an Ethiopian studying at Moscow University, who writes to his sister that Moscow is 'the capital of the first socialist state in the world. Many people in Asia, Africa and Latin America, who are fighting for their liberation, have learned an important lesson from the great October Revolution.' Another lesson is about a British girl—Peggy Miller—who is a member of the British Communist party working in a library in Dresden, East Germany. Then, since English after all originated in England, we come to London, most famous of course for being the 'birthplace of capitalism' and the place where Karl Marx lived for over 30 years and wrote *Capital*.

The type of history taught in Cuban schools is no less didactic. The main text used is the *Historia de Cuba* (1967) which was written for the political board of the Revolutionary Armed Forces and sets out to portray the principal aspects of Cuban history under a Marxist, revolutionary focus. Unfortunately it falls into the easy trap of substituting clichés and propaganda for the serious study of Cuban history. Another revealing aspect of the nature of secondary education in Cuba can be seen in the *Salón de Historia* which exists in each school. In this room, which has all the aura and appearance of a shrine, badges and trophies won by the school in emulation contests are kept, as well as artefacts and information about Cuban revolutionary history. Above all stands a quotation from the theses and resolutions of the first Congress of the Communist party: 'The objective of the Communist formation of the new generation is to create harmoniously developed men and women to live in the new society and to participate in its construction and subsequent advance.'

In the visitor's book, I came across an entry by Angela Davis, the black American militant whom the philosopher Herbert Marcuse once called his best pupil and who later became a personal guest of Castro in Cuba. She wrote on 26 February 1972: 'The visit has been an extraordinary experience. The enthusiasm of the students for their studies, their work, is evident everywhere you turn. This is indeed the spirit of the Cuban Revolution, the spirit of struggling for and building communism. Solidarity!'

Other foreign visitors to secondary schools in the country have been less enthusiastic and reported that the students were living under a semimilitary regime with strict discipline. This was not my impression. Discipline is maintained by a system of rewards and punishments. No corporal punishment is allowed, not even slaps. Badly behaved students are obliged to do extra work or study. The greatest sanction is the black mark which goes into their cumulative file.

I left with the impression of having seen some very beautiful, fit, cheerful, confident and relaxed young people. Despite the intense atmosphere of Marxist-Leninist indoctrination and the high expectations, they did not seem cowed or crushed in any way. In a physics lesson I attended, they laughed and chatted to each other while the teacher was trying to explain the use of a piece of electrical equipment. Their relations with their teachers—only a few years their superior—were easygoing and informal, and the teachers appeared more like friendly guides than authoritarian taskmasters. They mixed unconsciously with each other whatever their racial background, and I saw more than one couple holding hands in front of their teachers while quietly queueing for lunch. Their mutual trust was demonstrated by the absence of doors on their cupboards in their dormitories.

Cuban officials wax lyrical whenever they hear mention of the schools in the country. While being impressed by the combination of work and study, I could not help thinking however that such a competitive and narrow system of education was hardly conducive to producing young people with critical and independent minds and creative imaginations. Hard-working and self-sacrificing they might be, but the New Men and Women being forged in the secondary schools in the country will not necessarily be innovating and effective workers of the future.

Secondary schools in the country are not only available to Cuban students. The Isle of Youth, formerly a pirate's haven, dictator's penal colony and American real estate paradise, has become the scene of a unique international educational experiment. Since 1976, the Cuban government has offered free education to students from developing countries who have some kind of socialist system at home and an 'anti-imperialist' foreign policy. Apart from Nicaragua and South Yemen, all the students come from Africa: Angola, Mozambique, Namibia, Congo-Brazzaville, Guinea-Bissau, Ethiopia, Sahara Democratic Republic, São Tomé and Príncipe, and, most recently, Ghana. The portraits of the presidents of these countries line the road to the area where most of the schools are situated. Over 12,000 of the 30,000 students on the island are foreigners. The schools are not, as rumoured, training camps for guerrillas, but a direct expression of Cuba's internationalist spirit. Waldo Medina, the director of the island's education programme, explained to me why the Cuban government supported the foreign schools:

We want to pay back our debt, our historical debt. Internationalism is the most beautiful flower of our Revolution. The ancestors of these students were brought here as slaves. Now they can come here freely to study in order to become professionals, technicians, teachers, engineers. For us it constitutes an honour to offer help to those countries who have difficulties with their economic and social development.

After an intensive course in Spanish, the foreign students undergo the same curriculum and work as Cubans in their secondary schools in the country. However, the aim is primarily to help the country which sends students over. 'We want to make better Ghanaians,' Director Medina insisted, 'not Cuban Africans. They should be able to act and think like Ghanaians and only require from us more technical skills in accordance with the needs of their country.'

Teachers from each country therefore teach their own language, history, geography and politics with their own materials. Each school is encouraged to retain its national identity by practising its own religion and culture. Each takes charge of its own discipline. At the same time, regular exchanges take place between the schools, especially for sports, although Cubans jokingly lament that Africans prefer football to baseball. I saw a football match between Mozambicans and Angolans which drew a vast and enthusiastic crowd.

This unique programme is entirely free, except for transport to and from the students' homeland. Not only clothes and books are provided, but even pocket money. The result is that the foreign students receive an education which might have been difficult if not impossible to come by in their own countries. The students are chosen by their governments but the governments are encouraged to choose young people from poor backgrounds and from different regions in order to get as great a cross-section as possible. Unlike many Africans educated in the West, they are more likely to return to work in their own countries than to join an intellectual elite abroad. In the Windhoek School for Namibians, for instance, the majority were orphans from refugee camps who had lost their parents in the War of Independence, including several survivors of the massacre at Kassinga refugee camp in southern Angola during a raid by South African troops in 1978. These children, who had lost everything, are now eager to return home to help build an independent nation.

After spending four years in secondary school, and a year at pre-university school, many foreign students join their Cuban counterparts to go on to the polytechnics and the universities. But only those with the highest marks and the best conduct are allowed to climb the higher rungs of Cuban education. Those who are chosen undoubtedly form a privileged group in the country; they are, as the great sign at the entrance to the central university of Las Villas declares, the VANGUARDIA NA-CIONAL. During their five years of study, they receive their education, accommodation and food free of charge. They are exempted from military service, although they must undergo military training once a week, and automatically become officers on graduation in the army reserve. It is from their ranks that the managers, technicians and bureaucrats are chosen.

Although the students were at the forefront of the opposition to Batista, and even armed themselves and occupied Havana University on his downfall, they were soon taken over by Castro and his July 26 Movement. Their autonomy, which had been fought for bitterly throughout the century, was lost once and for all in July 1960. Two-thirds of the professors went into exile. Henceforth the university was ruled by a *Junta de Gobierno* (government commission). Every professor had to demonstrate the 'revolutionary fidelity of the faculty' and the teaching of Marxism-Leninism became obligatory. A rebel army officer was appointed president of the Federation of University Students (FEU) and the former leader of the Communist party, Juan Marinello, became rector of the University of Havana. When Castro was asked, while on a visit to Chile in 1971 during Allende's rule, whether Cuban universities were independent of the government—an important issue for the students in Latin American countries where dictators ruled—he replied that the question no longer applied: 'Maybe we should pass a law giving the government autonomy from the students,' he joked. 'They're into everything, they run everything, you can't keep them away.'[18]

There has been an enormous expansion of higher education in Cuba. Las Villas University had 615 students in 1952; it now has 10,200, of which 200 are foreign students. Half of all students are women. But despite the impressive development in facilities and numbers, no independent centre of higher education exists in Cuba today except for a few seminaries. The students' union, like other unions, is used mainly as a means of communicating directives to the student body. The government of the university itself is entirely in the hands of the state. The professors are obliged to follow the official curricula, and the students are chosen nearly as much for their correct attitude, obedient behaviour and ideological orthodoxy as for their academic excellence. There is now no genuine freedom of enquiry or thought.

On the steps of Havana university, under the stern eye of a seated woman intended to represent the Alma Mater, the students gather in their faculty uniforms, where they once fought with Batista's police. The only demonstrations which take place are carefully orchestrated, like the one on March 13 each year to commemorate the death of the student leader José Antonio Echeverría, who seized a radio station during an attack on Batista's presidential palace in 1957. The omnipresent eye of the state is symbolized by a tank which stands as a monument in the courtyard of the university. It contrasts strangely with the neo-classical elegance of the surrounding stone buildings, engraved with the names of 'Linneo', 'Pasteur', and 'Cuvier', which celebrate the progress of humanism in the arts and sciences. The tank, too, demonstrates the close link between the university, the army and the state in modern Cuba.

Since I am particularly interested in the subject, I chose to investigate the type of philosophy being taught in the university. A booklet, the 'Programme of the History of Philosophy', is highly revealing. Its approach and content are unmitigatedly Marxist. The first thing for philosophy students to consider is the 'Marxist conception of the history of philosophy as science' and the 'laws of its progress' as well as the history of philosophy seen 'in the deforming mirror of actual bourgeois philosophy'. The course cannot be criticized for not being comprehensive, for it virtually covers the whole of Eastern and Western philosophy, from Taoism via German idealism to existentialism. But the only book offered in the reading for the course is a translation of a *Compendium of History of Philosophy* by the Russians Iovchuk, Oizerman and Shchipanov.

This is not however entirely representative of all the courses at university. A young teacher I met who had graduated in English explained that in his course they had studied the history of England up to the industrial revolution, and then moved on to the history of the USA up to the present day. His reading included Chaucer, Milton, Dickens, Joyce, Virginia Woolf, Somerset Maugham and Graham Greene, although Lawrence and Orwell were noticeably absent. Despite the anti-imperialist propaganda he had imbibed he was nevertheless delighted to meet a 'native' of England and to practise his competent English.

The Cuban education system has undoubtedly made some impressive strides in ending illiteracy and extending its services to the whole of the population. But the desire of the Communist party to make the New Man and Woman into 'good Communists' has meant that the education system has become the principal tool of the state to indoctrinate its citizens. The students might read *Juventud Rebelde*, but they are certainly not rebelling against the new authorities in school and university. The Cuban novelist Edmundo Desnoes once complained that before their Revolution Cubans were subtly colonized by Western literature; now they are directly influenced by Soviet propaganda. Teachers must work in a pedagogical strait-jacket and ensure that the unimaginative orthodoxy of the party prevails. By trying to shape the 'malleable clay' of Cuban youth into one mould, they have been forced to restrict the growth of the creative imagination and the independent and critical mind. The model of the hard-working, obedient Cuban that is being created is a poor substitute for the enlightened and transformed individual who develops the full harmony of his being envisaged by the early Marx and Guevara.

Moreover, there is a danger that the selection of the most promising students for special schools and higher education will create a new elite of bureaucratic cadres and skilled technicians. As early as 1978, Castro foresaw this danger and encouraged adults to control competitive behaviour amongst their children, but since then the education system has aggravated it all the more.[19] Indeed, while the successful attempt to combine work and study is genuinely original on such a large scale, Cuban education with its stress on emulation, discipline and obedience to superiors, is not very different from the traditional, competitive, authoritarian and hierarchical system of the West. Enormous material resources have been poured into education, but the assault on the 'most difficult Moncada of them all', as Castro has called the old ways of thinking, has only just begun.[20]

9

SEXUAL POLITICS

When Cubans talk of the New Man, they use it to cover both men and women. This is a common enough linguistic habit but here it reflects the particularly deep-seated *machismo* typical of Latin American countries. However, Cuba has made a unique and impressive attempt to liberate women from their customary role of mothers in the home. Castro has called the emancipation of women the 'revolution within the Revolution', and Cuban women now undoubtedly have more sexual freedom and economic independence than ever before.

The traditional position of woman in Cuba derives its particular character from Catholicism and Spanish culture, which linked virginity with honour, and the institution of slavery, which broke up the ties of the African family and denied the father responsibility for his children. Amongst the upper classes, centuries of traditional Spanish patriarchy ensured that the prevailing view of woman was that she was a man's appendage and property: *'La mujer honrada, la pierna quebrada y en casa'* (The honourable woman stays in the house with a broken leg) is a nineteenth-century Cuban saying.

A woman's traditional role in Cuba was defined by a complicated value system of *honor* and *vergüenza* (shame) which had been inherited from the Spanish and developed in a colonial setting with its particular nuances of class and race. A white woman was meant to be a model of virtue and modesty; divorce was forbidden by the Catholic church. A father's principal family duty was to protect the purity of his daughters. Since the loss of virginity was a major calamity, a single girl was chaperoned with the utmost zeal. The myth of female sexual vulnerability became part of Cuba's moral order; a girl was considered defenceless without her father or brother, and it was also their duty to avenge her *honor* if it were besmirched and the family suffered *vergüenza*.

The double standard reigned supreme. It was essential to defend the honour of one's own women, family, class and race, but seducing women was seen as affirmation of virility, especially if the woman was a virgin. In the eighteenth century it was quite acceptable for an upper-class male to seduce and not to marry a woman of inferior status; since it could not dishonour her family, it was held that 'such an offence is of an individual and does not harm the Republic'.[1] If the victim were of good family, however, it was considered to be 'an offence of such gravity that it will denigrate an entire family'. As the Council of the Indies declared in 1783, 'any stain in one or other of the ancestors contaminates the whole generation'.[2] While these attitudes grew less rigid, they still continued to exert an influence in the twentieth century.

Before the Revolution, the lot of the middle- or upper-class woman in Cuba had changed little. After being turned over by fathers to their husbands women could then look forward to gossip, four walls and the double standard. Their social inequality was enshrined in law. The Civil Code of 1902 declared that the husband had an exclusive right to their joint property and finances, and could demand her obedience: 'The husband must protect the wife, and the wife obey the husband'. When divorce was eventually introduced in 1918 for the first time it was allowed automatically on the grounds of the wife's adultery, but it only applied if a husband's adultery resulted 'in a public scandal or the neglect of the wife'. (In practice it meant that the husband could discreetly take a mistress with impunity, but if his wife dared to take a lover then she was thrown out.) Although women obtained the right to vote and the right to sue for divorce in the Civil Constitution of 1934, Articles 59 and 60 which made the husband the administrator of the conjugal property and demanded the wife's obedience, remained until 1958. The new Constitution of 1940 accepted the principle of equal pay for equal work, made sexual discrimination illegal, offered equal civil rights to married women, and protected the working mother; but these remained empty letters of the law.

Poorer women in Cuba suffered, from earliest times, the double exploitation of class and sex. In the city they lived in shanty towns and crowded tenements. If they did go out to work, it was as prostitutes or as domestic servants with little defence against their employers. In the 1953 census, only 13.7 per cent of the female population was defined as economically 'active'. By 1959, less than 10 per cent of women had jobs. The result was that they eked out an uncertain life in which meeting Mr Right or winning the lottery seemed the only way out. Conditions were worse in the country. Peasant women were condemned to working in the fields and to bearing innumerable children in primitive huts. The men would eat separately, and would expect absolute obedience from their wives and daughters.

For black women, it was even worse. Slaves were considered as by definition persons *sin vergüenza*—with no honour or respect to lose. In the mid-nineteenth century the ratio of male to female slaves was two to one. When the labour shortage led to black women being brought into the sugar mills, they had to work like men for up to 16 hours a day. Under the barrack system the sexes lived separately and were able to meet only briefly and clandestinely. The female slaves could be raped by overseers and masters at will; if they gave birth, they had to be back at work after a few days. *Mulatas* in particular were sought after: *No hay tamarindo dulce ni mulata señorita* (There is no sweet tamarind fruit, nor a virgin mulatto girl) is a Cuban saying. At the same time, with slavery destroying the Africans' own cultural resources for defining self-worth, domestic slave women gained prestige by becoming mistresses of well-off whites, especially as they could buy their freedom. Black women also sought to have children with white men so that their children could have a higher social status.

After the abolition of slavery, many black men and women lived together in unstable relationships without marriage: in 1934 about a quarter of the entire Cuban population was illegitimate. Since this meant that women often had to bring up children on their own, a tradition emerged in which, although despised in the wider society symbolized by the street, the black or mulatto woman became a powerful figure in the family and home.

There were of course women in Cuban history who refused to accept their inferior status and passive role. During the Wars of Independence in the nineteenth century, women not only supported their menfolk but also fought in the rebel army. The Wars have been correctly described as Family Wars: many wives of combatants took to the mountains. Mariana Grajales, mother of the black general Antonio Maceo, is remembered for having lost her husband, 12 of her 13 sons and many of her grandchildren to the cause; when the fighting broke out, she made her sons swear they would fight for independence until they were free or killed.

It was Ana Betancourt who first raised the call for women's emancipation in Latin America, at the Guáimaro Assembly in 1869 which met to draw up a new Cuban constitution:

Citizens: Cuban women, in the dark and quiet corners of their homes, have patiently awaited this sublime hour, in which a just revolution breaks free and spreads its wings. Everything was slavery here— the cradle, colour, sex. You want to destroy the slavery of the cradle by fighting to death. You have destroyed the slavery of colour by emancipating the slave. The moment of women's liberation has arrived![3]

José Martí, who helped organize the second War of Independence in 1895, also looked forward to a time when 'women will live as equals of men, as a comrade, and not at their feet as a pretty toy'.[4]

The First National Congress of Women was held in 1923. Its demands were reformist rather than revolutionary, mainly concerned with improving the legal position and opposing male oppression on an individual basis. The failure to implement the 1940 Constitution under Batista's dictatorship led an increasing number of young women to join the clandestine groups opposed to his rule. Haydée Santamaría and Melba Hernández, jailed for their part in the attack on the Moncada Barracks in 1953, afterwards became leading figures in the Revolutionary government. Vilma Espín, an organizer of the July 26 Movement in Santiago, eventually joined the guerrillas and married Raúl Castro. Cecilia Sánchez, who became Fidel Castro's secretary, is also remembered for her part in the campaign in the Sierra Maestra. So many women joined the guerrillas that in the end a Mariana Grajales platoon of women fighters was formed. Haydée Santamaría later recalled the tremendous family pressures on women at the time who involved themselves in politics: 'My own mother was the kind of woman who thought that only men had the right to make a revolution.'[5]

From his experience of living and fighting with women in the Sierra Maestra, Che Guevara wrote in *Guerrilla Warfare*:

> The woman is capable of performing the most difficult tasks, of fighting beside the men; and despite current beliefs, she does not create conflicts of a sexual type in the troops. She can work the same as a man and she can fight; she is weaker, but no less resistant than he.[6]

Nevertheless, Guevara assumes that combatant women will naturally remain a minority. He therefore recommends the use of women as messengers, teachers, nurses, seamstresses, as well as participants in all the aspects of civil administration. He particularly stresses their role as teachers and organizers of schools, since they 'arouse more enthusiasm among children and enjoy more affection from the school community.' Guevara is sufficiently enlightened to see no reason why 'persons who are otherwise free and love each other' should not live as man and wife in the guerrilla band. But the old Latin American *machismo* cannot remain entirely silent in him, and he calls for the female guerrilla to 'perform her habitual tasks of peacetime'; in particular, 'the woman as cook can greatly improve the diet and, furthermore, it is easier to keep her in these domestic tasks'![7]

It was in order to improve the lot of women and to incorporate them in the social, economic and political life of the country, that the Federación de Mujeres Cubanas (FMC) (Federation of Cuban Women) was set up in 1960 with Vilma Espín as its president. It has become one of the most important and influential mass organizations in the country; in 1986 it had a membership of 83 per cent of the total female population in Cuba between the ages of 14 and 65.

Its first great task after the Revolution was to help to rehabilitate prostitutes and to prepare maids in day and night schools for non-domestic work. It then provided for the first time education for country women through the Ana Betancourt school. Its most impressive activity, however, was its involvement in the literacy campaign of 1961. Women not only made up a good proportion of the teachers, but 55 per cent of those who learned to read and write for the first time were women. It was for many teachers a deeply liberating experience. It was the first time that women had been given an equal role in bringing about a major social change.

Not surprisingly, the new role of women met with profound resistance from conservative men. The last part of the film *Lucía* made by Humberto Solás in 1968, brilliantly portrays the dilemma of the young heroine whose husband tries to prevent her from attending literacy classes and from being alone with her male teacher from the city. For thousands of women like Lucía, to be able to read and write was a major step to greater self-confidence and dignity. To go out to work was an even greater step. The male protests which went up led Guevara to declare in 1963 that 'the proletariat has no sex' and to castigate severely those workers who would not let their women go out alone. He recognized that a change in women's own perception of themselves was as necessary as the political changes:

The liberation of women should consist of the achievement of their total freedom—their *inner* freedom. It is not only a matter of a physical restriction which is placed on them to hold them back from certain activities. It is also the weight of a previous tradition.[8]

Women were not only freed from the home and from their illiteracy, but were also encouraged, after the Bay of Pigs attack, to join the militia and, later, the Revolutionary Armed Forces. The logo of the FMC became a woman carrying a baby in her arms with a rifle over her shoulder; many older women and men were shocked to see women in uniform and carrying guns. At the third Congress of the FMC, the leaders sat under the banner: 'Let us convert flowers into arms for the defence of the homeland'. Since 1984 there has been an all-women combat unit in the Revolutionary Armed Forces. At the Congress of the FMC in 1985, Castro praised them as being more efficient than men. Women also now form half of the territorial troop militia.

After full employment had been achieved for men in 1964, the FMC played a key role in preparing women for work as well as fighting for equal access to jobs, equal rights and equal pay. The positive female images presented in bulletins of the FMC are of women cutting cane, working in factories, reading, performing ballet, and carrying rifles in the militia. At the same time the government uses the organization to integrate women into the Revolutionary process through 'ideological education' to raise 'the cultural, technical, political and ideological awareness of women'.[9] It has close links with the other mass organizations, particularly the CDRs. It has formed Mutual Help Brigades with the private farmers. Above all, it has worked closely with the Communist party to eliminate attitudes and practices which discriminate against women.

At the fifth national plenary of the FMC held in 1966, Castro publicly gave his support to women's liberation. He argued that the Revolution had involved a double liberation, since in the old days women had been discriminated against not only in their role as workers but also as wives, mistresses, and mothers. At the same time he warned against women having too high an expectation of the Revolution, for the full development of women in society and authentic equality of rights would require 'the material foundations of economic and social development'.[10] In other words, the ladies would have to wait a little until the gentlemen had sorted out the economic base of socialist society. At the second Congress held in November 1974, Castro admitted that 15 years after the Revolution, the country was still politically and culturally behind in the emancipation of women. Women were legally equal with men and, he observed, not morally or intellectually inferior, but they had not become fully integrated into Cuban society. They only made up 25 per cent of the workforce and 13 per cent of the Communist party at the time. While Castro has backed the emancipation of women, he partly encourages an adherence to their former image and role by his own dominant position. It is Castro, and not his sister-in-law Vilma Espín, who is principally responsible for shaping the main policies for women. He delights to charm the women of Cuba *en masse*, who respond with apparent enthusiasm. The negative hero of Latin American *machismo* is the dictator; the positive hero is the rebel: Castro combines something of both.

At the second Congress of the FMC, Castro stated his view of the relationship between the sexes and placed himself, like Martí, firmly within the tradition of courtly love. Certainly man must be woman's comrade, and man's happiness is not possible without woman's happiness. At the same time, the pursuit of equality should not be an excuse for rudeness; there is room, Castro asserted to loud applause, for 'proletarian chivalry'. If there is to be any inequality in society, it should take the form of 'certain small privileges' in favour of women. He further celebrated the importance of woman in her role as mother: in an oft-quoted phrase, he declared women to be 'nature's workshop where life is forged'.[11] The ovation which followed amongst the women showed perhaps that Castro was appealing to old prejudices within them rather than to a new order of genuine sexual equality.

Following Castro's flattery, a more extensive and thoughtful document, *On the Full Exercise of Women's Equality*, was presented at the first Congress of the Communist party in 1975. It offered a traditional Marxist analysis of sexual discrimination by tracing it back to the period when: '. . . with the disintegration of the primitive community, the establishment of private property and the division of society into classes, men attained economic supremacy, and with it, social predominance'. While calling for the full participation of women in the Revolutionary process, at work, and in 'leadership positions', it recognized that the necessary and proper changes in people's consciousness had not yet come about. The media in particular still presented the image of woman inherited from capitalism as 'a sexual and decorative object, passive, confined to the tasks of the home, whose highest aspiration is marriage'. The authors of the document further argued that women and men have both to be equally free and responsible in determining their sexual relations. But rather than advocating free love, the authors maintain that 'socialist morality' does not define freedom as 'licentiousness'. The ideal put forward thus remains the old, familiar one of 'a stable and happy marriage based on love and honesty'.[12] Indeed, rather than sparking off a sexual revolution, the Cuban Revolution has strengthened the institution of marriage and emphasized the importance of the family as the fundamental unit of society. 'Socialist morality' moreover, as practised in Cuba, has proved remarkably puritanical and conservative, by celebrating the virtues of heterosexual and monogamous relationships, by condemning homosexuality and lesbianism as vicious and unnatural, and by discouraging free unions. Even talk of sex for woman's pleasure as well as man's was a taboo subject until recently.

The Cuban Revolution has even ignored the radical sexual politics which exist within the Marxist tradition. The party accepts Engels' view in *The Origin of the Family, Private Property and the State* (1884) that marriage is first and foremost an economic institution, and as such is responsible under capitalism for the exploitation of women. But the arguments of Alexandra Kollontai, who saw legal marriage as a function of the bourgeois society made necessary by private property relations, and who believed that it would be superfluous in a new egalitarian and socialist order, have not been raised publicly.

The institution of marriage was traditionally relaxed amongst poor people and blacks in Cuba. Even Castro was born out of wedlock, although his parents eventually married. Yet at the beginning of the Revolution, the regime actively encouraged people living together to marry. As a result of the campaign, many 'collective' marriage ceremonies took place in the country, especially in Oriente where the rate of marriage increased threefold. 'Wedding Palaces' were established as in the Soviet Union, often in old colonial houses which make available to the poorest couple a semblance of all the extravagance of the bourgeois wedding. To encourage couples to marry, the ceremony has been streamlined into a straightforward yet superficially showy affair. The ceremony only costs 50 pesos and lasts about 30 minutes. Popular Cuban music is played in the background; the bride wears white, if it is the first time; red, the second; purple, the third; and black, if she is widowed. She can come back dressed in different colours up to six times, when the state will have no more of it! Resorts like Soroa in Pinar del Río province have also been developed especially for honeymoons.

No doubt the drive to get people to marry has been partly inspired by a desire for stability and for social justice, in that certain status symbols formerly reserved for the upper classes were being made available to the lower classes. To prevent counter-revolutionary feeling, the regime was also eager to show that it was not planning to abolish the family or to encourage promiscuity amongst the young. At the same time, the stress on marriage has undoubtedly resulted from the state's wish to regulate and control people's private lives and sexual morality, since they can threaten its absolute rule.

After much public discussion, the Family Code of 1975 and the Constitution of 1976 further legislated for the monogamous, nuclear family. The Family Code defines the family as the 'elementary cell of society' and the 'centre of relations of common existence', while the Constitution sees the prime responsibility of the state as 'to protect the family, maternity and marriage' (Article 34). But by thus enshrining the concept of the nuclear family, the state has pre-empted experiments in new forms of living. Many people still live together outside marriage, but the 'pair bond' is the expected norm. A woman, too, is chiefly defined by her marital status.

It cannot be denied, however, that some elements in the Constitution and the Family Code relating to women are progressive. In the first place, the legal concept of bastardy has been abolished once and for all by the principle in the Constitution that 'all children have equal rights' (Article 36) whether born within or outside of wedlock. Secondly, the conjugal couple have 'absolute equality of rights and duties' (Article 35) in looking after the home and bringing up the children. Indeed, the most radical aspect of the Family Code is that it specifically engages both men and women in housework and child care. Women and men have equal rights, but no more than equal duties at home: both partners must therefore care for the family they have created and must participate 'to the extent of their capacity or possibilities' in the running of the home (Article 26).

If the marriage has 'lost its meaning', either partner can seek divorce on the same grounds, and both must continue to be responsible for supporting their children. Since divorce is also easy and cheap, it comes as no surprise that four out of ten marriages are dissolved. No other country has such advanced legislation on the relations between the sexes within the institution of marriage.

It is the call in the Family Code for an equal share in housework and child care that has proved the most controversial and difficult to implement. The party likes to quote Lenin's view that 'petty housework crushes [a woman], strangles, stultifies and degrades her, chains her to the kitchen and nursery, and she wastes her labour on barbarous, unproductive, petty, nerve-racking, stultifying and crushing drudgery'.[13] The *Full Exercise of Women's Equality* insists on men participating in this drudgery. It also insists that masculinity is not in contradiction to housework, taking care of children, and 'mutual co-operation in all fields of revolutionary activity, but rather is reaffirmed through them'. Equally, it points out that femininity is 'not counterposed to any activity of work, of educational improvement, or of the responsibilities of daily life'.[14]

Unfortunately, despite these noble sentiments, the *machismo* elaborated by Spanish institutions and confirmed by slavery over centuries, is not so easy to wipe out overnight. In a debate promoted by the paper *Juventud Rebelde* in March 1984 on the equality of rights of women, it was recognized that the social development of women had been more rapid than that of men since 1959, but the theoretical equality of the sexes had not become practice. The mother still has a predominant role in looking after children; if a child is ill, she is expected to stay off work. When it comes to household tasks, at best the man will 'help' the woman; he does not see housework as his responsibility. Husbands go out with women other than their wives, but not vice versa. At the same time, women are often as *machista* as men, and by their own behaviour mothers instil *machisto* attitudes and practices in their children. But at least some of the young were challenging these attitudes. One student girl challenged directly Castro's call for 'proletarian chivalry' and 'special privileges' for women by asking: 'Why should there be a different etiquette for men and women?'[15] The fact that these questions are being discussed openly and the contradictions are recognized shows at least how there is a growing public awareness of sexual politics.

But the archetypal hero in Cuba remains the *macho* figure of the boxer, the baseball star, the cane cutter and, more recently, the guerrilla. Homosexuality is despised, but with such virulence that it suggests the men fear it within themselves. The prevalence of *machismo* in Cuba goes hand-in-hand with a deep paranoia about homosexuality; even Castro has idealized rural life on the grounds that 'in the country, there are no homosexuals'.[16]

Homosexuality in Cuba was common in the past because of the ratio of men to women and the separation of the sexes enforced by slavery. Havana was the 'red light district' of the Caribbean before the Revolution, which encouraged homosexual prostitution on a large scale. At first, many homosexual intellectuals supported the Revolution, seeing it as part of an overall movement for social, cultural and sexual freedom. But the leaders from the Sierra Maestra, who had lived rough without women, were not sympathetic. The cultural magazine, *Lunes de Revolución*, which was largely run by homosexuals, was closed down. José Lezama Lima's last novel, *Paradiso* (1966), which contained explicit homosexual passages, was very nearly refused publication.

In the late 1960s there was a public campaign against homosexuals, who were rounded up without charge or trial and sent to work in the country, to labour camps, and to join the Military Units to Aid Production. The night raids against homosexuals have stopped, but there is still strong official disapproval. No homosexual is allowed to become a member of the Communist party, since homosexuality is considered incompatible with Communist morality. A careful watch is kept for homosexuals in 'dangerous' professions like ballet or music. A rumour that first appeared in the 1960s still circulates, that the Beatles were homosexuals and that they required special permission from the King of England to get married!

A lawyer acquaintance told me how the son of a neighbour who showed effeminate tendencies was hounded by his school fellows and criticized by his parents. 'Why, it is unnatural! Horrible!' she exclaimed. 'I can't understand it. Why should the middle boy in a family of three sons become effeminate? He's had the same background and schooling as his brothers, and yet he turns out like that! As far as I'm concerned, we don't want any homosexuals in Cuba today. They can all go to the United States.' She went on to quote approvingly her own son's sentiments, who had declared: 'If I had a son who turned out to be homosexual, I'd kill him!'

The same incomprehension and hostility are faced by lesbians. At an international film festival in Havana in 1984, a foreign film with a discreet lesbian scene raised nervous laughs amongst the Cuban audience. The embarrassment hides a deep-seated horror. It was only with great difficulty that one divorced woman I met confided in me that she had had lesbian experiences with a foreigner: 'I would never admit this to a Cuban, but you are a foreigner, you understand; in your country that kind of love is not a crime. But here—I would be finished if anybody knew I liked to go to bed with a woman. It's not against nature, as they say here, it's quite natural, absolutely natural. You can't do anything in this country now!'

To find out more what the Cuban Federation of Women (FMC) was doing about *machismo* and these related topics, I visited its headquarters in Havana. It occupies a sumptuous palace in an elegant boulevard of the Miramar district. The overall impression inside is one of pink luxury, although a proper Revolutionary tone was set by large portraits on the walls of Che Guevara and his companion in Bolivia, Tamara Bunke (although exposed as a spy in the Western press, she is still revered as a Revolutionary in Cuba). A young woman welcomed me into an elegantly furnished room and gave the official line on female emancipation in Cuba. She spoke with the fluency and monotony of one who had told the tale many times, keeping as close as possible to her chosen text. After reeling off details of the work of the FMC in education, health and jobs, she declared breathlessly that 'our ideological work involves collaboration with the CDRs and circles of study, solidarity with women of other countries, support for the government, and the elimination of prejudice against women'. I then raised the key issue of *machismo*.

Legally, women and men are equal in Cuba. There is equality in work and the family, with equal rights and duties. In practice, however, equality does not yet exist because of *perjuicio macho* [male prejudice]. But *machismo* cannot be eradicated by campaigns; it is a question of persuading and convincing people. *Machismo* exists in women as well as men; indeed, mothers often teach it to their boys.

I then asked her about the different types of work which are still allocated to men and women. 'We are tackling that problem right now,' she replied. 'There are plans for men to work, for instance, in day-care centres, or to stay at home and look after the children when they are ill. Men must become accustomed to do domestic tasks. But it is a moral problem, and should be seen from both the man's and the woman's point of view.'

To my enquiry as to whether men worked in the FMC offices, she said yes, but as gardeners and cleaners only. We then discussed the question of feminist separatism. The president of the FMC, Vilma Espín, had gone out of her way to criticize the first National Congress of Women organized in 1923 for raising the problem of woman's emancipation 'from the false angle of women against men' instead of focussing on the struggle as a 'fight of women against socio-economic oppression together with men, which is the working-class point of view'.[17] My young interlocutor confirmed this point of view: 'The struggle is not *against* man but *with* man . . . In this we have the full support of the party, and especially Fidel.' To my further urging that in some circumstances it may be necessary for women to form a separate group in order to define themselves and their interests, she suddenly grew impatient: 'You Europeans always ask this question. As I said before, the FMC is not a separatist organization. It works for the emancipation of women in co-operation with men.'

And that was the end of that. As expected, the literature of the FMC describes the personal revolt of women against male oppression in the West as a 'diversionary tactic' aimed at concealing the 'terrible problems of an exploitative social system'. The path laid out by the FMC for the Cuban woman is therefore to become the educated equal of man but to remain his wife in a nuclear family. When I asked which thinkers most inspired the philosophy of the women's movement in Cuba, the FMC representative replied: 'Our philosophy is not inspired by a particular thinker; we are Marxist-Leninist first and foremost.' She added, on second thoughts, 'Fidel is the most influential. We would also listen to Angela Davis, but not Simone de Beauvoir.' The admission was revealing: Angela Davis had been a personal guest of Castro in the 1970s, while de Beauvoir was banned because of her criticism of the Cuban government's literary censorship.

As for the institution of marriage, the FMC official argued that there was no prejudice in Cuba against living together:

Marriage is not legally necessary although it is part of our tradition. People still marry very young, and there is a 40 per cent divorce rate. Men and women now of course have the same status within marriage. We do not defend marriage for itself; we are neither for nor against marriage, but we recognize the family as the fundamental unit of society. We are keen, however, to see that having children is a voluntary decision for the mother: abortion is therefore free and easy to obtain, and contraception is widely available.

Many Cuban men had joked to me that women were taking over. But she assured me that this was not the case in Cuba: 'Nor are we trying to turn women into men. Although we have *macheteras* (female sugar-cane cutters), some work is not for women or for mothers. We also want to be feminine; we wear trousers for work, but we also wear skirts and like to use make-up'. I mentioned Castro's call for men to practise 'proletarian chivalry' in dealing with women. 'Yes, that's very important,' she smiled. 'It is very easy for men to forget to give their seat to old ladies or to mothers with babies.' As for the *pirópo*, or street compliment, the young woman explained that it must be understood in terms of Cuban culture: 'It is part of our cultural tradition inherited from Spain to see woman as an object, but the *pirópo* can also be a sympathetic and affectionate compliment. Indeed, we are making a documentary study of the *pirópo*. One day it will be possible for a woman to make a *pirópo* to a man.' The interview had come to an end. To my parting question about how long female emancipation would take in Cuba, my hostess declared: 'It depends on the young; we are optimistic, not utopian.'

There are good grounds to be optimistic. Women make up 40 per cent of the workforce. In higher education, they make up more than half of the students, and 43 per cent of university lecturers. They are particularly strong in education (68 per cent of teachers), health (67 per cent of doctors and nearly all nurses), and in the technical and scientific professions (54 per cent). Even in industry and in the agricultural co-operatives, they make up more than a third of the workforce.

Castro has been particularly impressed by women's military potential: 'This is not only a congress of women,' he declared at the fourth Congress of the FMC in 1985, 'but also a congress of the representatives of half of our territorial troop militia, a congress of the homeland's defenders, a congress of the new combatants and soldiers of the Revolution'.[18] He also claimed that women's 'social behaviour' was far better than men's, which could be a backhanded compliment since it implies that female soldiers are simply more obedient and disciplined.

But despite these real changes in the work patterns of women, the President of the FMC, Vilma Espín, has strongly attacked the vestiges of discrimination which allow certain trades and professions, especially in industry and construction, to be considered only fit for men. There are many parents, she has pointed out, with backward ideas who want their daughters to work only in a shop or an office. At the fourth Congress of the FMC, Castro further acknowledged that certain jobs are still only given to men simply because of concern over the possible pregnancies of women employees. On the other hand, some women are chosen for jobs because of their looks rather than their capabilities. Rejecting the 'irrational prohibition' which designates certain tasks for men, Castro called for additional facilities to enable women to go out to work. But while the Revolution has given rise to new values, he insisted that 'we must go on educating and creating an awareness not just among the men but also—and I would dare say above all—among the women.'[19]

The political power of women is also limited, as reflected in the figures of leadership positions in Cuba. Certainly in the Pioneers Organization girls have three-quarters of the positions of responsibility, and almost half in the Union of Young Communists. They also form 43 per cent of leadership in trade unions at local level and 50 per cent in the CDRs. But when it comes to direct participation in political decision-making, the picture is different. Women representatives in People's Power Assemblies at the municipal level only made up 8 per cent in 1981, a figure which only marginally improved to 11 per cent in the 1985 elections. These are the most significant figures, since candidates are not nominated by the party. Women make up 22 per cent of the National Assembly, but that is due to party encouragement and influence. Nevertheless, women still only make up about a fifth of party membership. In 1986, there were only three women in the 24-strong Politburo, and only 41 out of 225 in the Central Committee.

Castro's observation in 1980 that 'our party is still largely a party of men, and our state is still largely a state of men' is as valid as ever. The most influential women, moreover, come from the old guard of the Sierra Maestra and are closely related to the men in power: Vilma Espín is Raúl Castro's wife, Haydée Santamaría was the wife of Foreign Minister Armando Hart, and Cecilia Sánchez used to be Fidel's secretary. Just as the National Ballet is dominated by the ageing prima donna Alicia Alonso, so the mass organizations at top level are ruled by women who refuse to release the reins. Castro rightly admitted at the fourth Congress of the FMC that while the course was well-charted, the struggle against the discrimination of women will be 'one of the most difficult, prolonged and long-ranging tasks of the Revolution'.[20]

There is clearly a long way to go. Women run the day care centres and there are few male primary school teachers. Girls as well as boys are trained to be mechanics and technicians, though the girls are not expected to do dirty or dangerous work. The career of traffic warden seems to be the preserve of women, but it is men who tear about on the police motor cycles. The schools are mixed and everyone uses the same toilets, but the work brigades are sexually divided; the girls are given lighter tasks because they are considered physically weaker. Legal equality does not require the state to provide work for all women, hence they are exempt from the draft for military service and the law of 1970 which requires all able-bodied men to work. But it is the women, not the men, who have the choice to work in or outside the home on a full-time basis.

Attitudes are slow to change in other respects also. Women's bodies are noticeably absent on hoardings to advertise and sell products as in the West, although the glamourized images of women are still used sometimes in political propaganda. Television is largely free from the type of entertainment that mixes sex with violence. Delegates at the second Congress of the FMC held in 1975 called for an end to the use of sexist images of women in the media, and criticized the practice of choosing beauty queens for carnivals.[21] The party, too, has condemned the 'exhibition of women' in beauty contests and carnivals, which 'besides being negative and absurd in our society, sometimes becomes vulgar and grotesque'.[22] But the beauty contests still flourish and *estrellas* or stars, chosen by their workmates, still grace the carnival floats in alluring undress. And of course in the wildly popular cabarets, chorus girls, scantily clad and gorgeously plumed, continue to dance erotically in the best Folies Bergères tradition.

Another sexist tradition that continues is the practice (once belonging to the Spanish upper classes) of celebrating the girls' fifteenth birthdays by dressing them up like the most frivolous of dolls. All taffeta and revealing adolescent bosoms, the girls are made up with a rainbow of cosmetics. The parents then take their daughters to the most luxurious hotel nearby to immortalize their offspring on celluloid for the family album. While this no doubt has a certain anthropological significance as a rite of passage into womanhood, the girl is made to look like a passive, enticing sex object. Fussing mothers and proud fathers look on as the wily photographer encourages the poor blushing girl to take up alluring and seductive poses. The competition between these girls on a busy Saturday in Du Pont's mansion at Varadero or in the lobby of the Riviera Hotel in Havana, contrasts strangely with the socialist principles of equality and austerity espoused by the leaders of the Cuban Revolution.

Women are still subject to assault by men. An English friend of mine, whilst returning home to her hotel with an elderly couple, was mugged—hit on the head and her bag stolen. I also met a young Cuban woman who said she had been raped when she was 16 by an acquaintance in his twenties. She claimed that he only got two months' imprisonment, and that she still occasionally saw him in the streets of Havana. But these may be just isolated examples. Rape, especially of minors, is considered a serious crime and offenders may be executed by firing squad. Havana is said to be one of the safest cities in the world for women to walk in at night, and the incidence of rape in Cuba as a whole is low. However, the maxim 'women in the home, the men in the street' still prevails to a degree. It is extremely rare to see a single girl or even a group of women out in a bar or restaurant. Night clubs in Havana insist that entrance is for couples only.

The Cuban woman has rightly been called a 'psychic one-crop economy'.[23] She is psychologically dependent on men and defines herself largely in relation to them. The ideal model for girls is to form a heterosexual relationship leading to marriage and the nuclear family. While complaining about the double standard, Cuban women are reluctant to accept that men's adultery is only possible by their acquiescence in the conspiracy. The single woman is rarely discussed officially and little emphasis is placed on sisterhood or female solidarity. In the circumstances, it is not surprising that the revolutionary heroine Haydée Santamaria felt compelled to commit suicide when her husband began a public affair with a younger woman.

But for all the prevalence of *machismo* amongst both men and women, and the continuing sexual discrimination in Cuba, it cannot be denied that the position of Cuban women has improved dramatically since the Revolution. A comprehensive system of welfare looks after them from the cradle to the grave and the new opportunities for work decrease their economic dependence on men. It is affection rather than necessity that now holds a family together. Household chores have been lightened by the provision of collective laundries and canteens and by the campaigns to get men involved. The care of children is increasingly shared by men, while the day care centres, nursery schools, weekly boarding schools and youth organizations take them away from the home for long periods.

The 1974 Maternity Law provides three months' paid maternity leave, and guarantees mothers the same job to return to for up to a year. Contraception and abortion are freely available, regardless of marital status, which has led to a high abortion rate and reduced the birth rate to less than two per cent a year. Divorce is easily available on equal grounds for men and women, and no longer carries any stigma. Prostitution has been virtually eradicated, along with sexist advertising.

The result is that women have greater control over their bodies, increased sexual freedom, and more economic independence. They have the opportunity to fulfil themselves in education and work outside the home. The traditional patriarchal family is changing: parents are losing exclusive control over their children who are more independent and self-sufficient, and husbands and wives are increasingly separated by their work and participation in the various organizations. Above all, the 'revolution within the Revolution' has meant that *machismo* has become a daily topic of analysis and criticism, and that most young Cuban women now have an understanding of sexual politics and a wish for complete equality.

10

RACIAL EQUALITY

The black and mulatto population of Cuba has undoubtedly gained most from the egalitarian policies of the Cuban Revolution. After centuries of white male patriarchy in which the dominant relationship was the master and the slave, a major task of the regime has been to bring about racial as well as sexual equality. The New Man and Woman are being brought up to define themselves not by the different colour of their skins, but by their common humanity.

Racial feeling was never so strong in Cuba as in neighbouring British Protestant islands—the Spanish had, after all, lived for centuries under the Moors, and the Catholic church recognized that all souls are equal before God. From the beginning of the Spanish conquest, there was considerable mixing between the races; the upper-class families had mulatto cousins; indeed, the higher the status of the family, the more likely this was. Since few white women were amongst the Spanish immigrants, the men had little alternative but to turn to the black population for their women. As in most countries in the New World, however, it remained more common for white men to marry black women than for white women to marry black men. If a white woman went with a black, she would be isolated from 'respectable' society. The old saying, 'white women for marriage, mulatto women for love and black women for work', reflected sexual behaviour.

The church preferred marriage between the races to concubinage, but in the 1760s and 1770s, inter-racial marriage was prohibited by the state because of the fear of Africanization with the new influx of slaves for the expanding sugar industry. From the early 1790s, the black population began to grow faster than the white one. Although whites began again to outstrip blacks through immigration, there was still a widespread fear of *ennegrecimiento*, absorption of whites by blacks. As slavery expanded, racism became more entrenched. The resulting acute racial awareness is demonstrated in the tortuous definition in Pichardo's dictionary of 1836 of a *trigüeno* as:

The person of slightly darker colour or similar to that of wheat [*trigo*] in the same way as the person of lighter complexion colour, milky with a pink hue is called *white*. . . . In a racial context the word *white* is used even if the person is *trigüeno*, in order to differentiate him from *negro* or *mulato*; although there are some of the latter who are whiter than many of the white race.[1]

When 140,000 Chinese labourers were brought into Cuba in the mid nineteenth century, marriage was forbidden between Asiatics and people of African descent.

White immigration increased in the latter half of the nineteenth century: in 1861, blacks and mulattos made up 43 per cent of the population; by 1899, it was only 32 per cent—of which 15 per cent were black and 17 per cent were mulattos. By 1861 only 16.7 per cent of the black and mulatto population were *libertos* (freed slaves). Cuba in 1886 was the last country to abolish slavery in the Caribbean. Although racial discrimination was afterwards made illegal in schools, bars and the cities, it flourished elsewhere in all walks of life. The discrimination was partly fired by a constant fear of black rebellion; for instance, during the US occupation from 1898 to 1902, blacks were forbidden to join the Havana Police. The fear was made real by a 'Negro rising' throughout Cuba in 1904, which was only put down by the help of US marines.

With the influx of new Spanish immigrants early this century, and the growing influence of North America during the period of the Pseudo Republic, racial barriers became more pronounced. As a result, whites and blacks mixed mainly in church, in the semi-secret African religious sects sometimes attended by upper-class whites, cockfighting events, and in illicit sex and drugs. With over three centuries of black slavery, racial stereotyping continued to exist. As a popular saying reveals, blacks were seen by whites as having intractable natures, especially when it came to white property: 'Children are born to be happy; blacks are born to steal chickens'. Again, another saying carefully defined the social hierarchy of colour: 'White is a career, mulatto is an illusion, black is coal that you find anywhere'.

The racial barriers were reflected in jobs. Although many trades and crafts became the preserve of the black population, they were not strongly represented in the professions or politics at the beginning of the century. A Comité de los Derechos del Negro (Committee for the Negro's Rights) in 1934 noted that blacks were not employed in commerce, industry or the great foreign enterprises, but rather where the work was hardest and the pay lowest. The most menial jobs remained the preserve of black people; for the most part they were 'hewers of wood and bearers of water'. They were not to be found in public jobs like sales clerks or receptionists. The major exception was in sports and entertainment, where 'black sensuality' was prized.

In the country, the small tobacco farmers were white while the blacks worked in the sugar fields and mills. According to the 1931 census, black Cuban farmers owned only 11 per cent of the land; whites, 74 per cent. They suffered the same exploitation as poor whites but with the added burden of racism. However, the blacks were not prepared to accept this. They could take inspiration from many black leaders in the nineteenth-century Wars of Independence, especially the 'Bronze Titan' General Antonio Maceo. They were prominent in the trade unions, with Lázaro Peña as General Secretary of the Confederation of Cuban Workers from 1939 to 1947, and Jesús Menéndez as head of the powerful sugar workers in the 1930s and 1940s. In the same period, they were well represented in health (making up a fifth of all doctors) and in the teaching profession and in the army. Blacks dominated the leadership of the Communist party in the early days after its foundation in 1935. Even Cuba's most famous dictator, Fulgencio Batista, who first came to power in 1934 and dominated Cuban politics until 1959, was a mulatto; his government included the mulatto General Francisco Tabernilla as chief of the armed forces, as well as a black minister of justice.

Although there was no formal segregation in Cuba before the Revolution, there were white areas. In Havana, blacks congregated at the bottom end of the Paseo del Prado near the waterfront, while whites strolled along the rest of the promenade. Discrimination was even more intense in the provinces. In Las Villas, blacks tended to walk on one side of the central square and whites on another; in Santiago de Cuba, blacks and whites sat on different benches. Again, there were no black ghettoes as in the United States, but the blacks tended to live in the shanties while the high income areas like Miramar, Country Club and Biltmore in Havana were almost completely white. There were also 'white only' private clubs, bars, restaurants, hotels, beaches, schools, swimming pools and hospitals. After the abolition of slavery, racial discrimination in Cuba was based on class as well as colour: if you were poor and black, then brother, get back; but if a black became rich or obtained political power, only the most exclusive private clubs would close their doors to him.

On the political left, there has always been a considerable degree of solidarity between blacks and whites. In the late nineteenth century, José Martí had declared: *'Cubano es más que blanco, más que negro'*

(Being Cuban is more than being white or black). Both races fought alongside each other in the Wars of Independence to expel the Spanish. They shared a common colonial experience of oppression and on many subjects held similar beliefs. The black historian Fernando Ortíz argued in the 1930s that Cuban culture is mulatto, a dynamic synthesis between African and Spanish traditions. More recently the black poet Nicolás Guillén has spoken of the love affair between the Spanish guitar and African drum which has produced Cuban music. Following Martí, he calls himself neither black nor white but Cuban. Relationships between black and white on the left may have contained some resentment, guilt and even fear, but there was little overt hatred.

Racial politics in Cuba have always tended to remain behind a veil. Before the Revolution, there was no reference to the race question by the Revolutionaries, possibly because Batista had support among some blacks and mulattos. In his speech made to the tribunal after the abortive attack on the Moncada Barracks, Castro made no mention of racial discrimination. Apart from Juan Almeida, most of the guerrilla leaders in the Sierra Maestra and of the July 26 Movement in the cities were, like Castro himself, middle-class whites.

One of the first and most popular acts of the new Revolutionary regime was to open the private beaches and clubs to people of all races: the maids and waiters could now play with their own children in the warm waters of the Caribbean. The Urban Reform Law, which reduced rents to ten per cent of income, and the Agrarian Reform Law which distributed land to tenants, were immensely popular, especially amongst the poorest, who tended to be black. Nicolás Guillén expressed the feelings of many of his fellow black Cubans when he wrote:

> When I look at myself and everything
> I, Juan Without Anything only yesterday,
> and now Juan with everything
> and today with everything,
> I look around, I look,
> I see myself and everything
> and I ask myself how it happened.

> What I have, let's see,
> is that I, just because I'm black,
> can't be stopped by anyone
> at the door of a cabaret or bar . . .
> Or else at the hotel desk,
> to shout at me that there are no rooms,

just a little room, not a big one,
a tiny little room where I can rest.

What I have, let's see,
is that there are no police
to grab me and lock me up in a barracks,
or to uproot me and throw me off my land
in the middle of the highway.

What I have is land, I have sea,
not country club,
not high life,
not tennis and not yacht
but from beach to beach and wave to wave
gigantic blue open democratic:
In short: the sea.[2]

Castro first dealt directly with the race issue in a speech on 22 March 1959. He particularly focussed on the need to end racial discrimination at work:

It should not be necessary to pass a law to establish a right which a person has by the simple fact of being a human being and a member of society. It should not be necessary to pass a law against prejudice. What must be legislated is anathema for and public condemnation of everyone who is full of prejudices from the past . . . We are going to end racial discrimination in the work centres by making a campaign to end that hateful and repulsive system, with one motto: Work opportunities for all Cubans, without discrimination of race or sex . . . Let white and black unite to end racial discrimination. And thus we shall proceed, step by step, to create our new homeland.[3]

He finished his speech by also calling for an end to an educational system which separated black and white.

The speech was well received by blacks, was approved by most white Revolutionaries, but many of the white bourgeoisie were horrified. A rumour spread like wildfire that the revolutionary government would soon be forcing the daughters of whites to marry black men. 'If blacks have the same rights and opportunities as us', many white racists declared, 'They will become simply impossible!' Concern was so great that Castro felt it necessary to go on television a few days later to clarify his position. He reassured people that the Revolution was not going to tell them who they must dance with, but he went on to attack vehemently racists of every political degree and class, including 'those who call themselves Christians and are racists; those who call themselves followers of Martí and are racists; those who think they are educated and are racists'.[4]

The press followed up Castro's speech with similar statements. As the handbook *Alfabeticemos* used by the teachers in the literacy campaign in 1961 further declared: 'Racial discrimination has no *raison d'être*. Science has shown that all men are equal, that there are no essential differences between a white man, a negro, or a man of yellow race.' The official position was that racism, like exploitation, is a product of capitalist society and that socialism will eradicate them both in time.

Discussions about the race question were soon dropped from government publications. By early 1966, Castro was talking as if racism and sexism were diseases of the capitalist past:

In a class society, which is to say, a society of exploiters and exploited, there was no way of eliminating discrimination for reasons of race or sex. Now the problem of such discrimination has disappeared from our country, because the basis for these two types of discrimination which is, quite simply, the exploitation of man by man, has disappeared.[5]

The veil had been drawn once again over racial politics.

Unfortunately, wishful thinking was not enough to eradicate centuries of racial prejudice in which blackness was invariably associated with slavery, evil, cunning and ungratefulness. The black Communist Carlos Moore soon became disenchanted, and in an article in the Parisian journal *Présence Africaine* in 1965, complained that the Cuban Revolution was simply a victory of the white national bourgeoisie and that racial prejudice still continued. He further criticized school history textbooks for underestimating the role of blacks in the Wars of Independence, and for undermining the significance of African-based religions by transforming them into folklore.

There is undoubtedly some truth in this. Earlier this century, the black writer Fernando Ortíz, and the black poet, Nicolás Guillén, both argued correctly that Cuban culture is a creative fusion, a dynamic synthesis of both African and Spanish elements. But while the African contribution to Cuban culture is now widely recognized by scholars, two opposing attitudes have prevailed since the Revolution, both of which underplay, in their different ways, the importance of the African influence.

In the first place, Carlos Franquí (who believes that Cuban consciousness will come into its own only when it discovers its African
origins) has accused the regime of continuing the old distinction between
high 'white' culture and low 'black' culture. Castro, he argues, still
believes that the dominant white culture is best; he prefers waltzes and
boleros to the *rumba*: 'When the Castro brothers and the hard-line
Communists heard the Internationale played in *conga* rhythm, they
raised the roof.'[6] In addition, the religious rites which gave birth to
Cuban music are defined by them as superstition. At the same time,
the official cultural policy of the government argues that by abolishing
classes, the Revolution has created a unified national, socialist and
working-class culture. As Miguel Barnet has recently argued: 'When
class distinctions cease, when all vestiges of stratification are abolished,
popular traditional culture is one and indivisible.'[7] Yet this myth of a
common Cuban culture not only denies the real cultural diversity within
Cuba, but suppresses the experience and origins of black Cubans.

Because slavery was abolished so late, and because different groups
from Africa were allowed to form *cabildos* (groups) of their nations or
tribes, African culture has exerted a more lasting and purer influence
in Cuba than elsewhere in the Caribbean. Not only are many African
languages still spoken, especially in the semi-secret religious sects, but
it is even said that Yoruba is spoken in Cuba in a more correct form
than in Nigeria today. Cuba is the only place in the Americas where
African proverbs are found in everyday conversation. Many African
words are also used rather than their Spanish equivalents: for instance,
jimagua for twin, rather than the Spanish *gemelo*.

It cannot be denied that Cuba's national culture is profoundly and
inextricably linked to its African roots. Some blacks, however, resent
the fact that African cultural traditions have been downgraded to the
status of folklore, becoming either the subject of historical research in
the Institute of Ethnology and Folklore, or a major tourist attraction.
The metaphysical significance of the religious sects is dismissed as
superstition, but the dances and rites which are an integral part of them
are performed regularly by the National Folklore Group to tourists. The
spectacle is billed as an 'Afro-Cuban Night'.

Yet the very term 'Afro-Cuban' implies that there is another Cuban
culture to which African elements have been added. Cuban culture is
in fact a blend of African and Spanish, 'Afro-Spanish' no less. From
the present perspective in Cuba, the ballet is considered high culture,
but African dance is seen as picturesque folklore; one is part of a genuine
living tradition, the other a primitive form, of historical interest only.

Cuban blacks continue to suffer from a residue of racism in the economic and social as well as the cultural spheres. John Clytus, a radical American sympathizer who lived in Cuba from 1964 to 1967 and worked as an English teacher at Havana University and a translator on *Granma*, complained in *Black Man in Red Cuba* (1970) that blacks in any responsible capacity were conspicuously absent from hotels, stores and restaurants. He dismissed Juan Almeida's position as a vice minister in the army at the time as a 'piece of window dressing'.[8] Elizabeth Sutherland, another enthusiastic black American writer, spent the summer of 1967 in Cuba and concluded that while overt racism had been eliminated, certain forms of aesthetic racism continued. The Jamaican playwright, Barry Reckord, also wrote in 1971 after a visit that while there was no public racism in Cuba, 'a lot of private racism' existed.[9] My own experience confirms these views. Blatant institutionalized racism is a thing of the past in Cuba, but the more subtle elements continue.

The exact proportion of the black population is difficult to establish since official statistics are no longer broken down on racial lines. In the 1953 census, the black and mulatto population was put at 27 per cent, but other estimates reach as high as 45 per cent. Mulattos are generally thought to outnumber blacks by about two to one; for understandable reasons since the abolition of slavery, the mulatto population has been growing steadily. Although 'mulatto' is considered an offensive term in the United States, its use is common and acceptable in Cuba. It is employed to cover a great variation in features and colour, and means nothing more than dark or light brown.

The Revolution has changed the language of race in one crucial area. Whites have been freed from their racism, in that they no longer use *niche* or *macri* (nigger) or *negrada* (niggers); polite euphemisms like *gente de color* have been replaced by the straight descriptive term *negros*.

The figures for the different races are vague for, unlike in the United States where anyone with the slightest amount of 'black blood' is considered black, in Cuba if a person looks whitish then he or she is considered white. Moreover, there is a general recognition that after centuries of interbreeding, African blood runs in everyone's veins: '*El que no tiene de Congo, tiene de Carabalí*' (He who does not have something from the Congo, has something from Calabar). The crossbreeding between the races over the centuries has made Cuba's population the most racially mixed in the Caribbean. Almost every shade of colour and every racial characteristic are visible, from the felicitous blending of European, African and, to a lesser extent, Indian and Chinese. It is not uncommon to see a person with green oriental eyes, straight black Indian hair, African features and a light brown skin. The Cuban population is a living testimony to the beauty of racial mixing.

But the way officials refuse to discuss racism by denying it exists is a sign in itself of a certain malaise. 'Racism is simply no longer a problem,' they declare. 'Everybody is equal here; we are all human beings, neither black nor white.' It has become a taboo subject. Some blacks even complain that they have become more conspicuous since the Revolution and resent being pointed out as examples of racial integration.

In public places, especially in parks, old birds of a feather still tend to flock together, and families are usually of the same colour. The students and schoolchildren, however, seem far less conscious than their parents of racial differences: they mix freely in groups in the streets, and young mixed couples hold hands. But marriage between the races is still comparatively rare and provokes interest. The fact that I, a white Englishman, should live with a West Indian lady and have two children, was greeted with incredulity on more than one occasion. This may partly have been because I am English, for it is undoubtedly more acceptable for a white man to be with a brown woman rather than the other way round.

John Clytus recalled that when he lived in Cuba in the late 1960s he constantly saw black women strolling with white men, but saw no white women with black men. The situation has not changed a great deal since. Walking through the streets of Havana with a brown woman, I was never questioned, but a Zimbabwean acquaintance who was on a visit with his Swedish wife was stopped by police several times on suspicion of being a Cuban chatting up a foreigner. Would he have been stopped if he were a white Cuban? Despite the official silence of the Cuban government, race is clearly still an issue.

As I found out when travelling with Cuban men, especially if brown themselves, it is assumed that every white wants to 'make it' with a *mulata*. The thought of sex between the races clearly continues to raise the temperature. Indeed, the social nuances of sex across racial barriers still enthral. This no doubt explains the unprecedented popularity of the epic Brazilian television series *La Esclava*, in which the white son of a rich plantation owner wishes to marry a freed slave girl (suitably light-skinned) in opposition to the local white society. The dramatic twists of this soap opera kept the people of Santiago off the streets at eleven o'clock at night at the height of the Carnival, and neighbours and passers-by crowded around open windows to see the next cliff-hanging climax.

The slogan 'black is beautiful' does not seem to have caught on in Cuba, perhaps because black self-esteem is already high. Black women do try and straighten their hair with massive curlers most of the time. I saw hardly anyone growing their hair naturally or in Afro style. Indeed, when a young black girl got on a bus in Havana with long beaded plaits virtually all the women near her, whether black or white, were pointing her out, sniggering and joking uneasily about it. Fashions clearly do not travel to the island from Florida or Jamaica. At the same time, people are refreshingly unconcerned with the colour of their skin; young blacks and mulattos enjoy lying on the beach with their white friends, in a way rarely seen in other Caribbean countries where children are warned by their parents not to go in the sun 'because you are black enough already'. I saw no girls using skin lightener.

In addition to private racism, a certain amount of racial stereotyping continues to exist. I was told by a white Cuban that black Cubans talk, behave and walk differently and will always do so. The myth of 'black sensuality' is also prevalent; they are considered better drummers, dancers and lovers. Certain jobs still seem to be distributed on racial lines; the barmen in the hotels tend to be white, while the drivers are black. Cuban blacks are well represented in sport—from their ranks come the great boxers and runners—while under-represented in the professions. The cabaret dancers are nearly all *mulatas*, while the Cuban National Ballet is almost entirely white. Blacks are still not well represented in the top leadership, except for the old-timers like Juan Almeida and Dr Carlos Rafael Rodríguez who are prominent members of the Communist party. Another exception is Cuba's black Poet Laureate, Nicolás Guillén, who is President of the Unión de Escritores y Artistas de Cuba (UNEAC) (Union of Cuban Writers and Artists).

It has to be recognized, however, that the regime has consistently advocated racial equality and encouraged black political participation. Castro went out of his way in the late 1960s to support the black power movement in the United States, and welcomed many of its leaders, although this policy slightly backfired when the outspoken Stokely Carmichael caused a considerable stir during a visit in 1967 by appealing to the blacks of Cuba as a separate group with its own grievances and aspirations.[10] In 1983 the Reverend Jesse Jackson was warmly received.

In recent years the part played by blacks in Cuban history has been increasingly commented on and appreciated. Although the Marxist-Leninist state, committed as it is to promoting historical materialism in education and culture, dismisses the African religious sects as superstition, and treats their rituals as 'folklore', scholars are recognizing the crucial importance of the African contribution to Cuban culture, especially in music and dance. The heavy military involvement in Africa since 1975, especially in Angola and Ethiopia, has been welcomed as a way of expressing solidarity between peoples who share a common ancestry. Above all, the Revolution has received its greatest support from the black and mulatto sections of the population, who clearly see it as improving their lot and expressing their interests.

In the new generation at least, it might be quite possible for open, direct and relaxed relationships to develop between black and white in Cuba. Indeed, perhaps more than in any other place on earth, it seems likely that a genuinely egalitarian, multicultural and non-racist society could emerge in the not too distant future. To witness this process at work was one of the most refreshing aspects of my whole stay in Cuba.

In most countries, to be black and female is to be at the bottom of the pile. In Cuba, the women and the blacks, and especially the black women, are now largely incorporated in a society which they feel is their own. As the black poet, Nancy Morejón, has written:

This is the land where I was thrashed and whipped.
I journeyed the length of its rivers.
Beneath its sun, I sowed and reaped but of its harvest ate not.
My home was the slave quarters
I brought stones to build,
but I sang in natural tune to the nation's birds.
I rose up. . . .

I came down from the Sierra
to end capital and usury,
generals and bourgeoisie.
Now I am: only now do we have and create.
Nothing is beyond our reach.
Ours is the land.
Ours is the sea and the sky.
Ours the magic and the chimera . . . [11]

While vestiges of sexual and racial discrimination undoubtedly remain, the regime is actively pursuing a policy of equality. The education system is trying to bring up a new generation without sexual or racial prejudice. The New Man and Woman will not be defined by the accident of their racial origins, but above all by their humanity and conscience. The project has still a long way to go, and there are many obstacles in the way. But compared to the race-torn societies of the USA and Great Britain, it is a delight to visit a country where institutionalized racism has been virtually eradicated, and where black and white work together for a common goal, defining themselves not so much by the shade of their skins but by the colour of their political aspirations.

11

CULTURAL POLICY

At the beginning of the Revolution, the heady sense of euphoria, renewal and freedom felt throughout society gave a new impetus to literature and art. Outstanding Cuban writers like Alejo Carpentier returned from self-imposed exile, while the black poet Nicolás Guillén and the Catholic writer José Lezama Lima made common cause with the Revolutionaries. The cadres of the July 26 Movement included young intellectuals who were passionately interested in modernist aspects of Western culture— American cinema, French philosophy and Spanish surrealism—as well as their own dance and music and African roots. There was already a thriving subculture of writers and artists living a bohemian life in Havana who opposed Batista.

Lively theoretical and cultural journals were started up. *Revolución*, under the editorship of Carlos Franquí, was 'anti-militarist, pro-culture, pro-art, in favour of free trade unions, tolerant of homosexuals, and totally opposed to terrorism of any kind'.[1] Its Monday literary supplement *Lunes*, which achieved a circulation of over 200,000, was original and dynamic. Motivated by José Martí's motto, 'Culture brings Freedom', it issued huge editions with pictures and texts by Borges, Neruda, Marx, Faulkner, Lezama Lima, Martí, Breton, Picasso, Miró, Virginia Woolf, Trotsky and Brecht in its bold attempt to renew Cuban culture. For local inspiration, it turned to Cuban black and peasant folk traditions. It stood for new literature, new art and freedom of expression.

In addition, there were intelligent and searching theoretical journals like *Cuba Socialista* and *Revista Económica* which carried the debate between Charles Bettelheim and Che Guevara on the role of money in planning a socialist economy, and *Pensamiento Crítico* which concentrated on a wide range of foreign thinkers and writers. The government financed a Cuban Film Institute, the Instituto Cubano del Arte e Industria Cinematográficos (ICAIC), and a major publishing house Casa de las Américas, which offered new outlets for creative work.

But it did not last. Already by 1961, the tight inner leadership including the Director of Cultural Affairs Edith García Buchacha, President Dorticós and Armando Hart, began to direct cultural policy. The brilliant Cuban film *PM*, which had little overt Revolutionary content, was banned and denounced as decadent because it depicted Cuban people who had no awareness of national problems but preferred to dance and drink.

The threat of counter-revolution became an excuse for the regime to tighten its ideological controls. On 12 February 1961, Guevara published in *Verde Olivo*, the magazine of the armed forces, a chilling article repudiating all compromise with opponents. Angered by the failure of the independent second front in the Escambray mountains to accept the ultimate authority of the Sierra Madre group, Guevara declared that the 'sin of the Revolution' was the 'sin of compromise' in the face of the lack of 'Revolutionary spirit'. The second front should not therefore have been tolerated, but eliminated. Indeed, he insisted, 'We must be inflexible in the face of error, weakness, deceit, bad faith . . . we must stand up to denounce and punish wherever we find any vice which sullies the high principles of the Revolution.'[2]

Soon after the Bay of Pigs invasion in April 1961, Cuba's leading intellectuals, artists and writers (including Nicolás Guillén and Alejo Carpentier) were called to a meeting with the Council of Culture, held on 30 June in the National Library in Havana and attended by Armando Hart, Castro, President Dorticós and others. The issue was cultural freedom. The Communist Alfredo Guevara, who as Director of the Cuban Film Institute had seized and censored the film *PM*, accused the publications *Lunes* and *Revolución* of

> trying to split the Revolution from within; of being enemies of the Soviet Union; of revisionism; of sowing ideological confusion; of having introduced Polish and Yugoslavian ideas; of having praised Czech and Polish films; of being spokesmen for existentialism, surrealism, US literature, bourgeois decadence, elitism; of refusing to see the accomplishments of the Revolution; of not praising the armed forces.[3]

Castro's *Address to the Intellectuals* was more measured. He recognized the need for culture in a socialist society: 'Just as we have wanted for the people a better life on the material level, we'll want for the people a better life on all the spiritual levels; we'll want for the people a better life on the cultural level.' But culture, he insisted, should be the 'real patrimony of the people'. He went on to attack individualism and called on intellectuals to support the Revolutionary effort. While

allowing that some artists and writers who are not genuine Revolutionaries can 'find within the Revolution a place to work and create', he
established the criterion for permissible freedom: *'Dentro de la Revolución, todo; contra la Revolución, nada'* (Everything within the Revolution, nothing against the Revolution).[4] Soon after, the government
set up the Unión de Escritores y Artistas de Cuba (UNEAC) (Union of
Cuban Writers and Artists) with the message in its declaration of principles that: 'It is absolutely essential that all writers and artists, regardless of individual aesthetic differences, should take part in the great
work of defending and consolidating the Revolution.'[5]

According to Carlos Franquí, the former editor of *Revolución*, Castro
is a cultural philistine who prefers sports to the arts. But while he is
certainly no poet, artist, thinker or writer—his talents are those of a
soldier, an orator and a teacher—he has always been fully aware of the
importance and power of culture. As he observed in 1985 to the visiting
British Labour politician Neil Kinnock: 'In history, the poets can live
without politicians, but without poets the world cannot go on.'[6] Whereas
Franquí laments the fact that Castro is seemingly more interested in
visiting the zoo than an art gallery, Cabrera Infante's *bon mot* is possibly
more accurate: 'Castro is not indifferent to art; it would be better for
art if he were.'[7] Indeed, Castro not only felt that art should have a
moral purpose in making people happier and better, but that even truth
should be useful: 'These gentlemen who write "Truth never hurts", I
don't know whether they conceive of truth as an abstract entity. Truth
is a concrete entity in the service of a noble cause.'[8]

Guevara's contribution to the discussion on culture was more subtle
but not as influential or long-lasting as Castro's strictures. Guevara
always stressed the need to tell the truth, whatever the short-term benefit
of lies might be in terms of propaganda. In his *Reminiscences of the
Cuban Revolutionary War*, he recalled approvingly how: 'Preoccupation
with the truth was always a central theme in reports from the Rebel
Army, and we attempted to imbue our men with a profound respect for
truth and a feeling of how necessary it was to place truth above any
transitory advantage.'[9] In the section on propaganda in his manual
Guerrilla Warfare, Guevara equally insisted that the fundamental principle must be that 'truth in the long run is the best policy'. Whether on
the radio or in the newspapers, Guevara would have no truck with
utilitarian defences of falsehood: 'It is preferable to tell the truth, small
in its dimensions, than a large lie artfully embellished'.[10]

But while insisting that the writer must write the truth, he rejects
outright the call of some cultural officials for socialist realism and
political didacticism. He also condemns the school of 'artistic freedom'

created by alienated individuals under capitalism as escapist. What is needed, he argues, is the development of

> an ideological-cultural mechanism which permits both free enquiry and the uprooting of the weeds which multiply so easily in the fertile soil of state subsidies . . . We must not bring into being either docile servants of official thought, or scholarship students who live at the expense of the state—practising 'freedom'.[11]

But as usual, Guevara's feel for truth and freedom is counter-balanced by his penchant for state intervention in cultural matters. Like Castro he, too, believed 'There is no life outside the Revolution'.[12] Unfortunately, his condemnation of bourgeois 'artistic freedom' and his call for uprooting anti-revolutionary weeds were remembered more than his concern for new forms to express the songs of the new society.

Soon after Castro's *Address to the Intellectuals* which defined the position of the state *vis-à-vis* the writer and artist, the regime began to limit creative activity. Although Castro had at first promised free media, he defended his new policy of censorship by talking in his disconcerting way about the Revolution as if it were an independent being whose survival sanctions all: 'The Revolution is the first to lament that individual guarantees cannot be granted . . . The Revolution explains that to concede those guarantees would serve that powerful enemy who has tried to destroy the Revolution and to drown it in the blood of the people.'[13]

The lively literary supplement *Lunes* was suppressed in November 1961, supposedly because of a lack of paper. Its editor, Cabrera Infante, who wrote the powerful novel about pre-revolutionary Havana *Tres tristes tigres* (1964), was first banished to Brussels as cultural attaché before eventually defecting in 1965. *Revolución* was also closed down; its editor, Carlos Franquí, who had helped run Radio Rebelde in the Sierra Mastre, became sufficiently disillusioned to go into exile in 1964. Adopting Castro's line, President Dorticós summed up the situation in the same year: 'Our principal idea has been full freedom for those who support the Revolution and nothing for those who are opposed.'[14]

For those writers who stayed, life became difficult if they could not find it in themselves to be wholehearted supporters of the regime and its cultural policy. Lezama Lima managed to publish his novel *Paradiso* in 1966, a Joycean novel of homosexual experiences with no mention of the Revolution, but it only passed the censor (at a time when homosexuals were being 'rehabilitated' in labour camps) because of Lima's international reputation as a poet, and because it was difficult to read.

There was a small print run and no second edition; it would not easily get into the hands of the people.

By the beginning of 1968, the advocates of artistic freedom had not yet been silenced; there were even some positive signs of a loosening of ideological control. At the International Cultural Congress held in Havana early in 1968, the capital was invaded by all manner of radical writers and artists from Europe, with interests ranging from Trotskyism and Maoism in politics to surrealism and modernism in art and poetry. It was still a time when editions of Proust, Joyce and Robbe-Grillet could be found in the bookshops, and Antonioni and Bergman films played at the cinemas. There were passionate discussions of art and revolution, the New Man, artistic freedom, and the role of the intellectual in society, as Andrew Salkey's *Havana Journal* written during the congress, so vividly shows.

At the closing ceremony on 11 January 1968, Castro's speech seemed to augur a new era of intellectual freedom. Attacking the 'calcified leaders' of a 'pseudo-revolutionary church', he insisted that Marxism needed to develop itself, 'to come out of a certain stiffening of the joints, to interpret today's realities in an objective and scientific sense . . . Nobody can say that he has all the truth.' Indeed, Castro went so far as to assert: 'Nothing is more anti-Marxist than dogma and petrified thought. No one has a monopoly of ideas, and of revolutionary ideas least of all. No one is a repository of all revolutionary truths.'[15]

But Castro's speech was largely inspired by certain disagreements with orthodox Communists within the Cuban Communist party which led to the trial of Anibal Escalante and eight others at the end of January for creating a pro-Soviet faction within the party. The critic Ambrosio Fornet's paper on *The Intellectual in the Revolution* presented to the congress was a more accurate account of the regime's position. He not only calls upon the poet to become 'a master-communicator and a cultural duty-officer' but insists that the task of the intellectual is 'to lead the way, to address himself and his work to the soul of the people, to conquer nature and to create new highways and visions of reality; and that cannot be achieved in isolation from the concrete responsibility to the other sectors of the Revolution.'[16]

But while the International Cultural Congress was in progress, the conflict between the cultural *apparatchiks* who wanted to make literature narrowly to serve the Revolution and those who demanded artistic freedom in form and content was intensifying. Towards the end of 1967, a critical debate had been rumbling in the literary magazine *El Caimán Barbudo* about the literary merit of the novel *Pasión de Urbino* by Lisandro Otero (a high-ranking cultural official). The poet and former editor of *Granma*, Heberto Padilla wrote a letter debunking the work and praising Cabrera Infante's *Tres tristes tigres*. The resulting controversy ended with the resignation of the editorial board of the magazine and Padilla losing his job. When Padilla was chosen by an international jury as the winner of the annual poetry prize of the Union of Cuban Writers and Artists (UNEAC), the decision was respected, but UNEAC published a political disclaimer with his book of critical poems, *Fuera del juego*. Padilla was then bitterly criticized in *Verde Olivo*, the magazine of the armed forces. His crime was having dared to raise a note of criticism about the course of the Revolution. The playwright Anton Arrufat, who also won a prize, suffered a similar fate to Padilla. It was made clear at the first Congress of UNEAC in October 1968 that: 'the writer must contribute to the Revolution through his work and this involves conceiving of literature as a means of struggle, a weapon against weaknesses and problems which, directly or indirectly, could hinder this advance.'[17]

In the following year, Haydée Santamaría, President of the Casa de las Américas publishing house which had hitherto been comparatively free of political prejudice, explained to the juries who were to judge the annual prizes that no artist could remain non-political, and recommended that Latin Americans residing in their own countries should be preferred. The prize that year went to a lamentable novel about Guevara in Bolivia. Henceforth, priority would be given to 'Revolutionary' authors. Nicolás Guillén, president of UNEAC, also reminded his audience at an award ceremony in 1969 that the contest had taken place in an era of acute political crisis and that: 'Cuban writers and artists have the same responsibilities as the soldiers, with respect to the defence of the nation . . . He who does not [fulfil his duty] regardless of his position will receive the most severe Revolutionary punishment for his fault.'[18] Just as society was under the control of the soldiers, so literature was becoming militarized. Military magazines like *Verde Olivo* could pronounce on literary matters; unfortunately, the opposite was not permitted: writers could not criticize the military.

The punishment threatened by Guillén eventually fell on Heberto Padilla in March 1971 when he was jailed. He was released 37 days later but not until he had signed a long statement of self-criticism of his 'serious transgressions'. He delivered it personally at a meeting of UNEAC and called on other Cuban artists to follow suit. An international outcry followed this second 'Padilla affair' and a letter of protest was sent to Castro on 9 April 1971, signed by a large number of European and Latin American intellectuals (including Sartre, Gabriel García Márquez, Octavio Paz and Carlos Fuentes).

Castro was furious. He chose the first National Congress on Education and Culture to state his views publicly, when he savagely attacked in his closing speech on 30 April 1971 those 'pseudo-leftist bourgeois intellectuals' who had dared to criticize Cuba's cultural policy and to liken the regime's proceedings with the worst moments of the Stalinist era. Rejecting art for art's sake as forcibly as ever, he declared: 'We value cultural and artistic creations in their usefulness for the people, in what they bring to man, in what they bring to the recovery of man, to the liberation of man, to the happiness of man. Our valuation is political. There can be no aesthetic value without human content. There can be no aesthetic value against man.'[19]

Rather than expanding artistic freedom, the intervention of Western intellectuals had the opposite effect of increasing the regime's ideological control and cultural insularity. A new hard line emerged which has prevailed ever since. The congress called for an end to what it called 'ideological diversionism' (not following the straight and narrow Marxist-Leninist path) and 'cultural imperialism' (all foreign influences, especially from the West). Henceforth, cultural media would not be allowed to serve 'as an instrument for the proliferation of false intellectuals who pretend to transform snobbery, extravagance, homosexuality and other social aberrations into expressions of Revolutionary art, alienated from the masses and from the spirit of our Revolution.'[20] On the contrary, the congress insisted that 'art is an arm of the Revolution' and the great tasks of the writer must therefore be to fight elitism and develop the cultural progress of the masses.

This hard line on the over-riding political purpose of culture was reaffirmed in the thesis and resolution on artistic and literary culture of the first Congress of the Communist party held in 1975. Culture, it insists, must be directed to the formation of the New Man in the new society. The role of the critic must be 'to stimulate the wide diffusion of art for the masses, to serve the Revolution'. Criticism of socialist culture will not therefore be found in 'anarcho-bourgeois individualism' but in the principles of Marxism-Leninism. It follows that UNEAC must 'close ranks against imperialist cultural penetration and collaborate closely with the organs of the state and mass organizations in the elevation of the cultural level of our people'. And just as literature is expected to serve the Revolution, the Revolution, for which read 'state', has the right and duty 'to reject any attempt to use the work of art as an instrument or pretext to diffuse or to legitimize ideological positions adverse to socialism'.[21]

Official cultural policy in Cuba has evolved from the arguments in Castro's *Address to the Intellectuals* of 1961, the main conclusions of the first Congress of Education and Culture in 1971, and the thesis and resolution on culture of the first Congress of the Communist party in 1975. Its fundamental principles were outlined succinctly in the Constitution of the Republic drawn up in 1976. The state is given a central role in orientating, encouraging and promoting culture, the sciences and education. Its cultural policy itself is based unequivocally on 'the scientific conception of the world, established and developed by Marxism-Leninism' (Article 38). Artistic creation is free, the Constitution states, but with the familiar rider 'as long as its content is not against the Revolution' (Article 38).

In order to implement these policies, the Ministry of Culture was founded in 1976. The hard-line Communist and veteran of the Sierra Maestra, Armando Hart Dávolos—who had once declared that the USSR had become 'the undisputed technical and scientific leader in the world'—was appointed Minister of Culture.[22] At the second Congress of UNEAC held in March 1977, Minister Hart made his cultural views crystal clear. The essential objective and the *raison d'être* of intellectual work, he declared, 'is its ideological and political importance'. As such, he called on writers to be attentive to the ideological line of the Communist party, to combat 'ideological deviationism' and to adhere to the historical line of Cuban literature which he saw as being fundamentally realistic and progressive. Not fearful of making sweeping judgements in aesthetics as well as politics, the new functionary told the Congress (presided over by Nicolás Guillén) not only that 'the most beautiful way of writing is that which will serve the interests and aspirations of the people', but that literature which 'is decidedly counter-revolutionary cannot have any value, not even as literature'.[23]

More recently, Hart has expounded further the cultural policies of the Cuban government during a European tour. Aware of Cuba's Western critics, he argues that it is not the business of his ministry to tell writers and artists what to create, but 'to facilitate the development of all viable artistic forms, based on the country's cultural history and its resources'. But while stressing the need to avoid bureaucracy and to develop the 'broadest possible freedom for artistic creativity', he echoes the words of the Constitution by defining the role of the state in the cultural sphere as 'to co-ordinate, promote and encourage'. For him, the goal of the ministry is to create the necessary conditions for a socialist culture to flourish which is both diffuse (penetrating 'all aspects of life') and popular ('with deep roots in the people').[24]

In order to discover more about the present position of the writer and artist in Cuba, I went along to the Unión de Escritores y Artistas de Cuba (UNEAC), the Union of Cuban Writers and Artists, which rep-

resents film makers and dancers as well. Its president is still Nicolás
Guillén who entirely endorses and promotes the government's cultural
policies.

The headquarters of UNEAC is set in a sumptuous and luxurious
villa in the Vedado district of Havana. I was met by Joaquín G. Santana,
Director of Public Relations, a thoughtful bureaucrat, and by Luis Pavon, Director of International Relations, a mild white-haired man who
seemed more interested in literature than politics, although in Cuba the
two clearly cannot be separated.

Since UNEAC is a publishing house and publishes two lively journals,
Unión and *Gaceta de Cuba*, I began by asking about the way in which
a work is selected for publication. The work is first read by two or three
readers, Santana explained, but a final decision is made by an editorial
committee. The most important criterion is that the book must be well-
written; next, it must have imaginative value and originality. Santana
added:

> There is no problem with the political focus. We may not be always
> in agreement with the author, and may think that he could be better
> politically. We look for a universal focus; capitalism produced great
> art, but socialism has widened the scope of arts and made them more
> legitimate and true. Our editorial policy is very wide. It does not
> matter whether a writer is Catholic or socialist, as long as he is
> working within the Cuban Revolution. At the same time, there are
> those who write against the values of humanity. Some are sponsored
> by the enemies of socialism. We won't allow writers to misuse their
> liberty, or give them the right to fight socialism or to distort reality.

We then turned to the question of 'socialist realism' and I mentioned
Guevara's criticism of its 'frozen forms'. He recognized that the two
greatest Cuban writers to remain within the Revolution, Alejo Carpentier
and Nicolás Guillén, had a love of magic and fantasy. And although
he claimed that Cuban literature had a *tendencia realista*, especially
since the Revolution, this did not mean that writers are compelled to
be realistic: 'We do not impose a style on writers and artists; they
express themselves as they want. We are not for a capitalist form or a
socialist form. We think they can assimilate a heritage—surrealism,
pop art and so on—and reproduce it in a new way; you have to create
new forms for a new society.'

When we came to the thorny question of the freedom of expression,
my interlocutor became serious and didactic:

All discussions about liberty are based on a concept of liberty. Our own conception of liberty is not new; it has not evolved since the triumph of the Revolution but was formed centuries ago in our fight for independence. Felix Varela, the early nineteenth-century Catholic philosopher [who became a radical humanist and utilitarian] originated our concept of liberty. We were the last people in the Americas to free ourselves from colonialism and the first to free ourselves from imperialism. Since the Revolution, there has been a national awareness of liberty expressed in our direct knowledge of being free. Our liberty of course has its limits; in the prohibition of racial and sexual discrimination, for instance, or the use of drugs which diminish the dignity of man. But our notion of liberty has no point of contact, indeed it is in a state of everyday confrontation with, the American concept of liberty. When the Spanish first came here, the Indian leader Hatuey was offered the Christian idea of heaven—if the Spanish were to be found there, he wanted no part of it. Five centuries later, we say the same. If liberty is the liberty which Reagan offers us, we don't want it.

The Cuban concept of liberty, in this sense, would seem to mean primarily the freedom from external interference, whether military, economic or cultural.

After this long preamble about Cuba's historic conception of liberty, I tried to turn the conversation back to our opening theme of freedom of expression. The UNEAC director declared simply: 'If the book is not counter-revolutionary, or antagonistic, we can publish it. The author hasn't got to reflect directly the Revolution, he can even be a Catholic writer, but he cannot be *against* the Revolution.' We were back to Castro's criterion again. The key question is, what is it to be 'against the Revolution'? In practice, it seems to be whatever the Communist party ideologues in power define it to be. It is an elastic concept, which changes with the degree of confidence and security of the Revolutionary regime itself. In an attempt to clarify the concept, I asked what would happen to a writer who was brilliant but who might be a psychopath and even counter-revolutionary. The quiet old man, Luis Pavon, took up the question: 'Yes, that clearly is a problem—in the case of a Kafka, a Dostoevsky, or a Van Gogh, who were great writers and artists but also psychopaths. Their works should be presented to the people. Writers and artists are extra-sensitive people, and are acutely aware of the problems around them. We must respect them and help them to create.' Taking the bull by the horns, I raised the issue of exiled writers who had fallen foul of the Cuban authorities and whose cases had been widely publicized in the West, especially Heberto Padilla, Cabrera Infante and Armando Valladares. Santana was aware of the minefield he was treading:

Padilla is a prehistoric figure who acted against the Revolution and people. He was a sycophant and full of personal resentment. He preferred to leave Cuba because of his impotence and became the centre of an anti-Cuban campaign. His friend Cabrera Infante is another one, who by betraying the Revolution thought he would do well. He is now complaining of lack of success in capitalist Britain! As for Valladares, that is a truly scandalous case. Valladares was one of Batista's policemen and found guilty of counter-revolutionary terrorism, but our enemies made a poet out of the policeman. Padilla and Infante may have been writers, but not him!

Of course, many writers like the black poet Nancy Morejón remain. She earns her living as an editor of UNEAC's publishing house Letras Cubanas. She is quite clear about the social role of the writer: 'A writer has a distinct role in Cuban society. That role is to write well and to be useful. All writers should be useful to our people.' Indeed, she sees intellectuals as forming an elite who have a social duty to enlighten and inform the rest of society. She, of course, is 'within the Revolution' and finds no problem with being free to write what she chooses: 'I feel free with myself and my country. I am a product of this society and I agree with our political policy. I would never think of writing a verse or a poem against the realities of this Revolution, because I am proof of this Revolution. It would be suicide. These things are very poetic, sometimes people don't understand.'[25]

But apart from the difficulties encountered by writers who are not entirely wedded to Marxism-Leninism, or who do not write for the people in the approved way, there are other handicaps. The writer's economic as well as political lot is not a happy one. In 1967 Castro proposed that copyright on books should no longer be respected and that royalties to authors should not be paid, even to foreign writers. Private notions of property, he declared in a speech on 29 April 1967, were being replaced by collective ones in Cuba. This applied to 'intellectual property' as well as physical objects. Knowledge therefore should not be considered the property of an individual but as 'the patrimony of mankind'.[26] In addition, from a practical point of view, the excessive expense of paying royalties on foreign works often checked the pace of economic development in poor Third World countries. There is much which is accurate in this criticism of Western notions of intellectual property, but Cuba's decision to refuse to respect international copyright law meant that foreign writers did not receive royalties for their works published or 'pirated' in Cuba. Although international copyrights have been honoured since 1978, Cuban writers still do not receive royalties or retain copyright on their works.

Since the state does not pay writers a salary either, there are no professional writers in Cuba. They must earn their bread by other means—as journalists, editors, teachers, and so on. This is not always easily done; Ernesto Cardenal, for instance, found the great poet Lezama Lima living in poverty. 'Royalties,' the director of UNEAC told me, 'are a form of blackmail, since they appeal to the commercial instincts of writers and encourage them to write what sells rather than what is good. But even if royalties did exist in Cuba, they would not be great, as Cuban books are made and sold cheaply.' Although not paid according to their popularity or quality, however, Cuban writers are paid something. The present yardstick for pecuniary awards is quantity—the number of pages they write. A Cuban Dickens or Tennyson would thus do considerably better than a Kafka or a T. S. Eliot.

The limits of freedom of expression have of course given rise to some of the bitterest criticisms of Cuba in the West. But Cuban officials openly admit that the state practises censorship and limits criticism. Castro justified the policy because of the strength of the counter-revolution. He explained his position frankly in July 1977 in an interview with the American journalist Barbara Walters. When asked why he did not allow dissent in the media or an opposition paper, he replied:

> Naturally, our concept of freedom of the press is different from yours, and I tell you so honestly, since I have absolutely nothing to hide. If you were to ask whether a paper against socialism could be published here, I will tell you frankly that the answer would be no. The government, party and people would not allow it . . . Our mass media serve the Revolution.[27]

Castro's slogan 'Everything within the Revolution; nothing against the Revolution' is sufficiently general to be applicable to virtually any work or person Cuban officials choose to condemn. What is meant by the Revolution is left vague, but it has taken on an abstract, independent force. The 'Revolution' sanctions and excuses all; it is the ultimate court of appeal. In practice, the leaders often use the term as if it were synonymous with the state, for whatever is for or against the Revolution is really whatever is for or against the state.

The attitude of the regime in its cultural as well as its educational policies is thus highly paternalistic. A considerable degree of freedom of expression would seem to exist at the elite level, but the government tends to treat the citizens of Cuba as if they were children incapable of recognizing moral or intellectual truths, and in constant danger of being misled. The way to deal with the threat of 'cultural imperialism' and 'ideological deviationism' is simply to shut the doors on them. Yet this is clearly a sign of weakness, not strength. It would appear that the present Cuban leaders have no great confidence in the ability of Marxism-Leninism to defeat its intellectual critics, otherwise they would allow opposition, satire and criticism. Cubans may have been given the tools with which to think, but they have not been allowed to use them freely.

12

CULTURE WITHIN THE REVOLUTION

Every Saturday night the Calle Heredia in Santiago de Cuba is closed to traffic and becomes the venue for a dynamic expression of Cuba's Revolutionary culture. A black woman sings arias from Falla in the foyer of the city library; a folklore group performs ancient slave dances on the patio of one of their former masters; through the open windows of a restored colonial mansion the strains of a tango can be heard. The house where the early nineteenth century writer José María de Heredia was born has been turned into a museum illustrating the life and work of Cuba's first great poet. Spacious buildings with painting exhibitions and poetry readings entice the passers-by. A puppet theatre and an open-air cinema vie for the attention of the children, opposite the Museum of the Carnival. Under a starry sky, late revellers gather round a *rumba* band playing in front of Santiago's music centre, the Casa de la Trova, its walls plastered with photographs of Cuba's famous troubadours. When the lights go out in the early hours, groups of black and white *santiagüeros* wander home chatting and laughing, their heads full of music, poetry, rum and stars in the balmy night. The whole event is put on free by the government to promote Cuba's culture and it is clear that people of all ages, not merely a few intellectuals, enjoy the entertainment and enlightenment on offer.

Well aware of the need to change people's consciousness as well as the economic life of the country, Castro's regime has made considerable efforts to develop a socialist culture. With no private market for art works or royalties for books, no independently run theatre or gallery, the state is the one and only sponsor in cultural activities. But it has not been parsimonious in its patronage. There is a National Symphony Orchestra, National Chorus, National Dance Group, National Ballet and National Folklore Group. In most major towns the government provides a library, museum, art gallery, theatre, Casa de la Cultura and Casa de la Trova. In addition to the national groups and museums, the government regularly promotes cultural activities throughout the country. There are regular poetry, ballet and music performances. Travelling libraries, cinemas and even theatres bring the benefits of high culture to the suburbs and the countryside. International festivals of music and film are held annually, attracting great numbers of visitors. But behind this enormous outburst of state-sponsored culture, there is an overriding purpose—to serve and consolidate the Revolution.

From the moment Radio Rebelde crackled into the airwaves in 1958 from the Sierra Maestra, Castro and his comrades recognized the prime importance of the mass media in shaping the people's ideas and values. It was recognized at the first National Congress on Education and Culture in 1971, that: 'Mass media are powerful tools for ideological formation. They help develop social consciousness and their utilization and development should not be the result of chance improvization and spontaneity.'[1]

The principal national newspaper is *Granma*, the official organ of the Central Committee of the Communist party. It has been called an exhortation sheet. It is certainly full of speeches by Castro and the party faithful and Marxist-Leninist in orientation. Unlike Western newspapers, it dwells on social and economic processes rather than current events or personalities. It gives full coverage to news about economic development in the country—urging, for instance, the provinces to produce more through 'socialist emulation' during the sugar harvest. There is only a sprinkling of carefully sifted foreign news, with features illustrating the decadence of capitalism in the United States such as drug abuse or ghetto poverty, or reports on the heroic achievements of socialism such as the Soviet space programme or the Angolan Revolution. But while predictable, *Granma* is not as dull as *Pravda* on which it is modelled; its design is better and its style is more flamboyant. Above all, its level is generally more intelligent than the tabloids of the West. People queue in the morning to get their copy of *Granma* and it quickly sells out.

Granma is followed daily by an evening paper of the Union of Young Communists called *Juventud Rebelde*. In addition there are trade union papers such as *Trabajadores* of the CTC, papers of the mass organizations like *Mujeres* of the FMC, children's papers like *Pionero*, regional papers like *Sierra Maestra* in Oriente, sports papers and comics. The armed forces have the influential *Verde Olivo*. *Bohemia* has been a long-standing general weekly, while *Prisma* and *Tricontinental* are aimed at an internationalist audience to extol Cuba's cultural and revolutionary achievements. In all, there are more than a hundred newspapers, magazines and specialized journals published in Cuba. Each one has primary responsibility for editorial policy but they can be relied on to toe the party line. The bookstalls are also full of publications from Communist countries, but no Western papers are on sale.

While the press is undoubtedly a government tool used to control and educate the people, it serves different functions and provides opportunities for some feedback from readers. Indeed, a new spirit of criticism has recently become discernible in the press. The statutes of the Communist party insist on the 'practice of criticism' and the 'self-criticism of our own errors' in the dialectic of becoming a good Communist.[2] The government has even called upon journalists to be more aggressive in rooting out grievances and abuses. Therefore *Granma* is beginning to carry articles and letters calling attention to abuses of power or shortages and disruptions in the economy: lack of beer during carnivals, dirty beach hotels, and *machismo* have all become subjects of discussion. A lively consumer monthly *Opina* also invites readers to criticize services and distribution networks.

But while criticism is encouraged, it is always 'within the Revolution'; it must only touch upon practical difficulties and ideological deviations. The ambivalent position of journalists was summed up inadvertently by Raúl Castro at the fourth Congress of the Union of Cuban Journalists in March 1980. As he left the rostrum, he shouted to the journalists: 'Criticize all you want; the party is behind you!'[3] But the party, as its statutes make clear, remains faithful to Marxism-Leninism and will defend its particular interpretation of the ideology 'against all rightist and leftist deviations and against attacks and deformations of the bourgeois theorists, revisionists and pseudo-Marxist dogmatists'.[4]

The regime has not only used the press for its propagandist purposes. The Cuban Revolution is the first major one to have made full use of television to spread its influence. Castro was fortunate in inheriting a broadcasting service that was well established by Latin American standards. Quickly realizing its potential, he made regular weekly appearances on television, often speaking for up to four hours, explaining the goals of the Revolution in the country's longest running one-man show. Under the directorship of Major Jorge Serguera, the Judge Advocate in the Rebel Army, the television service was cut down from seven to two channels. Programmes were completely reorganized to reinforce the people's political motivation, to raise cultural awareness, and to supplement school and adult education. The network became controlled by the Instituto Cubano de Radiodifusión. It now ensures that educational and cultural programmes have twice as much time as news and information, while light entertainment follows in third place. About 60 per cent of programmes are now made locally; the rest are mainly imported films and documentaries. The whole exercise is aimed, as Castro made clear at the first Congress of the Communist party in 1975, at 'fulfilling a social function, informing, entertaining, developing good taste'.[5]

The programmes can be quite varied, entertaining and internationalist in content. It is possible to see during a night's viewing a Spanish cartoon, a tango competition, a Czech film, a pirated pop video, a local documentary on civil defence, and an English comedy series. Instead of commercials, information bulletins cut in to criticize schoolboys loafing in the streets, or to persuade the overweight to take exercise. There is a regular 'Science and Health' feature, and one called 'Towards New Victories' celebrating the achievements in building socialism. Music and sports are particularly well catered for. The news is analysed from a clear Marxist-Leninist viewpoint, with the main emphasis placed on economic progress, social events and cultural activities in Cuba. International news tends to be limited to good stories from socialist countries. Films, particularly Western films, are often shown usually with a commentary to explain their ideological content. In recent years these have included international hits such as *Tom Jones*, *ET*, *Gandhi*, and *Jaws*. An immensely popular programme at the weekend is *Historia de la Película* when a famous film is shown with a commentary by a critic from the ICAIC: I saw him deftly reduce *Flash Gordon* to the theme of fascist superman produced by monopoly capitalism.

The radio network is more widely dispersed but has a similar ideological function. There are nine channels, some with revolutionary names such as Radio Rebelde, Radio Liberación, Radio Progresivo. They usually offer a diet of groovy music, political homily, public information, popular culture and, of course, news. Radio Reloj, which has a clock ticking constantly in the background, offers a 24-hour news service while trying to make Cubans more time-conscious and productive. There is Radio Municipal Nacional which offers music concerts, and Radio Enciclopedia which broadcasts only instrumental music from around the world.

Havana has its own Radio Metropolitan. The guerrillas' Radio Rebelde, first heard transmitting from the Sierra Maestra in 1958, is now the 'home service' station, mixing music, magazine items, sport, drama, and interviews. Radio Habana Cuba broadcasts to the region and has an extensive overseas service with programmes in Spanish, English, French, Portuguese, Arabic, Creole and other languages.

In terms of quantity of output of literature there has been remarkable progress. Since the first publishing venture of an edition of Cervantes' *Don Quijote*, Cuba now publishes some 50 million books a year, 35 million of which are for education and the rest in the fields of art, literature, science, economics and politics. Before the Revolution there were no Cuban publishers. There are also 13 state-controlled publishing houses (ten of which come under the umbrella of the Minister of Culture) which include Editorial Política, Letras Cubanas of UNEAC, Casa de las Américas, and Editorial José Martí for books in foreign languages. Whereas the national distribution of books before the Revolution was 0.6 per capita, it is now 5.6. There has been a massive effort to edit forgotten Cuban texts as well as Latin America's most important books. Many translations of the classics of European and North American literature have appeared. But there are strange lacunae. Writers like Jorge Luis Borges, Octavio Paz and Pablo Neruda, who have been at the centre of cultural activity in the Hispanic world since the Revolution, are noticeably absent. They are, like Jean-Paul Sartre or George Orwell, no doubt suspect on ideological grounds, whatever their literary merit.

In Havana's main bookshop, La Poesía Moderna, there are vast stands devoted to the works of Martí, Guevara, Castro, as might be expected. Dominating all is the section on *Marxismo-Leninismo*. When I asked for the philosophy section, I was directed to this section; there is no other devoted to the subject. But even here the choice is limited. There are Marx, Lenin and Engels, but no Mao or Trotsky. Pablo Lafargue, better known as Paul, a radical doctor of Cuban ancestry who married Marx's daughter Laura, has many editions of his selected works available.

Castro once complained that before the Revolution in stores in the mountains you could find books on philosophy—even Marx and Engels—but not on farming.[6] The Revolution has changed all that, but now there are books on farming and not on philosophy. Indeed, most of the books on sale are of a technical and scientific nature. There is a substantial section on poetry, but mainly of Nicolás Guillén and other patriotic poets. Popular novels come in the form of mass-produced political thrillers which show heroic Cubans outwitting CIA agents or defeating their enemies. New titles are snatched up in a flash. While there are many books from the Communist bloc, I saw only one or two works from the West. This is perhaps not surprising because of the fear of 'capitalist subversion', the shortage of foreign exchange to buy the books, and the refusal of the Cuban government from 1968 to 1979 to recognize the international law on copyright. Nevertheless, despite the shortage of foreign books to buy in the shops, the literature available in the public libraries does not seem to have been purged or censored so radically.

But despite the phenomenal increase in book production and the availability of local and foreign literary classics, there has not been a corresponding flowering of Cuban writers in recent years. The towering figures of the Cuban literary scene—José Lezama Lima, Alejo Carpentier and Nicolás Guillén—all established their reputations well before the Revolution. The Catholic poet Lima founded (with Fayad Jamís and Roberto Fernández Retamar) *Orígenes* (1944–57), the most important literary magazine of the pre-revolutionary period. Lima supported the Revolution at first, but after his novel *Paradiso* (1966), fell into disrepute. Ernesto Cardenal found him living in virtual internal exile, although more recently Minister of Culture Armando Hart Dávalos has denied that he was isolated from the mainstream of Cuban life.

Alejo Carpentier, undoubtedly Cuba's greatest novelist this century, was criticized for remaining silent during his self-imposed exile during the Batista era, but he supported the Revolution from afar and became Cuba's cultural attaché in Paris. He was eventually elected as a deputy to the National Assembly before he died. Nicolás Guillén, a long-standing Communist, has flourished most under the Revolutionary regime, narrowly applying the government's restrictive cultural policy as President of UNEAC. The poet Roberto Fernández Retamar, vice president of the Casa de las Américas publishing house, and Fayad Jamís are also uncritical supporters of the regime.

Younger writers have not fared so well. Those associated with El Puente publishing house from 1960 to 1965 were accused of sins which were aesthetic (transcendentalism), moral (homosexuality) and political (liberalism). The purer Nancy Morejón and Miguel Barnet, however, went on to merit state patronage. Other writers who fell foul of the regime, like Cabrera Infante, who left in 1965, Heberto Padilla and Reinaldo Arenas, who both left in 1980, were unable to flourish in the repressive cultural atmosphere. Some good novels appeared in the 1960s by new writers like Edmundo Desnoes' *Memorias del subdesarallo* (1965) and José Soler Puig's *El derrambe* (1964), but they did not deal directly with the Revolution, rather the world of private experience. In a famous interview in Paris in 1964, Alejo Carpentier said the burden of creating revolutionary novels would fall on the shoulders of the next generation: 'Twenty years from now we will be able to read the literary products of the New Cuba'.[7] As yet, no great new poet or novelist has emerged to earn an international reputation. The main new development in Cuban literature has been in the form of the documentary and reportage.

The literary system since the 1970s has been characterized as nothing more than 'the spotting [of] books that will serve as tools of mass indoctrination'.[8] There has however been a relative liberalization this decade, no doubt due to a growing sense of political security and awareness that artistic freedom is essential if literature is to flourish.[9] The

Colombian novelist Gabriel García Márquez, for instance, who once incurred Castro's wrath by signing the letter of protest about Padilla's persecution, is now a regular presence in literary Havana. As in the the Soviet Union, there is a new feeling of openness in the air.

Before the Revolution, there was little tradition of drama in Cuba, although small private theatres in Havana were showing plays by Sartre, Genet and Lorca. In 1959, the National Theatre was created in an attempt to develop new Cuban theatre, but like the other branches of literature it suffered from the new Revolutionary puritanism from about 1963. Apart from José Triana's *La noche de los asesinos* few memorable plays have emerged. Political themes are expected from young playwrights, while the backbone of the repertoire is safe international classics. However, one interesting development has been the Escambray Theatre Group, founded in 1968, which takes plays to the countryside and sees theatre as a Revolutionary activity.

In a country where the regime sees itself as an inevitable outcome of historical forces and which looks to its history to forge a national identity, it is not surprising that historical studies should have flourished. Marxist historians like Manuel Moreno Fraginals, author of *El ingenio* (1964), Julio de Riverend, author of *Historia económica de Cuba* (1974), and Juan Pérez de la Riva, editor of the scholarly *Revista de la Biblioteca Nacional*, have developed the high standards set by Ramiro Guerra and Fernando Ortíz. The journal *Cuba Socialista* also published some original articles on Cuban labour history before it was discontinued. Unfortunately, the regime's desire to highlight the revolutionary aspects of Cuba's past and to justify the historical destiny of Castro and the Communist party has led to some distortions. This approach comes through in *Historia de Cuba* (1967), the main historical text used in secondary schools, which was first compiled by the political board of the Revolutionary Armed Forces. As a result, the so-called Marxist study of history is turned into a vehicle of political propaganda with a crude emphasis on economic forces. The Instituto de Historia del Movimiento Comunista y de la Revolución Socialista, set up in 1975, continues this trend.

Because it is less overtly ideological, art (especially painting) has been less prone to censorship. With outstanding painters like Marcelo Pogolotti in the 1930s, and Wilfredo Lam, René Portocarrero, Luis Martínez Pedro, Amelia Peláez and Jorge Arche in the 1940s and 1950s, Cuba had already earned an international reputation for fine art before the Revolution. Despite the efforts of diehard Communists like Blas Roca to impose a form of realism in art, the Revolutionary regime permitted a considerable degree of artistic freedom.

Che Guevara's comments on art in *Socialism and Man* provided solid revolutionary grounds for experimentation. Adopting a classic Marxist position, Guevara argues that man tries to defend his 'oppressed individuality' and to free himself from alienation in capitalist society through culture and art. With the Revolution, however, artistic enquiry gains a new impulse. While condemning the escapist concept of total artistic freedom as bourgeois idealism, Guevara equally rejects the 'frozen forms' of socialist realism which arose in the nineteenth century. He warns against putting a strait-jacket on the artistic expression of the New Man. Indeed, the New Man in the new society must be able to express himself in new forms: 'To sing the song of the New Man in the true voice of the people'.[10]

Castro would have nothing to do with art for art's sake; it must have a moral if not a political purpose: 'Art', he stressed, 'is not an end in itself. Man is the end. Making men happier, better.'[11] His personal taste is reflected in the realistic Mural de la Prehistoria which he sponsored Leovigildo González to paint on a limestone knoll in Viñales Valley. Yet even Castro defended artistic freedom in a formal sense. When 'Russia's satellites in Havana' asked him to ban abstract painting as Khrushchev had done (Khrushchev believed that only homosexuals could be abstract painters) Castro declared: 'Our enemies are capitalism and imperialism, not abstract painting'.[12]

It was still possible for the Parisian Salon de Mai to exhibit its work in July 1967 in Havana. In an outburst of Revolutionary fervour, an immense scaffold was erected in the Vedado district for some 60 artists from different countries to create a collective mural in front of a large crowd of *habaneros*. Dancers from La Tropicana enacted Revolutionary scenes on stage in the street during this surrealist happening, to entertain the crowd as they witnessed the collective work of art slowly taking shape.

This artistic freedom is reflected in the rooms devoted to post-revolutionary art in the National Museum of Fine Art in Havana. They are a delight to the eye. There is abstract expressionism, surrealism, abstract art, pop art, op art. But the styles absorbed from Europe and North America have been made their own by the Cuban artists, as can be seen in the work of Servando Cabrera Moreno, Raúl Martínez and Raúl Milían. In the 1970s there can be discerned a move towards primitivism as in Manuel Mendive's work, or to ultra-realism, as in that of Flavio Garcíandia and Aldo Menéndez.

Sculpture, unlike painting, has become an art form heavily sponsored by the state. The functionaries in the Ministry of Culture most approve of works like the bust of Lenin hewn from a great mass of stone which stands in Lenin Park outside Havana. Designed by a Russian artist and executed by Cuban craftsmen, it is completely lifeless in its heroic pose; the statue of José Martí by the Cuban sculptor Sicre in Revolutionary Square is certainly more vibrant.

The most prolific sculptress is Rita Longa, whose works can be seen in public places all over the country, whether they be of Indians in Guamá village, a cock in Morón, or a fountain in Las Tunas. The latter town is scattered with sculptures, left after a congress held there in 1978, which give an idea of the officially approved sculpture. José Antonio Díaz Peláez has celebrated a beloved theme in his 'Monument to Work', while a strong nationalist theme is to be found in Manuel Chiong's tall 'Liberation of the People' which is placed opposite the provincial People's Power Assembly, and shows two rifles breaking a chain. However, the most interesting works are of an Indian and of a country troubadour by Ángel Iñigo Blanco. Blanco has also carved a remarkable stone zoo of animals out of the side of a hill near Guantánamo.

Cuban architecture has long been famous for its distinctive and varied styles. The colonial architecture of Havana, Trinidad or Santiago de Cuba was the pride of the New World; the baroque followed the Moorish style, only to vie with the neo-classical in the nineteenth century. The remarkable profusion of styles earlier this century is evident in the Christopher Columbus cemetery in Havana, where ornate baroque contrasts with Le Corbusier-style modernism. In the 1920s and 1930s the extravagance of the rich gave rise to a delightful range of architectural eccentricities although the neo-classical column remained a dominant motif. Then in the 1950s the new skyscrapers in Havana took on a sub-Miami style. Since the Revolution, however, the new buildings have been starkly functional and utilitarian. The new low-rise housing estates have been built to a Bulgarian design known locally as the Girón system. Made from pre-fabricated blocks, they have spawned themselves like clones throughout the island. Most of the new hotels, hospitals, and schools are also prefabricated and based on a common 'H' plan; their monotony is only occasionally relieved by a splash of plain colour or a mural. There are no major new buildings which can be considered architectural masterpieces.

Cuban design in general is good. There is no great tradition of carving or weaving, and the local arts and crafts—as a search of the tourist shops reveals—tend to be roughly made. Graphic design, on the other hand, has come into its own. This is apparent in paper and book design: the literary magazine *Lunes* for instance used to play with letters in a Dadaist way. Such experimentation has been suppressed, but even the

Communist tabloid *Granma* uses clean graphics in a futurist manner. Above all, Cuban posters have been rightly praised for their boldness and originality.

They fall roughly into four categories: cultural posters, posters about different national liberation struggles, posters about the political history of Cuba, and posters about everyday life, exhorting the Cuban people to build a better world. Many commentators like Susan Sontag have placed a misleading emphasis on cultural posters which publicize film, ballet and other events, but the political ones dominate by far. The verges of the main roads in the countryside are plastered with great hoardings pointing out how different regions are building socialism. Castro's profile lights up in red neon on the Malecón in Havana, but the most famous figures are Martí and Guevara who have been reduced to highly stylized icons. The stamps, formerly printed abroad, are also impressively designed. A complete collection of those printed since the Revolution can be seen in the Stamp Museum in Havana. Like the posters, they are used unashamedly for propaganda purposes.

The Cuban film industry, without a tradition or history before the Revolution, has earned a well-deserved international reputation. The Instituto Cubano del Arte e Industria Cinematográficos (ICAIC) was set up in 1959 to develop and supervise the industry. As an important means of mass communication, the cinema is under tight control. Nevertheless, directors like Tomás Gutiérrez Alea, Sara Gómez, Humberto Solás, Manuel Octavio Gómez and Sergio Giral have been able to make astonishingly original works. Tomás Gutiérrez Alea came to prominence with his remarkable *La muerte de un burocrata* (Death of a Bureaucrat) in 1966, a brilliant satire about a corpse which has difficulty getting buried. This was followed by *Memorias del subdesarallo* (Memories of Underdevelopment) in 1968 based on the novel by Eduardo Desnoes about an uncommitted intellectual who observes the Revolution from the fringes. More recently, Alea has directed *La ultima cena* (The Last Supper) (1976), an ironic fable about a plantation owner who decides to celebrate Holy Week by inviting 12 of his slaves to dinner: his demonstration of Christian charity misfires and a slave revolt follows.

The most famous film to come out of revolutionary Cuba is *Lucia* (1968) by Humberto Solás. It is an epic in three episodes about three women called Lucía who come from different social classes and are involved to varying degrees in Cuba's struggles for independence in different epochs. On a different theme, *Retrato de Teresa* (Portrait of Teresa): (1979) by Pastor Vega is concerned with the struggle of a modern young Cuban woman with her *macho* husband. Sergio Giral has directed an impressive trilogy on slavery in *El otro Francisco* (The

Other Francisco) (1974), *Rancheador* (Slave Hunter) (1976) and *Maluala* (1979). Manuel Octavio Gómez in *La prima carga al machete* (The First Machete Charge) (1969) has also used experimental techniques to portray an episode at the start of the Wars of Independence.

Aware of the popularity of film, the ICAIC was quick to realize its value as an instrument of political education. Sophisticated techniques are used to reach a mass audience, as can be seen in the documentaries of Santiago Alvarez, such as *Hanoi Tuesday 13th* (1967) and *LBJ* (1968); or of Sara Gómez, such as *Local Power, Popular Power* (1970), *Pre-Natal Attention* (1970) and *On Overtime and Voluntary Work* (1973). Octavio Cortazar's *For the First Time* (1967) about mobile cinemas bringing films to peasants, and Sergio Giral's *The Death of J. J. Jones* (1966) about an American GI in Vietnam, have remained classics. Other documentaries have covered subjects as wide-ranging as the literacy campaign, African religion, Castro's trip to Africa, and Cuban women. In addition to the wave of social documentaries and educational films, there have been newsreels and cartoons of impressive quality.

Recent feature films have been concerned with relations between the sexes, and especially the position of women in Cuban society. Humberto Solás in *Amada* (1983) has used the historical period of 1914 to portray a repressed gentlewoman who falls in love with her radical young cousin but is unable either to consummate their relationship or escape her situation. She wastes away, a victim of her own class and time, while the real political action takes place in the streets. On the other hand, Rolando Díaz's comedy, *Los pájaros tirándole a las escopetas* (Birds Will Fly) (1985) is set in contemporary Havana and deals with the theme of widowed or single parents being entitled to love again. It not only has a sideswipe at overcrowding in Havana, where lovers young and old have great difficulty in finding privacy, but also attacks ever-present *machismo* (the hopes of the entire family for a son are dashed when the heroine gives birth to twin girls). A more profound analysis of *machismo* comes in Alea's *Hasta cierto punto* (Up to a Point) (1984) which explores the affair between a scriptwriter researching for a film about *machismo* in the docks and an unmarried mother who is a dock worker and trade unionist.

Cuban film directors, like all other artists and writers, work within certain permitted limits. Jorge Fraga, head of production at ICAIC, prefers to talk of self-censorship rather than censorship. Directors have absolute artistic control over what they produce but their freedom is tempered by their 'collective sense of responsibility'—in other words, they know what can or can't be shown in the Cuban context. The directors are expected 'to rescue and affirm the identity of Latin American and Caribbean countries' and 'to defend their peoples' cultural values and shared characteristics against deforming imperialist interference'.[13]

While the Cuban film industry has notched up some remarkable achievements, the sophisticated Cuban audiences enjoy foreign as well as local films. In the early days of the Revolution, there was a great interest in avant-garde, existentialist movies from France and Italy. But the cultural *apparatchiks* soon started to control the flow—Communist party secretary Blas Roca tried, unsuccessfully at the time, to stop the import of Fellini's films, especially *La dolce vita*, because of its allegedly corrupting influence. Modern films which are universal box office hits still get through, such as *Jaws*, *Gandhi* and *ET*. During my journey round the island, I saw *Lolita* and *The Seven Samurai* on show in the provincial town of Santa Clara. In an open-air cinema for children in Santiago de Cuba there was a showing of the Robin Hood series made in Elstree Studios in England in the 1950s.

Television has not yet replaced the cinema as mass public entertainment. All major cities have at least one cinema, and admission is never more than a peso. It is the queue rather than the price which is offputting. Small towns and villages in the country are visited by *cine moviles*, travelling cinema shows. Cuban audiences are incredibly enthusiastic by European standards, clapping, shouting and laughing at dramatic moments during the films.

But for all the new emphasis on the written word and the visual symbol, Cuban culture is still overwhelmingly oral. Music is the opium and the ecstasy of the people. Wherever you go in Havana you hear music: in restaurants, in bars, in taxis, in the streets, on the beach, you hear music, music. The most popular seems to fall into four categories: romantic crooners of the Spanish and American varieties; ballad singers and troubadours, known as *trovadores*; jazz; and African-inspired Cuban sounds. Strangely enough, although perfectly in keeping with the American-style skyscrapers, I repeatedly heard Glen Miller's wartime classic 'In the Mood'. Black American soul music is very popular, but reggae from nearby Jamaica (despite Bob Marley's stature as a cultural hero and Eddie Grant's rapturous welcome at the 1985 International Music Festival) does not seem to have caught on. However, as a friend told me, the most important aspect of music for Cubans is the rhythm: 'You Europeans like music to listen to; we Cubans must have music to dance to.' Whenever music was played, I noticed Cubans would unconsciously tap their fingers or feet to the beat. Fernando Ortiz has rightly called Cuban music the offspring of the love affair between the Spanish guitar and African drums.

The Spanish elements of Cuban music are clear in *guajira* or country music in which the singer also plays guitar. Its greatest exponent was Joseito Fernández, whose country song of the 1940s, *Guantanamera*, was made internationally famous by the American folk-singer Pete Seeger. It is derived via Spain from the French *contredanse* and has a formal structure with a strict rhythm but its melodies are often varied. More recently, the verses of José Martí have been put to the music of *Guantanamera*, to produce one of the most popular songs in Cuba today.

The ballad, or *trova*, the Cuban version of the medieval European ballad form, has also had a long history in the country, but developed into a popular form in Oriente towards the end of the last century. The ballads often recount stories of love, or great historical events. Almost every major city has a Casa de la Trova, a music centre where *trovadores* perform regularly. Since the Revolution, a *nueva trova* or new ballad movement has developed, in which young Cubans have set their politically-conscious poetry to renovated musical forms. Professionals and amateurs participate, revitalizing an old tradition and conveying new messages. The most famous singers like Pablo Milanés and Silvio Rodríguez are at one with the regime, putting on a show during my visit in 1984 to journalists the night before Castro's key 26 July speech.

Classical music is much appreciated; a national orchestra makes the best of European music available to the people. Ballet, too, has become a Cuban passion. I managed to watch a brilliant performance of Alicia Alonso, now almost blind, in her most celebrated role, *Giselle*. After a meteoric career in the American Ballet Theatre, Alicia Alonso, the 'First Lady of Cuba' as she is known, founded the ballet in Havana in 1948. During the Batista dictatorship she went into exile, declaring in a manifesto of the company in 1953 that: 'No longer will ballet be the art of kings and rulers, but rather the art of the people and for the people.' With the triumph of the Revolution six years later, she and her company returned to Havana. The guerrillas led by Castro and Guevara recognized in 1959 that 'ballet is without doubt one of the finest and most beautiful forms of art expression', and awarded a generous grant to form a National Ballet.[14] Not long after, the British critic Arnold Haskell hailed the ballet as a 'Cuban miracle'.[15] The company now has grown to over one hundred members, half of whom travel abroad, while the other half stay at home performing not only in theatres but also in workplaces.

Jazz, made popular in Cuba by great exponents like Benny Moré in the 1940s, is still much appreciated. Local bands fuse Cuban rhythms with jazz improvization, taking advantage of the latest electronic sounds. The first English voice I happened to hear in my hotel in Havana was that of the leading British jazz musician Ronnie Scott, who had brought his group to play at the annual International Jazz Festival in Havana. He felt that Cuba's political isolation from the West had in no way impaired its appreciation of the latest developments in Western jazz. He was so impressed by what he had heard that he invited the top musician Chucho Valdés and his group Irakere, and the groups of Arturo Sandoval and the up-and-coming Gonzalo Rubalcava to play in London in 1985. They were received with great critical acclaim and dispelled earlier criticisms that Cuban jazz was losing its originality. Irakere in particular is looking to classical European music for inspiration, while retaining its powerful Cuban drive.

Cuba, of course, has one of the richest and most original traditions of music and dance. It has given the world, before the Revolution, the *conga*, *cha cha cha*, *mambo*, *rumba*, *son* and *guaracha*. *Salsa* (meaning sauce), the urban music combining many different rhythms which is sweeping Latin America and the United States today, is also claimed by Cubans to be of Cuban origin, developed by exiles abroad. Its rhythms are very close to the rhythms of the *son*.

Some Cuban dances contain European elements like the *danzón*, which uses very formal movements from the eighteenth-century French and English *contredanse*. Since its rhythm is a little like ragtime, it was principally accepted by the white bourgeoisie towards the end of the last century. It came up with the inimitable *Manisero* (Peanut Vendor) in the thirties.

However, most of Cuba's dances and music come from African sources, particularly via the African-inspired religious cults. The cults not only continue to exist clandestinely, but since the Revolution the music and dance traditions have been kept alive in their pure form by the National Folklore Group. Santería, a blend of Yoruba religion and Catholicism, for instance, has supplied many songs sung in Yoruba by a male lead singer leading a chorus to the rhythm of *conga* drums, while dancers dressed in different colours express the attributes of the different *orishas* or saints of the sect. The Abakuá or Carabalí sect has also made an important contribution to Cuban music, although its secret drums or *batas* were never played outside the sect before 1930. Their orchestra is made up of four drums of different sizes, the largest beaten with two sticks, a pair of tambourines, and a curved metallic disc instrument played with a stick. These make a distinctive contribution to the Santiago Carnival. The *iremes* or *diablitos* (little devils) who represent the spirits of the dead and who communicate with movements of their hands, have become important folk dancers. It is the most secret and sinister sect, Palo Monte or Regla Mayombé, whose members use human remains in their worship of nature, that has most contributed to Cuban music. Their drums are cylindrical in shape, and the intricate rhythms they create in their sacred houses have echoed across the world in one form or another. The famous *rumba, conga, mambo* and *son,* can all be traced back to *palero* dances.

Many of Cuba's popular dances which developed before the Revolution have maintained their appeal. There are still *cha cha cha* and *tango* competitions, slow *boleros* are danced with as much enthusiasm as fast *mambos.* Popular groups like Los Van Van have set new themes to the old rhythms, such as a recent hit which declared that overcrowded 'Havana can take no more'. The *son,* which has taken elements from the *danzón,* is particularly popular as a musical form; it is, I was told, 'the most sublime way of touching the soul'.

Be that as it may, the country which produced so many fresh dances early in this century has developed little distinctively new since the Revolution apart from the *nueva trova* movement. Many young people are frankly bored with the traditional sounds, and listen to Western pop beamed from the US for entertainment. Some commentators have seen this as the failure of the new socialist culture, with its limits on artistic freedom, to generate a creative environment. The phenomenal originality of Cuban music earlier this century however was probably due to the sudden discovery of the musical forms of the African religious cults. There is now no such tradition to stimulate a new musical wave.

Even so, the old traditions of music and dance are as strong and popular as ever. The *rumba,* born in the slums of Havana at the turn of the century, remains a central Cuban institution. *'Yo soy rumbero',* I was told by one young fan. It not only means that he likes to dance the *rumba,* but that the *rumba* expresses a whole view of life, with its own particular loves, dreams and hopes. *'Cuba es rumba',* I was also told. 'Study the *rumba* and you can learn what makes Cubans tick.'

The popular expression of Cuban music and dance is undoubtedly the carnival, which is put on in every town in Cuba after the *zafra* or sugar harvest, in July or August. The biggest carnival takes place in Havana on the Malecón, but the most authentic and colourful carnival in Latin America takes place in the city of Santiago de Cuba in the country's Oriente region. For five days and nights in the latter half of July, Santiago, sweltering in tropical heat, vibrates to the clatter and thud of tom toms, to the cries of men and women in the ecstasy of dance, to the gyrating presence of its African ancestors.

The Santiago carnival originated in the eighteenth century when it was customary to mark the end of the Catholic religious ceremony on 25 July with noisy outbursts of dance and song. These outbursts were originally known as *fiestas de los mamarrachos*, as the participants would dress up in extravagant clothes. Street parties soon turned into processions, or *comparsas* through the city, and while organized chiefly for and by the blacks and mulattos, many whites would join in.

Neighbourhood groups were formed of dancers from different sects who would compete with each other and develop distinctive styles of their own. The most famous local dance tradition is the *tumba francesa* (French drum), which has its origin in the culture of the slaves brought to the east of Cuba by French planters fleeing the revolution in Haiti at the end of the eighteenth century. These slaves, mainly Arara people from Benin, maintained their traditional music but adopted French eighteenth-century *contredanses* from the *salons* of their white masters. As a result their elegant and formal dancing, usually performed by a king and queen and their court, dancing alone or in pairs, contrasts with the African rhythms of their drums and rattles. The *carabalís* of the Abakuá cult are particularly influential in providing the drums of different sizes and the curved metallic disc-shaped instrument known as the *ekon* which is played with a stick—now replaced by a brake-disc from a car, beaten with an iron rod. It is the *paleros* of Regla Mayombé, however, who have contributed the most distinctive dances of the carnival—the *conga* and the *rumba*. The cornet, brought by the indentured Chinese workers in the middle of the last century, has also become an essential complement to the traditional drums and rattles, while trumpets, trombones, clarinets and, more recently, electric guitars all make their contribution to the magnificent racket of the carnival.

Early in this century, the carnival took on an increasingly commercial turn, with private companies financing different groups in order to promote their goods. Since the Revolution, the character of the carnival has changed again and today it is encouraged not so much as a tourist attraction or commercial jamboree, but rather as an authentic expression of the *pueblo trabajador*. The *comparsas* represent trade unions and mass organizations and are supported by state subsidies. There has been every attempt, as the Museum of the Carnival points out, to 'integrate the carnival into the revolutionary process, expressing success in socialist reconstruction'. For instance, the grand finale of the 1984 carnival had costumes from all over the world, clearly intended to demonstrate 'proletarian internationalism'.

Beyond this, however, the carnival has always been an expression of pent-up energy and frustrations, a safety valve for yesterday's slaves and today's workers. It comes after the gruelling toil of the sugar harvest, and is a way of both celebrating and relaxing. It has been known to get out of hand, a time when old scores can be settled or crimes perpetrated under cover of the general confusion. Castro and his comrades deliberately chose 26 July, at the height of the carnival, for their attack on the Moncada Barracks in Santiago in 1953, hoping that the soldiers would be incapacitated by the merrymaking. The modern Apollonian state has not been entirely able to impose order on the Dionysian rites. Anti-social elements still use the carnival to cause public disorder and sabotage. Recently members of the Abakuá sect are said to have cut the dresses and backsides of women with sharpened coins, causing so much trouble that some of the local street processions have been banned. The festival now takes place around stages or along carefully-policed avenues. But the Santiago carnival has had setbacks many times before: no matter how much governments try to channel its energy, it will exist as long as the drums, brought from Africa all those centuries ago, continue to beat.

It would appear that the Cuban government's policy of promoting culture which only serves the Revolution, and suppressing that which opposes it, has had mixed results. There has been a remarkable expansion of cultural activity and a genuine attempt to make it available to the people. But the media remains tightly controlled and is mainly used as a vehicle for official propaganda. Despite an initial outburst of creativity, literature has suffered from the heavy hand of state patronage. Art, mainly because it is less overtly ideological and more limited in influence, has been able to break new ground. Posters, in particular, have been highly original. The cinema has flourished and become internationally famous. The National Ballet is an impressive achievement. Popular music and dance have maintained their vigour, although apart from the *nueva trova*, few new forms have been developed. In general, there is undoubtedly a tremendous artistic and literary potential in Cuba which could only benefit from greater freedom of expression and exposure to outside influences.

13

CHURCH AND STATE

In Communist countries, relations between church and state are often fraught with tension, and Cuba is no exception. Both organizations compete with each other for the total commitment of their members. Despite the recent marriage of Christianity and Marxism in the liberation theology of radical priests in Latin America, Christianity traditionally offers a system of spiritual belief which is very different from the official Communist doctrine of historical and scientific materialism as developed by Marxism-Leninism. It therefore comes as no surprise that organized religion in Cuba is only tolerated if it does not actively threaten the state or oppose the Revolution.

The Constitution of 1976 recognizes in principle the neutrality of the state in religious matters and the freedom of individual conscience: 'the right of each person to profess any religious belief and practice within the respect of the law, or to practise the cult of his or her choice'. But it adds immediately that it is 'illegal and punishable to oppose religious faith or belief against the Revolution' (Article 54).

The Leninist principle of the separation of the state and party in religious matters would seem to be recognized by the official acceptance of the freedom of individual conscience. It is, however, written in the Constitution that the state is to form the basis of its educational and cultural policies on 'the scientific concept of the world, established and developed by Marxism-Leninism' (Article 38). The institutions of the state, as well as the party, are therefore entirely secular.

As in all the countries of the West Indies, religion in Cuba has deep roots. The pre-Columbian Indians worshipped a supreme being and appealed to spirits as intermediaries. The Africans naturally brought their own religious beliefs with them across the Atlantic in the slave ships, and their descendants have continued to practise cults in one form or another ever since. Catholicism in Cuba has always been associated with the Spanish colonialists. Every Revolutionary Cuban will tell you that Columbus came with the cross and the sword; the *conquistadores* put the rebel Indian leader Hatuey to death precisely because he refused to accept the Christian God and a heaven where Spaniards might be found.

During the colonial period which followed, the church and the state were indivisible, and Catholicism was directly identified with the Spanish ruling class. Nearly all the priests were Spanish, not Cuban; they sided with their compatriots during the bitter Wars of Independence, thereby encouraging anti-clerical sentiment amongst the rebels. When they did venture outside their comfortable livings in the towns, it was usually only to baptize children for a fee. But while trying to replace African religions, the Catholic church in Cuba was itself Africanized. The bells of the splendid cathedral in Havana would ring, but few would attend Mass. The highlight of the year was Holy Week, but this was mainly because of the processions, which had all the atmosphere of a pagan carnival. The Catholic church in Cuba proved to be the weakest in Latin America.

Under the constitution of the First Republic, the church was separated from the state and was therefore deprived of its state income and direct political influence. At the same time, Protestant groups from North America began to become active in Cuba, and they eventually converted about a tenth of the population. A small number of Jews settled in Havana. But the Catholic church remained weak; few Cubans were attracted to the priesthood, and 80 per cent of the lower clergy remained Spanish. They showed little interest in the well-being of the poor, and limited their pastoral visits in rural areas to about one a year. The result was that, according to a survey made in 1954, while virtually everyone said they believed in God, they paid no more than lip service to the Catholic church and its ceremonies.[1] The Catholic church was especially weak in the rural areas, where nearly half the population were indifferent to religion, and amongst the blacks who had their own sects. Its main influence was exerted through private schools for the middle class in the towns. In 1954, only 16 per cent of marriages were formalized in church.

At the beginning of the Revolution, there was a reciprocal and no doubt self-interested acceptance amongst Catholics and the Revolutionaries. Indeed, many Christians took part in the Revolutionary movement—the leader of the Directorio Revolucionario, José Antonio Echeverría, killed during the attack on the Presidential Palace in March 1957, was a Christian as was Frank País, the son of a Baptist priest, who led the abortive uprising in the same year in Santiago de Cuba. Castro, who had a strict Jesuit education, is said to have worn a colourful crucifix around his neck in the Sierra Maestra. He certainly presented himself as an earthly Messiah, and with twelve apostles who survived the *Granma* expedition, came down from the mountains to lead his people to the promised land. So as not to alienate any possible support, Castro declared soon after his triumphant entry into Havana that 'the Catholics of Cuba have lent their dedicated co-operation to the cause of liberty'.[2] Several days later he was photographed shaking hands with the Archbishop of Havana, Evelio Díaz, who had come to attend the anniversary of the birth of José Martí on 28 January 1959, a photograph of which was given wide circulation. In the first Declaration of Havana, he further called for 'honest' Christians to join in the Revolution and asserted that 'whoever betrays the Revolution, betrays Christ'.[3]

At first the Church was willing to accept what appeared to be a nationalist and liberal Revolution. But as the new regime grew more radical in its policies, threatened the Church's activities and properties, and increased state control of the press and education, the two came into direct confrontation.

On 6 December 1960, Castro accused the Catholic church and schools of waging criminal campaigns against the Revolution. The following year proved a turning point. The Revolutionary government in June 1961 closed the Catholic church's two universities and nationalized its 324 primary and secondary schools. When a religious procession led by the auxiliary bishop of Havana, Boza Maspidal, turned into an anti-Communist demonstration, all religious activities outside the church were banned. Saints' days, Holy Week, Epiphany and even Christmas were abolished. Any priest involved in politics would henceforth be deported: about a third of the priests (about 3,000) left, and nearly all the nuns. Nevertheless Castro insisted in March 1961 that in Revolutionary Cuba: 'A good priest will have no problems. What is a good priest? One who dedicates himself to exercising his religious duties without conspiring and without promoting terrorism.'[4]

The growing fear of an organized Catholic resistance to the regime was made real a month later when it was discovered that three Cuban priests had accompanied the CIA-backed invasion force at the Bay of Pigs. Afterwards, Castro read out the leaflet signed by the head chaplain which the invaders had intended to distribute:

The liberating forces have landed on the beaches of Cuba. We come in the name of God, Justice and Democracy to restore the rights that have been abridged, the freedom that has been trampled upon, and the religion that has been subjugated and slandered . . . Our struggle is that of those who believe in God against the atheists, the struggle of spiritual values against materialism, the struggle of democracy against Communism . . .

Catholics of Cuba: our military might is crushing the invincible, and even greater is our moral strength and our faith in God and in His protection and His help. Cuban Catholics: I embrace you on behalf of the soldiers of the liberating army. Families, relatives, friends: soon you shall be reunited. Have faith, for victory is ours, because God is with us, and the Virgin of Charity cannot abandon her children. Catholics: long live Cuba, free, democratic, and Catholic! long live Christ the King! Long live our glorious patroness![5]

At the time of the missile crisis in October of the following year, a shipment of bibles arrived in Cuba wrapped in US anti-Cuban newspapers. These and other counter-revolutionary documents emanating from Catholics opposed to the regime were used as an excuse to crush the church; its traditional weakness and sullied image made it an easy victim. It was seen, however, more as a nuisance, as an independent body within the state, than a real threat to the regime. It suffered along with the media and trade unions as a pressure group with a potential to create an alternative source of power protecting the individual from the triumphant will of the state. Once the confrontation had led to the defeat of the church, there followed a period of uneasy coexistence. On the anniversary of the death of student leader José Antonio Echeverría on 13 March 1962, Castro acknowledged that revolution and religion are not necessarily antithetical: 'A revolutionary can hold a religious belief', he declared. Four years later he went out of his way to insist that religious toleration did exist: 'Cuba is a large family in whose bosom all her sons work for a happy future . . . the churches remain open, the priests say mass every day; in sum, the state does not hinder any of the works of the church. Any religious man or woman can walk through the streets of Havana with his or her habit . . . '[6]

He was now sufficiently confident to reopen a dialogue with Cuban Christians, especially if they were prepared to join in the Revolutionary process. At the International Cultural Congress held in December 1968 in Havana, a message was read out from a group of Catholic priests who had decided to follow the example of Camilo Torres, the Colombian priest and professor of sociology who had joined the guerrilla movement. In his closing speech, Castro, with power struggles in the party on his mind, poured scorn on dogmatic Marxists:

It is not one of the least paradoxes of history that, at a time when certain sectors of the clergy have seen fit to become revolutionaries, certain Marxist sectors have turned themselves into a pseudo revolutionary church. I only hope that by drawing attention to this fact I shall not myself be excommunicated, or delivered over to the Holy Inquisition.[7]

Thereafter, Castro went out of his way to encourage Revolutionary Christians. In the city museum of Havana, in the former governor general's palace, a whole room was dedicated to the memory of Camilo Torres. When Castro opened a poly-clinic and school named after the Colombian priest in January 1969, he declared:

> All men of progressive thought, of human thought, of just thought, are those called to carry out this [the Revolutionary] task. And in that task—as we said in the Declaration of Havana once—Marxists and honest Christians will gather, men of the broadest ideas and most varied beliefs will gather.[8]

The Christians who remained in Cuba quickly realized that they would either have to go underground or else collaborate with the regime. They chose the latter path. Some theologians moreover began to draw a parallel with Guevara's vision of the New Man and the message of Christ, at least in this world. Dr Sergio Arce Martínez, Professor of the Protestant Evangelic Seminary of Theology in Matanzas, called for a renovation in the structure, language, perspective, teaching and witness of the church, arguing that the Christian Revolutionary could play an active part in the Christian church in Cuba. Since work is the 'spiritual fulfilment of man', he even said work on Sunday was permissible—an issue which had previously been a thorny question for Christians.[9]

In similar vein, the Protestant-affiliated Christian student movement representing students from the universities of Havana, Santa Cruz and Santiago de Cuba, linked the New Man of Cuban socialism with the New Man of Christian theology. In 1968 they issued the declaration: 'We maintain that the Christian faith has a contribution to make to this process by its presence and participation. We affirm that the New Man is one who practises solidarity, struggles by all means within his grasp to establish justice, and loves all work which is for the benefit of humanity.'[10]

The Cuban Episcopal Conference distributed a communiqué on 29 April 1969 to be read out by priests to the laity, which denounced the injustice of the economic embargo, called for a renovation in Christian ethics, and asserted that 'work has been beloved and blessed by God [because] every worker is a creator'.

The Christian clergy in Cuba had thus, towards the end of the 1960s, adopted a policy of collaboration rather than opposition, and took up Castro's offer of dialogue. Although some Christian exiles in the US fulminated against the treachery of the clergy, more sympathetic observers saw it as an honest attempt by Cuban Christians to free themselves from the oppressive religious patterns of a previous era and to participate in the new movement of Latin American Christianity which combines religious faith with a confidence in man's power to shape the world. While differing in final goals, many Christians felt that they could share common ground with Guevara in the rejection of material incentives, the emphasis on co-operation, the desire to promote equality, and the view of work as primarily a means of developing the human personality rather than of earning a living.

Even Castro has been keen to underplay the atheistic materialism which is at the core of Marxist-Leninist philosophy. In conversation with the visiting Nicaraguan poet Ernesto Cardenal, he once argued passionately: 'Look, Marxist philosophy and Christianity coincide in 90 per cent of things, don't they? And dialectical materialism is more spiritual than positivism, isn't it?'[11] More recently, he told the Brazilian priest Frei Betto: 'There are 10,000 more coincidences between Christianity and Communism than there could be with capitalism.'[12]

But despite the growing tolerance between church and state towards the end of the 1960s, the power of the churches had been seriously diminished. In 1959 there were about four million Catholics; by 1970 less than a million, although two-thirds of the population were still being baptized and buried in the church. Protestant numbers were also down: from 250,000 in 1959 to about 50,000 in 1970.[13] The Jamaican playwright Barry Reckord noted after a visit in 1971 that in Cuba 'God is dead'.[14]

But while Christians have undoubtedly suffered a blow, it has not been fatal. In its thesis on 'ideological struggle' the first Congress of the Communist party held in 1975 confirmed the Leninist line that:

> Our party, by revolutionary principle, practises the respect of the right of citizens to participate or not in any religious belief. But its conception of the world and nature is scientific, and educates its militants and the people in this conception, which excludes any mystical or religious interpretation of natural, social and human phenomena.[15]

The position was ratified and confirmed in the Constitution of 1976. Catholics can still practise in their homes and behind the closed doors of their churches. Cuba has maintained diplomatic relations with the Vatican, and the Papal Nuncio has an office in Havana.

To find out more about the state of the Catholic church today, I visited a young Catholic priest who was in charge of the cathedral in Baracoa, the first capital of the country but now a remote town in the most easterly tip of the island. He had entered the Catholic Seminary in Havana at the age of 12 where he received a thorough grounding in philosophy and theology. He admitted that the 1960s had proved a difficult period in the affairs of the church and the state, for the church had become a focus of opposition. Confrontation had been followed by silence, although he thought relations with the government were improving now and there were signs of a new dialogue. Indeed, the Catholic church was now in agreement with the government on its basic social goals.

The church however was not in a very healthy state according to the priest. There were only 200 priests and nine bishops, two of whom were in Rome. In addition there was a crisis of vocation amongst young priests, with only about 30 students in the two remaining seminaries. The church received no money from the state and had to count on donations from abroad, especially from West Germany, to continue its work. There was even a dire shortage of bibles. As for the congregations themselves, elderly women were the most numerous; the proportion of women was four times that of men, while black and white came to church in equal numbers. More than half the population were not baptized. His own congregation totalled about 400 faithful, who would come to church during Holy Week, although half that number would come regularly to Sunday mass. The rest of the week the cathedral would remain locked.

In its diminished state, the Catholic church is therefore keen to maintain contact with other religious groups, and to work out a Cuban theology which took into account the prevailing social and political circumstances. 'Catholicism and Marxism are not entirely incompatible,' the priest told me. 'It is possible to be a Catholic and a Revolutionary at the same time. We are both concerned with the harmonious development of man, and there can be no salvation without living for others. There are Catholics in the armed forces and in the militia. But Catholics cannot be in the party. And when it comes to theology, certain principles are inflexible and must be upheld with the utmost discipline.' This point of view was reiterated in a document drafted by bishops and priests and released on 17 December 1985 which declared that the Cuban Catholic Church supported the basic social goals of the government. Nevertheless, it lamented the fact that Christians were denied the right to educate their children and were rarely seen by political leaders as patriotic citizens.

Most of the Protestant sects have survived slightly better than the Catholics, and have been more willing to throw in their lot with the Revolution. Baptists, Presbyterians, Episcopalians, Pentecostals, Christian Scientists, Quakers and the Salvation Army all continue their work, especially in the country. Some Catholics have become Protestants in recent years, and there is a widespread feeling among party officials that Protestants are more accessible to the ideas of socialism. No longer suspecting a serious threat, the government in the summer of 1984 allowed the import of 12,000 new bibles, the fourth shipment from the United Bible Societies since 1970.

At the same time, the Jehovah's Witnesses have suffered sorely under the Revolutionary government. This sect believe that all war is immoral and that the civil law must be resisted wherever it conflicts with their own religious principles. This means that they firmly refuse to work on Sundays, salute the flag, bear arms or wear prison uniforms. They have been banned since 1974, ostensibly because of their counter-revolutionary behaviour, but chiefly because of their refusal to conform to the dictates of the state. According to Amnesty International in 1986, many Jehovah's Witnesses were sentenced to imprisonment as a result of their religious activities.

It is for such religious sects that the clause has been added to Article 54 in the Constitution which declares that it is 'illegal and punishable to oppose religious faith or beliefs against the Revolution, education, or the accomplishment of the duties to work, to defend the homeland with arms, to reverence its symbols and the other duties established by the Constitution.'

Ironically, just as the African religions absorbed Catholicism, so Cuban Marxism has become a kind of religion. Like Catholicism, it demands uncritical acceptance of the central doctrines as a test of faith. There is close similarity between the hierarchy of the Catholic church and the Communist party, with members selected for their loyalty and purity. The chosen few then preach the new socialist morality to the corrupt and fallen masses who, if they work hard and keep to the straight and narrow, will be led to the heaven on earth of Communist society. The party has its martyrs and saints whose anniversaries are commemorated each year and whose exemplary lives are held up for the edification of youth. Che Guevara appears everywhere in the image of a new Christ, who gave his life to save the oppressed of the earth. His writings have become holy writ. Castro, too, performs a messianic role, both punishing and rewarding his people, surrounded by the twelve apostles, the guerrillas of the Sierra Maestra who formed the nucleus of the rebel army.

Be that as it may, traditional Christianity is undoubtedly dying out. In Havana most of the Roman Catholic churches still hold mass on Sunday mornings; there are a Presbyterian church, a Baptist church and a synagogue still open, but nothing else. There are perhaps only 80,000 active Catholics left. Castro can praise Jesus as an extraordinary figure, but God is to all intents and purposes dead and buried in Cuba, and there seems little likelihood that the Cuban church will provide a centre of opposition to the state as in Catholic Poland. The churches are not even social centres any more; the focus of local activity has been taken over by the CDRs and other mass organizations. The church buildings are still maintained, but more as architectural museums rather than places of worship. The few seminaries which remain have trouble in attracting students, and there is now only one private Catholic hospital for the mentally ill left in Cuba.

It is clear that many Cuban Christians feel persecuted by the regime. This sense of persecution is vividly reflected in the claim that in 1982 the Virgen de la Caridad del Cobre, Cuba's patron saint, appeared walking on the waves off Havana only to be shot down by Castro's troops. The actual wooden statue of the Virgin Mary was discovered floating in the sea by three sailors in the early seventeenth century. Looking like a *mulata*, she has been matched in Santería with Ochún, the Yoruba goddess of love and beauty. The statue is kept in the Catedral del Cobre near Santiago de Cuba, with a replica in Havana Cathedral; it remains a powerful symbol even for non-Christian Cubans.

Officially, Castro continues to maintain a 'dialogue' with Christians in Cuba, but it is a dialogue in which he tends to do all the talking and which takes place on his own terms. It was reported that he told a US Congressman in January 1985 that 'I am a Christian [because Christianity provides] people with hard, concrete values.'[16] In December 1985, he published some conversations with the Brazilian priest Frei Betto in which he stressed his Christian upbringing and described liberation theology as 'one of the most fundamental happenings that have occurred in our epoch'. It is nothing less than a 're-encounter of Christianity with its roots, with its most beautiful, heroic and most glorious history'.[17] Castro's statements on Christianity, however, are invariably vague and ambivalent. There is no evidence that he believes in God, and his interest in Christianity would seem to be primarily motivated by his interest in ethics. If the Church were to pose a threat to his rule, he certainly would not tolerate it. It is precisely because the Church is almost moribund in Cuba that Castro felt able to ease restrictions on visiting clergy and to invite the Pope in December 1985 to visit the country.

Marxism and Christianity have of course overlapped in South and Central America to form the dynamic new liberation theology which portrays Christ as a rebel fighting oppressive forces in his attempt to realize the kingdom of God on earth. Many Catholic priests now identify with the interests of Latin American workers and the peasants, while some bishops have declared that for oppressed people violence may be considered as a last resort. In the shanty towns of Brazil, Che's portrait often appears alongside Christ's. Even priests have served in the Nicaraguan government which is trying to forge a society very similar to Cuba's. Some visitors to Cuba have interpreted events in the light of liberation theology. The Christian Bruce Kenrick declared after a visit to Cuba in 1979 that Castro was even leading a 'secular religious movement'. Deeply impressed by the attempt to create the New Man who thinks of others rather than of himself, Kenrick suggested that the Cubans were living 'the spirit of the Gospel' and that the teaching of Christ was emerging in their lives without them knowing it. Indeed, he saw no fundamental difference between Guevara and Christ in that they both tried to create the New Man on a new earth; for many Cubans, Che is thus the 'twentieth-century image of God'.[18]

My own impressions are very different. Only recently has there been any public discussion of liberation theology in Cuba and then it was only after Castro published his widely distributed conversations on religion with Frei Betto in December 1985. Catholic priests are not only expressly forbidden to engage in politics, but they are themselves eager to keep religion and politics separate. Far from being religious in any meaningful sense, Castro's movement has been both secular and anticlerical. The regime has not only effectively crushed any religious activity beyond closed doors, but the Communist party ensures that the militant atheism enshrined in the Constitution is diffused in education and culture. Although there may be some superficial similarities between Christ's New Man and Guevara's New Man, they are ultimately very different models of humanity. Guevara's New Man may be self-sacrificing and ready to help others but he is also a trained fighter who will unquestionably kill and obey the orders of his superiors. Cuban youth are taught to love their neighbours and to help their socialist allies, but they are equally brought up to hate their enemies and to enact revenge on them in a way which hardly tallies with the Christian message of goodwill unto all men and turning the other cheek.

While the Revolution has virtually eradicated organized Christianity in Cuba, the semi-secret, African-based religious sects are flourishing. The slave ships from Africa of course not only brought bodies but also beliefs and gods, dances and songs. Despite the devastating impact of the journey, the subsequent breaking-up of families and the suppression of many of their cultural traditions, a great many of these slaves' religious beliefs survived. This was partly due to the *cabildos*, religious and social associations organized on tribal lines which their Spanish masters permitted. Cuba was also the last country to abolish slavery in the Caribbean and slaves were being shipped from Africa as late as 1875 with all their cultural values still fresh in their minds. The result was that African beliefs and practices have continued in Cuba with a purity and strength unequalled elsewhere in the Caribbean.

The religious cults not only helped the slaves maintain an image of their self-worth and retain their cultural identity, but offered them the possibility of creating a magical order out of the social disorder of the plantation society to which they were condemned. The cults reflected that society by confirming that the only way to improve one's lot was to oblige a master or a superior power. But they also contrasted with it. While in slave society human beings were treated as objects, the slaves saw all objects as living. The practice of ancestor worship and the belief in reincarnation further enabled them to feel part of a wider historical and natural community. The cults were thus responsible for forming in Cuban culture an ethos of brotherhood, holism, and harmony with nature.

Before the Revolution, the cults were directed and guarded by the blacks, but many poor whites attended as well as some whites from the upper classes. Strict Catholics dismissed the whole thing as *brujería* or witchcraft; but it is more usually called loosely *santería* or the cult of gods. At least one Cuban out of four went to such celebrations prior to the Revolution—although they felt compelled to assert: '*Yo no creo, pero lo repito*' (I do not believe, but I repeat the ritual). I was told that although most people do not believe in *santería*, they know all about it. My own interest was first aroused by seeing a middle-aged black woman dressed entirely in white crossing a square in Havana: she was a *santera*, I was told. Then, by chance, in a flower bed under the great silk-cotton tree or *ceiba* in Friendship Park in the city centre, I found a dead pigeon cut open and stuffed with a cigar and some small coins. 'It is to bring luck,' I was told, but again no further explanation was forthcoming, and the conversation was changed rapidly. It appears that the religious cults have survived principally in three groups known respectively as Santería, Abakuá and Regla Mayombé. They originated from particular tribes in Africa but have been developed and transformed to differing degrees in the New World.

The largest cult is a development from the Yoruba or Lucumí religion, known in Cuba as Santería or the Regla de Ochoa. The cult, as its name suggests, was brought from Western Nigeria to Cuba by the Yoruba people. It has had the greatest impact on Cuban culture mainly because unlike the other religions it absorbed many elements from Catholicism. Since they were unable to practise their beliefs openly, the Yoruba identified their own gods with Catholic saints. It was a process actively encouraged from the sixteenth century by Spanish priests who hoped that their religion would eventually replace the African one. In the eighteenth century, the tribal *cabildos* were allowed as a way to divide and rule the slaves and to redirect energies which might otherwise explode in revolts. Sunday on the plantations was often a day of drinking, love making, drumming, dancing and dressing up. *Día de los Reyes* or Epiphany was a time of unbridled licence and jubilation, while Holy Week became an excuse for processions and parties which eventually became carnivals. In the event, Cuban Catholicism became Africanized, while the Yoruba religion was strengthened by the new influences.

The Yoruba believe in the existence of a celestial empire ruled by Olofí, a being so great that he is beyond human conception. He cannot therefore be worshipped directly: it is necessary to use intermediaries, known as *orishas*, who have human virtues and defects but can protect or punish, kill or give life. With this structure, it was not difficult for Yoruba to link some of the 400 or more *orishas* with Catholic saints. Although the gods can be bi-sexual and good or bad, they are all direct manifestations of the creative principle, and as such are spirits of light not darkness. There are seven principal *orishas* which are believed to control every aspect of human life, especially health, purity and fertility. The *orishas* are rather like Greek gods and goddesses, in that they reflect human weaknesses and strengths, but are closely identified with their Catholic counterparts. Thus Eleguá, a two-faced god representing good and evil, is known as El Dueño de los Caminos (Master of Paths) and is matched with St Antonio. Changó, the red god of war, virility, fire, thunder and drums, is identified with St Barbara. He worships his opposite, Yemaya, the blue goddess of the moon and maternity, who is linked with Our Lady of Regla, the patron of Havana. Ochún, the yellow goddess of love, beauty and fresh water, is linked with Cuba's patron saint, the Virgin of Charity known as La Virgen de la Caridad del Cobre. Then Oyá, a multicoloured goddess of vengeance, metals and the rainbow, is identified with St Teresa; Obatalá, the white creator of the world and symbol of peace, with Christ or the Virgin of Mercedes, and, finally, Babalú Ayé, god of illness, with St Lazarus; the latter has been called 'the patron saint of the negroes'.

Different groups worship different gods and goddesses, and on their equivalent Catholic saints' days, devotees celebrate with dance and music. The rituals sometimes appear completely Catholic, with Hail Marys, Our Fathers, incense and candles. On other occasions *santeras* put on the clothes of the *orishas* and become possessed. Although fundamentally conservative, Santería this century assimilated Red Indian Chiefs from North America into their mythology, and the stones on which cocks are sacrificed, said to have been brought from Africa, took on greater significance. The priests of the cult, known as Babaláos, are men. Indeed, it is the men who have the sacred knowledge, who divine the gods' wishes, who lead the praying and chanting, and who play the drums and maracas. Women take on a more passive role, dancing, forming most of the chorus, and falling into trances. They are the spiritual intermediaries and the major receptacles of the gods. Both *santeros* and *santeras* inhabit the same world, in which matter is not divorced from spirit but one and the same. An *orisha* can therefore pass easily in or out of a human body. The *ceiba* or silk-cotton tree is sacred, for instance, because it houses Changó and other spirits of the dead— it symbolizes, even in the middle of the busiest square in Havana, the terrible omnipotence of a god.

Despite the disapproval of the government, Santería exerts a growing power as a religious sect. It has also had an extraordinary cultural influence. The rhythms and songs of the Yoruba are some of the most complex and lyrical produced by any of the African sects, and have greatly influenced the *rumba* and other dances. The archetypal character of the *orishas*, which offer ways of understanding human behaviour, have equally contributed to Cuban folklore. But above all, the cult reflects the remarkable process of cultural synthesis at work in Cuba, a country described by Nicolás Guillén as 'This mulatto land of African and Spanish, St Barbara on one side, on the other side, Chango.'

The sect which has the greatest influence on Cuban music is the Regla Mayombé, also known as Palo Monte, and often called *brujería* or witchcraft. It was first founded by slaves from the Congo, and its adepts are called *paleros* or *congos*. Like Santería, it matches its gods with Catholic saints: the Virgin of Charity becomes Mama Chola, the mother of the sect; Zarabanda, the god of war and iron, becomes St Barbara. Supernatural forces are given the colours and attributes of their Yoruba equivalents. Fetishes in human form are used to cast spells: in order to break up a couple, for instance, two figures would be tied together back to back and placed in a small box. The priests, known as *tatas n'ganga*, make offerings or *n'gangas* in large pots which contain magical powers from objects such as twigs from sacred trees, instruments of work such as machetes, and railway line nails, as well as earth, the blood of cocks and goats, stones from the north, south, east and west corners of a cemetery, and the brain from buried human corpses. Before any ceremony, the godfathers, or *tatas*, write their names on the ground in a complex sign language of circles, lines, curves, arrows, crosses, thorns, skulls, suns and moons. This enables them to manipulate the forces of nature.

In the last century, overseers on the plantations treated the *tatas* with respect and would even join in the dancing of the sect on Sundays. Indeed, intricate rhythms played on their cylindrical drums to accompany their rites have had an enormous influence: the famous *rumba*, *mambo*, *conga* and *son*, can all be traced to Palo Monte dances. Each sect has between 30 and 40 members who recognize each other by special handshakes. If any one member is offended, then the others will take revenge. As they are the most clandestine and least organized, it is difficult for the state to persecute them.

The most distinct, original and feared of the cults is Abakuá, whose members are called *ñáñigos* or *carabalís*. It originated amongst the Efik people from the Calabar region on what is now the border of Nigeria and Benin, who thought they were a chosen race. They formed secret, all-male, mutual aid societies which were called powers, lands, or nations. Members are bound together by an oath and call each other *ecobio*, *acere* or *monina*, African terms for friend, brother and comrade. They re-enact in their ceremonies the rediscovery of Ekué, the voice of the sacred fish Tanze, who is the incarnation of the supreme god, Abasi. They also believe that souls can rest permanently in limbo rather than be constantly reincarnated. They have developed a series of complex hieroglyphics based on circles and crossed lines which, since the 1860s, have incorporated the cross.

Central to the cult are *iremes*, or little devils, which represent the spirits of the dead returning to supervise rites. Blind and deaf, the *iremes* are supposed to communicate with men by movement of their hands. Dancers dressed as *iremes* have become one of the most popular expressions of Cuban folklore. The cult has a sacred room or *famba* in which live 15 devils. The most interesting manifestations of these devils are Eribanganelo, who wears cowbells around his waist and carries in his right hand a short stick symbolizing the law and in his left hand a branch representing discipline; and Enamagui, rarely seen by the uninitiated, who wears black with symbols of death on his head and chest and only dances in special ceremonies with muffled bells. The drums, or *batas*, which accompany the ritual dances are considered sacred. I saw one made out of a trepanned human skull. No woman or homosexual is allowed to touch them or take part in the ceremonies. The subtle rhythms made by their drums and tambourines are essential ingredients of any carnival.

The *ñáñigos* have been feared by Cubans with good reason, for at the beginning of the century an initiate would have to kill the first passer-by he met. Before the Revolution, nannies would warn their rich charges that if they misbehaved the *ñáñigos* would come and take them away. Half the murders in Havana in the 1960s were said to be connected with the sect. Their numbers are said not to be great—it is estimated that there are about 2,000 members, especially in Havana around the docks, Guanabacoa and Matanzas. But the sect is extremely secret (the exact nature of their ceremonies is known only by two members at a time) and is impossible to subvert. They have undoubtedly become a rallying point for opposition to the regime, especially amongst the disaffected blacks. They have also become a scapegoat. The government often puts down counter-revolutionary acts of vandalism and sabotage to the sects. The secrecy of the sects not only makes them intolerable in a Communist state, but their sinister rites evoke widespread fear, like the Voodoo sects in neighbouring Haiti.

These cults as organized religion are officially discouraged. Santería is tolerated if its members keep to themselves, and Catholic priests still hope they can purify it of its African origins. The Regla Mayombé and Abakuá, however, by their very nature are considered a threat. The government cannot deny their enormous contribution to Cuban dance and music, so it does its best to rescue the cultural values in the African traditions which have played such a great part in forming the national identity, while removing their mystical element. The authorities have tried to eradicate the anti-social and dangerous practices of the past.

This is partly done by drawing a veil over their real nature. I found it impossible to organize officially a meeting with any practitioner or attend any of their ceremonies. Even the unique Guanabacoa Historical Museum just outside Havana has under lock and key its *salas etnográficas* which represent the three main cults. I could only see them with special permission as a researcher and by making prior arrangements. The knowledgeable guide stressed before the visit that the exhibits were of historical interest only, and was at pains to demonstrate the 'ridiculousness' of such beliefs. But she warmed to her theme and, like most Cubans, clearly held the cults in respect.

The other way to emasculate the cults is to turn them into picturesque folklore and give them a historical and sociological explanation. The deeply rooted nature of the cults in Cuba is explained by the needs of the slaves, and later other underprivileged sectors, 'to defend themselves against an oppressive society'. The high point of an 'Afro-Cuban' night as, for instance, performed by the National Folklore Group, is the sacrifice of a cock or some other live animal. The programme notes explain to the uninitiated: 'The slave seeks a bit of peace and hope after much suffering and harassment. With rites, offerings and the sacrifice of blood, he invokes the gods of redemption, from whom he has been brutally separated by inhuman slavery.'

For the present, the state has undoubtedly got the upper hand over the churches and sects in Cuba. Every effort in the past has been made to suppress Christianity by denying it a public voice, and to dissolve the African cults by transforming them into colourful folklore. There is no real intellectual dialogue between church and state, only a practical accommodation. It is official policy to incorporate believers in the task of building a Communist society, based on the historical materialist conception of the universe. It is hoped by the party, moreover, that the new system of social and scientific education will counter the ignorance on which all religions are allegedly based, and the economic development of the country will eventually destroy the conditions in which they supposedly thrive. Only the moral basis of Christianity is accepted in so far as it coincides with Communist values.

But it may not prove so easy to eradicate the metaphysical and magical consciousness of the Cuban people which is so deeply rooted in their culture and collective experience. As the saying goes: 'Abakuá will last in Cuba as long as there are drums.'

14

LAW AND DISORDER

Under Batista, the police and army often acted as a law unto themselves, arbitrarily arresting people, detaining them without trial, and torturing them at will. Dawn in Havana would often reveal the bodies of students thrown into the gutters. It has been estimated that up to 20,000 people lost their lives in the period before the Revolution.

The administration of justice amongst the guerrillas was harsh, but not so arbitrary. Informers and bandits were executed by firing squad, and on Castro's orders symbolic executions were carried out as an exemplary punishment. Castro also announced that the 'crimes' of insubordination, desertion and defeatism would be punishable by death. The accused had a chance to defend themselves and the guerrillas would often act as a jury.

On coming to power, the guerrillas transformed the old legal system. Law was administered by *tribunales populares*, local courts which dealt with minor cases like labour disputes or public disorders. They were presided over by three reliable Revolutionaries who had ten days' training and who were able to imprison people for up to six months. There were no juries. The decisions of the tribunals were often arbitrary and the accused were sometimes not allowed to defend themselves. More serious crimes were dealt with by the *audiencias*, the formal court structure inherited from before the Revolution. Ironically in a country ruled largely by ex-lawyers, there was considerable antipathy towards the law which was seen as part of the 'capitalist superstructure'. By 1969, only 11 law students were enrolled in the University of Havana.

While the judicial system dealt with disputes and misdemeanours, for political crimes there were no clear cut procedures. The law of *habeas corpus* was not respected and people could be held indefinitely without trial. In the initial flush of the Revolution, hundreds of Batista's henchmen were executed, but this was soon stopped following international protests; no major Revolutionary terror occurred in Cuba. Even so, it has been estimated that 2,000 people were executed by early 1961, and perhaps 5,000 by 1970. Political trials also remained highly irregular, particularly those of Hubert Matos in 1959, Marcos Armando Rodríguez in 1964, and Aníbal Escalante and others in 1968. In the latter case, Castro acted as prosecutor as well as witness and judge.

There was no separation of the powers of the executive, the legislature and judiciary, and the independence or neutrality of the judiciary was not respected. With no legal code, it was not clear what was and what was not a political offence, which made for a sense of personal insecurity. And with the line between civil and political crimes so blurred, the regime was able to charge individuals with political offences—such as black market activities or damage to public property—which might be considered civil or common-law offences.

Just as the economy was set on a new footing in the early 1970s, so there was a thorough reform of the judicial system undertaken in 1973. After the original drafts had been circulated for discussion amongst the mass organizations, work centres and party members, a series of laws was enacted, including the Criminal Procedure Code, Civil and Administrative Procedure Code, Family Code, and Youth and Children Code. The 1970s proved a period of intense legislation aimed at building new foundations for Cuba's judiciary. It formed part of a general trend towards greater order and authority in the government of Cuban society. The legal code which emerged was no longer based on Roman-Spanish law, but on the judicial system of East European states. This became clear in the new Criminal Code of 1979, which grouped crimes according to their similarity, so that crimes against the state are differentiated from those against public order, or labour crimes. It reclassified crimes such as burglary, theft, and the impersonation of officials, as common-law crimes. It also fixed a maximum sentence of 20 years for crimes not punishable by the death penalty and 30 years as a possible alternative to the death penalty.

The process of establishing 'socialist legality' culminated in the adoption of the new Constitution in 1976. The Constitution guarantees the independence of the judiciary: 'The judges, in their function of imparting justice, are independent and owe no obedience other than to the law' (Article 125). But the judiciary itself cannot check the powers of the executive, legislature or Communist party. The courts moreover are not intended to safeguard certain individual rights or freedoms against the potential tyranny of government, but rather they are intended to ensure that the laws passed by the government are enacted. The Constitution clearly states that the objectives of the courts are: 'to maintain and to reinforce socialist legality . . . to safeguard the economic, social and political regime established in the Constitution'; and 'to educate citizens in the conscientious and voluntary observance of their duties of loyalty to the country, to the cause of socialism and the socialist norms of living together' (Article 123).

Under the new Constitution, the autonomy of the courts has been reduced and legal power concentrated into executive hands. The Law of Organization of the Judicial System of 1977 recognizes equality before the law and the right of the accused to a defence (Article 13). Yet, as before, there is no recognition of the separation of powers, and the courts are ultimately subordinate to the National Assembly and the Council of State. By any previous Cuban standards, the powers of the Revolutionary government are consequently enormous. And Castro does not hesitate to interfere. In 1979 he complained about the leniency of the courts, which were dismissing over a third of cases, saying that they created 'guarantees for the criminal'. Instead, he urged that they should enable the 'rights of society' to prevail, by which he meant the will of the government.[1] In the following year, at the second Congress of the Communist party held in December, he insisted that the 'demand for orderliness should never be neglected in a revolution'.

In the administration of law, there are now three levels of courts. At the municipal level, the cases are evaluated by three judges, two of whom are non-professionals elected by the local People's Power Assembly for a two-and-a-half-year term. At the provincial and national level, five judges preside, with only two non-professionals. There is a lawyer for the defence and one for the prosecution. The judges do not have to reach a unanimous decision; a simple majority is enough, although the accused can appeal to a higher court. While no jury system exists, there is an element of popular participation through the elected non-professional judges. Beyond the municipal court, however, these are in a permanent minority.

In the People's Supreme Court the judges are elected by the National Assembly, but its president and vice president are nominated by the head of state. Since this is the foremost judicial body and its decisions final, the state therefore has the last word. All the lay and professional judges are nominated by the Ministry of Justice. There are in addition special courts run on the same principles at the provincial and national levels that deal with labour crimes, military crimes and crimes against state security.

The courts can impose five orders of sanctions against a criminal: admonitions, fines, limitation of liberty, deprivation of liberty, and the death penalty. In the case of fines, the judges can decide the amount to impose according to the circumstances, within the limits set by a quota. They can also choose between prison and fines (six months, for instance, equals 270 quotas). The limitation of liberty is a new experiment in which the criminal is kept within the community and his conduct is surveyed by the mass organizations who report back to the courts. Imprisonment is considered an unfortunate necessity, but sentences can be draconian: seven years for possessing marijuana, 15 to 20 years for theft, or 20 years for raiding a store. There is a maximum of 30 years. In the hierarchy of crimes, the least serious are those which are non-violent. The more serious, in ascending order, are crimes against persons, then 'organized delinquency', and finally and gravest of all, 'counter-revolution'.

The primary aim of the penal system is to reform the criminals and to re-integrate them into society. The principal means of rehabilitating prisoners is through work. All prisoners are obliged to work and can often be seen around Cuba in grey uniforms, employed in agriculture or construction. In Holguín I saw a group building their own prison; near Santiago they were erecting statues of prehistoric animals in a tourist park. Their work is not only similar to that performed in the wider society, but they are paid like all Cubans according to the amount of work done. In this way it is hoped that prisoners will become productive members of society once again. And if they behave well, they are allowed home to visit their families as a way of rehabilitating them into the community.

The most controversial aspect of prison is the re-education programme which every prisoner must undergo. While undoubtedly a form of political indoctrination, it does not seem to go as far as actual brainwashing. It is enough for a dissident or wrongdoer to accept the present Marxist-Leninist State of Cuba, and the dictatorship of the proletariat. He or she must also be willing to work productively without actively opposing the regime.

Despite lengthy negotiations with the Ministry of the Interior, I was not allowed to attend a court in session. I managed to see, however, in the Teatro Principal in Camagüey a remarkable play by Lourdes Gómez Canes called *Causa numero.* . . . It not only shows how theatre is used to convey a political message, but vividly illustrates the course of justice since it is based on a real case. The play centres on the predicament of Rosa, a mother working in a factory, who is abandoned by her husband. She subsequently takes a new lover, turns to drink and neglects the upbringing of her children. The climax of the play takes place in court where Rosa is condemned for the delinquent behaviour of her children, although it is made clear that they are as much the responsibility of the father who gets away scot free. The play gives an interesting insight into collective life in modern Cuba. Both parents are held up as examples of anti-social and non-revolutionary conduct. The chief witness for the prosecution is president of the local CDR who lays into poor Rosa for not looking after her children properly. Rosa, in her desperation, turns to a *santero* in order to win back her man, prays to St Barbara (whose equivalent in Santería is Changó, the Yoruba god of virility and war) and dabbles in the black market. The father, for his part, takes to drink, music and wild parties.

In the summing up, the judge stresses that Rosa's behaviour is not 'compatible with Marxist-Leninist society' and reminds her that there is 'nothing more important than a child' (a common slogan). He then condemns her to six months in prison. Her children are sent to a boarding school in the country. At the end of the play, the defence and prosecution lawyers come forward and ask the audience for their view of the case. The audience, as jury, were quick to participate. One elderly woman speaking in careful Spanish and dressed in pre-revolutionary finery, got up and said that the woman got what she deserved and, if anything, warranted more. 'She's one of the old bourgeoisie,' my companion whispered. 'They often pretend to be the most revolutionary in public so that they can retain their privileges.'

Other members of the audience were more lenient. It was pointed out that the accused was alone, that she should be helped rather than condemned, that every effort should have been made to incorporate her into society, and that the local CDR had not been sufficiently under-standing or helpful. I was impressed. It was the young working class element in the audience, and especially the young women, who were the most compassionate and forgiving. It is unfortunate, for the pros-ecuted at least, that the jury system does not now exist in Cuba.

In order to learn more about the new judicial and penal system pre-vailing in Cuba, I met Quirós Pírez, a loquacious and eloquent lawyer who was a spokesman for the Ministry of Justice. He started by ex-plaining the philosophy underlying the new legal code:

The fundamental concept of justice in Cuba is that *la pena es una crítica por un hecho*, that is, punishment is a way of criticizing a person's actions, not beliefs or thoughts. It is not administered as a form of revenge but as a sanction applied by society against an individual's anti-social behaviour. The sanction therefore has a social mission. It does not have an absolute character, but depends on a close dialectical relationship with the prevailing social conditions. The true function of sanctions is that they should help develop society and that society in turn should develop them. The sanctions applicable in the transitional period from a capitalist to a socialist society will not therefore necessarily prevail in a Communist society. At present, in our penal code, the state sets the laws and the courts work out the dialectical relationship between the law and the social conditions in which it is applied. There are no case laws or precedents, not even in civil actions. At the basis of our penal code there are three principles: socialist humanism, socialist legality and socialist democracy. The first principle recognizes that man is the product of his work; the second, that no one can be punished unless he has committed a crime in law; the third, that there is popular democracy in the application of the law.

In order to forestall the obvious criticisms I might have made regarding earlier legal practice in Cuba, the lawyer went on: 'All citizens in Cuba are considered innocent until they are proved guilty. Confession has no value whatsoever in a court. A person is sentenced in law according to his crime. If he has not committed a crime, he cannot be punished.'

I then asked about the principle of *habeas corpus*. 'It is written in the penal code; a suspect must be brought before a judge or court within ten days of his detention. The judiciary is absolutely independent; it is written in Article 125 of the Constitution; no one has the right to interfere. The principle is not merely formal; there is a constant struggle to take it to its ultimate consequences.'

I next raised the issue of the death penalty, by firing squad, which still exists for persons over 20-years old for murder, assaults on minors, and 'crimes against state security'. The latter catch-all phrase has been understandably controversial, and has been applied to include industrial sabotage and attempts on Castro's life, as well as unofficial trade union activity. In April 1981, 67 people were reportedly under sentence of death in the Combinado del Este, and by August 1981, 54 had been executed for crimes such as attempting to burn a bus, attempting to burn down a sugar factory, and for taking hostages in an embassy. On 1 October 1982, 29 were accused of attempting to assassinate Castro and were in La Cabaña prison under threat of execution. Ten prisoners sentenced to death in 1959 are still said to be in prison with their cases unreviewed. In 1983, the Western press also took up the case of five Cubans who were allegedly sentenced to death on 25 April 1983 for trying to form a Solidarity-style trade union, although it was subsequently reported that they were probably involved in a local dispute with management, and their sentences commuted to imprisonment. The spokesman for the Ministry of Justice realized the sensitivity of the issue of capital punishment, and chose his words carefully:

No one is in favour of the death penalty; it is a necessary evil. Yes, we have it on the statute book, but there is a great difference between the law and its practice. Before 1958, there was no legal death penalty in Cuba but in seven years more than 20,000 of the most honest, heroic and pure Cubans were killed under Batista's dictatorship. In Nicaragua there was no greater assassin and criminal than Somoza and yet the death penalty was illegal. On the other hand, in El Salvador no legal death penalty exists, yet it is applied in law. So you see, there is a great difference between the law and its practice. Here in Cuba, with the triumph of the Revolution, the death penalty was used against torturers, assassins and war criminals, but the accused were allowed their own defence and were judged by popular tribunals. Although we still have the death penalty, its implementation is now disappearing.

The other controversial aspect of the Cuban judicial system is the 'crime against state security'. Despite official claims to the contrary, such crimes involve religious beliefs and political views. For instance, writings which are interpreted as against the Revolution in any way are considered crimes against the state. In the early days of the Revolution, when Cuba was threatened by a US invasion and counter-revolutionaries were active in the Escambray mountains, there were thousands of political prisoners detained, often denounced by the CDRs. The well-organized Ministry of the Interior, run on the lines of the KGB, painstakingly maintains security and sifts out potential counter-revolutionaries. In 1965 Castro admitted that there were 20,000 political prisoners being held.[2] Ex-prisoner Pierre Goldendorf maintained there were as many a decade later.[3] During the brief dialogue between the Cuban government and members of the exiled community in the US, Castro declared in November 1978 that he was willing to release 3,000 people imprisoned for 'crimes against state security' as well as an additional 600 jailed for 'illegal departures' which allegedly represented 80 per cent of the total number of political prisoners. Castro insisted however on 28 July 1983 to visiting French and American journalists that

From our point of view, we don't have any human rights problem. Here we don't have any people who've disappeared, people who've been tortured, people who've been murdered. Throughout the 25 years of the Revolution in spite of the difficulties and the dangers we've experienced, there has never been a person tortured; there has never been a crime.

The issue of political prisoners is, of course, one of the West's principal weapons in the cold war against Communist states, and Cuba is no exception. Individual cases which come to light are given maximum coverage in the Western press. The case of Armando Valladares, who was released in October 1983 having served almost 22 years of a 30-year sentence for allegedly being a counter-revolutionary, has been widely reported after the publication of his prison memoirs *Against All Hope* (1985). The claims of torture and atrocious prison conditions made by Jorge Vallas in May 1984 after serving a 20-year sentence for giving evidence in defence of a friend accused of being a Batista informer, was also given widespread coverage. Cuba's prisoners continued to make the headlines when the Reverend Jesse Jackson flew out in June 1984 with 26 prisoners, and the French explorer Jacques Cousteau left with 17 early in 1986.

But despite the publicity, it is impossible to confirm the number of political prisoners held in Cuban jails, or the conditions in which they are kept, as no international commission is allowed into the country to check. Estimates vary between several hundred and several thousand, and the higher figure seems more likely. They are held for crimes ranging from refusing to do military service, trying to leave the country without permission, and expressing counter-revolutionary views. Amnesty International is still concerned about the continued detention of some 80 long-term political prisoners (known as *plantados* for refusing to co-operate with the prison authorities or undergo political re-education) who had completed their original sentences. They are chiefly held in the Combinado del Este prison in Havana, in Kilo Siete near Camagüey and in the Boniato prison in Santiago. Amnesty International has also been worried about 'the increase in judicial executions for allegedly political crimes; and prolonged detention without charge in the custody of the state security police of people suspected of political activities'.[4] The organization adopted five prisoners of conscience in 1986 who were arrested allegedly for being members of the unofficial Cuban Committee for Human Rights.

When I raised the controversial subject of political prisoners, the spokesman of the Ministry of Justice answered again with great care:

We do not have political prisoners as such. There are prisoners who have acted against the security of society or engaged in counter-revolutionary activity such as espionage, sabotage, terrorism, piracy, divulging state secrets, propagating enemy propaganda. They are treated the same as common criminals and undergo the same regime of work and re-education. You have to realize that dictatorship is necessary in order for us to survive. We are a small, poor nation, next door to the US, the greatest power in the world. For the past 26 years, they have been looking at us all the time. From 1959 to 1969, there were 1,500 US interventions in Cuba alone. Thousands of saboteurs and counter-revolutionaries have infiltrated our schools, factories and farms. There have been at least 30 attempts on Fidel's life. In these circumstances we have to defend ourselves from aggression and take the necessary precautions.

Despite the constant threat of subversion and sabotage, it cannot be denied that in general the due process of law now takes place in Cuba, and that the treatment of prisoners is much better than under Batista. Detentions and executions usually take place within the framework of legality. Prison conditions have improved and considerable efforts are made to rehabilitate the wrongdoer into society. Although no official figures are published, the crime rate is said to have more than halved since the Revolution, and the rate of recidivism is said to be low. There is virtually no prostitution, gambling or drug trafficking. Women feel safe to walk on the streets at night.

Of course, crime still exists. I was told by an acquaintance always to lock my things in a car: 'I know my people,' he told me. 'Don't tempt them.' A BBC journalist friend had all her recording equipment stolen at a private function. Nevertheless, it is impossible to generalize from such incidents, and there has undoubtedly been a considerable decrease in crime. It has been achieved to a large extent by the changes in society that make theft less of a temptation, and the use of violence more dangerous. Moreover, the power of public opinion, as expressed in the mass organizations, strengthens the rule of law to such an extent that some find it oppressive.

But while there is less crime in Cuba today and the judicial system is more stable, delinquency still remains a significant problem. Even Castro admitted at the fourth Congress of the Federation of Cuban Women in March 1985 that Cuba still has an unacceptable number of 'children with criminal tendencies'.[5]

However the problem of delinquency is not new. In the sixties, Cuba had its problems with 'hippy' youths who neither studied nor worked and committed 'anti-social' acts, particularly in Havana around the La Rampa area.[6] They formed groups with names like *Los Chicos Now*, (The Now Boys) *Los del Tercero Mundo* (Those of the Third World), *Los Chicos Melenudos* (The Hairy Boys), or even *Los Sicodélicos* (The

Psychedelic Ones). 'There was no respect for Cuban culture,' I was told by a former member of the 'Happy Boys'. 'We listened to the Beatles and the Rolling Stones, and were attracted to American culture. I even wore tight pants and a long-haired wig. We had parties lasting all night, and spent our time looking for pleasure.'

Hair, as in the West, was symbolic. The guerrillas swore not to cut their hair until they were victorious, and swept into the elegant boulevards of Havana like so many young hippies, with beads around their necks. *Los Barbudos* they were called, and people even grew beards to appear Revolutionary, although Cubans have traditionally been clean-shaven. As Sartre observed, the beard meant to the supporters of Batista and the bourgeoisie, 'ambush, the law of the jungle, and extermination'.[7] But the order then went out for the Revolutionaries to cut their beards, symbolically marking the regime's transition from Revolution to administration. Except for Castro himself, beards were not even allowed in the army. The long hair of youth in the late 1960s had the same symbolic value as the dreadlocks of the Rastafarians in neighbouring Jamaica. For those in power, it implied chaos, revolt and individualism.

From 1964 to 1968, the struggle between the regime and disaffected youth intensified. Like their counterparts in the West, their attempt to drop out and create their own sub-culture was seen as a threat to the state. In Cuba it also led to a criminalization of the youth: from 1960 to 1968, 41 per cent of all crimes were committed by minors. Truancy was also high: in 1969, it was admitted that there were 400,000 children between the age of 6 and 16 who neither attended school nor worked.[8]

The response of the regime was to clamp down on the youth in order to prevent them from developing fully an alternative culture. In the 1968 Revolutionary Offensive against small traders, many so-called hippies were arrested. An Army of Working Youth was created to set delinquents to work under military discipline although this was abandoned in 1973 partly because of its inefficiency and partly because of continuing escapes and desertions. At the same time legislation against delinquency was stiffened. The Cuban Defence Code recognized that some criminal responsibility was applicable to children at the age of 12; full responsibility was reduced from 18 to 16 years. In 1971 truancy was made a criminal act.

There was a parallel increase in the control and surveillance of the young. Cumulative student files were introduced and the youth organizations—the Pioneers and the Union of Young Communists—were strengthened in order to divert energies in an approved direction. The parents' associations and the CDRs have also been asked to keep an eye on families with children who develop 'anti-social' tendencies and to make sure that all children attend school.

While the law and institutions have been used to impose sanctions against delinquency, there has been a long public debate on the causes of the phenomenon, particularly as its continued existence is an implicit criticism of the Revolutionary regime and its attempt to create the New-Man. The family is considered the fundamental unit of society in Cuba and therefore the primary agent for the socialization of the young. Since parents tend to educate their children according to their own moral standards, it is considered the institution which bears the greatest responsibility for children and the creation of the New Man. In this context, the roots of delinquency have been traced to the parental errors of over-protection, rejection, neglect, over-domination and irregular discipline.[9] Parents are also constantly reminded to feel love and affection for their children: 'Love them, they're yours' declare the posters. And while officials call for greater parental discipline, corporal punishment has been rigorously condemned and forbidden in schools, and the best form of discipline is recognized to operate through parental example.

Castro has recently contributed to the debate on delinquency by stressing the responsibility of the family. 'The Revolution,' he told the fourth Congress of the Federation of Cuban Women on 24 March 1985, 'has constantly called and demanded the co-operation of the family, the family unit, in everything related to the upbringing of the new generations.' Education is not just a task for schools and teachers, he reminded the mothers in his audience, since 'education greatly depends on the work of the home and the parents'. In the same speech, Castro gave the findings of recent Cuban research about the causes of delinquency. These suggest that children are more likely to be anti-social and do less well at school if they come from families with a high rate of divorce, with large numbers living in overcrowded accommodation, and with poor discipline, or discipline based on physical punishment. All children with 'criminal tendencies' come from families who have relatives with a history of anti-social behaviour so that 'criminal conduct becomes a sort of legacy'. There is also evidence to show that delinquents come from families with 'poor revolutionary integration', with the consequent 'lack of positive role models, lack of supervision in the fulfilment of established norms'.[10] Above all, a close correlation has been observed between truancy and delinquency. It is clear, to Castro at least, that if parents live in small stable families, set a proper Revolutionary example, and get their children to school, then the widespread problem of delinquency would decline and the ideal of the New Man be closer to realization.

Castro's stress on the inadequacy of family life as the primary cause of delinquency is not shared by all Cuban specialists. Firstly, there is a view widely held by psychologists and educationalists that children are 'malleable clay', as Guevara put it, who are entirely shaped by their environment.[11] On this model, all abnormal behaviour of individuals is learned and therefore can be unlearned, especially by 'the use of social pressure by the group which acts over them, incorporating in them positive attitudes which permit them to be useful in society'.[12] Secondly, there is a common assumption about males, based on a developmental approach to personality, that 'boys will be boys' and that anti-social behaviour is a phase in their maturing process. Thirdly, social causes such as the remains of capitalist society, the continued influence of the US, and the inevitable social disharmony created by radical change, have all been put forward as explanations for the continued existence of delinquency.[13]

But despite the recognition of the importance of these psychological and social causes in shaping the behaviour of the young, the Cuban state refuses to accept any blame for delinquency. For all the stress placed on the environment by educationalists, the law assumes that a youth over 16 is a rational being possessed of free will and is entirely responsible for his or her acts. Since the state by definition is good, and the party line correct, it therefore follows that the responsibility for crime and delinquency can only be blamed on adverse historical influences and the family. In fact it would appear that Cuban delinquency, primarily involving urban, poorly educated males coming from disrupted homes, has developed in forms similar to those found in capitalist countries. Delinquency is certainly still very visible in Havana. Outside the hotels in La Rampa, young men hang about and openly accost you with '*¡Cambio, Cambio!*' offering pesos for your dollars at three or four times the official exchange rate. They all want to do business even though if caught they could get two or three years in prison. One day, walking along a side street with another European friend, two young Cubans approached us and enquired, '*¿Sovieticos, Sovieticos?*' and offered under their breath *plata mejicana* or Mexican silver.

Although delinquency is widespread, there is no organized dissent in Cuba. The problem of dissent has of course been partly solved by the periodic exodus of malcontents. The first great surge occurred between 1959 and 1960, when the wealthy, the professionals and the powerful who had benefited under Batista's regime left as socialism began to bite into their privileges. The second wave was in 1968 after the Revolutionary Offensive nationalized the small businesses and many shopkeepers and artisans left. The third great exodus of the *gusanos* or worms, as they are called, took place in 1980 and 125,000 Cubans left when Castro briefly opened the door. Many continue to wait to have exit visas processed so that they can join their relatives abroad. The result of these movements has meant that a million Cubans, ten per cent of the population, now live abroad, mainly in the USA and to a lesser extent in Spain and Mexico. But there is little organized resistance amongst *émigrés*. In Miami, the largest centre of exiled Cubans, the old opposition groups have lost their way and most young Cubans are more interested in making it in US society rather than attempting the seemingly impossible task of toppling Castro's regime.

It is still possible to hear dissident voices in Cuba. One young woman, a child of the Revolution, who was waiting for a visa to leave, had no illusions about the regime. 'There is no freedom in Cuba,' she told me. 'You can't say what you want. Everybody is checking on what you are doing. You can't move without being watched.' Other more loyal Cubans complained to me about the unnecessary level of surveillance in the country. Ironically, however, research amongst Cuban exiles in the US shows that their chief complaint is not so much about the limits on expression but the absence of the freedom to do business in Cuba. Indeed, the main reasons stated for leaving are pragmatic rather than ideological.[14]

The greatest outburst of dissidence, an outburst which still disturbs Cubans by its strength and extent, occurred during the Mariel exodus of 1980. Castro is reported to have been particularly shocked. Ironically, the year before, Castro had tried to begin a dialogue with Cuban exiles in the US and talks with President Carter about the reunification of families were well under way. Even the Cubans who had left were no longer being called *gusanos* but *mariposas*, butterflies, by the Cuban press. The affair began when the Peruvian Embassy was occupied by a group of dissidents wanting to leave the country. The news spread like wildfire; people came on foot, in cars and in trucks. Soon as many as 10,000 people were squeezed together in the embassy grounds. Other Western embassies, especially those of Venezuela, Ecuador and the Vatican, were occupied. President Carter declared an open door policy to anyone with a family in the US. More than 1,250 ships came to Mariel harbour near Havana to ferry them across to Florida. Eventually Carter was forced to restrict their flow, concerned, so the Cubans say, about the number of spies joining the crowds.

For the Cuban authorities, it seemed at first a golden opportunity to clear out all the dissidents, delinquents, homosexuals, political prisoners and mental patients who wanted to leave the country. Immigration officers were directed by the ever-watchful CDRs to the houses of suspected dissidents. Those who wanted to leave were then given passes and allowed to sleep in their homes until they were called for to be escorted to Mariel harbour. To avoid a brain drain, certain jobs were classified so that a doctor or an engineer could not leave unless he or she could pay for training. Mental patients were sent, it is claimed, only if their family in exile requested it, but allegedly many were just added to the lists to embarrass Carter.

The affair clearly got out of hand and turned Havana into an uproar. Cuban crowds besieged the embassy and fought with Cubans trying to gain admittance, one bus crashing through the gates of the Peruvian embassy and killing a Cuban guard. If a defector was caught, he would be beaten up by the crowd. Both sides would hurl continual abuse at each other. At one stage 50 to 70 ex-political prisoners took refuge in the US Interests Section building. The CDRs and FMC called out women who laid siege to the place; the situation became very tense when a woman was killed by a truck. Further bloodshed was only avoided when the police were allowed to rearrest the ex-prisoners.

For many Cubans, especially for those who had not witnessed the Revolution itself, the experience proved traumatic. The faith of the patriotic was deepened by the spectacle. As one young Communist militant told me:

They were all anti-social bums, homosexuals, lesbians. After a bus knocked down and killed a Cuban guard, the embassies were circled by the police and angry crowds. Once inside the embassy grounds, they began to behave as if in another country; they had no respect for the government or the Revolution. They smoked marijuana openly and girls were raped by ex-prisoners. They made Abakuá and *ñáñigo* tattoos on themselves—big hearts and pictures of St Barbara. The government agreed to feed them, but the strong took the food parcels from the weak. They started making knives from bits of metal. They were doing all sorts of dirty things. It was the first time that I realized what the dictatorship of the proletariat meant—that the majority has a right to force the minority. When one of them fell out of a tree on the wrong side of the embassy wall, he was beaten up by the Rev-olutionaries. I get very excited when I talk about those days because we were so directly affected. Two of my cousins left, and then my aunt (who was the president of the local CDR) left because of her children. One of the people at work also wanted to go to see his father. About a hundred fellow workers came out to throw eggs and

shout abuse at him: 'Traitor! Son of a bitch! Homosexual!' That is
the dictatorship of the proletariat. It was incredible; whatever you
could imagine, happened. Kids were leaving their parents and vice
versa—although a mother couldn't take her kids, if the father didn't
want them to go.

In the end, it is estimated that 125,000 Cubans left. Most of them
were young working men won over to the American dream. More than
300,000 put down their names to go, and Cubans say that there were
probably half a million *escoria* (scum) which the country could have
done very well without. As the numbers began to swell, it became
increasingly embarrassing for Castro and more difficult for Carter, so
the lists were cut short and the lid put back on the can of disaffected
worms. But Cubans are still on the waiting list to go and negotiations
continue with the US administration. Cuba thus still has its safety valve
and the US a glove labelled 'dissent' to box the ears of its most hated
adversary.

Disorder in the shape of crime, delinquency and dissent thus still
exists in Cuba, but the state has ensured that the rule of Soviet-style
law prevails. Delinquency remains a significant problem, but no more
than in other countries. The crime rate has halved, and the use of the
death penalty is less frequent. The number of political prisoners has
been reduced considerably. Dissent continues, but it is not organized,
and many of the most disaffected have managed to go into exile. Above
all, the majority of Cubans support the present judicial system and see
the police as protecting their interests rather than acting as an independent tyrannical force. The result is that the Cuban state has never been
so strong, and little short of a foreign invasion seems likely to shake
its firm rule.

15

INTERNATIONAL SOLIDARITY

Cuba has been called a small nation with a big nation's foreign policy. From the beginning, Castro's regime followed a distinctive but erratic path in its dealings with other nations. It has not only made its voice heard but, despite its size, plays a major role in international affairs. Few weeks pass by without the mention of Cuba in the world's press.

Although the Cuban Revolution was at first an 'olive green', nationalist revolution, it rapidly became internationalist in outlook. Cuba presented itself as a revolutionary model for other oppressed nations of the world, and the Cuban leaders called for a global struggle against US imperialism. The country continues to pride itself on its internationalist spirit, and its Constitution enshrines 'the principles of proletarian internationalism and the combative solidarity of peoples' (Article 12).

The independent nature of the Cuban Revolution and the experience of guerrilla warfare enabled the Cuban leaders to offer a new path to national liberation and social revolution. Castro was quick to try and assume the leadership of the struggle against US imperialism. The first Declaration of Havana, issued by Castro on 2 September 1960, asserted Cuba's right to export revolution and 'the duty of each nation to make common cause with all the oppressed, colonized, exploited peoples, regardless of their location in the world'.[1] Castro responded to the decision of the Organization of American States (OAS) to suspend Cuba as a member state by asserting in the second Declaration of Havana on 4 February 1962 that 'the duty of every Revolutionary is to make Revolution'.[2] The call seemed to catch fire in Latin America at least; guerrilla movements arose in Venezuela and Guatemala in 1962 and in Colombia in 1964. The landing of US marines in the Dominican Republic in April 1965 only seemed to confirm Castro's claims that US imperialism posed an international threat which could only be countered by armed struggle.

Guevara, in the meantime, stressed that the real contradiction in the world was not between capitalism and Communism, but between the developed and underdeveloped countries. He called for a trade union of the poor nations who made up the Third World in the continents of Africa, Asia and Latin America, insisting that the developed countries of East and West were opposed to the interests of the Third World. In a speech to the General Assembly of the United Nations on 11 December 1964 he declared that there could be no peaceful coexistence between 'the exploiters and the exploited, the oppressor and the oppressed'.[3] At the Afro-Asian Solidarity Conference held in Algiers on 26 February 1965, he further asserted: 'There are no boundaries in this struggle to the death . . . The practice of proletarian internationalism is not only a duty for the peoples struggling for a better future, it is an inescapable necessity.'[4]

Sharing Guevara's views, Castro established the headquarters of the Latin American Solidarity Organization (OLAS) and the Afro-Asian Latin American People's Solidarity Organization (OSPAAAL) in Havana after the Tricontinental Solidarity Organization (TSO) Conference was held there in January 1966. From somewhere in Bolivia, Guevara sent a message to the next TSO conference held in April 1967, calling on the peoples of Latin America, Africa and Asia to liberate themselves at any cost. Since imperialism was a world system, it could only be defeated by a global confrontation. All must therefore fight together in genuine proletarian internationalism and try to create 'two, three, many Vietnams' on the face of the globe.[5]

The OLAS Conference held in August of the following year adopted as its key slogan: 'The duty of every Revolutionary is to make Revolution' and reaffirmed, much to the alarm of the USSR and the USA, that armed struggle must be the fundamental strategy. The conference also coincided with the appearance of Régis Debray's *Revolution in the Revolution?* which rejected the leadership of the traditional Communist parties, presented the Cuban Revolution as the only correct path, and argued that the guerrilla force should be 'the party in embryo'.[6]

Castro's response to the death of Guevara in Bolivia on 8 October 1967 was initially to become even more of a maverick in the Communist camp. At the International Cultural Congress held in Havana in January 1968, he belittled orthodox Communism for its lack of militancy and called for an updating of Marxism to meet the present situation: 'Nothing can be more anti-Marxist than dogma', he declared, 'Nothing can be more anti-Marxist than the ossification of ideas . . .' While admitting that the Cuban Revolution 'never claimed a monopoly on revolutionary truths', he nevertheless made it clear that he considered it in a better position than the 'ecclesiastical forces' within Marxism to interpret and express the aspirations of the Third World.[7] He then proceeded to accuse

Aníbal Escalante and his 'micro-faction' in the party of spreading Soviet propaganda. Relations with Moscow could not have been at a lower ebb.

And yet a few months later in August 1968, the Year of the Heroic Guerrilla, Castro was approving of the Soviet intervention in Czechoslovakia and condemning the 'inadmissible romantic and idealistic attitude' of the Czech leaders.[8] Towards the end of the year, a Cuban-East German communiqué was signed on the necessity of fighting 'against all forms of revisionism and opportunism'.[9] In July 1969 a Soviet naval squadron visited Cuba for the first time. This growing accommodation with the Soviet Union seems to have resulted from a sense of disillusion and loss of will after the death of Guevara in 1967, and the failure of 'many Vietnams' to flower in the Latin American continent. Cuba also was suffering from severe economic problems, and all its energies were directed to making the ten-million ton sugar harvest in 1970. After the collapse of this project, Castro abandoned his and Guevara's dreams of fermenting world revolution and of building socialism and Communism at the same time.

He accepted the conditions offered by the Soviet Union for his country's economic survival. *Pravda* noted approvingly in October 1970 that the 'Cuban people and the Cuban Communists realize that Cuba's main contribution to the world socialist system and the general revolutionary process now lies in economic building—creating a developed society on this base . . .'[10]

In the same year a Cuban-Soviet Commission of Economic, Scientific and Technical Collaboration was created, and in 1972 Cuba became the only member of COMECON in the West. With Cuba's new-found economic orthodoxy went a political realignment with the Soviet Union which culminated in the new Cuban Constitution of 1976 which was modelled on the East European pattern. In its preamble it acknowledged specifically the 'fraternal friendship, help and co-operation of the Soviet Union'.[11] In the 1980s the Cuban Revolution has emerged as a centrally planned regime, fully integrated in the Soviet bloc economies and dependent on the Soviet Union for its economic prosperity and military security.

It cannot be denied that the Soviet Union has immense leverage on the Cuban economy. Soviet aid runs to about 4 billion US dollars a year. The overall debt with the Soviet Union, according to Western experts, is between 7.5 and 10 billion US dollars. Cuba further exchanges, at prices fixed well above the world market, its sugar, nickel and citrus fruits for Soviet oil at subsidized prices. COMECON accounts for over 70 per cent of Cuban sugar exported, and 90 per cent of its value. Cuba is the first to admit that it has been sheltered by the long-term trade agreements with the Soviet Union and its allies. In 1979 Raúl Castro acknowledged that 'it is only because of the existence of a socialist regime here and our close economic relations with the socialist world, particularly the Soviet Union, that the effects of the present world crisis have not led us into economic bankruptcy'.[12] But the economic advantage is not all one-sided. The Soviet Union needs Cuban sugar and COMECON its citrus fruits, and when the Cuban crop falls short they are obliged to buy them for hard currency and often at premium prices. The Soviet Union may make some small sacrifice in swopping oil for sugar, but it can get rid of a whole range of manufactured goods virtually unsaleable elsewhere. All the barter trade is fixed bilaterally.

Again, while Cuba has remained a one-crop enclave and the USSR has replaced the US as its principal trading partner, there are some important differences. Whereas the United States previously owned the largest sugar mills, major enterprises, mines and banks, these are all now in Cuban hands. Soviet aid is intended to help the country to develop an industrial base rather than to keep it dependent. Indeed, the trading relationship between Cuba and the Soviet Union is closer to the kind of equitable exchange demanded by many Third World countries between the developed North and the developing South. Soviet aid to Cuba is no more than US aid to Puerto Rico.

On the other hand, with the increasing economic aid, the ideological and cultural influence of the Soviet Union has undoubtedly grown. There is a massive propaganda campaign in favour of the Soviet Union. Most scientific, technical and philosophical textbooks are translations from Russian. Russian is now as important as English in the secondary schools. The shops are full of Russian books, from official biographies of Marx to books like *The Folk Art of the Ukraine*. The Marx-Engels-Lenin triumvirate have had parks, factories, schools and hospitals named after them all over the country.

Yet despite the close ties, Cubans have not always got on well with the Russians on a personal level. When the Russians first came during the missile crisis, the Cubans were apparently not impressed by their shoddy clothes and drunken behaviour on the rare occasions they were let out of their bases. The Russian temperament is a mystery to most Cubans. On the paper stands it is the Soviet and Eastern European magazines and papers which gather dust. In Havana, it is the American films, not the Russian ones, which attract the longest queues. It will take a long time before it will be possible to talk of Russian cultural imperialism at work in Cuba.

Cuba is as Cuban as ever, and remains fundamentally a Latin American and Caribbean country. This obvious fact is often overlooked.

Many Cubans are now learning Russian, but Cuba shares with the countries of Latin America common ties of language, Iberian-Catholic culture, and colonial experience. Castro sprang from this matrix and, like Bolívar and Martí before him, has a vision of the united and independent Americas—*nuestra América*—which shapes its own destiny and is not dictated to by greater powers.

Despite the ideological and economic ties, it would therefore be wrong to conclude that Cuba is a Soviet satellite 90 miles off the coast of the US. A strong sense of Cuban history has made Castro fiercely independent: 'This Revolution', he declared in March 1967, 'will never be anybody's satellite or yes-man. It will never ask anybody's permission to maintain its position, either in the matters of ideology, or in domestic or foreign affairs.'[13] He is only too well aware of Martí's dictum: 'The nation that sells only to one nation dies.' Indeed, Castro insisted in July 1984 that: 'Some things are sacred: independence, the sovereignty of our country, its Revolutionary principles, its political and social system, and its right to build a future. These are things we will never give up, and those who try to destroy them will have to fight us.'[14]

There is a general harmony in Cuba with Soviet foreign policy, especially when it comes to defending attacks from the West on human rights and Marxist-Leninist doctrine. Soviet and Cuban operations overseas are co-ordinated, but Castro insists that Cuba is independent and sovereign. Just as the Soviet Union disapproved in the 1960s of Cuban calls for armed struggle in Latin America, so it would seem to prefer Cuba to be more moderate in the region in the 1980s. Cuba's forays in Africa since 1976, especially in Ethiopia and Angola, seem to have been largely of its own initiative and undoubtedly stretch its limited resources and personnel. Cuba backed the USSR in the United Nations on the 14 January 1980 vote that condemned the Soviet invasion of Afghanistan, but it has been notably silent about its continued occupation. On the other hand, it has criticized the Polish Communist party for losing its contact with the masses. And although China accused Cuba of sending mercenaries to Angola, since 1984 relations have improved.

At the same time, Cuba has been careful to nurture its links with the West. It has successfully renegotiated its debts of $3.2 billion, and has been scrupulous in repaying its commitments when they fall due. It is keen to develop trade, running at present at 15 per cent of Cuba's total trade, with the West, especially Canada, Western Europe (particularly France and Spain) and Japan. It would like to improve its tourism with the West to its pre-revolutionary level.

If anything, Castro would appear to be increasingly irritated by his country's dependence on the Soviet Union and the claim of his enemies that he is merely a puppet of the Russians. He not only refused to attend the funeral of Konstantin Chernenko in March 1985, but has shown few signs of being impressed by Mikhail Gorbachev's new style of leadership. It seems that he wants to transform his image from being the agent of the Communist East to a champion of the underdeveloped South.

Following Guevara's vision Castro still sees the major conflict in the world more between the North (developed countries) and the South (developing countries) rather than between the Communist East and the capitalist West. The recent self-image of Cuba in speeches and publications is as a member of the Third World, committed as ever to participate in the struggles of the wretched of the earth. After being elected president of the non-aligned movement, Castro was careful to voice the consensus of its members at the summit of the movement held in Havana in September 1979, and in his address as its official spokesman to the 34th session of the United Nations General Assembly held the following month. Castro further insisted to US and French journalists in July 1983 that 'we are socialists but we also belong to the Third World . . . we have common interest with it'.[15] He therefore enthusiastically supports a new economic order between North and South, black liberation in South Africa, and the struggle against Zionist imperialism and racism in the Middle East. In his closing speech to the seventh session of the Cuban parliament, he further declared in January 1985: 'The world needs détente and needs peace. Otherwise, thousands of millions of human beings in the Third World won't have the slightest hope of a solution.'[16]

Cuba's commitment to what the Constitution calls 'proletarian internationalism and the combative solidarity of peoples' has meant that hundreds of thousands of volunteers have served on missions abroad. They have helped build schools, hospitals and roads in countries as disparate as Peru, Jamaica, Grenada, Nicaragua, Tanzania and North Vietnam. They have helped with military programmes in Syria, South Yemen, Algeria and Somalia. They have supported the national liberation movement in Mozambique in 1963 and in Guinea-Bissau and the Congo in 1965. Although the Cubans work for low salaries, in some cases they have earnt hard currency by building, for instance, in Iraq and Libya.

However, Cuba's greatest involvement has been in Angola and Ethiopia since 1975. Cubans see their role as not only 'settling their debt with humanity' but as expressing solidarity with the people of Africa with whom they share a common ancestry. Guevara also set a precedent by training and fighting alongside the freedom fighters in the Congo for most of 1965. In Ethiopia, Cuba helped check the advance of the Somalis in the Ogaden War in 1978, but after refusing to fight the Eritreans, whom it once supported, it reduced its presence from about 10,000 to about 2,000 advisers in 1985. Cuba has been even more committed in Angola, engaging about 25,000 troops to help the MPLA government contain the South African-backed UNITA rebels. It has also provided about 6,000 civilian technicians. Considerable assistance has also been given to SWAPO, fighting for the independence of Namibia. The South African government claims that the chief stumbling block to a settlement in Namibia is the presence of Cuban troops in Angola. Castro certainly boasts that in all some 60,000 Cubans have been through Angola, and he is ready to commit another 60,000. At the third Congress of the Communist party in February 1986, he insisted that he would not withdraw Cuban troops until the system of apartheid was dismantled.

Cubans insist that they are not in Africa as Soviet surrogates, even though the operations of the two countries are co-ordinated to a degree. They also reject the accusation that they are a new kind of imperialist. An imperialist, they point out, invades Africa and takes what he can. Cubans are invited to Africa to give all they can. While the imperialist lives off the country he occupies, the internationalist helps develop it for the future benefit of its people. The Cubans remain however the leading foreign military force in Africa.

After the death of Guevara in 1967, Castro became more cautious in Latin America. In the 1970s Cuba assiduously sought ties with countries which recognized its right to exist. Relations with Chile were renewed in 1970, and Castro paid a triumphant visit to the country a year later; however, the fall of Allende in 1973 put paid to the friendly relations between the two countries. Cuba's new reticence in the region led to the OAS effectively lifting sanctions in the middle of the 1970s. By 1977, Cuba enjoyed cordial relations with Panama, Peru, Colombia, Guyana and Venezuela in Latin America, and with the Bahamas, Barbados and Trinidad and Tobago in the Caribbean. After the fall of Galtieri, diplomatic links have been renewed with Argentina. Cuba's increasingly warm involvement with Manley's Jamaica was cut short by a change of government in 1980. Its close ties with the Jewel movement in Grenada were abruptly ended by the US invasion of the island in 1983. Although President Duvalier was forced to flee in 1986 in neighbouring Haiti, there was little evidence of Cuban influence at work. In June 1986, Brazil was sufficiently impressed by Cuba's record to reopen diplomatic ties.

Cuba's economic and military support for the Sandinistas in Nicaragua is considerable. It involves sending 2,000 teachers, doctors and advisers, according to Cuban sources, although the US claims it has at least 6,000 military advisers on the ground. Although the Sandinista government increasingly resembles Cuba's, with CDRs, censorship, and schools creating the New Man and Woman, Castro insists that Cuban advisers are not there to teach Marxism-Leninism and that they 'do not interfere in the least in the people's political convictions'.[17] Much to the annoyance of the US, Castro flew to Nicaragua in January 1985 for the inauguration of President Daniel Ortega. Cuba also actively helps the Farabundo Martí Front fighting in El Salvador. Nevertheless, Cuba has ruled out any direct involvement in the event of an overt US military intervention there, and supports the call of the Contadora group of countries, Venezuela, Panama, Mexico and Colombia, for a negotiated settlement to the conflict in Central America.

Cuba continues to influence the revolutionary sub-cultures of the continent. In June 1984, for instance, at a meeting of 31 leftist parties in Havana—hailed as the 'first consultative meeting of the Caribbean and Central American anti-imperialist organizations'—Cuba reasserted its hegemony and called for the dismantling of all foreign military bases and a zone of peace in the region.

Cuba's relations with most Latin American governments have improved in the wake of its support for Argentina in the Malvinas war. Castro has dropped talk of the need for armed struggle in his speeches and now advocates a broad front for his policies just like the orthodox Communists in the 1950s and 1960s. A conference of Latin American and Caribbean countries held in Havana on the international debt in August 1985 was notably attended by several right-wing politicians, military officers and prominent churchmen from Latin America who, in former times, might have been expected to visit the country only after a US invasion. Nevertheless, they did not prevent Castro from calling for a general strike of debtor nations, insisting 'we must win our freedom and not indemnify our oppressors'.[18]

Cuba's foreign policy is of course dominated by the brooding presence of the US. The United States refuses to abandon its large naval base at Guantánamo which, according to the Cuban government, 'has only served to offend the honour of our nation, to harbour counter-revolutionary forces, to introduce arms into the country with which to fight the liberating revolution, to concentrate troops wherever the liberation movements in Caribbean countries have threatened imperialist domination'.[19] The Cuban government further accuses the CIA of a continued campaign of subversion and sabotage, and of repeated attempted assassinations of Castro. It even claims that it is guilty of biological warfare by introducing swine fever in 1979, and dengue fever and blue tobacco mould in 1980. Television and radio beamed from Florida and Washington create a barrage of anti-revolutionary propaganda.

Cuba, for its part, constantly views the US as enemy number one. Whenever the US is mentioned in Castro's speeches, his audience still breaks out into the chant: 'Fidel, Fidel, Give the Yankees Hell!' Clearly, in a military sense, Cuba cannot give the US hell, but the country takes the threat of a US invasion seriously. The result is that the whole of Cuba has become militarized and boasts the best equipped armed forces in Latin America. After the invasion of Grenada in 1983, the country was put on a war footing, with its regions organized into defence zones as in Vietnam. Civil defence exercises were organized involving the whole of the population. In all, Cuba felt compelled to double its planned defence spending in the first half of the 1980s. During a visit of the United Nations Secretary General Pérez de Cuellar in May 1985, Castro declared: 'We are all ready to fight. We have created conditions for that and consider ourselves invincible.'[20] Like Reagan, Castro believes in the paradox that the best way to achieve peace is to prepare for war.

While building up the country's defences, however, Castro has been more ready to talk with the US. An anti-hijacking pact was signed in 1973. With the election of President Carter and the ending of the Vietnam war, relations began to thaw a little. A US Interests Section was opened in the former US Embassy in Havana in 1977, and in the following year direct commercial flights were resumed. Castro opened the door to visits from Cuban exiles in Florida. In November 1978, Castro said he was willing to release 3,000 people imprisoned for crimes against state security, as well as an additional 600 jailed for illegal departures—which allegedly represented 80 per cent of the total number—in his attempt to woo the Cuban community in the US. But the Mariel exodus of 125,000 disaffected Cubans in 1980 and the subsequent election of President Reagan soon put relations back into deep freeze.

Yet Castro has continued to present himself as wanting better relations with the US, making out that it is Washington which is consistently unfriendly. He stresses that he will never break Cuba's ties with the socialist countries, but he has gone out of his way to be conciliatory: 'Just as we are willing to die and fight,' he declared in his key annual address on 26 July 1984, 'we have no fear of talks and discussion.'[21] In December 1984, a few days after Reagan's reelection, it was agreed that Cuba would take back 2,700 common criminals and mental patients included in the Mariel exodus of 1980, and that the US would accept at least 20,000 Cuban immigrants each year. But when the new Spanish-language José Martí radio station ordered by Reagan broke into the airwaves on Cuba's Independence Day on 20 May 1985, Castro immediately suspended the immigration pact, halted visits by Cuban Americans except for 'humanitarian reasons', and threatened to end co-operation on hijacking between the two countries. US-Cuba relations were plunged again into a deep rift. Yet only a few months later in September 1985, Castro agreed to release another 70 political prisoners following an appeal by visiting American Roman Catholic leaders.

After 28 years of attempted destabilization, Cuba's 'paranoia' about the United States as an imperialist bully is undoubtedly well-founded. The recent US intervention in Grenada and Nicaragua only confirms the worst fears of what the colossus of the north might do. But the constant US threat has not been without its advantages for the Cuban regime. Ever since the 1962 missile crisis, there has been a tacit agreement between the superpowers that Cuba will not be invaded. Yet the apparent threat has played into Castro's hands. It has enabled him to rally his people behind him against a common enemy, and renew their Revolutionary energies. The economic embargo has further provided an excuse for the shortages his people have suffered. The threat of a CIA-backed counter-revolution makes it possible for the state to control and survey its people. Above all, the periodic exodus of malcontents and dissidents to the US has provided a perfect safety valve for the regime.

Despite the Cuban government's implacable opposition to the US system of capitalism and imperialism, there is a considerable amount of curiosity and goodwill towards the American people. The Cuban Revolution has, of course, divided many families, and of the estimated one million Cubans now living in exile, the vast majority have chosen the US as their land of adoption. While many of the older generation still rail at the Castro regime, its seeming invulnerability has led the exiled Cuban community to look to a future elsewhere. The new generation of Cubans born in the US no longer dream of returning to the home of their parents, let alone of organizing an invasion. Their newfound American identity was symbolized by the election early in 1986 of the Harvard-trained Cuban lawyer Xavier Suárez as the mayor of Miami, where Cubans make up nearly half of the city's population of 750,000. He was the first Cuban to become mayor of a medium-sized American city, and with the US becoming increasingly Hispanic, is unlikely to be the last. Like their elders, the younger generation tends to be obsessively anti-Communist and to adhere to the conservative wing of the Republican party.

Cuba, therefore, approaches the end of the 1980s with its adventurous foreign policy largely intact. After the collapse of its offensive in Latin America, it has turned to Africa to refurbish its revolutionary image. It is willing to help revolutionary movements in the Western hemisphere at a distance, but is careful to court the goodwill of reformist governments. Its close economic and ideological ties with the Soviet Union have not prevented it from pursuing an independent path in foreign policy. Above all, while remaining a colourful feather in the cap of the Soviet Union and a painful thorn in the side of the US, it has continued to be a voice for the 'wretched of the earth' and remains a respected member of the socialist community for its support of fledgling socialist regimes throughout the world.

16

BREAKING THE CHAINS

After nearly three decades of Revolution, Cuba has come a long way. It has developed a stable Marxist-Leninist regime in which the ruling elite has the support of the great majority of the people. It has made some remarkable economic and social achievements, especially in the provision of education and health care. From being little more than a corrupt colony before the Revolution, it has become a major voice in international affairs. It is a country to be reckoned with, both ideologically and militarily.

But for all its achievements, can it really be said that Cuba is at the head of the Americas? Does it provide an exemplary model for Third World development? Are the Cuban people, as Guevara argued, more complete because they are more free, and more free because they are more complete?

It cannot be denied that Cuba has to a large extent broken the chains of underdevelopment. Despite the US blockade, the country has notched up an impressive growth rate while other Latin American countries have slipped back. It still remains a predominantly agricultural country, but the industrialization programme is continuing apace. Excessive bureaucracy and waste continue, and there are continuing shortages and a flourishing black market, but the rationing and queues are at least a sign of equitable distribution. In recent years there has been something of a consumer boom. With an innovating attitude to new technology and a well-trained and hard-working labour force, the country is in a good position for sustained industrial growth in the next century.

The greatest achievement of the Revolution has undoubtedly been its agrarian reform. It has proved widely popular and was achieved without the bloody collectivization which took place in the Soviet Union, or the forced removal of scattered farmers into villages as in Tanzania. From the beginning, the regime was careful to respect the wishes of the private farmers, who still form almost a third of the rural workforce. The new co-operative movement developing since 1977 has been encouraged through persuasion rather than force and proved a great success. The regime however sees the co-operatives as only a stepping stone to the full nationalization of all land in Cuba. Farmers will then become salaried workers on state farms rather than members of self-governing communes.

The considerable economic gains have been matched by even greater social achievements. The basic material needs of the Cuban people have been met. They are fully employed, adequately housed, and well fed. Illiteracy has been eradicated. An impressive welfare system has been developed to care for people from the cradle to the grave. No one in Cuba has to worry about where his next meal is coming from or where he will lay his head at night.

The goal of equality has also been achieved to a considerable extent. The differences between town and country, and between workers and peasants, have been lessened enormously. While *machismo* is still widespread, women are no longer confined to the house. They live in a positive atmosphere of encouragement and are participating more and more in the economic and political life of the country. Public racial discrimination has been more or less eradicated, and although private racism still exists, it is becoming increasingly unacceptable. If the white, urban, wealthy intellectual has suffered at the hands of the Revolution, the black, illiterate country woman has gained. There remains the danger, however, that a new educated elite of technocrats and party members will replace the old bourgeoisie, but at least they are likely to have the good of the country rather than the health of their bank accounts in mind. All Cubans suffer from the present conditons of austerity and frugality, but all are poised to share the spoils of future well-being.

These impressive social and economic gains, especially for a Latin American and Third World country, have been achieved at some cost. The country has been unable to break its reliance on sugar, and is dependent on the goodwill of one trading partner, the USSR. The original ideals of the 1960s, when it was hoped that work would become meaningful play, money would be abolished, and Revolutionary will would overcome all obstacles, have been replaced by material incentives and productivity quotas. The goals of social justice and equality have increasingly given way to those of economic growth and militarism. The watchwords of the Revolution are now 'production' and 'defence'.

The attempt to forge the New Man is still considered the greatest task of the Revolution. But there is a danger that the means employed will distort the desired ends. Although it might be concerned more with the group than the individual, 'socialist emulation' as a driving force still encourages competition with its inevitable catalogue of failures and winners. The stress on 'socialist morality' which distinguishes Cuban Communism reveals an unpleasant streak of revolutionary puritanism and intolerance. Corruption still bedevils the bureaucracy; the Old Man, as well as the New, is still around, money-conscious, consumer-orientated and power-seeking.

Nevertheless, much still remains of Guevara's noble vision. It is too idealistic to suggest that the teachings of Christ are emerging in the everyday lives of Cubans without them knowing it, but many have certainly overcome the rapacious greed and materialism which flourished in Cuba before under capitalism. Many people in Cuba have undoubtedly come to think in terms of the general good rather than of personal gain. A great deal of work is still done voluntarily. Thousands volunteer to fight or serve abroad in order to 'repay their debt to humanity' and often risk their lives in a display of 'proletarian solidarity'. The altruistic and egalitarian principles of the Revolution are not mere slogans, but deeply felt.

If, as the Cubans insist, the goal of Communism is to have all the spiritual as well as the material needs of humanity satisfied, then the picture is less bright. While freeing the people from the chains of material underdevelopment, the present regime would seem to have imposed what William Blake called 'mind-forged manacles' of its own. This is principally due to its excessively narrow educational and cultural policy which is based on a dogmatic 'scientific conception' of the world as established and developed by Marxism-Leninism. By denying a metaphysical dimension to human thought and imagination, the cultural commissars in Cuba leave it a poorer place.

On the face of it, the present education system—which is universal, free and continuous—is a remarkable achievement. It has freed the Cuban people from the darkness and silence of illiteracy. It has provided a genuine equality of opportunity whatever the pupil's background. But its restricted ideological framework and narrow curriculum do not encourage critical analysis or creative imagination. Sloganeering is no substitute for free enquiry. It is in danger of forging a New Man or Woman who is one-dimensional, aggressive and obedient. Cuban children are not only brought up in the shadow of the tank, but are expected to fight in a Manichean world in which all good is represented by Communism and all evil by Capitalism. As a result, the schools and universities resemble the training camps of Sparta as much as the community of scholars of ancient Athens. The continuing problem of delinquency shows just how far a significant proportion of the country's youth are still alienated from the Cuban state.

In culture there is widespread state patronage and a concerted effort to reach the people and reflect their lives through the arts. But the narrow application of Castro's dictum, 'Nothing against the Revolution' means that artists, writers and thinkers must serve the Revolution. The state claims to define not only what is *right* but what is *true*. No institution, group or individual is allowed to challenge its monopoly on defining what is reality. This state of affairs has had a stultifying effect on the growth of culture for the mind and imagination, like certain wild animals, cannot breed well in captivity. An adversary or alternative culture simply does not exist. As a result, there is a real danger that the drive for ideological orthodoxy will stifle the creativity and innovation which were the exciting hallmarks of the Revolution in its early stages.

It is possible that the regime's cultural policy will become more liberal as the Revolution grows more secure, and it may not yet be too late for a genuine popular culture to emerge which will draw on Cuba's rich Spanish and African roots and will sing new songs for the new society. While Soviet cultural influence is increasing, Cuban culture is at least sufficiently powerful to retain its own dynamic identity.

The restrictions on the freedom of expression and thought have, of course, given rise to some of the most bitter and telling criticisms of the Cuban Revolution in the West. Cuban officials do not deny that there are restrictions on liberties in Cuba. People are allowed to criticize the means of implementing the goals of the Revolution, but not the goals themselves. At the elite level, there would seem to be a substantial degree of freedom of expression, and behind the closed doors of the National Assembly there is sometimes vigorous and forthright debate. But censorship in general is strict and the media tightly muzzled. It is the Communist party which decides what is the correct ideological line; any other deviation is simply not permitted. Cubans not only have to suffer from the oppression of the law in intellectual and cultural matters, but also the tyranny of public opinion: the mass organizations, especially the CDRs, maintain a constant vigilance and surveillance over potential nonconformists and dissidents. The CDRs not only keep their eyes and ears open but are not reluctant to point their fingers.

However, the restrictions on the freedom of thought and expression are seen by the regime as a necessary sacrifice in the building of Communism. They have consciously adopted the paradox that it is necessary to control the minds of the population in a transitional period towards a free society. Kant's dictum that a people can only become free if they are allowed to practice freedom, is not heeded. Nor is Mill's view that truth can only emerge in the clash of opposing opinions, and that truth is strengthened when criticism is allowed. Even Guevara's position that truth is the best policy in the long run has been forgotten. The regime simply considers that Revolutionary 'truth' to be too fragile and vulnerable to fight its own battles, and therefore needs the support of the policeman's gag and the censor's blue pencil.

Cuban officials, like Deputy Foreign Minister Ricardo Alarcón, defend the policy by arguing that Cuba is at war. 'When Britain was at war with Germany,' he argued in December 1983, 'You had to accept censorship and special measures which impinged on civil liberties.'[1] The analogy, however, is not entirely apt; Cuba is not yet directly at war with anyone.

At the same time, officials argue that Cubans enjoy more fundamental freedoms than the 'bourgeois freedom' advocated by its Western critics. Bourgeois freedom, it is asserted, is mainly concerned with the right of the capitalist to exploit the worker, and the right of the rich to oppress the poor. This view of freedom as economic *laissez-faire* is plainly inadmissible in Cuba's brand of state socialism; indeed, the chief complaint of Cuban exiles has been that one is no longer 'free' to do business in Cuba.[2] Cubans, on the other hand, are said to enjoy 'socialist freedoms' in the sense that they have the opportunity to develop fully as individuals and citizens in a social environment. There may be no right to private property, but there is a right to life, to work, to health and education. As for political freedom, which in the West is reduced to the freedom of voting for different parties, it is claimed that Cubans not only have universal suffrage but their popular assemblies are now more representative than Western parliaments, since they are vehicles of the 'dictatorship of the proletariat' rather than being merely committees for managing the affairs of the 'bourgeoisie'. From this point of view, Minister of Culture Armando Hart finds it possible to argue that 'for the vast majority of the people there's more freedom in Cuba now than ever before'.[3]

Like all the arguments between East and West, it depends of course on what people mean by freedom and whose freedom they are talking about. Certainly there is no 'economic freedom' in Cuba's centrally planned and state-controlled economy. When it comes to political and social freedom, the position is not so clear-cut. Cubans are to a large extent free *from* the ancient ills of their country—from disease, racial discrimination, unemployment, hunger and poverty. At the same time, they are denied many positive freedoms taken for granted in the West: they are not fully free *to* express themselves, to practise their religions, to bring up their children as they see fit, to do nothing, to travel, to be homosexual, to be pacifists, to organize even non-violent opposition to the government and state. They may have gained some negative freedoms, but they have lost other positive ones.

As for Guevara's claim that people in socialist Cuba are freer because they are more complete, and more complete because they are freer, his vision has only been partially realized. Certainly, Cubans have more opportunity for fulfilling their nature as social beings, but this would seem to have been at the expense of their individuality. Again, they all have the opportunity to work, but it cannot be said that their work entirely fulfils the creative aspect of their nature. They may benefit from the collective wealth, but it is the state, not themselves, which owns and manages the means of production. Alienation exists, as expressed in absenteeism and go slows, and for some, work is still avoided like the plague.

It is a commonplace in liberal political philosophy that equality threatens liberty. But there is no intrinsic reason why an equal society should threaten freedom; an equal society should involve an expansion of human freedom by allowing all members of society an equal opportunity to realize their potential. Equality and liberty, moreover, come together in the proposition that everyone has an equal right to be free, and in the principle that the freedom of one is the necessary condition for the freedom of all.

For all its bright promise, it would unfortunately seem to be the case that the Cuban Revolution has sacrificed the freedom of thought and expression and individual freedom in pursuit of social equality. Cuba cannot be called a fully democratic country, either in the liberal sense of being governed by elected representatives of the people, or in the socialist sense, of the people governing themselves through popular assemblies where the real power lies. Critics from the right and left have called it a totalitarian state; it is, in the sense of having an all-powerful, centralized state which plans the economy, controls culture and education, allows no dissent, and endeavours to extend into all parts of society. The 'direct democracy', which so fascinated Sartre and others in the early days of the Revolution, has proved a myth; notions such as workers' control or self-management have not been part of the Cuban Revolutionary vocabulary. At best, Cuba's political system might be described as a 'consultative oligarchy' in that it is a society ruled by a few leaders who have centralized economic and political power but who consult some members of society, especially in the upper echelons of the Communist party.[4] Citizens, too, can make contact with the leadership through the popular assemblies and mass organizations, although their real influence on policy-making remains limited.

Both Guevara and Castro were committed to the idea of the guerrilla group forming a vanguard party in power. Cuba is steered by a small, tightly knit, strongly centralized Marxist-Leninist party which controls the state and imposes its directives on the people. It has a sophisticated system of surveillance through the mass organizations, especially the CDRs and the FMC, and trade unions. All students and workers have fully documented files. No independent intermediary bodies are allowed between the state and the people in the form of mass media, non-Marxist political associations, schools, tribunals, trade unions and churches. All is justified by an appeal to the demands of the Revolution which increasingly seems to be a synonym for the state. The only feasible route for the disaffected is now overseas into exile.

In addition, the country has become militarized from top to bottom, with children, women and old people undergoing military training. The army itself has become hierarchical and authoritarian, modelled on and trained and supplied by the Soviet Red Army. A chauvinistic hatred of the US enemy is encouraged on every possible occasion. The line between the civilian and military realms has been smudged, if not erased. Castro has replaced his crumpled olive-green fatigues for a resplendent military uniform.

The model of development Cuba offered to the world in the 1960s was a co-operative society of workers and peasants in which each person worked for the good of all. In the 1980s, it is that of a centrally planned, highly militarized and tightly controlled society. It is fully integrated into the Soviet bloc economies, and dependent on the Soviet Union for its economic well-being and military security. But there are some positive signs of change. Castro at least would seem eager to increase the government's accountability and to extend popular participation. He has urged the party not to coerce but to persuade people: 'That should always be the style of our party and state: not to impose but to persuade or be persuaded . . . because the greatest wisdom has been, is and will always lie in the people.'[5] He has even warned of the dangers of creating a new technocracy; that is, of creating a group of experts who will pronounce on all matters. It would, he declared in 1980, turn 'the dictatorship of the proletariat into a dictatorship of the secretariat'.[6] Slogans have recently appeared throughout the country declaring: 'The strength of the party lies in its close link with the masses.'

Moreover, a reorganization of the Communist party was undertaken in 1985. It culminated in the third Congress held in February 1986 when 10 of the 24 members of the Politburo (including the veterans Ramiro Valdés and Blas Roca) and about a third of the 225-strong Central Committee were replaced in order to bring more women, blacks and youth into the leadership. There was also an attempt to separate further the party and government and reduce the role of the former in everyday affairs. The move would appear to represent a victory for the nationalist line in Cuban politics which seeks to lessen the country's dependence on the Soviet Union. The old guard from the Sierra Maestra still hold supreme political power, and occupy the key posts in the armed forces, party, state apparatus and secret services. But they are making way for a new generation of technocrats, known as 'Fidel's golden boys' who have had a thorough Marxist training and have worked their way up through the youth organizations. It is hoped in this way to avoid the type of recent leadership crisis in the Soviet Union when three ageing leaders died in rapid succession.

There remains, however, the towering figure of Castro who, while mobilizing and uniting the Cuban people in a unique way, undoubtedly continues to check popular initiative and responsibility. He may not be the active supporter of a personality cult—the reproduction of his image is officially discouraged—but he is certainly its victim. However, there are signs that there are limits to his charisma. His speeches are shorter and do not inspire the rapt attention and wild enthusiasm as before. In recent years he has increasingly been assuming a presidential role, concentrating on international affairs. While he may still arbitrate between the competing organizations and interest groups, it is difficult to see him as embodying a kind of permanent opposition, as has been suggested in the past. Even so, no one challenges his position as the supreme leader, the *jefe máximo*, a role he performs with all the panache of a traditional Latin American *caudillo*.

Although Castro jokes that if he is assassinated, there are thousands in the party to take his place, his succession will inevitably prove difficult. His brother Raúl has been named as his successor, but has neither the personal charisma nor the political insight of his elder brother. He has from the time of the guerrilla campaign been one of the most orthodox Communists in the Cuban leadership; he has even been known to insist in an angry outburst: 'Nobody offends Stalin when I'm around.'[7] As the chief of staff of the armed forces, he is first and foremost a soldier, and under his rule the militarization of Cuba will undoubtedly continue. For all the talk of popular democracy, it would appear that a Castro dynasty is in the making in Cuba. Castro's son, Fidelito, is waiting on the sidelines as head of the atomic energy commission.

It is of course comparatively easy to criticize the Cuban Revolution from the outside, and it should be remembered that Cuba has had to make a Revolution in difficult circumstances. The leadership has been besieged by constant US hostility and subversion, and has had to transform an economy which was entirely shaped by foreign interests. Democracy in the Western sense of parliamentary, representative democracy, has never existed in Cuba, either during the republican or colonial period. It is, moreover, unfair to judge social change in a particular country by some abstract model of excellence rather than by its own past.

Compared to what occurred before the Revolution, the Cuban people have undoubtedly gained in human dignity, economic well-being, and social justice. The great majority of Cubans, who had so little to begin with, are behind the regime; if this were not the case, they would not be armed in popular militias. The real material gains and the constant threat from abroad, as well as the ideological indoctrination, have rallied the people around the Castro regime. The restrictions on certain freedoms, the monopoly on political thought, the control of expression, the continuing austerity, are seen by many as necessary sacrifices in building Communism. The people no longer work just to survive, but to make something which they feel belongs to themselves. Cubans, in fact, are proud of their Revolutionary achievements and make up an optimistic nation.

Unlike Europe and the US with their prevailing mood of decline and despondency, there is still in Cuba a tremendous sense of renewal. Most Cubans live in the confident knowledge that the present is better than the past and that the future is likely to be better still. Castro remains as convinced as ever that 'Whatever goal we set ourselves, we will achieve it.'[8] It would be wrong to dismiss Cuba as yet another satellite of the USSR which merely repeats its tired and stale forms. The prevailing orthodoxy might be imported, but it is played to a distinctly Cuban beat—the weight of five centuries of history and culture cannot be shrugged off lightly. Cubans are well aware of the truth of Martí's saying that 'To change the master is not to be free.'

It is still possible that the new institutions set up in the late 1970s could be developed in a more democratic and libertarian direction. The judicial system offers the accused the opportunity of defending themselves, a clearer definition of what is a crime, and could have more lay representatives in the form of juries. The People's Power Assemblies have provided a degree of decentralization, and a channel for the people to express their views, and could be used to exert more power on the leadership and party. The CDRs might develop more as genuine neighbourhood committees for mutual aid rather than for collective vigilance and social control as at present. The trade unions, now mere bodies to aid management, could be turned into genuine organs of workers' control. The ultimate withering away of the state is still on the agenda.

The Cuban Revolution has provided a rare example of genuine experimentation outside the control of superpowers. It may not be too late for it to rediscover its original trajectory and create a society which puts equality and freedom before economic growth and defence, and which attempts to provide the conditions for all men and women to realize their natures as unique individuals and as social and creative beings. It may still be able to extend human imagination and experience by showing that models of social reality have not been definitively shaped by the US or the USSR, and that it is possible to build a society in the Third World which is both equal *and* free. Ultimately, the Cuban Revolution will not be remembered for its military strength or economic progress, but for the power of its example to inspire the wretched and the oppressed of the earth to throw off their chains.

NOTES

Notes

Introduction

1. Ernesto Che Guevara, *Socialism and Man* (New York, 1968) p. 22.
2. Fidel Castro, Speech on 2 May 1959.
3. Quoted by Andrew Sinclair, *Guevara* (London, 1970) p. 47; Jean-Paul Sartre, *Sartre on Cuba* (New York, 1961) p. 110.
4. Herbert L. Matthews, *Cuba* (New York, 1964) p. 17.
5. Leo Huberman and Paul M. Sweezey, *Socialism in Cuba* (New York, 1969) p. 204.
6. Heberto Padilla, 'Instructions for Admission into a New Society', *Sent off the Field: A selection from the Poetry of Heberto Padilla*, trans. by J. M. Cohen (London, 1972) p. 84.
7. *Granma Weekly Review*, 9 May 1971.
8. Sam Dolgoff, *The Cuban Revolution: A Critical Perspective* (Montreal 1976) p. 5.
9. Hugh Thomas, *The Revolution in the Balance* (London, 1983) p. 19.
10. Federico García Lorca, 'Son de negros de Cuba', *Poeta en Nueva York, Obras completas* (Madrid, 1980) I, 84.
11. Guevara to Peter Marucci, 4 May 1963, *Reminiscences of the Cuban Revolutionary War* (Harmondsworth, 1969) p. 244.

Chapter 1

1. Quoted by John Griffiths, *Let's Visit Cuba* (London, 1983) p. 8.
2. Pedro Mártir de Anglería, *Décadas del Nuevo Mundo* (1530) (Buenos Aires, 1946).
3. Quoted by Paula Di Perna, *The Complete Travel Guide to Cuba* (New York, 1979) p. 40.
4. Quoted by Marius André, *Columbus* (New York, 1928) p. 139.
5. Bartolomé de las Casas, *Historia de las Indias* (Mexico, 1951) I, 62–4.
6. Quoted by Rodríguez Expósito César, *Hatuey, el primer libertador de Cuba* (Havana, 1944) p. 120.
7. Quoted by Philip S. Foner, *A History of Cuba and its Relations with the United States* (New York, 1962) I, 26.
8. See Günter Grau, *La Habana* (Leipzig, 1982) p. 15.
9. Fernando Ortiz, *Cuban Counterpoint: Tobacco and Sugar* (New York, 1947) p. 286.
10. Quoted by Manuel Moreno Fraginals, *The Sugar Mill: The Socioeconomic Complex of Sugar in Cuba 1760–1860* (New York, 1976) p. 149.
11. Ibid., pp. 146–7.
12. Ibid., pp. 142–3.
13. See Verena Martínez-Alier, *Marriage, Class and Colour in Nineteenth-Century Cuba: A Study of*

Racial Attitudes and Sexual Values in a Slave Society (Cambridge, 1974) p. 101.

14. Fraginals, *The Sugar Mill*, op.cit., p. 55.
15. Quoted by Terence Cannon, *Revolutionary Cuba* (Havana, 1981) p. 16.
16. Quoted by Foner, *A History of Cuba*, op.cit., p. 145.
17. Ibid., p. 148.
18. Maceo to Coronel Federico Pérez, quoted by Antonio Núñez Jiménez, *Cuba: La naturaleza y el hombre* (Havana, 1982) I, 608.
19. *Boletín FMC* (Havana, 1982) p. 5.
20. Quoted by W. Adolphe Roberts, *Havana: The Portrait of a City* (New York, 1953) p. 87.
21. Quoted by Fraginals, *The Sugar Mill*, op.cit., p. 135.
22. Ibid., p. 166.
23. Quoted by Maurice Halperin, *The Rise and Decline of Fidel Castro: An Essay in Contemporary History* (Berkeley, 1972) p. 7.
24. Quoted by Jaime Suchlicki, *Cuba from Columbus to Castro* (New York, 1974) p. 87.
25. Quoted by Foner, *History of Cuba*, op.cit. II, 351n.
26. Ibid., II, 342.
27. Quoted by Hugh Thomas, *Cuba, or The Pursuit of Freedom* (London, 1971) p. 310.
28. Inscribed on the monument to Maceo erected in 1919 on the shores of the River Duaba.
29. Inscribed on Martí's tomb in Santa Ifigencia Cemetery, Santiago de Cuba.
30. *Constitución de la República de Cuba* (Havana, 1976) p. 19.
31. Inscribed on Maceo's monument by the River Duaba.
32. Quoted by Thomas, *Cuba*, op.cit., p. 404.

Chapter 2

1. Quoted by Cannon, *Revolutionary Cuba*, op.cit., p. 38.
2. Quoted by Matthews, *Cuba*, op.cit., p. 88.
3. Quoted by Roberts, *Havana*, op.cit., p. 105.
4. See Julio de Riverend, *Cuba, Socialista*, (February 1965) and Maurice Zeitlin, *Revolutionary Politics and the Cuban Working Class* (Princeton, 1967) pp. 3, 13.
5. Quoted by *Solidaridad Gastronómica*, 15 August 1955.
6. Quoted by Suchlicki, *Cuba*, op.cit., p. 139.
7. Quoted by Thomas, *Cuba*, op.cit., p. 770.
8. Castro, *La historia me absolverá* (Havana, 1981) p. 97.
9. Ibid., p. 98.
10. See Jiménez, *Cuba*, op.cit., I, 627–8.
11. Quoted by Cannon, *Revolutionary Cuba*, op.cit., p. 52.
12. Castro to Nati Revnelta, 23 March 1954, Carlos Franquí, *Fidel: A Family Portrait* (London, 1984) Appendix, p. 248.
13. Castro to Luis Conte Aquero, 14 August 1954, ibid., p. 250.
14. Letter dated 4 April 1954, ibid., p. 241.
15. Letter dated 27 January 1954, ibid., p. 240.
16. *Daily Worker* (New York), 10 August 1953.
17. Quoted by Cannon, *Revolutionary Cuba*, op.cit., p. 66.
18. Ibid., p. 67.
19. Quoted by Sinclair, *Guevara*, op.cit., pp. 9–10.
20. Ibid.
21. Guevara, *Reminiscences*, op.cit., pp. 43–4.
22. Quoted by Thomas, *Cuba*, op.cit., p. 930.
23. Guevara, *Reminiscences*, op.cit., p. 171.
24. Ibid., p. 96.
25. Ibid., pp. 183–4.
26. Guevara, *Guerrilla Warfare* (New York, 1961) p. 15.
27. Castro, speech on 1 January 1959.
28. Franquí, *Fidel*, op.cit., p. 3.

Chapter 3

1. Roberto Fernández Retamar, 'No word does you justice', *Writing in Cuba since the Revolution*, ed. Andrew Salkey (London, 1977) p. 36.
2. Castro, speech on 2 May 1959.
3. Franquí, *Fidel*, op.cit., p. 13.
4. Castro, speech on 15 April 1959.
5. Franquí, *Fidel*, op.cit., p. 37.
6. Castro, speech on 8 January 1959.
7. Guevara, *Reminiscences*, op.cit., p. 195.
8. Nicolás Guillén, 'Land in the Sierra and Below', *Writing in Cuba*, op.cit., p. 17.
9. Quoted by Sinclair, *Guevara*, op.cit., p. 47.
10. Quoted by Dolgoff, *The Cuban Revolution*, op.cit., p. 103.
11. *Sartre on Cuba*, op.cit., pp. 135, 144.
12. Castro, speech on 2 December 1961.
13. Simone de Beauvoir, quoted by Yves Guilbert, *Castro, l'infidéle* (Paris, 1961) p. 170.
14. Régis Debray, *Revolution in the Revolution?* (London, 1968) p. 108.
15. Jiménez, *Cuba*, op.cit., I, 601.
16. See Matthews, *Cuba*, op.cit., p. 112.
17. Guevara to René Ramos Latour, 14 December 1957, in Franquí, *Fidel*, op.cit., p. 243.
18. Castro to the students of University of Concepción, Chile, 18 November 1971.
19. Castro to Celia Sánchez, 5 June 1958, in Franquí, *Fidel*, op.cit., pp. 247–8.
20. Castro, speech on 5 March 1960.
21. Quoted by Cannon, *Revolutionary Cuba*, op.cit., p. 142.
22. Castro, speech on 28 September 1960.
23. Castro, speech on 15 April 1961.
24. Fayad Jamís, 'The Victory of Playa Girón', *Writing in Cuba*, op.cit., p. 46.
25. Castro, speech on 2 January 1961.
26. Franquí, *Fidel*, op.cit., p. 105.
27. Second Havana Declaration, issued on 4 February 1962.
28. Castro, speech on 23 October 1962.
29. Franquí, *Fidel*, op.cit., p. 195.
30. Quoted by Sinclair, *Guevara*, op.cit., p. 58.
31. Ibid., p.61.
32. Guevara, *Socialism and Man*, op.cit., p. 22.
33. Castro, speech on 26 July 1968.

Chapter 4

1. Debray, *Revolution in the Revolution?* op.cit., p. 105.
2. Guevara, *Socialism and Man*, op.cit., p. 4.
3. Ibid., p. 5.
4. Ibid., pp. 5, 19.
5. Ibid., p. 7.
6. Guevara, 'On Revolutionary Medicine' (1960) *Venceremos! The Speeches and Writings of Ernesto Che Guevara*, ed. John Gerassi (London, 1968) p. 115.
7. Guevara, *Socialism and Man*, op.cit., p. 22.
8. Guevara, 'On Creating a New Attitude' (1964), *Venceremos*, op.cit., p. 337.
9. *Che Guevara Speaks: Selected Speeches and Writings*, ed. George Lavan (New York, 1967) p. 99.
10. Ibid., p. 107.
11. Ibid., p. 159.
12. Castro, speech on 18 October 1967, *Venceremos*, op.cit., pp. 435, 441.
13. Guillén, 'Che Comandante', *Writing in Cuba*, op.cit., p. 19.
14. Guevara to his parents, mid 1965, *Reminiscences*, op.cit., p. 264.
15. Guevara to Castro, April 1965, ibid., p. 262.
16. See Lee Lockwood, *Castro's Cuba: Cuba's Fidel* (New York, 1969): Theodore Draper, *Castroism: Theory and Practice* (New

York, 1965); Jean Lamore, *Le Castrisme* (Paris, 1983).

17. Matthews, *The Cuban Story* (New York, 1961) pp. 105–6.
18. K. S. Karol, *Guerrillas in Power: The Course of the Cuban Revolution* (New York, 1970) p. 489.
19. Franquí. *Fidel*, op.cit., p. 170.
20. Ibid., p. 78.
21. *The Times*, 13 January 1985.
22. Elizabeth Sutherland, *The Youngest Revolution* (London 1971) p. 19.
23. Castro, speech on 26 July 1970.
24. Castro, speech on 4 April 1982.
25. Castro, speech on 17 May 1982.
26. Matthews, *Cuba* op. cit. pp. 105–6.
27. Castro, speech on 30 June 1961.
28. Lockwood, *Castro's Cuba*, op.cit., p. 141.
29. *Statutes of the Communist Party of Cuba* (Havana, 1981), p. 2.
30. Ibid., pp. 3–4.
31. Ibid., p. 3.
32. Ibid., p. 8.
33. Castro, speech on 17 December 1975.
34. Karol, *Guerrillas in Power*, op.cit., p. 482.
35. Franquí, *Fidel*, op.cit., p. 160.
36. Castro, speech on 8 January 1959.
37. Castro, speech on 4 November 1969.
38. Quoted by Cannon, *Revolutionary Cuba*, op.cit., p. 168.
39. Castro, speech on 24 March 1985.
40. *Granma Weekly Review*, 12 January 1986.

Chapter 5

1. Guevara, 'On Sacrifice and Dedication' (1960), *Venceremos*, op.cit., p. 101.
2. Guevara, 'Our Industrial Tasks' (1961), ibid., p. 199.
3. Quoted by Donald C. Hodges, *The Legacy of Che Guevara: A Documentary Study* (London, 1977) p. 95.

4. Guevara, 'On the Budgetary System of Finance' (1964), *Venceremos*, op.cit., p. 298.
5. Guevara, 'On Socialist Planning' (1965), ibid., p. 405.
6. Guevara, 'On Revolutionary Medicine' (1960), ibid., p. 116.
7. Guevara, 'On Creating a New Attitude' (1964), ibid., pp. 336–7.
8. Guevara, 'On Socialist Competition and Sugar Production' (1963). *Venceremos*, op.cit., p. 226.
9. Franquí, *Fidel*, op.cit., p. 262.
10. Guevara, 'Our Industrial Tasks' (1961), *Venceremas*, op. cit., p. 263.
11. Franquí, *Fidel*, op.cit., pp. 144, 146.
12. Guevara, 'The Cadre, Backbone of the Revolution' (1962), *Venceremos*, op.cit., pp. 205, 207.
13. Guevara, 'Against Bureaucratism' (1963), ibid., p. 225.
14. Franquí, *Fidel*, op.cit., p. 213.
15. Quoted by Karol, *Guerrillas in Power*, op.cit., p. 541.
16. Ibid., pp. 357–8.
17. Castro, speech on 13 March 1968.
18. *Granma*, 31 March 1968.
19. See Karol, *Guerrillas in Power*, op.cit., pp. 464–5n.
20. Ibid., p. 542.
21. Castro, speech on 11 January 1968.
22. Castro, speech on 28 September 1968.
23. *Granma*, 1 December 1968.
24. *Ogonek*, 21 June 1970.
25. Castro, speech on 1 May 1971.
26. Castro, speech on 26 July 1973.
27. Castro, speech on 17 May 1982.
28. See my chapter, 'Cuba', *Latin American & Caribbean Review* (London, 1983) p. 227.

Chapter 6

1. Castro, speech on 31 May 1961.
2. Castro, speech on 31 May 1977.
3. Guevara, 'On Sacrifice and Ded-

ication' (1960), *Venceremos*, op.cit., pp. 93–4.
4. Quoted by Dolgoff, *The Cuban Revolution*, op.cit., p. 99.
5. Quoted by Roberto E. Hernandez and Carmelo Mesa-Lago, 'Labor Organization and Wages', *Revolutionary Change in Cuba*, ed. C. Mesa-Lago (Pittsburgh, 1971) p. 212.
6. Guevara, 'On Creating a New Attitude' (1964), *Venceremas* op.cit., p. 336.
7. Castro, speech on 28 September 1968.
8. See Carmelo Mesa-Lago, *Cuba in the 1970s: Pragmatism and Institutionalization* (Albuquerque, 1974) pp. 33–4.
9. Quoted by Cannon, *Revolutionary Cuba*, op.cit., pp. 262–3.

Chapter 7

1. Quoted by Cannon, *Revolutionary Cuba*, op.cit., p. 206.
2. Eduardo B. Ordaz Ducungé, *The Psychiatric Hospital of Havana in the XI World Festival of Youth and Students* (Havana, n.d.) p. 1.
3. See Ordaz Ducungé *et al.*, *La terapéutica psiquiatrica en la salud mental: la rehabilitación del enfermo mental crónico en Cuba* (Havana, n.d.) pp. 14–16.
4. See Ordaz Ducungé, *The Sheltered Rehabilitation Center with Lodging* (Havana, n.d.) pp. 14–15.
5. See *Psicoballet* (Havana, n.d.).
6. Ordaz Ducungé, *The Sheltered Rehabilitation Center with Lodging*, op.cit., pp. 12–13.

Chapter 8

1. Guevara, *Socialism and Man*, op.cit., p. 7.
2. Ibid., p. 7.
3. Ibid., p. 13.
4. Ibid., pp. 10, 19.

5. *Children in Cuba: Twenty Years of Revolution* (Havana, 1979) p. 5.
6. Castro, speech on 26 July 1967.
7. Castro, speech on 13 March 1968.
8. Ernesto Cardenal, *En Cuba* (1972), p. 364.
9. *Children in Cuba*, op.cit., p. 15.
10. Ibid., pp. 16–17.
11. *Statutes of the Communist Party*, op.cit., p. 3.
12. *Granma*, 23 October 1977.
13. *Children in Cuba*, op.cit., p. 102.
14. Ibid., p. 84.
15. Ibid., p. 5.
16. Ibid., p. 20.
17. Ibid., p. 31.
18. Quoted by Cannon, *Revolutionary Cuba*, op.cit., p. 191.
19. See *Granma*, 30 January 1978.
20. Castro, speech on 26 July 1967.

Chapter 9

1. Martínez-Alier, *Marriage, Class and Colour*, op.cit., p. 101.
2. Ibid., p. 113.
3. *Boletín FMC*, op.cit., p. 5.
4. Quoted by Castro, speech on 29 November 1974.
5. Quoted by Margaret Randall, *Cuban Women Now* (Toronto, 1974) p. 317.
6. Guevara, *Guerrilla Warfare*, op.cit., p. 88.
7. Ibid., p. 89.
8. Guevara, 'On Party Militancy' (1963), *Venceremos*, op.cit., p. 241.
9. *Boletín FMC*, op.cit., p. 16.
10. Castro, speech on 9 December 1966.
11. Castro, speech on 29 November 1974.
12. 'Thesis: On the Full Exercise of Women's Equality' (1975), *Women and the Cuban Revolution: Speeches and Documents*, ed. Elizabeth Stone (New York, 1981) pp. 80, 102, 101, 104.
13. Ibid., p. 99.

14. Ibid., p. 100.
15. *Juventud Rebelde*, March 1984.
16. Franquí, *Fidel*, op.cit., p. 150.
17. Vilma Espín, 'The Early Years' (1960), *Women and the Cuban Revolution*, op.cit., p. 37.
18. Castro, speech on 8 March 1985.
19. Ibid.
20. Ibid.
21. See Introduction, *Women and the Cuban Revolution*, op.cit., p. 18.
22. 'On the Full Exercise of Women's Equality', *Women and the Cuban Revolution*, op.cit., p. 102.
23. Germaine Greer, 'Women and Power in Cuba', *Granta*, 16 (1985), p. 228.

Chapter 10

1. See Martínez-Alier, *Marriage, Class and Colour*, op.cit., p. 72.
2. Guillén, 'I have', *Cuba: An Anthology for Young People* (London, 1983) pp. 51–2.
3. Castro, speech on 22 March 1959.
4. Castro, speech on 25 March 1959.
5. Castro, speech on 9 December 1966.
6. Franquí, *Fidel*, op.cit., p. 106.
7. Miguel Barnet, 'The Culture that Sugar Created', *Latin American Literary Review*, 8, 16 (1980) p. 46.
8. John Clytus, *Black Man in Red Cuba* (Coral Gables, 1970) p, 41.
9. Barry Reckord, *Does Fidel eat More than Your Father?* (London, 1971) p. 127.
10. See Sutherland, *The Youngest Revolution*, op.cit., pp. 154–5.
11. Nancy Morejón, 'Black Women', *Cuba: An Anthology for Young People*, op.cit., p. 17.

Chapter 11

1. Franquí, *Fidel*, op.cit., p. 210.
2. *Verde Olivo*, 12 February 1961.
3. Franquí, *Fidel*, op.cit., p. 131.
4. Castro, speech on 30 June 1961.

5. *Hoy*, 23 August 1961.
6. *Spectator*, 26 January 1985.
7. *The Times*, 20 January 1985.
8. Quoted by Thomas, *Cuba*, op.cit., p. 1465.
9. Guevara, *Reminiscences*, op.cit., p. 114.
10. Guevara, *Guerrilla Warfare*, op.cit., p. 99.
11. Guevara, *Socialism and Man*, op.cit., pp. 17–18.
12. Ibid., p. 20.
13. *Hoy*, 23 August 1961.
14. Osvaldo Dorticós to Mark Schleiffer, *Monthly Review* (April, 1964) p. 655.
15. Castro, speech on 11 January 1968.
16. Ambrosio Fornet, 'The Intellectual in the Revolution', *Writing in Cuba*, op.cit., pp. 132, 135–6.
17. *Granma Weekly Review*, 27 October 1968.
18. Ibid., 7 December 1969.
19. Quoted by Rine Leal; 'Hacia una dramaturgia del socialismo', *La cultura en Cuba socialista* (Havana, 1982) pp. 242–3.
20. Salvador Arias, 'Literatura Cubana (1959–1978)', ibid., p. 18.
21. *La lucha ideológica y la cultura artística y literaria* (Havana, 1982) pp. 91–2.
22. *Granma*, 5 October 1969.
23. Armando Hart Dávalos, *Rencontre avec les écrivains* (Havana, 1977) pp. 14, 31, 33, 30.
24. Hart Dávalos, *Changing the Rules of the Game*, interviewed by Luis Baez (Havana, 1983) pp, 11, 16, 17, 36, 18.
25. *Cubatimes* (May–June 1984).
26. Castro, speech on 29 April 1967, reprinted in *Writing in Cuba*, op.cit., p. 149.
27. *Granma Weekly Review*, 17 July 1977.

Chapter 12

1. Quoted by Diana Mansfield, 'Television and Radio', *Cuba: The*

Second Decade, ed. John Griffiths & Peter Griffiths (London, 1982) p. 238.

2. *Statutes of the Communist Party*, op.cit., p. 4.
3. *Cuba Update* (June 1980), p. 10.
4. *Statutes of the Communist Party*, op.cit., p. 4.
5. *Granma Weekly Review*, 29 December 1975.
6. Castro, speech on 29 April 1967.
7. Quoted by Hugh S. Thomas, Georges A. Fauviol, Juan Carlos Weiss, *The Cuban Revolution 25 Years Later* (Boulder & London, 1984) p. 43.
8. Carlos Ripoll, *The Cuban Scene: Censors and Dissenters* (New York, 1982) pp. 11–12.
9. See Gonzalez Echeverría, 'Criticism and Literature in Revolutionary Cuba', *Cuban Studies*, 11, 1 (1984) p. 14.
10. Guevara, *Socialism and Man*, op.cit., pp. 15, 17, 18.
11. Lockwood, *Castro's Cuba*, op.cit., p. 207.
12. Castro, interviewed by Claude Julien, *Le Monde*, 23 March 1963.
13. Publicity for the 6th New Latin American Film Festival held in Havana in December 1984.
14. Law Number 812 (1959).
15. Pompeyo Pino, *Ballet Nacional de Cuba* (Havana, n.d.) p. 7.

Chapter 13

1. See Mateo Jover Marimon, 'The Church', *Revolutionary Change in Cuba*, op.cit., p. 400.
2. *Bohemia*, 18 January 1959.
3. First Declaration of Havana, 2 September 1960.
4. Castro, speech on 4 March 1961.
5. Quoted by Alice L. Hageman & Philip E. Wheaton (eds.) *Religion in Cuba Today: A New Church in a New Society* (New York, 1972) p. 29.

6. Castro, interview in *Sucesor* (Mexico) 10 September 1966.
7. Castro, speech on 11 January 1968.
8. Castro, speech on 5 January 1969.
9. See Hageman & Wheaton, *Religion in Cuba Today*, op.cit., p. 194.
10. Ibid., p. 283.
11. Cardenal, *En Cuba*, op.cit., p. 360.
12. *Fidel y la religión: conversaciones con Frei Betto* (Havana, 1985).
13. Hageman & Wheaton, *Religion in Cuba Today*, op.cit., p. 30.
14. Reckord, *Does Fidel Eat More than Your Father?* op.cit., p. 87.
15. *La lucha ideológica*, op.cit., pp. 30–1.
16. *The Times*, 28 January 1985.
17. *Fidel y la religión*, op.cit.
18. Bruce Kenrick, *A Man from the Interior: Cuba's Quest* (London, 1980) pp. 18, 79, 53.

Chapter 14

1. *Granma Weekly Review*, 15 July 1979.
2. Lockwood, *Castro's Cuba*, op.cit., p. 205.
3. Pierre Goldendorf, *7 años en Cuba, 38 meses en las prisiones de Fidel Castro* (Barcelona, 1977) p. 255.
4. *Amnesty International Report* (London, 1983) p. 128.
5. Castro, speech on 24 March 1985.
6. See *Bohemia*, 10 January 1969.
7. *Sartre on Cuba*, op.cit., p. 110.
8. See *Bohemia*, 10 January 1969.
9. See Ibid., 9 August 1969.
10. Castro, speech on 24 March 1985.
11. Guevara, *Socialism and Man*, op.cit., p. 19.
12. *Juventud Rebelde*, 17 June 1977.
13. See Luis P. Salas, 'Juvenile Delinquency in Post-revolutionary Cuba: Characteristics and Cuban Explanations', *Cuban Studies*, 9, 1 (1979) pp. 43–61.

14. See Geoffrey E. Fox, *Working Class Emigrés from Cuba* (Palo Alto, 1979) pp. 78, 19.

Chapter 15

1. Castro, speech on 2 September 1960.
2. Castro, speech on 4 February 1962.
3. Guevara, *Che Guevara Speaks*, op.cit., p. 99.
4. Ibid., p. 107.
5. Ibid., pp. 157, 159.
6. Debray, *Revolution in the Revolution?*, op.cit., p. 105.
7. Castro, speech on 11 January 1968.
8. Castro, speech on 23 August 1968.
9. Quoted by Karol, *Guerrillas in Power*, op.cit., p. 583.
10. *Pravda*, 20 October 1970.
11. *Constitución*, op.cit., p. 18.
12. Quoted by Cannon, *Revolutionary Cuba*, op.cit., p. 165.
13. Castro, speech on 13 March 1967.
14. Castro, speech on 26 July 1984.
15. Castro, *Talks with US and French Journalists* (Havana, 1983) p. 34.

16. Castro, speech on 13 January 1985.
17. Castro, speech on 24 March 1985.
18. *Granma Weekly Review*, 11 August 1985.
19. *Histoire d'une usurpation: la base navale des Etats-Unis dans la baie de Guantánamo* (Havana, 1982) p. 74.
20. *Daily Telegraph*, 31 May 1985.
21. Castro, speech on 26 July 1984.

Chapter 16

1. *Sunday Times*, 18 December 1983.
2. See Fox, *Working Class Emigrés from Cuba* op.cit., pp. 19, 38.
3. Armando Hart Daválos, *Changing the Rules of the Game* (Havana, 1983) p. 69.
4. Jorge I. Domínguez, *Cuba: Internal and International Affairs* (Beverley Hills, 1982) p. 15.
5. Castro, speech on 17 May 1982.
6. *Granma*, 4 July 1980.
7. Franquí, *Fidel*, op.cit., p. 129.
8. Castro, speech on 26 July 1984.

SELECT BIBLIOGRAPHY

1. *Cuban Publications*

Antúnez, Armando Chávez, *Del pensamiento ético de Che* (Havana: Editoria Politica, 1983)

Atlas de Cuba (Havana: Instituto Cubano de Geodesia y Cartografía, 1978)

Boletín FMC, Special Edition (Havana, n.d.)

Bosch, Juan, *De Cristobal Colón a Fidel Castro: El Caribe, frontera imperial* (Havana: Ediciones Casa de las Américas, 1981)

Cannon, Terence, *Revolutionary Cuba* (Havana: José Martí Publishing House, 1983)

Carpentier, Alejo, *La ciudad de las columnas* (Havana: Editorial Letras Cubanas, n. d.)

———, 'La moderna pintura cubana', *Pintura cubana contemporánea* (Havana: Colección Museo Nacional de Bellas Artes, n.d.)

———, *El siglo de luces* (Havana, 1963)

Castro Ruz, Fidel, *La historia me absolverá* (Havana: Editorial de Ciencias Sociales, 1981)

———, *Talks with US and French Journalists* (Havana: Editorial Politica, 1983)

———, *Fidel y la religión: conversaciones con Frei Betto* (Havana, 1985)

———, *Nada podrá detener la marcha de la historia* (Havana Editorial Politica, 1985)

———, Miscellaneous speeches as reported in *Granma*

César, Rodríguez Expósito, *Hatuey, el primer libertador de Cuba* (Havana, 1944)

Children in Cuba: Twenty Years of Revolution (Havana: Editorial de Ciencias Sociales, 1979)

Cinco años de esfuerzos y realizaciones: nueva división politico-administrativa, elaborado por la Agencia de Información Nacional (Havana: Editorial Política, 1983)

50 años de la revista de avance (Havana: Editorial Orbe, 1978)

Constitución de la República de Cuba (Havana: Editorial Orbe, 1976)

Cuba' 67: Image of a Country (Havana: Book Institute, 1967)

Fabelo, Alexis Cánavaros, *La nación Cubana: sus símbolos* (Havana: Gente Nueva, n.d.)

Family Code (Havana: Editorial Orbe, 1975)

González, Maritza (ed.), *Perfil histórico de las letras cubanas desde los orígenes hasta 1898* (Havana: Editorial Letras Cubanas, 1983)

Grau, Günter, *La Habana* (Leipzig, 1982)

Guanche, Jesús, *Procesos etnoculturales de Cuba* (Havana: Editorial Letras Cubanas, 1983)

Hart Dávalos, Armando, *Rencontre avec les écrivains* (Havana: Editorial Arte y Literatura, 1977)

———, *Changing the Rules of the Game*, interviewed by Luis Báez (Havana: Editorial Letras Cubanas, 1983)

Histoire d'une usurpation: La base navale des Etag-Unis dans la baie de Guantánamo (Havana: Editorial Política, 1982)

Historia de Cuba (1967) ed. Dirección Política de las FAR (3rd edn., Havana, 1971)

Jiménez, Antonio Núñez, *Geografía de Cuba* (3rd edn. Havana: Editorial Nacional de Cuba, 1965)

———, *En marcha con Fidel 1959* (Havana: Editorial Letras Cubanas, 1982)

———, *Cuba: La naturaleza y el hombre, Tomo I, El archipélago* (Havana: Editorial Letras Cubanas, 1982)

La cultura en Cuba socialista (Havana: Editorial Letras Cubanas, 1982)

La lucha ideológica y la cultura artística y literaria (Havana: Editorial Política, 1982)

León, Argeliers, *Música folklórica cubana* (Havana: Ediciones del Departamiento de Música de la Biblioteca Nacional José Martí, 1964)

Le Riverend, Julio, *Breve historia de Cuba* (Havana: Editorial de Ciencias Sociales, 1978)

———, *Historia económica de Cuba* (Havana: Editorial Pueblo y Educación, 1975)

Ley de organización del sistema judicial (Havana: Editorial Orbe, 1979)

Linares, María Teresa, *La música y el pueblo* (Havana: Editorial Pueblo y Educación, 1974)

Mayol, Raúl Gorrity, *Panorama de la cultura cubana* (Havana: Editorial Pueblo y Educación, 1982)

Ordaz Ducungé, Eduardo B. et al., *The Psychiatric Hospital of Havana in the XI World Festival of Youth and Students* (Havana: MINSAP. n.d.)

———, *The Sheltered Rehabilitation Center with Lodging: its characteristics and significance in the rehabilitation program of chronic mental patients in Cuba* (Havana: MINSAP, n.d.)

———, *Psicoballet* (Havana: MINSAP, n. d.)

———, *La terapéutica psiquiatrica en la salud mental, la rehabilitación del enfermo mental crónico en Cuba* (Havana: MINSAP, n.d.)

Ortíz, Fernando, *Les negros esclavos* (1916) (Havana: Editorial de Ciencias Sociales, 1975)

Pichards, Hortensia, *Documentos para la historia de Cuba*, 4 vols, (Havana: Editorial de Ciencias Sociales, 1977)

Pino, Pompeyo, *Ballet nacional de Cuba: arte del pueblo y para el pueblo* (Havana: Comité Organizador XIV Juegos Centroamericanos y del Caribe, n.d.)

Política cultural de la revolución cubana. Documentos (Havana: Editorial de Ciencias Sociales, 1977)

Stautes of the Communist Party of Cuba (Havana: Political Publishing House, 1981)

Villaverde, Cirilo, *Cecilia Valdés o la loma del ángel* (Havana: Editoriol Arte y Literatura, 1977)

2. Cuban Newspapers and Periodicals

Bohemia
Casa de las Américas
Cuba Socialista
Granma
Hoy
Juventud Rebelde
Los Trabajadores
Mujeres
Opina
Pensamiento Crítico
Pionero
Prisma
Revolución
Tricontinental
Verde Olivo

3. General Books

André, Marius, *Columbus* (New York, 1928)

Blackburn, Robin, *Slavery and Empire* (London: New Left Books, 1978)

Bonachea, Rolando E. & Nelson P. Valdés, *Cuba in Revolution* (New York: Anchor, 1972)

Boorstein, Edward, *The Economic Transformation of Cuba* (New York: Monthly Review Press, 1968)

Bourne, Peter G., *Fidel: A Biography* (New York: Dodd, Mead, 1986)

Cannon, Terence, *Free and Equal: The End of Racial Discrimination in Cuba* (New York: Venceremos, 1978)

Cardenal, Ernesto, *En Cuba* (Buenos Aires: Ediciones Carlos Lohlé, 1972)

Carpentier, Alejo, *La musique à Cuba* (1946) (Paris: Gallimard, 1985)

Caute, David, *Cuba, Yes?* (London: Secker & Warburg, 1974)

Chadwick, Lee, *A Cuban Journey* (London: Denis Dobson, 1975)

Chanan, Michael, *The Cuban Image: Cinema and Cultural Politics in Cuba* (London: BFI, 1985)

Clytus, John, *Black Man in Red Cuba* (Coral Gables, Florida: Univ. of Miami Press, 1970)

Cohen, J. M. (ed.), *Writers in the New Cuba: An Anthology* (Harmondsworth: Penguin, 1967)

Cuba: An Anthology for Young People, (London: Young World Books, 1983)

Danielson, Ross, *Cuban Medicine* (New Brunswick, N.J.: Transaction Books, 1979)

Debray, Régis, *Revolution in the Revolution?* (1967) (Harmondsworth: Pelican, 1968)

Del Aguila, Juan M., *Cuba: Dilemmas of a Revolution* (Boulder and London: Westview Press, 1984)

Di Perna, Paula, *The Complete Travel Guide to Cuba* (New York: St. Martín's Press, 1979)

Dolgoff, Sam, *The Cuban Revolution: A Critical Perspective* (Montreal: Black Rose Books, 1976)

Domínguez, Jorge I., *Cuba: Order and Revolution* (Cambridge, Mass.: Harvard Univ. Press, 1978)

———, *Cuba: Internal and International Affairs* (Beverley Hills, London, New Delhi: Sage Publications, 1982)

Draper, Theodore *Castro's Revolution: Myths and Realities* (New York: Praeger, 1962)

———, *Castroism: Theory and Practice* (New York: Praeger, 1965)

Dumont, René, *Cuba: Socialism and Development* (New York: Grove Press, 1970)

———, *Is Cuba Socialist?* (London: Deutsch, 1974)

Fagen, Richard R., *The Transformation of the Political Culture in Cuba* (Stamford: Stamford Univ. Press, 1969)

Foner, Philip S., *A History of Cuba and its Relations with the United States*, 2 vols. (New York: Monthly Review Press, 1962)

———, *Antonio Maceo: The Bronze Titan of Cuba's Independence Struggle* (New York: Monthly Review Press, 1978)

Fox, Geoffrey E., *Working Class Emigrés from Cuba* (Palo Alto, 1979)

Fraginals, Manuel Moreno, *The Sugar Mill: The Socioeconomic Complex of Sugar in Cuba 1760–1860*, trans. by Cedric Befrage (New York and London: Monthly Review Press, 1976)

Franquí, Carlos, *Diary of the Cuban Revolution (1976)* (New York: Viking, 1980)

———, *Fidel: A Family Portrait* (London: Cape, 1984)

Goldendorf, Pierre, *7 años en Cuba, 38 meses en las prisiones de Fidel Castro* (Barcelona: Plaza & Janes, S.A., 1977)

González, Edward, *Cuba under Castro: The Limits of Charisma* (Boston: Houghton Mifflin, 1974)

Green, Gil, *Cuba at 25: The Continuing Revolution* (New York: International Publishers, 1983)

González-Wippler, Migene, *Santería: African Magic in Latin America* (1973) (New York: Anchor Books, 1975)

Griffiths, John, *Fidel Castro* (London: Batsford, 1981)

——, *Let's Visit Cuba* (London: Burke, 1983)

Griffiths, John & Peter Griffiths (eds.), *Cuba: The Second Decade* (London: Writers and Readers, 1979)

Guevara, Ernesto Che, *Guerrilla Warfare* (New York: Monthly Review Press, 1961)

——, *Reminiscences of the Cuban Revolutionary War* (Harmondsworth: Pelican, 1969)

——, *Socialism and Man* (New York: Pathfinder Press, 1968)

——, *Venceremos! The Speeches and Writings of Ernesto Che Guevara*, ed. John Gerassi, (London: Weidenfeld & Nicolson, 1968)

——, *Che Guevara Speaks: Selected Speeches and Writings*, ed. George Lavan (New York: Pathfinder Press, 1982)

Guilbert, Yves, *Castro, l'infidèle* (Paris, 1961)

Hageman, Alice L. and Wheaton, Philip E. (eds.), *Religion in Cuba Today: A New Church in a New Society* (New York: Association Press, 1972)

Halebsky, Sandor & John M. Kirk (eds.), *Cuba: Twenty-five Years of Revolution* (1959–1984) (New York: Praeger, 1985)

Halperlin, Maurice, *The Rise and Decline of Fidel Castro: An Essay in Contemporary History* (Berkeley: Univ. of California Press, 1972)

——, *The Taming of Fidel Castro* (Berkeley: Univ. of California Press, 1981)

Hodges, Donald C., *The Legacy of Che Guevara: A Documentary Study* (London: Thames & Hudson, 1977)

Horowitz, Irving Louis, (ed.) *Cuban Communism* (1970) 2nd edn. (New Brunswick, New Jersey: Transaction Books, 1972)

Huberman, Leo & Sweezy, Paul M., *Socialism in Cuba* (New York and London: Modern Reader Paperbacks, 1969)

Karol, K. S., *Guerrillas in Power: The Course of the Cuban Revolution*, trans. Arnold Pomerans (New York: Hill & Wang, 1970)

Kenrick, Bruce, *A Man from the Interior: Cuba's Quest* (London: Epworth Press, 1980)

Knight, Franklin W., *Slave Society in Cuba during the Nineteenth Century* (Madison: Univ. of Wisconsin Press, 1970)

Lamore, Jean, *Cuba* (Paris: Presses Universitaires de France, 1970)

——, *Le Castrisme* (Paris: Presses Universitaires de France, 1983)

Las Casas, Bartolomé de, *Historia de las Indias* (Mexico, 1951)

Levine, Barry B., (ed.) *The New Cuban Presence in the Caribbean* (Boulder, Colorado: Westview Press, 1983)

Literatura y arte nuevo en Cuba (Barcelona: Editorial Estela, 1971)

Lockwood, Lee, *Castro's Cuba: Cuba's Fidel* (New York: Vintage, 1969)

Lowy, Michael, *The Marxism of Che Guevara: Philosophy, Economics and Revolutionary Warfare*, trans. Brian Pearce (London: Monthly Review Press, 1973)

MacGaffey, Wyatt & Barnett, Clifford, *Cuba: Its People, its Society, its Culture* (Newhaven: HRAF Press, 1962)

Marshall, Peter, *Into Cuba* (with photographer Barry Lewis) (New York: Alfred van der Marck Editions; Jondon: Zena, 1985)

Martínez-Alier, Verena, *Marriage, Class and Colour in Nineteenth-Century Cuba: A Study of Racial Attitudes and Sexual Values in a Slave Society* (Cambridge: CUP, 1974)

Matthews, Herbert L., *Castro: A Political Biography* (London: Allen Lane, 1960)

———, *The Cuban Story* (New York: George Braziller, 1961)

———, *Cuba* (New York: Macmillan, 1964)

———, *Revolution in Cuba: An Essay in Understanding (New York: Scribner's Sons, 1975)*

Menton, Seymour, *Prose Fiction of the Cuban Revolution* (Austin: University of Texas Press, 1975)

Mesa-Lago, Carmelo, (ed.), *Revolutionary Change in Cuba* (Pittsburgh: Univ. of Pittsburgh Press, 1971)

Mesa-Lago, Carmelo, *Cuba in the 1970s: Pragmatism and Institutionalization* (Albuquerque: Univ. of New Mexico Press, 1974)

———, *The Economy of Socialist Cuba: A Two-Decade Appraisal* (Albuquerque: Univ. of New Mexico Press, 1981)

Mills, C. Wright, *Listen, Yankee: The Revolution in Cuba* (New York: McGraw-Hill, 1960)

———, *Castro's Cuba: The Revolution in Cuba* (London: Secker & Warburg 1961)

Montejo, Esteban, *The Autobiography of a Runaway Slave* (1966), ed. Miguel Barnet, trans. Jocasta Innes (London: Bodley Head, 1968)

Nelson, Lowry, *Rural Cuba* (New York: Octagon Books, 1970)

———, *Cuba: The Measure of a Revolution* (Minneapolis: Univ. of Minnesota Press, 1972)

O'Connor, James, *The Origins of Socialism in Cuba* (Ithaca: Cornell UP, 1970)

Ortiz, Fernando Fenández, *Cuban Counterpoint: Tobacco and Sugar*, trans. Harriet de Onís (New York: Alfred A. Knopf, 1947)

———, *Hampa afrocubana: los negros brujos* (1906) (Madrid: Editorial America, 1917)

Padilla, Heberto, *Sent off the Field: A Selection from the Poetry of Heberto Padilla*, trans. by J. M. Cohen (London: Deutsch, 1972)

Radosh, Ronald, (ed.) *The New Cuba: Paradoxes and Potentials* (New York: William Morrow, 1976)

Randall, Margaret, *Cuban Women Now* (Toronto: Women's Press, 1974)

———, *Women in Cuba* (Brooklyn: Smyrna Press, 1981)

Reckord, Barry, *Does Fidel Eat More than Your Father?* (London: Deutsch, 1971)

Ripoll, Carlos, *The Cuban Scene: Censors and Dissenters* (Washington D. C.: Cuba–America National Foundation, 1982)

Roberts, W. Adolphe, *Havana: The Portrait of a City* (New York: Coward-McCann, 1953)

Ruiz, Ramón Eduardo, *Cuba: The Making of a Revolution* (New York: W. W. Norton, 1968)

Salkey, Andrew, *Havana Journal* (Harmondsworth: Penguin, 1971)

———, (ed.) *Writing in Cuba since the Revolution* (London: Bogle-L'Ouverture, 1977)

Sartre, Jean-Paul, *Sartre on Cuba* (New York: Ballantine, 1961)

Silverman, Bertrand (ed.), *Man and Socialism in Cuba: The Great Debate* (New York: Atheneum, 1971)

Sinclair, Andrew, *Guevara* (London: Fontana, 1970)

Stone, Elizabeth (ed.), *Women and the Cuban Revolution* (New York: Pathfinder Press, 1981)

Sobel, Lester A., (ed.) *Castro's Cuba in the 1970s* (New York: Facts on File, 1978)

Stermer, Durgald, (ed.), *Art in Revolution: 96 Posters from Cuba* (London: Pall Mall, 1960)

Suchlicki, Jamie, *Cuba from Columbus to Castro* (New York: Scribner's Sons, 1974)

———(ed.), *Cuba, Castro, and Revolution* (Univ. of Miami Press, 1972)

Sutherland, Elizabeth, *The Youngest Revolution* (London: Pitmans, 1971)

Szulc, Tad, *Fidel: A Critical Portrait* (New York: Morrow, 1986)

Thomas, Hugh, *Cuba, or The Pursuit of Freedom* (London: Eyre & Spottiswoode, 1971)

———, *The Revolution in the Balance* (London, 1983)

Thomas, Hugh S., Georges A. Fauriol, Juan Carlos Weiss, *The Cuban Revolution 25 Years Later*, (Boulder & London: Westview Press, 1984)

Valladares, Armando, *Against All Hope. The Prison Memoirs of Armando Valladares* (New York: Knopf, 1985)

Vallas, Jorge, *Twenty Years and Forty Days* (New York: Americas Watch Committee, 1985)

Wald, Karen, *Children of Che: Childcare and Education in Cuba* (Palo Alto: Ramparts Press, 1978)

Weinstein, Martin, (ed.) *Revolutionary Cuba in the World Arena* (Philadelphia: Institute for the Study of Human Issues, 1979)

Yglesias, José, *In the Fist of the Revolution: Life in a Cuban Country Town* (New York: Pantheon, 1968)

Zeitlin, Maurice, *Revolutionary Politics and the Cuban Working Class* (Princeton: Princeton UP, 1967)

4. *Articles*

Amnesty International, 'Political Imprisonment in Cuba' (November, 1986)

Azicri, Max, 'The Institutionalization of the Cuban Revolution: A Review of the Literature', *Cuban Studies*, 9, 2 (1979) 63–78

———, 'The Politics of Exile: Trends and Dynamics of Political Change among Cuban-Americans', *Cuban Studies*, 11, 2 (1981) 55–73

Barnet, Miguel, 'The Culture that Sugar Created', *Latin American Literary Review*, 8, 16 (Special Issue, Spring–Summer, 1980)

Bascom, William R., 'The Focus of Cuban Santería', *Peoples and Cultures of the Caribbean*, ed. Michael M. Horowitz (New York: Natural History Press, 1971)

Blackburn, Robin, 'The Economics of the Cuban Revolution', *Latin America and the Caribbean: A Handbook*, ed. Claudio Veliz (Oxford: OUP, 1968)

Camarand, Chris, 'On Cuban Women', *Science and Society*, 35, 1 (1971) 48–58

Greer, Germaine, 'Women and Power in Cuba', *Granta*, 16 (1985) pp. 207–229, reprinted in *Women: A World Report* (Methuen, 1985)

González, Echeverría, 'Criticism and Literature in Revolutionary Cuba', *Cuban Studies*, 11, 1 (1984) 1–18

Horowitz, Irving Louis, 'Authenticity and Autonomy in the Cuban Experience: Toward an Operational Definition of Revolution', *Cuban Studies*, 6, 1 (1976) 67–74

Marshall, Peter, 'Cuba', *Latin American & Caribbean Review 1983*, (World of Information, 1983) pp. 226–7

———, 'Cuba', *Latin American & Caribbean Review 1985*, (World of Information, 1985) pp. 189–92

———, 'Ernesto and Gregorio', *Observer Magazine*, (2 December 1984) pp. 84–89

Martínez-Alier, Juan, 'The Peasantry and the Cuban Revolution', *Latin American Affairs*, ed. R. Carr (Oxford: OUP, 1970)

Matas, Julio, 'Revolución, Literatura y Religión Afrocubana', *Cuban Studies*, 13, 1 (1983) 17–23

Peck, Graham, 'Sex Education in Cuba', *Cuba Sí*, 4 (1986), pp. 8–10

Pérez, Jr., Louis A., 'Toward a New Future, From a New Past: The Enterprise of History in Socialist Cuba', *Cuban Studies*, 15, 1 (1985) 1–13

Poyo, Gerald E., 'The Anarchist Challenge to the Cuban Independence Movement, 1855–1890', *Cuban Studies*, 15, 1 (1985) 29–42

Rojo, Antonio Benitez, 'Cultura Caribeña en Cuba: Continuidad versus Ruptura', *Cuban Studies*, 14, 1 (1984) 1–15

Salas, Luis P. 'Juvenile Delinquency in Postrevolutionary Cuba: Characteristics and Cuban Explanations', *Cuban Studies*, 9, 1 (1979) 43–61

Sims, Harold D., 'Cuban Labour and the Communist Party (1937–58)', *Cuban Studies*, 15, 1 (1985) 43–58

ABBREVIATIONS

Abbreviations

ANAP	Asociación Nacional de Agricultores Pequñios (National Association of Small Farmers)
CDR	Comité de Defensa de la Revolución (Committee for the Defence of the Revolution)
CTC	Central de Trabajadores de Cuba (Central Organization of Cuban Workers)
CTC	Confederación de Trabajadores de Cuba (Confederation of Cuban Workers)
FAR	Fuerzas Armadas Revolucionarias (Revolutionary Armed Forces)
FEU	Federación Estudiantil Universitaria (University Students Federation)
FMC	Federación de Mujeres Cubanas (Federation of Cuban Women)
ICAIC	Instituto Cubano del Arte e Industria Cinematográficos (Cuban Institute of Cinematographic Art and Industry)
INRA	Instituto Nacional de Reforma Agraria (National Institute of Agrarian Reform)
JUCEPLAN	Junta Central de Planificación (Central Planning Board)
MININT	Ministerio del Interior (Ministry of the Interior)
MINSAP	Ministerio de Salud Pública (Ministry of Public Health)
M-26-7	Movimiento 26 de Julio (July 26 Movement)
PCC	Partido Comunista de Cuba (Cuban Communist Party)
PSP	Partido Socialista Popular (People's Socialist Party)
UJC	Unión de Jóvenes Comunistas (Union of Young Communists)
UNEAC	Unión de Escritores y Artistas de Cuba (Union of Cuban Writers and Artists)

INDEX